"Lott turns conventional wisdom concerning violent crime and handguns on its head."
—*Chicago Tribune Books*

"John Lott has done the most extensive, thorough, and sophisticated study we have on the effects of loosening gun control laws. Regardless of whether one agrees with his conclusions, his work is mandatory reading for anyone who is open-minded and serious about the gun control issue. Especially fascinating is his account of the often unscrupulous reactions to his research by gun control advocates, academic critics, and the news media."
—**Gary Kleck, professor of Criminology and Criminal Justice, Florida State University**

"An intriguing and shocking look at crime, guns, and gun-control policy."
—*Kirkus Reviews*

"Armed with reams of statistics, John Lott has documented many surprising linkages between guns and crime. *More Guns, Less Crime* demonstrates that what is at stake is not just the right to carry arms but rather our performance in controlling a diverse array of criminal behaviors. Perhaps most disturbing is Lott's documentation of the role of the media and academic commentators in distorting research findings that they regard as politically incorrect."
—W. Kip Viscusi, Cogan Professor of Law and director of the Program on Empirical Legal Studies, Harvard Law School

"This book is a refreshing, well-documented case for responsible gun ownership."
—*Bookviews*

"John Lott's work to uncover the truth about the costs and benefits of guns in America is as valuable as it is provocative. Too much of today's public debate over gun ownership and laws ignores the empirical evidence. Based on carefully proven facts, Professor Lott shatters the orthodox thinking about guns and debunks the most prominent myths about gun use that dominate the policy debate. For those who are convinced that the truth matters in formulating public policy and for anyone interested in the role of guns in our society, *More Guns, Less Crime* is must reading."
—**Edwin Meese III, U.S. Attorney General 1985–88**

"The most important book ever published about firearms policy.... [I]t should be read by everyone who cares about firearms policy, which is literally a matter of life or death.... [T]he more people who read *More Guns, Less Crime*, the sooner streets in every state will become safe zones for good citizens, rather than for predators."
—**David B. Kopel,** *Chronicles*

"Lott's pro-gun argument has to be examined on the merits, and its chief merit is lots of data.... If you still disagree with Lott, at least you will know what will be required to rebut a case that looks pretty near bulletproof."
—**Peter Coy,** *Business Week*

"Until John Lott came along, the standard research paper on firearms and violence consisted of a longitudinal or cross-sectional study on a small and artfully selected data set with few meaningful statistical controls. Lott's work, embracing all of the data that are relevant to his analysis, has created a new standard, which future scholarship in this area, in order to be credible, will have to live up to."
—**Dan Polsby, Kirkland & Ellis Professor of Law, Northwestern University**

"Lott impressively marshals the evidence in support of his position in his best-selling (for an academic book) *More Guns, Less Crime*. As a result, Lott has become one of the few members of the legal academy whose name is now bandied about on talk shows, in legislative sessions, and in the print media. . . . [F]or those who argue that the serious evaluation of data is an important and underutilized guide to good public policy, this book poses a real challenge. For make no mistake, Lott has painstakingly constructed a massive data set, analyzed it exhaustively, and commendably shared it with scholars across the country. In these respects, he deserves high praise for following the scientific protocol so faithfully."
—**Ian Ayres and John J. Donohue III, *American Law and Economics Review***

More Guns, Less Crime

A volume in the series
STUDIES IN LAW AND ECONOMICS
EDITED BY *William M. Landes and J. Mark Ramseyer*

Previously published:

POLITICS AND PROPERTY RIGHTS: THE CLOSING OF THE OPEN RANGE
IN THE POSTBELLUM SOUTH, *By Shawn E. Kantor*

MORE GUNS, LESS CRIME: UNDERSTANDING CRIME AND
GUN-CONTROL LAWS, *by John R. Lott, Jr.*

JAPANESE LAW: AN ECONOMIC APPROACH, *by J. Mark Ramseyer and
Minoru Nakazato*

ARE PREDATORY COMMITMENTS CREDIBLE? WHO SHOULD THE
COURTS BELIEVE? *by John R. Lott, Jr.*

WHEN RULES CHANGE: AN ECONOMIC AND POLITICAL ANALYSIS OF
TRANSITION RELIEF AND RETROACTIVITY, *by Daniel Shaviro*

More Guns, Less Crime

Understanding Crime and Gun-Control Laws

Second Edition

John R. Lott, Jr.

The University of Chicago Press
Chicago and London

To Bill Landes and Sam Peltzman,
for all their support
and encouragement

The University of Chicago Press, Chicago 60637
The University of Chicago Press, Ltd., London
© 1998, 2000 by The University of Chicago
All rights reserved. Published 1998
Printed in the United States of America
07 06 05 04 03 02 01 00   5 4 3 2

ISBN: 0-226-49364-4 (paper)

Library of Congress Cataloging-in-Publication Data

Lott, John R.
      More guns, less crime : understanding crime and gun-control laws /
John R. Lott, Jr.—2nd ed.
          p.   cm. — (Studies in law and economics)
      Includes bibliographical references and index.
      ISBN 0-226-49364-4 (paper : alk. paper)
      1. Firearms—Law and legislation—United States.   2. Firearms and
crime—United States.   I. Title.   II. Studies in law and economics
(Chicago, Ill.)
      KF3941.L68   2000
      344.73'0533—dc21   00-020724

Contents

Preface to the Second Edition

The debate set off by this book was quite astonishing to me. Despite attacks early on when my paper was published in the *Journal of Legal Studies,* I was still rather unprepared for the publicity generated by the book in 1998. This expanded edition not only discusses the ensuing political debate and responds to the various criticisms, but also extends the data set to cover additional years. Replicating the results over additional years is important, so as to verify the original research. The new extended and broadened data set has also allowed me to study new gun laws, ranging from safe-storage provisions to one-gun-a-month purchase rules. It has also allowed me to extend my study of the Brady law and its impact to its first three years. Other extensions of the data set include entirely new city-level statistics, which made it possible to account more fully for policing policies.

Since I finished writing the first edition of this book in 1997, I have continued working on many related gun and crime issues. A new section of the book draws on continued research that I am conducting with numerous talented coauthors: William Landes on multiple-victim public shootings, John Whitley on safe-storage gun laws, and Kevin Cremin on police policies. Other work was published in the May 1998 *American Economic Review* under the title "Criminal Deterrence, Geographic Spillovers, and the Right to Carry Concealed Handguns," coauthored with Stephen Bronars. Also, an article of mine, "The Concealed Handgun Debate," was published in the January 1998 issue of the *Journal of Legal Studies.*

I am grateful for the many opportunities to present my new research in a variety of academic forums and for the many useful comments that I have received. The research on guns and crime has been presented at (a partial listing) Arizona State University, Auburn University, the University of Chicago, Claremont Graduate School, the University of Houston, the University of Illinois, the University of Kansas, the University of Miami, New York University, the University of Oklahoma, the University of Southern California, Rice University, the University of Texas at Austin, the University of Texas at Dallas, the University of Virginia, the College of William and Mary, and Yeshiva University School of Law, as well as at the "Economics of Law Enforcement" Conference at Harvard Law School, the Association of American Law Schools meetings, the American Economic Association meetings, the American Society of Criminology meetings, the Midwestern Economic Association meetings, the National Lawyers Conference, the Southern Economic Association meetings, and the Western Economic Association meetings. Other presentations have been made at such places as the Chicago Crime Commission, the Kansas Koch Crime Commission, the American Enterprise Institute, and the Heritage Foundation.

Finally, I must thank the Yale Law School, where I am a senior research scholar, for providing me with the opportunity to write the new material that has been added to the book. I must also especially thank George Priest, who made this opportunity possible. The input of my wife and sons has been extremely important, and its importance has only been exceeded by their tolerance in putting up with the long working hours required to finish this revision.

Does allowing people to own or carry guns deter violent crime? Or does it simply cause more citizens to harm each other? Using the most comprehensive data set on crime yet assembled, this book examines the relationship between gun laws, arrest and conviction rates, the socioeconomic and demographic compositions of counties and states, and different rates of violent crime and property crime. The efficacy of the Brady Law, concealed-handgun laws, waiting periods, and background checks is evaluated for the first time using nationwide, county-level data.

The book begins with a description of the arguments for and against gun control and of how the claims should be tested. A large portion of the existing research is critically reviewed. Several chapters then empirically examine what facts influence the crime rate and answer the questions posed above. Finally, I respond to the political and academic attacks leveled against the original version of my work, which was published in the January 1997 issue of the *Journal of Legal Studies.*

I would like to thank my wife, Gertrud Fremling, for patiently reading and commenting on many early drafts of this book, and my four children for sitting through more dinnertime conversations on the topics covered here than anyone should be forced to endure. David Mustard also assisted me in collecting the data for the original article, which serves as the basis for some of the discussions in chapters 4 and 5. Ongoing research with Steve Bronars and William Landes has contributed to this book. Maxim Lott provided valuable research assistance with the polling data.

For their comments on different portions of the work included in this book, I would like to thank Gary Becker, Steve Bronars, Clayton Cramer, Ed Glaeser, Hide Ichimura, Jon Karpoff, C. B. Kates, Gary Kleck, David Kopel, William Landes, Wally Mullin, Derek Neal, Dan Polsby, Robert Reed, Tom Smith, seminar participants at the University of Chicago (the Economics and Legal Organization, the Rational Choice, and Divinity School workshops), Harvard University, Yale University, Stanford University, Northwestern University, Emory University, Fordham University, Valparaiso University, the American Law and Economics Association

Meetings, the American Society of Criminology, the Western Economic Association Meetings, and the Cato Institute. I also benefited from presentations at the annual conventions of the Illinois Police Association and the National Association of Treasury Agents. Further, I would like to express my appreciation to the John M. Olin Law and Economics Program at the University of Chicago Law School for its generous funding (a topic dealt with at length in chapter 7).

One   **Introduction**

American culture is a gun culture—not merely in the sense that 75 to 86 million people own a total of about 200 to 240 million guns,[1] but in the broader sense that guns pervade our debates on crime and are constantly present in movies and the news. How many times have we read about shootings, or how many times have we heard about tragic accidental gun deaths—bad guys shooting innocent victims, bad guys shooting each other in drug wars, shots fired in self-defense, police shootings of criminals, let alone shooting in wars? We are inundated by images through the television and the press. Our kids are fascinated by computer war games and toy guns.

So we're obsessed with guns. But the big question is: What do we really know? How many times have most of us actually used a gun or seen a gun being used? How many of us have ever seen somebody in real life threatening somebody else with a gun, witnessed a shooting, or seen people defend themselves by displaying or firing guns?

The truth is that most of us have very little firsthand experience with using guns as weapons. Even the vast majority of police officers have never exchanged shots with a suspect.[2] Most of us receive our images of guns and their use through television, film, and newspapers.

Unfortunately, the images from the screen and the newspapers are often unrepresentative or biased because of the sensationalism and exaggeration typically employed to sell news and entertainment. A couple of instances of news reporting are especially instructive in illustrating this bias. In a highly publicized incident, a Dallas man recently became the first Texas resident charged with using a permitted concealed weapon in a fatal shooting.[3] Only long after the initial wave of publicity did the press report that the person had been savagely beaten and in fear for his life before firing the gun. In another case a Japanese student was shot on his way to a Halloween party in Louisiana in 1992. It made international headlines and showed how defensive gun use can go tragically wrong.[4] However, this incident was a rare event: in the entire United States during a year, only about 30 people are accidentally killed by private citizens who mistakenly believe the victim to be an intruder.[5] By comparison, police accidentally kill as many as 330 innocent individuals annually.[6] In neither the Louisiana case nor the Texas case did the courts find the shooting to be criminal.

While news stories sometimes chronicle the defensive uses of guns, such discussions are rare compared to those depicting violent crime committed with guns. Since in many defensive cases a handgun is simply brandished, and no one is harmed, many defensive uses are never even reported to the police. I believe that this underreporting of defensive gun use is large, and this belief has been confirmed by the many stories I received from people across the country after the publicity broke on my original study. On the roughly one hundred radio talk shows on which I discussed that study, many people called in to say that they believed having a gun to defend themselves with had saved their lives. For instance, on a Philadelphia radio station, a New Jersey woman told how two men simultaneously had tried to open both front doors of the car she was in. When she brandished her gun and yelled, the men backed away and fled. Given the stringent gun-control laws in New Jersey, the woman said she never thought seriously of reporting the attempted attack to the police.

Similarly, while I was on a trip to testify before the Nebraska Senate, John Haxby—a television newsman for the CBS affiliate in Omaha— privately revealed to me a frightening experience that he had faced in the summer of 1995 while visiting in Arizona. At about 10 A.M., while riding in a car with his brother at the wheel, they stopped for a red light. A man appeared wielding a "butcher's knife" and opened the passenger door, but just as he was lunging towards John, the attacker suddenly turned and ran away. As John turned to his brother, he saw that his brother was holding a handgun. His brother was one of many who had recently acquired permits under the concealed-handgun law passed in Arizona the previous year.

Philip Van Cleave, a former reserve deputy sheriff in Texas, wrote me, "Are criminals afraid of a law-abiding citizen with a gun? You bet. Most cases of a criminal being scared off by an armed citizen are probably not reported. But I have seen a criminal who was so frightened of an armed, seventy-year-old woman that in his panic to get away, he turned and ran right into a wall! (He was busy trying to kick down her door, when she opened a curtain and pointed a gun at him.)"

Such stories are not limited to the United States. On February 3, 1996, outside a bar in Texcoco, Mexico (a city thirty miles east of Mexico City), a woman used a gun to stop a man from raping her. When the man lunged at the woman, "ripping her clothes and trying to rape her," she pulled a .22-caliber pistol from her purse and shot her attacker once in the chest, killing him.[7] The case generated much attention in Mexico when a judge initially refused to dismiss murder charges against the woman because she was viewed as being responsible for the attempted rape, having "enticed" the attacker "by having a drink with him at the bar."[8]

If a national survey that I conducted is correct, 98 percent of the time that people use guns defensively, they merely have to brandish a weapon to break off an attack. Such stories are not hard to find: pizza deliverymen defend themselves against robbers, carjackings are thwarted, robberies at automatic teller machines are prevented, and numerous armed robberies on the streets and in stores are foiled,[9] though these do not receive the national coverage of other gun crimes.[10] Yet the cases covered by the news media are hardly typical; most of the encounters reported involve a shooting that ends in a fatality.[11]

A typical dramatic news story involved an Atlanta woman who prevented a carjacking and the kidnapping of her child; she was forced to shoot her assailant:

> A College Park woman shot and killed an armed man she says was trying to carjack her van with her and her 1-year-old daughter inside, police said Monday. . . .
>
> Jackson told police that the gunman accosted her as she drove into the parking lot of an apartment complex on Camp Creek Parkway. She had planned to watch a broadcast of the Evander Holyfield–Mike Tyson fight with friends at the complex.
>
> She fired after the man pointed a revolver at her and ordered her to "move over," she told police. She offered to take her daughter and give up the van, but the man refused, police said.
>
> "She was pleading with the guy to let her take the baby and leave the van, but he blocked the door," said College Park Detective Reed Pollard. "She was protecting herself and the baby."
>
> Jackson, who told police she bought the .44-caliber handgun in September after her home was burglarized, said she fired several shots from the gun, which she kept concealed in a canvas bag beside her car seat. "She didn't try to remove it," Pollard said. "She just fired."[12]

Although the mother saved herself and her baby by her quick actions, it was a risky situation that might have ended differently. Even though there was no police officer to help protect her or her child, defending herself was not necessarily the only alternative. She could have behaved passively, and the criminal might have changed his mind and simply taken the van, letting the mother and child go. Even if he had taken the child, he might later have let the baby go unharmed. Indeed, some conventional wisdom claims that the best approach is not to resist an attack. According to a recent *Los Angeles Times* article, "'active compliance' is the surest way to survive a robbery. Victims who engage in active resistance . . . have the best odds of hanging on to their property. Unfortunately, they also have much better odds of winding up dead."[13]

Yet the evidence suggests that the College Park woman probably engaged in the correct action. While resistance is generally associated with higher probabilities of serious injury to the victim, not all types of resistance are equally risky. By examining the data provided from 1979 to 1987 by the Department of Justice's National Crime Victimization Survey,[14] Lawrence Southwick, confirming earlier estimates by Gary Kleck, found that the probability of serious injury from an attack is 2.5 times greater for women offering no resistance than for women resisting with a gun. In contrast, the probability of women being seriously injured was almost 4 times greater when resisting without a gun than when resisting with a gun. In other words, the best advice is to resist with a gun, but if no gun is available, it is better to offer no resistance than to fight.[15]

Men also fare better with guns, but the benefits are significantly smaller. Behaving passively is 1.4 times more likely to result in serious injury than resisting with a gun. Male victims, like females, also run the greatest risk when they resist without a gun, yet the difference is again much smaller: resistance without a gun is only 1.5 times as likely to result in serious injury than resistance with a gun. The much smaller difference for men reflects the fact that a gun produces a smaller change in a man's ability to defend himself than it does for a woman.

Although usually skewed toward the dramatic, news stories do shed light on how criminals think. Anecdotes about criminals who choose victims whom they perceive as weak are the most typical. While "weak" victims are frequently women and the elderly, this is not always the case. For example, in a taped conversation with police investigators reported in the *Cincinnati Enquirer* (October 9, 1996, p. B2), Darnell "Bubba" Lowery described how he and Walter "Fatman" Raglin robbed and murdered musician Michael Bany on December 29, 1995:

> Mr. Lowery said on the tape that he and Walter "Fatman" Raglin, who is also charged with aggravated robbery and aggravated murder and is on trial in another courtroom, had planned to rob a cab driver or a "dope boy."
>
> He said he gave his gun and bullets to Mr. Raglin. They decided against robbing a cab driver or drug dealer because both sometimes carried guns, he said.
>
> Instead, they saw a man walking across the parking lot with some kind

of musical instrument. He said as he looked out for police, Mr. Raglin approached the man and asked for money.

After getting the money, Mr. Raglin asked if the man's car was a stick or an automatic shift. Then Mr. Raglin shot the man.

Criminals are motivated by self-preservation, and handguns can therefore be a deterrent. The potential defensive nature of guns is further evidenced by the different rates of so-called "hot burglaries," where a resident is at home when a criminal strikes.[16] In Canada and Britain, both with tough gun-control laws, almost half of all burglaries are "hot burglaries." In contrast, the United States, with fewer restrictions, has a "hot burglary" rate of only 13 percent. Criminals are not just behaving differently by accident. Convicted American felons reveal in surveys that they are much more worried about armed victims than about running into the police.[17] The fear of potentially armed victims causes American burglars to spend more time than their foreign counterparts "casing" a house to ensure that nobody is home. Felons frequently comment in these interviews that they avoid late-night burglaries because "that's the way to get shot."[18]

To an economist such as myself, the notion of deterrence—which causes criminals to avoid cab drivers, "dope boys," or homes where the residents are in—is not too surprising. We see the same basic relationships in all other areas of life: when the price of apples rises relative to that of oranges, people buy fewer apples and more oranges. To the non-economist, it may appear cold to make this comparison, but just as grocery shoppers switch to cheaper types of produce, criminals switch to attacking more vulnerable prey. Economists call this, appropriately enough, "the substitution effect."

Deterrence matters not only to those who actively take defensive actions. People who defend themselves may indirectly benefit other citizens. In the Cincinnati murder case just described, cab drivers and drug dealers who carry guns produce a benefit for cab drivers and drug dealers without guns. In the example involving "hot burglaries," homeowners who defend themselves make burglars generally wary of breaking into homes. These spillover effects are frequently referred to as "third-party effects" or "external benefits." In both cases criminals cannot know in advance who is armed.

The case for allowing concealed handguns—as opposed to openly carried handguns—relies on this argument. When guns are concealed, criminals are unable to tell whether the victim is armed before striking, which raises the risk to criminals of committing many types of crimes.

On the other hand, with "open-carry" handgun laws, a potential victim's defensive ability is readily identified, which makes it easier for criminals to choose the more vulnerable prey. In interviews with felony prisoners in ten state correctional systems, 56 percent claimed that they would not attack a potential victim who was known to be armed. Indeed, the criminals in states with high civilian gun ownership were the most worried about encountering armed victims.[19]

Other examples suggest that more than just common crimes may be prevented by law-abiding citizens carrying concealed handguns. Referring to the July, 1984, massacre at a San Ysidro, California, McDonald's restaurant, Israeli criminologist Abraham Tennenbaum described

> what occurred at a [crowded venue in] Jerusalem some weeks before the California McDonald's massacre: three terrorists who attempted to machine-gun the throng managed to kill only one victim before being shot down by handgun-carrying Israelis. Presented to the press the next day, the surviving terrorist complained that his group had not realized that Israeli civilians were armed. The terrorists had planned to machine-gun a succession of crowd spots, thinking that they would be able to escape before the police or army could arrive to deal with them.[20]

More recently, on March 13, 1997, seven young seventh- and eighth-grade Israeli girls were shot to death by a Jordanian soldier while visiting Jordan's so-called Island of Peace. Reportedly, the Israelis had "complied with Jordanian requests to leave their weapons behind when they entered the border enclave. Otherwise, they might have been able to stop the shooting, several parents said."[21]

Obviously, arming citizens has not stopped terrorism in Israel; however, terrorists have responded to the relatively greater cost of shooting in public places by resorting to more bombings. This is exactly what the substitution effect discussed above would predict. Is Israel better off with bombings instead of mass public shootings? That is not completely clear, although one might point out that if the terrorists previously chose shooting attacks rather than bombings but now can only be effective by using bombs, their actions are limited in a way that should make terrorist attacks less effective (even if only slightly).[22]

Substitutability means that the most obvious explanations may not always be correct. For example, when the February 23, 1997, shooting at the Empire State Building left one person dead and six injured, it was not New York's gun laws but Florida's—where the gun was sold—that came under attack. New York City Mayor Rudolph W. Giuliani immediately called for national gun-licensing laws.[23] While it is possible that even stricter gun-sale regulations in Florida might have prevented this and other shootings, we might ask, Why did the gunman travel to New York and not simply remain in Florida to do the shooting? It is important to study whether states that adopt concealed-handgun laws similar to those in Israel experience the same virtual elimination of mass public shootings. Such states may also run the risk that would-be attackers will substitute bombings for shootings, though there is the same potential downside to successfully banning guns. The question still boils down to an empirical one: Which policy will save the largest number of lives?

THE NUMBERS DEBATE AND CRIME

Unfortunately, the debate over crime involves many commonly accepted "facts" that simply are not true. For example, take the claim that individuals are frequently killed by people they know.[24] As shown in table 1.1, according to the FBI's *Uniform Crime Reports*, 58 percent of the country's murders were committed either by family members (18 percent) or by

Table 1.1 Murderers and victims: relationship and characteristics

	Percent of cases involving the relationship	Percent of victims	Percent of offenders
Relationship		—	—
Family	18%		
Acquaintance			
(nonfriend and friend)	40		
Stranger	13		
Unknown	30		
Total	101		
Race			
Black		38%	33%
White		54	42
Hispanic		2	2
Other		5	4
Unknown		1	19
Total		100	100
Sex			
Female		29	9
Male		71	72
Unknown		0	19
Total		100	100

Source: U.S. Dept. of Justice, FBI staff, *Uniform Crime Reports,* (Washington, DC: U.S. Govt. Printing Office, 1992

Note: Nonfriend acquaintances include drug pushers and buyers, gang members, prostitutes and their clients, bar customers, gamblers, cab drivers killed by their customers, neighbors, other nonfriend acquaintances, and friends. The total equals more than 100 percent because of rounding. The average age of victims was 33; that of offenders was 30.

those who "knew" the victims (40 percent). Although the victims' relationship to their attackers could not be determined in 30 percent of the cases, 13 percent of all murders were committed by complete strangers.[25]

Surely the impression created by these numbers has been that most victims are murdered by close acquaintances. Yet this is far from the truth. In interpreting the numbers, one must understand how these classifications are made. In this case, "murderers who know their victims" is a very broad category. A huge but not clearly determined portion of this category includes rival gang members who know each other.[26] In larger urban areas, where most murders occur, the majority of murders are due to gang-related turf wars over drugs.

The Chicago Police Department, which keeps unusually detailed numbers on these crimes, finds that just 5 percent of all murders in the city from 1990 to 1995 were committed by nonfamily friends, neighbors, or roommates.[27] This is clearly important in understanding crime. The list of nonfriend acquaintance murderers is filled with cases in which the relationships would not be regarded by most people as particularly close: for example, relationships between drug pushers and buyers, gang members, prostitutes and their clients, bar customers, gamblers, and cabdrivers killed by their customers.

While I do not wish to downplay domestic violence, most people do not envision gang members or drug buyers and pushers killing each other when they hear that 58 percent of murder victims were either relatives or acquaintances of their murderers.[28] If family members are included, 17 percent of all murders in Chicago for 1990–95 involved family members, friends, neighbors, or roommates.[29] While the total number of murders in Chicago grew from 395 in 1965 to 814 in 1995, the number involving family members, friends, neighbors, or roommates remained virtually unchanged. What has grown is the number of murders by nonfriend acquaintances, strangers, identified gangs, and persons unknown.[30]

Few murderers could be classified as previously law-abiding citizens. In the largest seventy-five counties in the United States in 1988, over 89 percent of adult murderers had criminal records as adults.[31] Evidence for Boston, the one city where reliable data have been collected, shows that, from 1990 to 1994, 76 percent of juvenile murder victims and 77 percent of juveniles who murdered other juveniles had prior criminal arraignments.[32]

Claims of the large number of murders committed against acquaintances also create a misleading fear of those we know. To put it bluntly, criminals are not typical citizens. As is well known, young males from their mid-teens to mid-thirties commit a disproportionate share of crime,[33] but even this categorization can be substantially narrowed. We know that criminals tend to have low IQs as well as atypical personalities.

For example, delinquents generally tend to be more "assertive, unafraid, aggressive, unconventional, extroverted, and poorly socialized," while nondeliquents are "self-controlled, concerned about their relations with others, willing to be guided by social standards, and rich in internal feelings like insecurity, helplessness, love (or its lack), and anxiety."[34] Other evidence indicates that criminals tend to be more impulsive and put relatively little weight on future events.[35] Finally, we cannot ignore the unfortunate fact that crime (particularly violent crime, and especially murder) is disproportionately committed against blacks by blacks.[36]

The news media also play an important role in shaping what we perceive as the greatest threats to our safety. Because we live in such a national news market, we learn very quickly about tragedies in other parts of the country.[37] As a result, some events appear to be much more common than they actually are. For instance, children are much less likely to be accidentally killed by guns (particularly handguns) than most people think. Consider the following numbers: In 1996 there were a total of 1,134 accidental firearm deaths in the entire country. A relatively small portion of these involved children under age ten: 17 deaths involved children up to four years of age and 25 more deaths involved five- to nine-year-olds.[38] In comparison, 1,915 children died in motor-vehicle crashes and another 489 died when they were struck by motor vehicles, 805 lost their lives from drowning, and 738 were killed by fire and burns. Almost twice as many children even drown in bathtubs each year than die from all types of firearm accidents.

Of course, any child's death is tragic, and it offers little consolation to point out that common fixtures in life from pools to heaters result in even more deaths. Yet the very rules that seek to save lives can result in more deaths. For example, banning swimming pools would help prevent drowning, and banning bicycles would eliminate bicycling accidents, but if fewer people exercise, life spans will be shortened. Heaters may start fires, but they also keep people from getting sick and from freezing to death. So whether we want to allow pools or space heaters depends not only on whether some people may be harmed by them, but also on whether more people are helped than hurt.

Similar trade-offs exist for gun-control issues, such as gun locks. As President Clinton has argued many times, "We protect aspirin bottles in this country better than we protect guns from accidents by children."[39] Yet gun locks require that guns be unloaded, and a locked, unloaded gun does not offer ready protection from intruders.[40] The debate is not simply over whether one wants to save lives or not; it involves the question of how many of these two hundred accidental gun deaths would have been avoided under different rules versus the extent to which such rules would reduce people's ability to defend themselves. Without looking at data, one can only guess the net effects.[41] Unfortunately, despite the best intentions, evidence indicates that child-resistant bottle caps actually have resulted in "3,500 additional poisonings of children under age 5 annually from [aspirin-related drugs] . . . [as] consumers have been lulled into a less-safety-conscious mode of behavior by the existence of safety caps."[42] If President Clinton were aware of such research, he surely wouldn't refer to aspirin bottles when telling us how to deal with guns.[43]

Another common argument made in favor of banning guns involves the number of people who die from guns each year: there were 17,790 homicides and 18,169 suicides in 1992 alone.[44] Yet just because a law is passed to ban guns, it does not automatically follow that the total number of deaths will decline. Given the large stock of guns in the country, and given the difficulties the government faces in preventing other illegal items, such as drugs, from entering the country, it is not clear how successful the government would be in eliminating most guns. This raises the important question of whether the law would primarily reduce the number of guns held by law-abiding citizens. How would such a law alter the relative balance of power between criminals and law-abiding citizens?

Suppose it were possible to remove all guns. Other questions would still arise. Would successfully removing guns discourage murders and other crimes because criminals would find knives and clubs poor alternatives? Would it be easier for criminals to prey on the weakest citizens, who would find it more difficult to defend themselves? Suicide raises other questions. It is simply not sufficient to point to the number of people who kill themselves with guns. The debate must be over what substitute methods are available and whether they appear sufficiently less attractive. Even evidence about the "success rate" of different methods of suicide is not enough, because questions arise over why people choose the method that they do. If people who were more intent than others on successfully killing themselves previously chose guns, forcing them to use other methods might raise the reported "success rate" for these other methods. Broader concerns for the general public also arise. For example, even if we banned many of the obvious ways of committing suicide, many methods exist that we could never really control. These substitute methods might endanger others in ways that shootings do not—for example, deliberately crashing one's car, throwing oneself in front of a train, or jumping off a building.

This book attempts to measure the same type of trade-off for guns. Our primary questions are the following: Will allowing citizens to carry concealed handguns mean that otherwise law-abiding people will harm each other? Will the threat of self-defense by citizens armed with guns primarily deter criminals? Without a doubt, both "bad" and "good" uses of guns occur. The question isn't really whether both occur; it is, rather, Which is more important? In general, do concealed handguns save or cost lives? Even a devoted believer in deterrence cannot answer this question without examining the data, because these two different effects clearly exist, and they work in opposite directions.

To some, however, the logic is fairly straightforward. Philip Cook argues that "if you introduce a gun into a violent encounter, it increases the chance that someone will die."[45] A large number of murders may arise from unintentional fits of rage that are quickly regretted, and simply keeping guns out of people's reach would prevent deaths.[46] Others point to the horrible public shootings that occur not just in the United States but around the world, from Tasmania, Australia, to Dunblane, Scotland.

The survey evidence of defensive gun use weighs importantly in this debate. At the lowest end of these estimates, again according to Philip Cook, the U.S. Department of Justice's National Crime Victimization Survey reports that each year there are "only" 110,000 defensive uses of guns during assaults, robberies, and household burglaries.[47] Other national polls weight regions by population and thus have the advantage, unlike the National Crime Victimization Survey, of not relying too heavily on data from urban areas.[48] These national polls should also produce more honest answers, since a law-enforcement agency is not asking the questions.[49] They imply much higher defensive use rates. Fifteen national polls, including those by organizations such as the *Los Angeles Times*, Gallup, and Peter Hart Research Associates, imply that there are 760,000 defensive handgun uses to 3.6 million defensive uses of any type of gun per year.[50] Yet even if these estimates are wrong by a very large factor, they still suggest that defensive gun use is extremely common.

Some evidence on whether concealed-handgun laws will lead to increased crimes is readily available. Between October 1, 1987, when Florida's "concealed-carry" law took effect, and the end of 1996, over 380,000 licenses had been issued, and only 72 had been revoked because of crimes committed by license holders (most of which did not involve the permitted gun).[51] A statewide breakdown on the nature of those crimes is not available, but Dade County records indicate that four crimes involving a permitted handgun took place there between September 1987 and August 1992, and none of those cases resulted in injury.[52] Similarly, Multnomah County, Oregon, issued 11,140 permits over the period from January 1990 to October 1994; only five permit holders were involved in shootings, three of which were considered justified by grand juries. Of the other two cases, one involved a shooting in a domestic dispute, and the other involved an accident that occurred while a gun was being unloaded; neither resulted in a fatality.[53]

In Virginia, "Not a single Virginia permit-holder has been involved in violent crime." [54] In the first year following the enactment of concealed-carry legislation in Texas, more than 114,000 licenses were issued, and only 17 have so far been revoked by the Department of Public Safety (reasons not specified). [55] After Nevada's first year, "Law enforcement officials throughout the state could not document one case of a fatality that resulted from irresponsible gun use by someone who obtained a permit under the new law." [56] Speaking for the Kentucky Chiefs of Police Association, Lt. Col. Bill Dorsey, Covington assistant police chief, concluded that after the law had been in effect for nine months, "We haven't seen any cases where a [concealed-carry] permit holder has committed an offense with a firearm," [57] In North Carolina, "Permit-holding gun owners have not had a single permit revoked as a result of use of a gun in a crime." [58] Similarly, for South Carolina, "Only one person who has received a pistol permit since 1989 has been indicted on a felony charge, a comparison of permit and circuit court records shows. That charge, . . . for allegedly transferring stolen property last year, was dropped by prosecutors after evidence failed to support the charge." [59]

During state legislative hearings on concealed-handgun laws, the most commonly raised concerns involved fears that armed citizens would attack each other in the heat of the moment following car accidents or accidentally shoot a police officer. The evidence shows that such fears are unfounded: although thirty-one states have so-called nondiscretionary concealed-handgun laws, some of them decades old, there exists only one recorded incident of a permitted, concealed handgun being used in a shooting following a traffic accident, and that involved self-defense. [60] No permit holder has ever shot a police officer, and there have been cases where permit holders have used their guns to save officers' lives.

Let us return to the fundamental issue of self-protection. For many people, the ultimate concern boils down to protection from violence. Unfortunately, our legal system cannot provide people with all the protection that they desire, and yet individuals are often prevented from defending themselves. A particularly tragic event occurred recently in Baltimore:

> Less than a year ago, James Edward Scott shot and wounded an intruder in the back yard of his West Baltimore home, and according to neighbors, authorities took away his gun.
>
> Tuesday night, someone apparently broke into his three-story row house again. But this time the 83-year-old Scott didn't have his .22-caliber rifle, and police said he was strangled when he confronted the burglar.
>
> "If he would have had the gun, he would be OK," said one neighbor

who declined to give his name, fearing retribution from the attacker, who had not been arrested as of yesterday. . . .

Neighbors said burglars repeatedly broke into Scott's home. Ruses [a neighbor] said Scott often talked about "the people who would harass him because he worked out back by himself."[61]

Others find themselves in a position in which either they no longer report attacks to the police when they have used a gun to defend themselves, or they no longer carry guns for self-defense. Josie Cash learned this lesson the hard way, though charges against her were ultimately dropped. "The Rockford [Illinois] woman used her gun to scare off muggers who tried to take her pizza delivery money. But when she reported the incident to police, they filed felony charges against her for carrying a concealed weapon."[62]

A well-known story involved Alan Berg, a liberal Denver talk-show host who took great delight in provoking and insulting those with whom he disagreed. Berg attempted to obtain a permit after receiving death threats from white supremacists, but the police first attempted to talk him out of applying and then ultimately rejected his request. Shortly after he was denied, Berg was murdered by members of the Aryan Nations.[63]

As a Chicago cabdriver recently told me, "What good is a police officer going to do me if you pulled a knife or a gun on me right now?"[64] Nor are rural, low-crime areas immune from these concerns. Illinois State Representative Terry Deering (Democrat) noted that "we live in areas where if we have a state trooper on duty at any given time in a whole county, we feel very fortunate. Some counties in downstate rural Illinois don't even have 24-hour police protection."[65] The police cannot feasibly protect everybody all the time, and perhaps because of this, police officers are typically sympathetic to law-abiding citizens who own guns.[66]

Mail-in surveys are seldom accurate, because only those who feel intensely about an issue are likely to respond, but they provide the best information that we have on police officers' views. A 1996 mail survey of fifteen thousand chiefs of police and sheriffs conducted by the National Association of Chiefs of Police found that 93 percent believed that law-abiding citizens should continue to be able to purchase guns for self-defense.[67] The Southern States Police Benevolent Association surveyed its eleven thousand members during June of 1993 (36 percent responded) and reported similar findings: 96 percent of those who responded agreed with the statement, "People should have the right to own a gun for self-protection," and 71 percent did not believe that stricter handgun laws would reduce the number of violent crimes.[68] A national reader survey conducted in 1991 by *Law Enforcement Technology* magazine found that 76 percent of street officers and 59 percent of managerial officers agreed that all trained, responsible adults should be able to obtain handgun-carry permits.[69] By similarly overwhelming percentages, these officers and police chiefs rejected claims that the Brady law would lower the crime rate.

The passage of concealed-handgun laws has also caused former opponents in law enforcement to change their positions. Recently in Texas, "vocal opponent" Harris County District Attorney John Holmes admitted, "I'm eating a lot of crow on this issue. It's not something I necessarily like to do, but I'm doing it on this."[70] Soon after the implementation of the Florida law, the president and the executive director of the Florida Chiefs of Police and the head of the Florida Sheriff's Association all admitted that they had changed their views on the subject. They also admitted that despite their best efforts to document problems arising from the law, they have been unable to do so.[71] The experience in Kentucky has been similar; as Campbell County Sheriff John Dunn says, "I have changed my opinion of this [program]. Frankly, I anticipated a certain type of people applying to carry firearms, people I would be uncomfortable with being able to carry a concealed weapon. That has not been the case. These are all just everyday citizens who feel they need some protection."[72]

If anything, the support among rank-and-file police officers for the right of individuals to carry guns for self-protection is even higher than it is among the general population. A recent national poll by the Lawrence Research group (September 21–28, 1996) found that by a margin of 69 to 28 percent, registered voters favor "a law allowing law-abiding citizens to be issued a permit to carry a firearm for personal protection outside their home."[73] Other recent national polling by the National Opinion Research Center (March 1997) appears even more supportive of at least allowing some law-abiding citizens to carry concealed handguns. They found that 53.5 percent supported "concealed carry only for those with special needs," while 45 percent agreed that permits should be issued to "any adult who has passed a criminal background check and a gun safety course."[74] Perhaps just as telling, only 16 percent favored a ban on handguns.[75]

The National Opinion Research Center poll also provides some insights into who supports tighter restrictions on gun ownership; it claims that "the less educated and those who haven't been threatened with a gun are most supportive of gun control."[76] If this is true, it appears that those most supportive of restrictions also tend to be those least directly threatened by crime.[77]

State legislators also acknowledge the inability of the police to be always available, even in the most public places, by voting to allow themselves unusually broad rights to carry concealed handguns. During the 1996 legislative session, for example, Georgia "state legislators quietly gave themselves and a few top officials the right to carry concealed guns to places most residents can't: schools, churches, political rallies, and even the Capitol."[78] Even local prosecutors in California strenuously objected to restrictions on their rights to carry concealed handguns.[79]

Although people with concealed handgun permits must generally view the police as offering insufficient protection, it is difficult to discern any pattern of political orientation among celebrities who have concealed-handgun permits: Bill Cosby, Cybill Shepherd, U.S. Senator Dianne Feinstein (D–California), Howard Stern, Donald Trump, William F. Buckley, Arthur O. Sulzberger (chairman of the *New York Times*), union bosses, Laurence Rockefeller, Tom Selleck, Robert De Niro, and Erika Schwarz (the first runner-up in the 1997 Miss America Pageant). The reasons these people gave on their applications for permits were quite similar. Laurence Rockefeller's reason was that he carries "large sums of money"; Arthur Sulzberger wrote that he carries "large sums of money, securities, etc."; and William Buckley listed "protection of personal property when traveling in and about the city" as his reason.[80] Some made their decision to carry a gun after being victims of crime. Erika Schwarz said that after a carjacking she had been afraid to drive at night.[81]

And when the *Denver Post* asked Sen. Ben Nighthorse Campbell (R–Colo.) "how it looks for a senator to be packing heat," he responded, "You'd be surprised how many senators have guns." Campbell said that "he needed the gun back in the days when he exhibited his Native American jewelry and traveled long distances between craft shows."[82]

EMOTION, RATIONALITY, AND DETERRENCE

In 1995 two children, ten and eleven years old, dropped a five-year-old boy from the fourteenth floor of a vacant Chicago Housing Authority apartment.[83] The reason? The five-year-old refused to steal candy for them. Or consider the case of Vincent Drost, a promising musician in the process of composing a symphony, who was stabbed to death immediately after making a call from a pay telephone to his girlfriend. The reason? According to the newspapers, "His five teenage attackers told police they wanted to have some fun and simply wanted 'to do' somebody."[84] It is not difficult to find crimes such as "the fatal beating of a school teacher" described as "extremely wicked, shockingly evil." The defense attorney in this crime described the act as one of "insane jealousy."[85]

The notion of "irrational" crime is enshrined by forty-seven states that recognize insanity defenses.[86] Criminal law recognizes that emotions can overwhelm our normal judgments in other ways.[87] For example, under the Model Penal Code, intentional homicide results in the penalty for manslaughter when it "is committed under the influence of extreme mental or emotional disturbance for which there is reasonable explanation or excuse."[88] These mitigating factors are often discussed in terms of the "heat of passion" or "cooling time," the latter phrase referring to "the interval in which 'blood' can be expected 'to cool'" or the time required for "reason to reassert itself."[89] Another related distinction is drawn between first- and second-degree murder: "The deliberate killer is guilty of first-degree murder; the impulsive killer is not."[90] In practice, the true distinction between these two grades appears to be not premeditation but whether the act was done without emotion or "in cold blood," "as is the case [when] someone who kills for money . . . displays calculation and greed."[91]

Some academics go beyond these cases or laws to make more general claims about the motives behind crime. Thomas Carroll, an associate professor of sociology at the University of Missouri at Kansas City, states that "murder is an irrational act, [and] we don't have explanations for irrational behavior."[92] From this he draws the conclusion that "there's really no statistical explanation" for what causes murder rates to fluctuate. Do criminals respond to disincentives? Or are emotions and attitudes the determining factors in crime? If violent acts occur merely because of random emotions, stronger penalties would only reduce crime to the extent that the people least able to control such violent feelings can be imprisoned.

There are obvious difficulties with taking this argument against deterrence to its extreme. For example, as long as "even a handful" of criminals respond to deterrence, increasing penalties will reduce crime. Higher probabilities of arrest or conviction as well as longer prison terms might then possibly "pay" for themselves. As the cases in the previous section have illustrated, criminal decisions—from when to break into a residence, whom to attack, or whether to attack people by using guns or bombs—appear difficult to explain without reference to deterrence. Some researchers try to draw a distinction between crimes that they view as "more rational," like robbery and burglary, and others, such as murder. If such a distinction is valid, one might argue that deterrence would then at least be effective for the more "rational" crimes.

Yet even if we assume that most criminals are largely irrational, deterrence issues raise some tough questions about human nature, questions that are at the heart of very different views of crime and how to combat it. Still it is important to draw a distinction between "irrational" behavior and the notion that deterrence doesn't matter. One doesn't necessarily imply the other. For instance, some people may hold strange, unfathomable objectives, but this does not mean that they cannot be discouraged from doing things that bring increasingly undesirable consequences. While we may not solve the deeper mysteries of how the human mind works, I hope that the following uncontroversial example can help show how deterrence works.

Suppose that a hypothetical Mr. Smith is passed over for promotion. He keeps a stiff upper lip at work, but after he gets home, he kicks his dog. Now this might appear entirely irrational: the dog did not misbehave. Obviously, Mr. Smith got angry at his boss, but he took it out on his poor dog instead. Could we conclude that he is an emotional, irrational individual not responding to incentives? Hardly. The reason that he did not respond forcefully to his boss is probably that he feared the consequences. Expressing his anger at the boss might have resulted in his being fired or passed up for future promotions. An alternative way to vent his frustration would have been to kick his co-workers or throw things around the office. But again, Mr. Smith chose not to engage in such behavior because of the likely consequences for his job. In economic terms, the costs are too high. He manages to bottle up his anger until he gets home and kicks his dog. The dog is a "low-cost" victim.

Here lies the perplexity: the whole act may be viewed as highly irrational—after all, Mr. Smith doesn't truly accomplish anything. But still he tries to minimize the bad consequences of venting his anger. Perhaps we could label Mr. Smith's behavior as "semirational," a mixture of seemingly senseless emotion and rational behavior at the same time.

What about changing the set of punishments in the example above? What if Mr. Smith had a "killer dog," that bit anyone who abused it (equivalent to arming potential victims)? Or what if Mr. Smith were likely to be arrested and convicted for animal abuse? Several scenarios are plausible. First, he might have found another victim, perhaps a family member, to hit or kick. Or he might have modified his outwardly aggressive acts by merely yelling at family and neighbors or demolishing something. Or he might have repressed his anger—either by bottling up his frustration or finding some nonviolent substitute, such as watching a video, to help him forget the day's events.

Evidence of responding to disincentives is not limited to "rational" humans. Economists have produced a large number of studies that investigate whether animals take the costs of doing things into account.[93] Animal subjects have included both rats and pigeons, and the typical experiment measures the amount of some desired treat or standard laboratory food or fluid that is consumed in relation to the number of times the animal must push a lever to get the item. Other experiments alter the amount of the item received for a given number of lever pushes. These experiments have been tried in many different contexts. For example, does an animal's willingness to work for special treats like root beer or cherry cola depend upon the existence of unlimited supplies of water or standard laboratory food? The results from these experiments consistently show that as the "cost" of obtaining the food increases, the animal obtains less food. In economic terms, "Demand curves are downward sloping."

As for human beings, a large economics literature exists that overwhelmingly demonstrates that people commit fewer crimes if criminal penalties are more severe or more certain. Whether we consider the number of airliners hijacked in the 1970s,[94] evasion of the military draft,[95] or international data on violent and property crimes,[96] stiffer penalties or higher probabilities of conviction result in fewer violations of the law. Sociologists are more cautious, but the National Research Council of the U.S. National Academy of Sciences established the Panel on Research on Deterrent and Incapacitative Effects in 1978 to evaluate the many academic studies of deterrence. The panel concluded as follows: "Taken as a whole, the evidence consistently finds a negative association between crime rates and the risks of apprehension, conviction or imprisonment. ... the evidence certainly favors a proposition supporting deterrence more than it favors one asserting that deterrence is absent."[97]

This debate on incentives and how people respond to them arises repeatedly in many different contexts. Take gun-buyback programs. Surely the intention of such programs is good, but why should we believe that they will greatly influence the number of guns on the street? True, the guns purchased are removed from circulation, and these programs may help to stigmatize gun ownership. Yet if they continue, one effect of such programs will be to increase the return to buying a gun. The price that a person is willing to pay for a gun today increases as the price for which it can be sold rises. In the extreme case, if the price offered in these gun-buyback programs ever became sufficiently high, people would simply buy guns in order to sell them through these programs. I am sure this would hardly distress gun manufacturers, but other than creating some socially useless work, the programs would have a dubious effect on crime. Empirical work on this question reveals no impact on crime from these programs.[98]

Introspection can go only so far. Ultimately, the issue of whether sanctions or other costs deter criminals can be decided only empirically. To what extent will concealed-handgun laws or gun-control laws raise these costs? To what extent will criminals be deterred by these costs? In chapter 2 we will consider how to test these questions.

AN OVERVIEW

The following chapters offer a critical review of the existing evidence on gun control and crime, with the primary focus on the central questions that concern us all: Does gun ownership save or cost lives, and how do the various gun laws affect this outcome?

To answer these questions I use a wide array of data. For instance, I have employed polls that allow us to track how gun ownership has changed over time in different states, as well as the massive FBI yearly crime rate data for all 3,054 U.S. counties from 1977 to 1992. I use additional, more recently available data for 1993 and 1994 later to check my results. Over the last decade, gun ownership has been growing for virtually all demographic groups, though the fastest growing group of gun owners is Republican women, thirty to forty-four years of age, who live in rural areas. National crime rates have been falling at the same time as gun ownership has been rising. Likewise, states experiencing the greatest reductions in crime are also the ones with the fastest growing percentages of gun ownership.

Overall, my conclusion is that criminals as a group tend to behave rationally—when crime becomes more difficult, less crime is committed. Higher arrest and conviction rates dramatically reduce crime. Criminals also move out of jurisdictions in which criminal deterrence increases. Yet criminals respond to more than just the actions taken by the police and the courts. Citizens can take private actions that also deter crime. Allowing citizens to carry concealed handguns reduces violent crimes, and the reductions coincide very closely with the number of concealed-handgun permits issued. Mass shootings in public places are reduced when law-abiding citizens are allowed to carry concealed handguns.

Not all crime categories showed reductions, however. Allowing concealed handguns might cause small increases in larceny and auto theft. When potential victims are able to arm themselves, some criminals turn away from crimes like robbery that require direct attacks and turn instead to such crimes as auto theft, where the probability of direct contact with victims is small.

There were other surprises as well. While the support for the strictest gun-control laws is usually strongest in large cities, the largest drops in violent crime from legalized concealed handguns occurred in the most urban counties with the greatest populations and the highest crime rates. Given the limited resources available to law enforcement and our desire to spend those resources wisely to reduce crime, the results of my studies have implications for where police should concentrate their efforts. For example, I found that increasing arrest rates in the most crime-prone areas led to the greatest reductions in crime. Comparisons can also be made across different methods of fighting crime. Of all the methods studied so far by economists, the carrying of concealed handguns appears to be the most cost-effective method for reducing crime. Accident and suicide rates were unaltered by the presence of concealed handguns.

Guns also appear to be the great equalizer among the sexes. Murder rates decline when either more women or more men carry concealed handguns, but the effect is especially pronounced for women. One additional woman carrying a concealed handgun reduces the murder rate for women by about 3–4 times more than one additional man carrying a concealed handgun reduces the murder rate for men. This occurs because allowing a woman to defend herself with a concealed handgun produces a much larger change in her ability to defend herself than the change created by providing a man with a handgun.

While some evidence indicates that increased penalties for using a gun in the commission of a crime reduce crime, the effect is small. Furthermore, I find no crime-reduction benefits from state-mandated waiting periods and background checks before people are allowed to purchase guns. At the federal level, the Brady law has proven to be no more effective. Surprisingly, there is also little benefit from training requirements or age restrictions for concealed-handgun permits.

Two

How to Test the Effects of Gun Control

THE EXISTING LITERATURE

Despite intense feelings on both sides of the gun debate, I believe everyone is at heart motivated by the same concerns: Will gun control increase or decrease the number of lives lost? Will these laws improve or degrade the quality of life when it comes to violent crime? The common fears we all share with regard to murders, rapes, robberies, and aggravated assaults motivate this discussion. Even those who debate the meaning of the Constitution's Second Amendment cannot help but be influenced by the answers to these questions.[1]

While anecdotal evidence is undoubtedly useful in understanding the issues at hand, it has definite limits in developing public policy. Good arguments exist on both sides, and neither side has a monopoly on stories of tragedies that might have been avoided if the law had only been different. While one side presents the details of a loved one senselessly murdered in a massacre like the December 1993 Colin Ferguson shooting on the Long Island Railroad, the other side points to claims that if only Texas had allowed concealed handguns, the twenty-two lives lost in Luby's restaurant in Killeen in October 1991 could have been saved. Less publicized but equally tragic stories have been just as moving.

Surveys have filled many important gaps in our knowledge; nevertheless, they suffer from many inherent problems. For example, how accurately can a person judge whether the presence of a gun actually saved her life or whether it really prevented a criminal from attacking? Might people's policy preferences influence how they answer the pollster's questions? Other serious concerns arise with survey data. Does a criminal who is thwarted from committing one particular crime merely substitute another victim or another type of crime? Or might this general deterrence raise the costs of these undesirable activities enough so that some criminals stop committing crimes? Survey data just has not been able to answer such questions.

To study these issues more effectively, academics have turned to statistics on crime. Depending on what one counts as academic research, there are at least two hundred studies on gun control. The existing work falls into two categories, using either "time-series" or "cross-sectional" data. Time-series data deal with one particular area (a city, county, or state) over many years; cross-sectional data look across many different geographic areas within the same year. The vast majority of gun-control studies that examine time-series data present a comparison of the average murder rates before and after the change in laws; those that examine cross-sectional data compare murder rates across places with and without certain laws. Unfortunately, these studies make no attempt to relate fluctuations in crime rates to changing law-enforcement factors like arrest or conviction rates, prison-sentence lengths, or other obvious variables.

Both time-series and cross-sectional analyses have their limitations. Let us first examine the cross-sectional studies. Suppose, as happens to be true, that areas with the highest crime rates are the ones that most frequently adopt the most stringent gun-control laws. Even if restrictions on guns were to lower the crime rates, it might appear otherwise. Suppose crime rates were lowered, but not by enough to reach the level of rates in low-crime areas that did not adopt the laws. In that case, looking across areas would make it appear that stricter gun control produced higher crime. Would this be proof that stricter gun control caused higher crime? Hardly. Ideally, one should examine how the high-crime areas that adopted the controls changed over time—not only relative to their past levels but also relative to areas without the controls. Economists refer to this as an "endogeneity" problem. The adoption of the policy is a reaction (that is, "endogenous") to other events, in this case crime.[2] To correctly estimate the impact of a law on crime, one must be able to distinguish and isolate the influence of crime on the adoption of the law.

For time-series data, other problems arise. For example, while the ideal study accounts for other factors that may help explain changing crime rates, a pure time-series study complicates such a task. Many potential causes of crime might fluctuate in any one jurisdiction over time, and it is very difficult to know which one of those changes might be responsible for the shifting crime rate. If two or more events occur at the same time in a particular jurisdiction, examining only that jurisdiction will not help us distinguish which event was responsible for the change in crime. Evidence is usually much stronger if a law changes in many different places at different times, and one can see whether similar crime patterns exist before and after such changes.

The solution to these problems is to combine both time-series and cross-sectional evidence and then allow separate variables, so that each year the national or regional changes in crime rates can be separated out and distinguished from any local deviations.[3] For example, crime may have fallen nationally between 1991 and 1992, but what this study is able to examine is whether there is an additional decline over and above that national drop in states that have adopted concealed-handgun laws. I also use a set of measures that control for the average differences in crime rates across places even after demographic, income, and other factors have been accounted for. No previous gun-control studies have taken this approach.

The largest cross-sectional gun-control study examined 170 cities in 1980.[4] While this study controlled for many differences across cities, no variables were used to deal with issues of deterrence (such as arrest or conviction rates or prison-sentence lengths). It also suffered from the bias discussed above that these cross-sectional studies face in showing a positive relationship between gun control and crime.

The time-series work on gun control that has been most heavily cited by the media was done by three criminologists at the University of Maryland who looked at five different counties (one at a time) from three different states (three counties from Florida, one county from Mississippi, and one from Oregon) from 1973 to 1992 (though a different time period was used for Miami).[5] While this study has received a great deal of media attention, it suffers from serious problems. Even though these concealed-handgun laws were state laws, the authors say that they were primarily interested in studying the effect in urban areas. Yet they do not explain how they chose the particular counties used in their study. For example, why examine Tampa but not Fort Lauderdale, or Jacksonville but not Orlando? Like most previous studies, their research does not account for any other variables that might also help explain the crime rates.

Some cross-sectional studies have taken a different approach and used the types of statistical techniques found in medical case studies. Possibly the best known paper was done by Arthur Kellermann and his many co-authors,[6] who purport to show that "keeping a gun in the home was strongly and independently associated with an increased risk of homicide."[7] The data for this test consists of a "case sample" (444 homicides that occurred in the victim's homes in three counties) and a "control" group (388 "matched" individuals who lived near the deceased and were the same sex and race as well as the same age range). After information was obtained from relatives of the homicide victim or the control subjects regarding such things as whether they owned a gun or had a drug or alcohol problem, these authors attempted to see if the probability of a homicide was correlated with the ownership of a gun.

There are many problems with Kellermann et al.'s paper that undercut the misleading impression that victims were killed by the gun in the home. For example, they fail to report that in only 8 of these 444 homicide cases could it be established that the "gun involved had been kept in the home."[8] More important, the question posed by the authors cannot be tested properly using their chosen methodology because of the endogeneity problem discussed earlier with respect to cross-sectional data.

To demonstrate this, suppose that the same statistical method—with a matching control group—was used to do an analogous study on the efficacy of hospital care. Assume that we collected data just as these authors did; that is, we got a list of all the people who died in a particular county over the period of a year, and we asked their relatives whether they had been admitted to a hospital during the previous year. We would also put together a control sample with people of similar ages, sex, race, and neighborhoods, and ask these men and women whether they had been in a hospital during the past year. My bet is that we would find a very strong positive relationship between those who spent time in hospitals and those who died, quite probably a stronger relationship than in Kellermann's study on homicides and gun ownership. If so, would we take that as evidence that hospitals kill people? I would hope not. We would understand that, although our methods controlled for age, sex, race, and neighborhood, the people who had visited a hospital during the past year and the people in the "control" sample who did not visit a hospital were really not the same types of people. The difference is pretty obvious: those hospitalized were undoubtedly sick, and thus it should come as no surprise that they would face a higher probability of dying.

The relationship between homicides and gun ownership is no different. The finding that those who are more likely to own guns suffer a higher homicide rate makes us ask, Why were they more likely to own guns? Could it be that they were at greater risk of being attacked? Is it possible that this difference arose because of a higher rate of illegal activities among those in the case study group than among those in the control group? Owning a gun could lower the probability of attack but still leave it higher than the probability faced by those who never felt the need to buy a gun to begin with. The fact that all or virtually all the homicide victims were killed by weapons brought into their homes by intruders makes this all the more plausible.

Unfortunately, the case study method was not designed for studying these types of social issues. Compare these endogeneity concerns with a laboratory experiment to test the effectiveness of a new drug. Some patients with the disease are provided with the drug, while others are given a placebo. The random assignment of who gets the drug and who receives the placebo is extremely important. A comparable approach to the link between homicide and guns would have researchers randomly place guns inside certain households and also randomly determine in which households guns would be forbidden. Who receives a gun would not be determined by other factors that might themselves be related to whether a person faces a high probability of being killed.

So how does one solve this causation problem? Think for a moment about the preceding hospital example. One approach would be to examine a change in something like the cost of going to hospitals. For example, if the cost of going to hospitals fell, one could see whether some people who would otherwise not have gone to the hospital would now seek help there. As we observed an increase in the number of people going to hospitals, we could then check to see whether this was associated with an increase or decrease in the number of deaths. By examining changes in hospital care prices, we could see what happens to people who now choose to go to the hospital and who were otherwise similar in terms of characteristics that would determine their probability of living.

Obviously, despite these concerns over previous work, only statistical evidence can reveal the net effect of gun laws on crimes and accidental deaths. The laws being studied here range from those that allow concealed-handgun permits to those demanding waiting periods or setting mandatory minimum sentences for using a gun in the commission of a crime. Instead of just examining how crime changes in a particular city or state, I analyze the first systematic national evidence for all 3,054 counties in the United States over the sixteen years from 1977 to 1992 and ask whether these rules saved or cost lives. I attempt to control for a change in the price people face in defending themselves by looking at the change in the laws regarding the carrying of concealed handguns. I will also use the data to examine why certain states have adopted concealed-handgun laws while others have not.

This book is the first to study the questions of deterrence using these data. While many recent studies employ proxies for deterrence—such as police expenditures or general levels of imprisonment—I am able to use arrest rates by type of crime and also, for a subset of the data, conviction rates and sentence lengths by type of crime.[9] I also attempt to analyze a question noted but not empirically addressed in this literature: the concern over causality related to increases in both handgun use and crime rates. Do higher crime rates lead to increased handgun ownership or the reverse? The issue is more complicated than simply whether carrying concealed firearms reduces murders, because questions arise about whether criminals might substitute one type of crime for another as well as the extent to which accidental handgun deaths might increase.

THE IMPACT OF CONCEALED HANDGUNS ON CRIME

Many economic studies have found evidence broadly consistent with the deterrent effect of punishment.[10] The notion is that the expected penalty affects the prospective criminal's desire to commit a crime. Expectations about the penalty include the probabilities of arrest and conviction, and the length of the prison sentence. It is reasonable to disentangle the probability of arrest from the probability of conviction, since accused individuals appear to suffer large reputational penalties simply from being arrested.[11] Likewise, conviction also imposes many different penalties (for example, lost licenses, lost voting rights, further reductions in earnings, and so on) even if the criminal is never sentenced to prison.[12]

While these points are well understood, the net effect of concealed-handgun laws is ambiguous and awaits testing that controls for other factors influencing the returns to crime. The first difficulty involves the availability of detailed county-level data on a variety of crimes in 3,054 counties during the period from 1977 to 1992. Unfortunately, for the time period we are studying, the FBI's *Uniform Crime Reports* include arrest-rate data but not conviction rates or prison sentences. While I make use of the arrest-rate information, I include a separate variable for each county to account for the different average crime rates each county faces,[13] which admittedly constitutes a rather imperfect way to control for cross-county differences such as expected penalties.

Fortunately, however, alternative variables are available to help us measure changes in legal regimes that affect the crime rate. One such method is to use another crime category to explain the changes in the crime rate being studied. Ideally, one would pick a crime rate that moves with the crime rate being studied (presumably because of changes in the legal system or other social conditions that affect crime), but is unrelated to changes in laws regulating the right to carry firearms. Additional motivations for controlling other crime rates include James Q. Wilson's and George Kelling's "broken window" effect, where less serious crimes left undeterred will lead to more serious ones.[14] Finally, after telephoning law-enforcement officials in all fifty states, I was able to collect time-series, county-level conviction rates and mean prison-sentence lengths for three states (Arizona, Oregon, and Washington).

The FBI crime reports include seven categories of crime: murder and non-negligent manslaughter, rape, aggravated assault, robbery, auto theft, burglary, and larceny.[15] Two additional summary categories were included: violent crimes (including murder, rape, aggravated assault, and robbery) and property crimes (including auto theft, burglary, and larceny). Although they are widely reported measures in the press, these broader categories are somewhat problematic in that all crimes are given the same weight (for example, one murder equals one aggravated assault).

The most serious crimes also make up only a very small portion of this index and account for very little of the variation in the total number of violent crimes across counties (see table 2.1). For example, the average county has about eight murders, and counties differ from this number by an average of twelve murders. Obviously, the number of murders cannot be less than zero; the average difference is greater than the average simply because while 46 percent of the counties had no murders in 1992, some counties had a very large number of murders (forty-one counties had more than a hundred murders, and two counties had over one thousand murders). In comparison, the average county experienced 619 violent crimes, and counties differ from this amount by an average of 935. Not only does the murder rate contribute just a little more than 1 percent to the total number of violent crimes, but the average difference in murders across counties also explains just a little more than 1 percent of the differences in violent crimes across counties.

Even the narrower categories are somewhat broad for our purposes. For example, robbery includes not only street robberies, which seem the most likely to be affected by concealed-handgun laws, but also bank rob-

Table 2.1 The most common crimes and the variation in their prevalence across counties (1992)

	Average number of crimes	Percent of crime category	Dispersion	Percent of variation in general category due to each crime	Number of counties
Violent crime	619.1		934.50		2,853
Murder	7.8	1.3%	11.60	1.2%	2,954
Rape	35.4	5.7%	48.96	5.2%	2,853
Robbery	224.8	36.3%	380.70	40.7%	2,954
Aggravated assault	367.5	59.4%	534.80	57.2%	2,954
Property crime	4,078.2		5,672		2,954
Auto theft	533.9	13.1%	868	15.3%	2,954
Burglary	969.1	23.8%	1,331	23.4%	2,954
Larceny	2,575.2	63.1%	3.516	62.0%	2,954

Note: Dispersion provides a measure of variation for each crime category; it is a measure of the average difference between the overall average and each county's number of crimes. The total of the percents for specific crimes in the violent-crime category does not equal 100 percent because not all counties report consistent measures of rape. Other differences are due to rounding errors.

beries, for which, because of the presence of armed guards, the additional return to permitting citizens to be armed would appear to be small.[16] Likewise, larceny involves crimes of "stealth," which includes those committed by pickpockets, purse snatchers, shoplifters, and bike thieves, and crimes like theft from buildings, coin machines, and motor vehicles. However, while most of these fit the categories in which concealed-handgun laws are likely to do little to discourage criminals, pickpockets do come into direct contact with their victims.

This aggregation of crime categories makes it difficult to isolate crimes that might be deterred by increased handgun ownership and crimes that might be increasing as a result of a substitution effect. Generally, the crimes most likely to be deterred by concealed-handgun laws are those involving direct contact between the victim and the criminal, especially when they occur in places where victims otherwise would not be allowed to carry firearms. Aggravated assault, murder, robbery, and rape are both confrontational and likely to occur where guns were not previously allowed.

In contrast, crimes like auto theft of unattended cars seem unlikely to be deterred by gun ownership. While larceny is more debatable, in general—to the extent that these crimes actually involve "stealth"—the probability that victims will notice the crime being committed seems low, and thus the opportunities to use a gun are relatively rare. The effect on burglary is ambiguous from a theoretical standpoint. It is true that if nondiscretionary laws cause more people to own a guns, burglars will face greater risks when breaking into houses, and this should reduce the number of burglaries. However, if some of those who already own guns now obtain right-to-carry permits, the relative cost of crimes like armed street robbery and certain other types of robberies (where an armed patron may be present) should rise relative to that for burglary or residential robbery. This may cause some criminals to engage in burglaries instead of armed street robbery. Indeed, a recent Texas poll suggests that such substitution may be substantial: 97 percent of first-time applicants for concealed-handgun permits already owned a handgun.[17]

Previous concealed-handgun studies that rely on state-level data suffer from an important potential problem: they ignore the heterogeneity within states.[18] From my telephone conversations with many law-enforcement officials, it has become very clear that there was a large variation across counties within a state in terms of how freely gun permits were granted to residents prior to the adoption of nondiscretionary right-to-carry laws.[19] All those I talked to strongly indicated that the most populous counties had previously adopted by far the most restrictive practices in issuing permits. The implication for existing studies is that simply using state-level data rather than county data will bias the results against finding any impact from passing right-to-carry provisions. Those counties that were unaffected by the law must be separated from those counties where the change could be quite dramatic. Even cross-sectional city data will not solve this problem, because without time-series data it is impossible to determine the impact of a change in the law for a particular city.[20]

There are two ways of handling this problem. First, for the national sample, one can see whether the passage of nondiscretionary right-to-carry laws produces systematically different effects in the high- and low-population counties. Second, for three states—Arizona, Oregon, and Pennsylvania—I acquired time-series data on the number of right-to-carry permits for each county. The normal difficulty with using data on the number of permits involves the question of causality: Do more permits make crimes more costly, or do higher crime rates lead to more permits? The change in the number of permits before and after the change in the state laws allows us to rank the counties on the basis of how restrictive they had actually been in issuing permits prior to the change in the law. Of course there is still the question of why the state concealed-handgun law changed, but since we are dealing with county-level rather than state-level data, we benefit from the fact that those counties with the most restrictive policies regarding permits were also the most likely to have the new laws imposed upon them by the state.

Using county-level data also has another important advantage in that both crime and arrest rates vary widely within states. In fact, as indicated in table 2.2, the variation in both crime rates and arrest rates across states is almost always smaller than the average within-state variation across counties. With the exception of the rates for robbery, the variation in crime rates across states is from 61 to 83 percent of their average variation within states. (The difference in violent-crime rates arises because robberies make up such a large fraction of the total crimes in this category.) For arrest rates, the numbers are much more dramatic; the variation across states is as small as 15 percent of the average of the variation within states.

These results imply that it is no more accurate to view all the counties in the typical state as a homogenous unit than it is to view all the states in the United States as a homogenous unit. For example, when a state's arrest rate rises, it may make a big difference whether that increase is taking place in the most or least crime-prone counties. Widely differing estimates of the deterrent effect of increasing a state's average arrest rate may be made, depending on which types of counties are experiencing the changes in arrest rates and depending on how sensitive the crime rates are to arrest-rate changes in those particular counties. Aggregating these

Table 2.2 Comparing the variation in crime rates across states and across counties within states from 1977 to 1992

	Percent of variation across states relative to the average variation within states
Crime rates per 100,000 population	
Violent-crime rate	111%
Murder rate	75
Murder rate with guns (from 1982 to 1991)	61
Rape rate	69
Aggravated-assault rate	83
Robbery rate	166
Property-crime rate	66
Auto theft rate	74
Burglary rate	69
Larceny rate	61
Arrest rates (number of arrests divided by number of offenses)*	
Violent crimes	21
Murder	21
Rape	17
Robbery	21
Aggravated assault	32
Property crime	18
Burglary	23
Larceny	15
Auto theft	15
Truncating arrest rates to be no greater than one	
Violent crime	44
Murder	30
Rape	34
Robbery	25
Aggravated assault	41
Property crimes	43
Burglary	33
Larceny	46
Auto theft	31

Note: The percents are computed as the standard deviation of state means divided by the average within-state standard deviations across counties.

*Because of multiple arrests for a crime and because of the lags between the time when a crime occurs and the time an arrest takes place, the arrest rate for counties and states can be greater than one. This is much more likely to occur for counties than for states.

data may thus make it more difficult to discern the true relationship between deterrence and crime.

Another way of illustrating the differences between state and county data is simply to compare the counties with the highest and lowest crime rates to the states with the highest and lowest rates. Tables 2.3 and 2.4 list the ten safest and ten most dangerous states by murder and rape rates, along with those same crime rates for the safest and most dangerous counties in each state. (When rates were zero in more than one county, the number of counties is given.) Two conclusions are clear from these tables. First, even the states with the highest murder and rape rates have counties with no murders or rapes, and these counties in the most dangerous states are much safer than the safest states, according to the average state crime rates for the safest states. Second, while the counties with the highest murder rates tend to be well-known places like Orleans (New Orleans, Louisiana), Kings (Brooklyn, N.Y.), Los Angeles, and Baltimore, there are a few relatively small, rural counties that, for very short periods

Table 2.3 Murder rates: state and county variation in the states with the ten highest and ten lowest murder rates (1992)

States ranked by level of murder rate (10 highest; 10 lowest)	Murder rate per 100,000	County with highest murder rate	Highest county murder rate per 100,000	Number of counties with zero murder rate
Louisiana (1)	15.3	Orleans	57	5
New York (2)	13.2	Kings	28	13
Texas (3)	12.7	Delta	64	116
California (4)	12.66	Los Angeles	21	8
Maryland (5)	12.1	Baltimore	46	4
Illinois (6)	11.21	St. Clair	31	67
Arkansas (7)	10.8	Chicot	53	19
Georgia (8)	10.7	Taliaferro	224	62
North Carolina (9)	10.4	Graham	56	16
South Carolina (10)	10.35	Jasper	32	4
Nebraska (41)	3.2	Pierce	13	72
Utah (42)	2.99	Kane	20	15
Massachusetts (43)	2.97	Suffolk	12	2
Montana (44)	2.22	Meager	55	32
North Dakota (45)	1.9	Golden Valley	53	44
Maine (46)	1.7	Washington	5.5	7
New Hampshire (47)	1.5	Carroll	5.5	5
Iowa (48)	1.1	Wayne	14	71
Vermont (49)	0.7	Chittenden	2.2	9
South Dakota (50)	0.6	Bon Homme	14	49

Table 2.4 Rape rates: state and county variation in the states with the ten highest and ten lowest rape rates (1992)

States ranked by level of rape rate (10 highest; 10 lowest)	Rape rate per 100,000	County with highest rape rate	Highest county rape rate per 100,000	County with lowest rape rate	Lowest county rape rate per 100,000
Alaska (1)	98	North Slope	473	Matanuska-Susitina	14
Delaware (2)	86	Sussex	118	New Castle	74
Michigan (3)	79	Branch	198	Keweenaw	0
Washington (4)	71	Ferry	237	Garfield	0
South Carolina (5)	59	Dillon	97	2 counties	0
Nevada (6)	55	Washoe	82	5 counties	0
Florida (7)	53.7	Putnam	178	3 counties	0
Texas (8)	53.5	Rains	130	70 counties	0
Oregon (9)	53	Multnomah	95	3 counties	0
South Dakota (10)	50	Pennington	136	24 counties	0
Mississippi (41)	29	Harrison	108	11 counties	0
Pennsylvania (42)	27.4	Fulton	85	2 counties	0
Connecticut (43)	26.8	New Haven	38	Windham	1
Wisconsin (44)	26.4	Menominee	98	10 counties	0
North Dakota (45)	25	Morton	81	33 counties	0
Maine (46)	23	Franklin	41	Sagadahoc	0
West Virginia (47)	22	Cabell	99	8 counties	0
Montana (48)	21	Mineral	179	24 counties	0
Iowa (49)	13	Buchanan	62	40 counties	0
Vermont (50)	12	Chittenden	47	Orange	0

of time, garner the top spots in a state. The reverse is not true, however: counties with the lowest murder rates are always small, rural ones.

The two exceptions to this general situation are the two states with the highest rape rates: Alaska and Delaware. Alaska, possibly because of the imbalance of men and women in the population, has high rape rates over the entire state.[21] Even Matanuska-Susitina, which is the Alaskan borough with the lowest rape rate, has a higher rape rate than either Iowa or Vermont. Delaware, which has a very narrow range between the highest and lowest county rape rates, is another exception. However, at least part of the reason for a nonzero rape rate in New Castle county (although this doesn't explain the overall high rape rate in the state) is that Delaware has only three counties, each with a relatively large population, which virtually guarantees that some rapes will take place.

Perhaps the relatively small across-state variation as compared to within-state variations is not so surprising, given that states tend to average out differences as they encompass both rural and urban areas. Yet when coupled with the preceding discussion on the differing effects of concealed-handgun provisions on different counties in the same state, these numbers strongly imply that it is risky to assume that states are homogenous units with respect either to how crimes are punished or how the laws that affect gun usage are changed. Unfortunately, this emphasis on state-level data pervades the entire crime literature, which focuses on state- or city-level data and fails to recognize the differences between rural and urban counties.

However, using county-level data has some drawbacks. Because of the low crime rates in many low-population counties, it is quite common to find huge variations in the arrest and conviction rates from year to year. These variations arise both because the year in which the offense occurs frequently differs from the year in which the arrests and/or convictions occur, and because an offense may involve more than one offender. Unfortunately, the FBI data set allows us neither to link the years in which offenses and arrests occurred nor to link offenders with a particular crime. In counties where only a couple of murders occur annually, arrests or convictions can be many times higher than the number of offenses in a year. This data problem appears especially noticeable for counties with few people and for crimes that are relatively infrequent, like murder and rape.

One partial solution is to limit the sample to counties with large populations. Counties with a large number of crimes have a significantly smoother flow of arrests and convictions relative to offenses. An alternative solution is to take a moving average of the arrest or conviction rates over several years, though this reduces the length of the usable sample period, depending on how many years are used to compute this average. Furthermore, the moving-average solution does nothing to alleviate the effect of multiple suspects being arrested for a single crime.

Another concern is that otherwise law-abiding citizens may have carried concealed handguns even before it was legal to do so.[22] If nondiscretionary laws do not alter the total number of concealed handguns carried by otherwise law-abiding citizens, but merely legalize their previous actions, passing these laws seems unlikely to affect crime rates. The only real effect from making concealed handguns legal could arise from people being more willing to use them to defend themselves, though this might also imply that they would be more likely to make mistakes in using them.

It is also possible that concealed-firearm laws both make individuals safer and increase crime rates at the same time. As Sam Peltzman has pointed out in the context of automobile safety regulations, increasing safety may lead drivers to offset these gains by taking more risks as they drive.[23] Indeed, recent studies indicate that drivers in cars equipped with air bags drive more recklessly and get into accidents at sufficiently higher rates to offset the life-saving effect of air bags for the driver and actually increase the total risk of death for others.[24] The same thing is possible with regard to crime. For example, allowing citizens to carry concealed firearms may encourage them to risk entering more dangerous neighborhoods or to begin traveling during times they previously avoided:

> Martha Hayden, a Dallas saleswoman, said the right-to-carry law introduced in Texas this year has turned her life around.
>
> She was pistol-whipped by a thief outside her home in 1993, suffering 300 stitches to the head, and said she was "terrified" of even taking out the garbage after the attack.
>
> But now she packs a .357 Smith and Wesson. "It gives me a sense of security; it allows you to get on with your life," she said.[25]

Staying inside her house may have reduced Ms. Hayden's probability of being assaulted again, but since her decision to engage in these riskier activities is a voluntary one, she at least believes that this is an acceptable risk. Likewise, society as a whole might be better off even if crime rates were to rise as a result of concealed-handgun laws.

Finally, we must also address the issues of why certain states adopted concealed-handgun laws and whether higher offense rates result in lower arrest rates. To the extent that states adopted the laws because crime was rising, econometric estimates that fail to account for this relationship will underpredict the drop in crime and perhaps improperly blame some of the higher crime rates on the new police who were hired to help solve the problem. To explain this problem differently, crime rates may have risen even though concealed-handgun laws were passed, but the rates might have risen even higher if the laws had not been passed. Likewise, if the laws were adopted when crime rates were falling, the bias would be in the opposite direction. None of the previous gun-control studies deal with this type of potential bias.[26]

The basic problem is one of causation. Does the change in the laws alter the crime rate, or does the change in the crime rate alter the law? Do higher crime rates lower the arrest rate or the reverse? Does the arrest rate really drive the changes in crime rates, or are any errors in measuring crime rates driving the relationship between crime and arrest rates? Fortunately, we can deal with these potential biases by using well-known techniques that let us see what relationships, if any still exist after we try to explain the arrest rates and the adoption of these laws. For example, in examining arrest rates, we can see how they change due to such things as changes in crime rates and then see to what extent the unexplained portion of the arrest rates helps to explain the crime rate. We will find that accounting for these concerns actually strengthens the general findings that I will show initially. My general approach, however, is to examine first how concealed-handgun laws and crime rates, as well as arrest rates and crime rates, tend to move in comparison to one another before we try to deal with more complicated relationships.

Who Owns Guns?

Before studying what determines the crime rate, I would like to take a look at what types of people own guns and how this has been changing over time. Information on gun-ownership rates is difficult to obtain, and the only way to overcome this problem is to rely on surveys. The largest, most extensive polls are the exit polls conducted during the general elections every two years. Recent presidential election polls for 1988 and 1996 contained a question on whether a person owned a gun, as well as information on the person's age, sex, race, income, place of residence, and political views. The available 1992 survey data did not include a question on gun ownership. Using the individual respondent data in the 1988 CBS News General Election Exit Poll and the 1996 Voter News Service National General Election Exit Poll, we can construct a very detailed description of the types of people who own guns. The Voter News Service poll collected data for a consortium of national news bureaus (CNN, CBS, ABC, NBC, Fox, and AP).

What stands out immediately when these polls are compared is the large increase in the number of people who identify themselves as gun owners (see figure 3.1). In 1988, 27.4 percent of voters owned guns.[1] By 1996, the number of voters owning guns had risen to 37 percent. In general, the percentages of voters and the general population who appear to own guns are extremely similar; among the general population, gun ownership rose from 26 to 39 percent,[2] which represented 76 million adults in 1996. Perhaps in retrospect, given all the news media discussions about high crime rates in the last couple of decades, this increase is not very surprising. Just as spending on private security has grown dramatically—reaching $82 billion in 1996, more than twice the amount spent in 1980 (even after taking into account inflation)—more people have been obtaining guns.[3] The large rise in gun sales that took place immediately before the Brady law went into effect in 1994 accounts for some of the increase.[4]

Three points must be made about these numbers. First, the form of

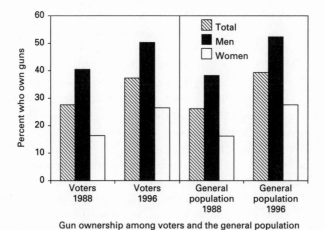

Gun ownership among voters and the general population

Figure 3.1. Percent of women and men who owned guns in 1988 and 1996: examining both voters and the general population

the question changed somewhat between these two years. In 1988 people were asked, "Are you any of the following? (Check as many as apply)," and the list included "Gun Owner." In 1996 respondents were asked to record yes or no to the question, "Are you a gun owner?" This difference may have accounted for part, though not all, of the change.[5] Second, Tom Smith, director of the General Social Survey, told me he guessed that voters might own guns "by up to 5 percent more" than nonvoters, though this was difficult to know for sure because in polls of the general population, over 60 percent of respondents claim to have voted, but we know that only around 50 percent did vote.[6] Given the size of the error in the General Social Survey regarding the percentage of those surveyed who were actual voters, it is nevertheless possible that nonvoters own guns by a few percentage points more than voters.[7]

Finally, there is strong reason to believe that women greatly underreport gun ownership. The most dramatic evidence of this arises from a comparison of the ownership rates for married men and married women. If the issue is whether women have immediate access to a gun in their house when they are threatened with a crime, it is the presence of a gun that is relevant. For example, the 1988 poll data show that 20 percent of married women acknowledged owning a gun, which doesn't come close to the 47 percent figure reported for married men. Obviously, some women interpret this poll question literally regarding personal ownership as opposed to family ownership. If married women were assumed to own guns at the same rate as married men, the gun-ownership rate in 1988 would increase from 27 to 36 percent.[8] Unfortunately, the 1996 data do not allow such a comparison, though presumably a similar effect is also occurring there. The estimates reported in the figures do not attempt to adjust for these three considerations.

The other finding that stands out is that while some types of people are more likely than others to own guns, significant numbers of people in all groups own guns. Despite all the Democrat campaign rhetoric during 1996, almost one in four voters who identify themselves as liberals and almost one in three Democrats own a gun (see figure 3.2). The most typical gun owner may be a rural, white male, middle-aged or older, who is a conservative Republican earning between $30,000 and $75,000. Women, however, experienced the greatest growth in gun ownership during this eight-year period, with an increase of over 70 percent: between the years 1988 and 1996, women went from owning guns at 41 percent of the rate of men to over 53 percent.

High-income people are also more likely to own guns. In 1996, people earning over $100,000 per year were 7 percentage points more likely to own guns than those making less than $15,000. The gap between those earning $30,000 to $75,000 and those making less than $15,000 was over 10 percentage points. These differences in gun ownership between high- and low-income people changed little between the two polls.

When comparing these poll results with the information shown in table 1.1 on murder victims' and offenders' race, the poll results imply

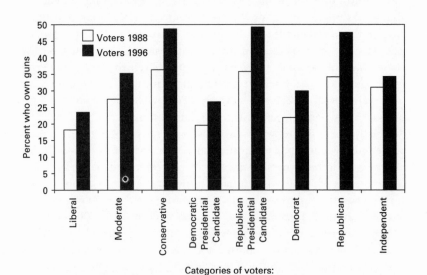

Figure 3.2. Percent of different groups of voters who owned guns in 1988 and 1996

that, at least for blacks and whites, gun ownership does not explain the differential murder rates. For example, while white gun ownership exceeds that for blacks by about 40 percent in 1996 (see figure 3.3), and the vast majority of violent crimes are committed against members of the offender's own racial group, blacks are 4.6 times more likely to be murdered and 5.1 times more likely to be offenders than are whites. Blacks may underreport their gun ownership in these polls, but if the white gun-ownership rate is anywhere near correct, even a black gun-ownership rate of 100 percent could not explain by itself the difference in murder rates.

The polls also indicate that families that included union members tended to own guns at relatively high and more quickly growing rates (see figure 3.3). While the income categories by which people were classified in these polls varied across the two years, it is clear that gun ownership increased across all ranges of income. In fact, of the categories examined, only one experienced declines in gun ownership—people living in urban areas with a population of over 500,000 (see figure 3.4). Not too surprisingly, while rural areas have the highest gun-ownership rates and the lowest crime rates, cities with more than 500,000 people have the lowest gun-ownership rates and the highest crime rates (for example, in 1993 cities with over 500,000 people had murder rates that were over 60 percent higher than the rates in cities with populations between 50,000 and 500,000).

For a subset of the relatively large states, the polls include enough respondents to provide a fairly accurate description of gun ownership even at the state level, as shown in table 3.1. The 1988 survey was extensive enough to provide us with over 1,000 respondents for twenty-one

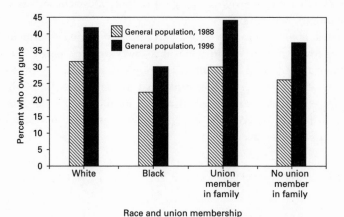

Figure 3.3. Percent of people by race and by union membership who own guns

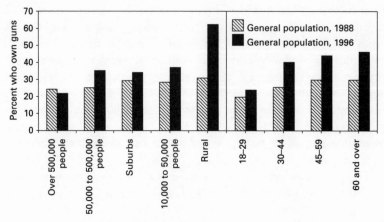

Gun ownership by size of community and by age

Figure 3.4. Percent of people living in different-size communities and in different age groups who owned guns in 1988 and 1996

states, and over 770 respondents for three other states. The 1996 survey was less extensive, with only fourteen of the states surveyed having at least 100 respondents. Since these fourteen states were relatively more urban, they tended to have lower gun-ownership rates than the nation as a whole.

The polls show that the increase in gun ownership was nationwide and not limited to any particular group. Of the fourteen states with enough respondents to make state-level comparisons, thirteen states had more people owning guns at the end of this period. Six states each had over a million more people owning guns. Only Massachusetts saw a decline in gun ownership.

States differ significantly in the percentage of people who own guns. On the lower end in 1988, in states like New York, New Jersey, and Connecticut, only 10 or 11 percent of the population owned guns. Despite its reputation, Texas no longer ranks first in gun ownership; California currently takes that title—approximately 10 million of its citizens own guns. In fact, the percentage of people who own guns in Texas is now below the national average.

UNDERSTANDING DIFFERENT GUN LAWS AND CRIME RATE DATA

While murder rates have exhibited no clear trend over the last twenty years, they are currently 60 percent higher than in 1965.[9] Driven by sub-

Table 3.1 Gun-ownership rates by state

| State | CBS General Election Exit Poll (November 8, 1988) surveyed 34,245 people | | | Voter News Service General Election Exit Poll (November 5, 1996) surveyed 3,818 people | | | Change in states over time | |
	Percent of voting population owning a gun[1] (1)	Percent of state's adults owning a gun[1] (2)	Estimated number of adults owning a gun, using column 2 (3)	Percent of voting population owning a gun[2] (4)	Percent of state's adults owning a gun[2] (5)	Estimated number of adults owning a gun, using column 5 (6)	Change in percent of adults owning a gun (7)	Change in the number of adults owning a gun (8)
United States	27.4%	26%	47.3 million	37%	38.9%	76.7 million	12.9%	29.4 million
California	23%	21%	6 million	33%	32%	10 million	11%	4 million
Connecticut	14%	10%	337,000	10%	12%	377,000	2%	40,000
Florida	28%	29%	3.6 million	35%	31%	4.4 million	2%	800,000
Illinois	19%	17%	1.9 million	34%	36%	4.3 million	19%	2.4 million
Indiana	29%	32%	1.74 million	32%	31%	1.8 million	−1%	60,000
Iowa	29%	31%	847,000	—	—	—	—	—
Maryland	23%	22%	1 million	—	—	—	—	—
Massachusetts	15%	16%	951,000	12%	11%	638,000	−5%	−313,000
Michigan	27%	28%	2.5 million	38%	37%	3.5 million	9%	1 million
Minnesota	33%	28%	1.2 million	—	—	—	—	—
Mississippi	40%	40%	1 million	—	—	—	—	—
Missouri	37%	31%	1.6 million	—	—	—	—	—
Nevada	30%	38%	404,000	—	—	—	—	—
New Jersey	12%	11%	810,000	14%	13%	1.04 million	2%	230,000
New Mexico	38%	41%	608,000	—	—	—	—	—

Table 3.1 Continued

	CBS General Election Exit Poll (November 8, 1988) surveyed 34,245 people			Voter News Service General Election Exit Poll (November 5, 1996) surveyed 3,818 people			Change in states over time	
State	Percent of voting population owning a gun[1] (1)	Percent of state's adults owning a gun[1] (2)	Estimated number of adults owning a gun, using column 2 (3)	Percent of voting population owning a gun[2] (4)	Percent of state's adults owning a gun[2] (5)	Estimated number of adults owning a gun, using column 5 (6)	Change in percent of adults owning a gun (7)	Change in the number of adults owning a gun (8)
New York	13%	11%	2 million	20%	18%	3.3 million	7%	1.3 million
North Carolina	35%	32%	2.1 million	45%	43%	4.8 million	11%	2.7 million
Ohio	25%	28%	2.97 million	32%	32%	3.57 million	4%	600,000
Oregon	40%	36%	996,000	—	—	—	—	—
Pennsylvania	24%	19%	2.2 million	30%	29%	3.5 million	10%	1.3 million
Texas	38%	37%	6.1 million	34%	34%	6.4 million	-3%	300,000
Vermont	34%	35%	193,000	—	—	—	—	—
Washington	33%	31%	1.5 million	—	—	—	—	—
Wisconsin	29%	29%	1.4 million	43%	45%	2.3 million	16%	900,000

Source: The polls used are the General Election Exit Polls from CBS (1988) and Voter News Service (1996). The estimated percent of the voting population owning a gun is obtained by using the weighting of responses supplied by the polling organizations. The estimated percent of the general population owning a gun uses a weight that I constructed from the census to account for the difference between the percentage of males and females; whites, blacks, Hispanics and others; and these groups by age categories that are in the voting population relative to the actual state-level populations recorded by the census.

[1]State poll numbers based upon at least 770 respondents per state.

[2]State poll numbers based upon at least one hundred respondents per state. Other states were surveyed, but the number of respondents in each state was too small to provide an accurate measure of gun ownership. These responses were still useful in determining the national ownership rate, even if they were not sufficient to help determine the rate in an individual state.

stantial increases in rapes, robberies, and aggravated assaults, violent crime was 46 percent higher in 1995 than in 1976 and 240 percent higher than in 1965. As shown in figure 3.5, violent-crime rates peaked in 1991, but they are still substantially above the rates in previous decades.

Such high violent-crime rates make people quite concerned about crime, and even the recent declines have not allayed their fears. Stories of people who have used guns to defend themselves have helped motivate thirty-one states to adopt nondiscretionary (also referred to as "shall-issue" or "do-issue") concealed-handgun laws, which require law-enforcement officials or a licensing agency to issue, without subjective discretion, concealed-weapons permits to all qualified applicants (see figure 3.6). This constitutes a dramatic increase from the eight states that had enacted nondiscretionary concealed-weapons laws prior to 1985. The requirements that must be met vary by state, and generally include the following: lack of a significant criminal record, an age restriction of either 18 or 21, various fees, training, and a lack of significant mental illness. The first three requirements, regarding criminal record, age, and payment of a fee, are the most common. Two states, Vermont and Idaho (with the exception of Boise), do not require permits, though the laws against convicted felons carrying guns still apply. In contrast, discretionary laws allow local law-enforcement officials or judges to make case-by-case decisions about whether to grant permits, based on the applicant's ability to prove a "compelling need."

When the data set used in this book was originally put together, county-level crime data was available for the period between 1977 and 1992. During that time, ten states—Florida (1987), Georgia (1989), Idaho (1990), Maine (1985),[10] Mississippi (1990), Montana (1991), Oregon (1990), Pennsylvania (1989), Virginia (1988),[11] and West Virginia (1989)—adopted nondiscretionary right-to-carry firearm laws. Pennsylvania is a special case because Philadelphia was exempted from the state law during the sample period, though people with permits from the surrounding Pennsylvania counties were allowed to carry concealed handguns into the city. Eight other states (Alabama, Connecticut, Indiana, New Hampshire, North Dakota, South Dakota, Vermont, and Washington) have had right-to-carry laws on the books for decades.[12]

Keeping in mind all the endogeneity problems discussed earlier, I have provided in table 3.2 a first and very superficial look at the data for the most recent available year (1992) by showing how crime rates varied with the type of concealed-handgun law. According to the data presented in the table, violent-crime rates were highest in states with the most restrictive rules, next highest in the states that allowed local authorities discretion in granting permits, and lowest in states with nondiscretionary rules.

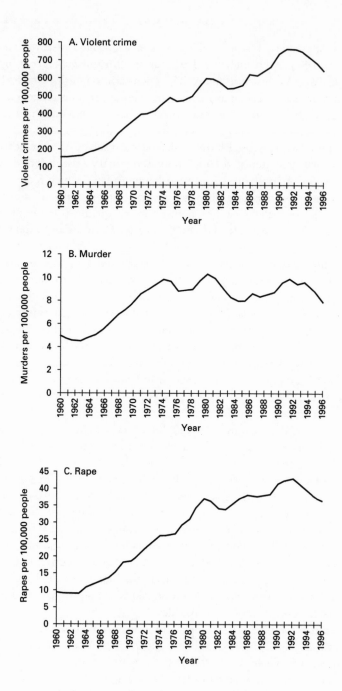

Figure 3.5. U.S. crime rates from 1960—1996 (from FBI's Uniform Crime Reports)

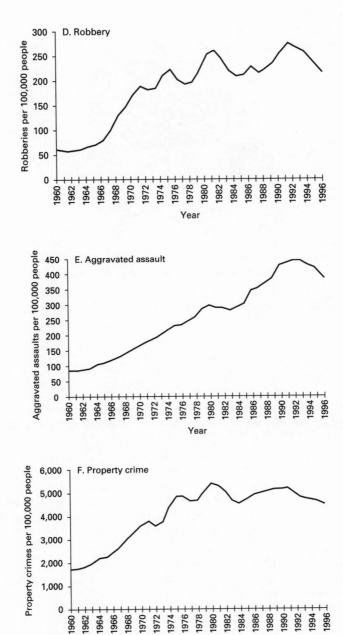

Figure 3.5. Continued

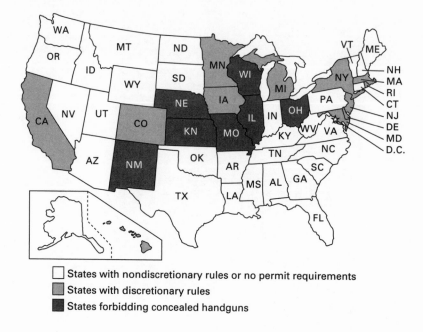

☐ States with nondiscretionary rules or no permit requirements
◼ (gray) States with discretionary rules
◼ States forbidding concealed handguns

Figure 3.6. State concealed-handgun laws as of 1996

Table 3.2 Crime rates in states and the District of Columbia that do and do not allow the carrying of concealed handguns (1992)

Type of crime	Crime rate per 100,000 population				
	States with nondiscretionary concealed-handgun laws	All other states	Percent higher crime rate in states without nondiscretionary laws	States with discretionary concealed-handgun laws	States forbidding concealed handguns
Violent crime	378.8	684.5	81%	653.1	715.9
Murder	5.1	9.5	86%	7.3	11.6
Rape	35	43.6	25%	43.3	43.9
Aggravated assault	229.9	417.4	82%	380.9	451.7
Robbery	108.8	222.6	105%	220.9	224.1
Property crime	3,786.3	4,696.8	24%	4,666.3	4,725.5
Auto theft	334.2	533.4	60%	564.6	504
Burglary	840.3	1,074.7	28%	1,035.8	1,111.3
Larceny	2,611.8	3,088.7	18%	3,065.9	3,110.1

The difference is quite striking: violent crimes are 81 percent higher in states without nondiscretionary laws. For murder, states that ban the concealed carrying of guns have murder rates 127 percent higher than states with the most liberal concealed-carry laws. For property crimes, the difference is much smaller: 24 percent. States with nondiscretionary laws have less crime, but the primary difference appears in terms of violent crimes.

Since the primary data that we will focus on are at the county level, we are asking whether crime rates change in counties whose states adopt nondiscretionary concealed-handgun laws. We are also asking whether the crime rates change relative to other changes in counties located in states without such laws. Using a reference library (Lexis/Nexis) that contains an extensive collection of news stories and state laws, I conducted a search to determine the exact dates on which these laws took effect. In the states that adopted the laws during the year, the effects for their counties were scaled to equal that portion of the year during which the laws were in effect. Because of delays in implementing the laws even after they went into effect, I defined counties in states with nondiscretionary laws as being under the these laws beginning with the first full year for which the law was in effect. While all the tables shown in this book use the second measure, both measures produced similar results.

The number of arrests and offenses for each type of crime in every county from 1977 to 1992 was provided by the FBI's *Uniform Crime Reports;* in addition, however, I contacted the state department of corrections, attorney general, secretary of state, and state police offices in every state in an effort to compile data on conviction rates, sentence lengths, and concealed-weapons permits by county. The Bureau of Justice Statistics also released a list of contacts in every state that might provide state-level criminal justice data. Unfortunately, county data on the total number of outstanding concealed-carry pistol permits were available only for Arizona, California, Florida, Oregon, Pennsylvania, and Washington, and time-series county data before and after a change in the law were only available for Arizona (1994–96), Oregon (1990–92), and Pennsylvania (1986–92). Since the Oregon nondiscretionary law was passed in 1990, I sought data on the number of permits in 1989 by calling up every county sheriff in Oregon, and 25 of the 36 counties provided that information. (The remaining counties stated that records had not been kept.)[13] For Oregon, data on county-level conviction rates and sentence lengths were also available from 1977 to 1992.

One difficulty with the sentence-length data is that Oregon passed a sentencing-reform act that took effect in November 1989 and required criminals to serve 85 percent of their sentences; thus, judges may have correspondingly altered their sentencing practices. This change was phased in over time because the law only applied to crimes committed after it went into effect in 1989. In addition, the Oregon system did not keep complete records prior to 1987, and their completeness decreased as one looked further into the past. One solution to both of these problems is to allow the sentence-length variable to have different effects in each year.[14] A similar problem exists for Arizona, which adopted a truth-in-sentencing reform in the fall of 1994. We must note, finally, that Arizona differs from Oregon and Pennsylvania in that it already allowed handguns to be carried openly before passing its concealed-handgun law; thus, one might expect to find a somewhat smaller response to adopting a concealed-handgun law.

In addition to using separate variables to measure the average crime rate in each county,[15] I collected data from the Bureau of the Census to try to control for other demographic characteristics that might influence the crime rate. These data included information on the population density per square mile, total county population, and detailed information on the racial and age breakdown of the county (percent of population by each racial group and by sex between 10 and 19 years of age, between 20 and 29, between 30 and 39, between 40 and 49, between 50 and 64, and 65 and over).[16] While a large literature discusses the likelihood that younger males will engage in crime,[17] controlling for these other categories allows us to account for the groups considered most vulnerable (for example, females in the case of rape).[18] Recent evidence reported by Glaeser and Sacerdote confirms the higher crime rates experienced in cities and examines the effects on these rates of social and family influences as well as the changing pecuniary benefits from crime;[19] the present study, however, is the first to explicitly control for population density (see appendix 3 for a more complete discussion of the data).

An additional set of income data was also used. These included real per-capita personal income, real per-capita unemployment insurance payments, real per-capita income-maintenance payments, and real per-capita retirement payments per person over 65 years of age.[20] Unemployment insurance and income-maintenance payments from the Commerce Department's Regional Economic Information System (REIS) data set were included in an attempt to provide annual, county-level measures of unemployment and the distribution of income.

Finally, I recognize that other legal changes regarding how guns are used and when they can be obtained can alter the levels of crime. For example, penalties involving improper gun use might also have been changing simultaneously with changes in the requirements for obtaining permits to carry concealed handguns. In order to see whether such changes might confound my ability to infer the causes of any observed changes in crime rates, I read through various editions of *State Laws and Published Ordinances—Firearms* (published by the Bureau of Alcohol, Tobacco, and Firearms: 1976, 1986, 1989, and 1994). Except for the laws regarding machine guns and sawed-off shotguns, the laws involving the use of guns did not change significantly when the rules regarding concealed-handgun permits were changed.[21] A survey by Marvell and Moody that addresses the somewhat broader question of sentencing-enhancement laws for felonies committed with deadly weapons (firearms, explosives, and knives) from 1970 to 1992 also confirms this general finding: all but four of the legal changes were clustered from 1970 to 1981.[22] Yet Marvell and Moody's dates still allow us to examine the deterrent effect of criminal penalties specifically targeted at the use of deadly weapons during this earlier period.[23]

States also differ in terms of their required waiting periods for handgun purchases. Again using the Bureau of Alcohol, Tobacco, and Firearms' *State Laws and Published Ordinances—Firearms,* I identified states with waiting periods and conducted a Lexis search on the ordinances to determine exactly when those laws went into effect. Thirteen of the nineteen states with waiting periods instituted them prior to the beginning of the sample period.[24]

Four

Concealed-Handgun Laws and Crime Rates: The Empirical Evidence

While our initial comparison of crime rates in states with and without concealed-handgun laws was suggestive, obviously many other factors must be accounted for. The next three chapters use common statistical techniques known as regression analysis to control for these factors. (For those who are interested, a more complete discussion of regressions and statistical significance is provided in appendix 1.) The following discussion provides information on a wide range of law-enforcement activities, but the primary focus is on the link between the private ownership of guns and crime. What gun laws affect crime? Does increased gun ownership cause an increase or a decrease in murders? What is the impact of more lenient laws regarding gun ownership on accidental deaths and suicide?

The analysis begins by examining both county- and state-level crime data and then turns to evidence on the benefits of gun ownership for different groups, such as women and minorities. To test whether crime-rate changes are a result of concealed-handgun laws, it is not enough simply to see whether these laws lower crime rates; changes in crime rates must also be linked to the changes in the number of concealed-handgun permits. We must remember also that the laws are not all the same: different states adopt different training and age requirements for obtaining a permit. These differences allow us to investigate whether the form of the concealed-handgun law matters as well as to test the importance of other gun-control laws. Finally, evidence is provided on whether criminals move to other places when concealed-handgun laws are passed.

The book is organized to examine the simplest evidence first and then gradually considers more complicated issues. The first estimates measure whether the average crime rate falls in counties when they adopt concealed-handgun laws. By looking across counties or states at the same time that we examine them over time, we can test not only whether places with the most permits have the greatest reductions in crime, but also whether those with the greatest *increases* in permits have the greatest reductions in crime. Similarly, we can investigate how total gun ownership is related to the level of crime. Tracking gun ownership in individual states over time allows us to investigate how a crime in a state changes as its gun-ownership rates change.

Using County and State Data for the United States

The first group of estimates reported in table 4.1 attempts to explain the crime rates for nine different categories of crime. Each column in the table presents the changes in the crime rate for the crime described in the column heading. The numbers in each row represent the impact that a particular explanatory variable has on each crime rate. Three pieces of information are provided for most of the explanatory variables: (1) the percent change in the crime rate attributed to a particular change in the explanatory variable; (2) the percentage of the variation in the crime rate that can be explained by the variation in the explanatory variable;[1] and (3) one, two, or three asterisks denote whether a particular effect is statistically significant at least at the 1, 5, or 10 percent level, where the 1 percent level represents the most reliable result.[2]

While I am primarily interested in the impact of nondiscretionary laws, the estimates also account for many other variables: the arrest rate for each type of crime; population density and the number of people living in a county; measures of income, unemployment, and poverty; the percentage of the population that is a certain sex and race by ten-year age groupings (10 to 19 years of age, 20 to 29 years of age); and the set of variables described in the previous section to control for other county and year differences. The results clearly imply that nondiscretionary laws coincide with fewer murders, aggravated assaults, and rapes.[3] On the other hand, auto theft and larceny rates rise. Both changes are consistent with my discussion of the direct and substitution effects produced by concealed weapons.[4]

The results are also large, indicating how important the laws can be. When state concealed-handgun laws went into effect in a county, murders fell by about 8 percent, rapes fell by 5 percent, and aggravated assaults fell by 7 percent.[5] In 1992 the following numbers were reported: 18,469 murders; 79,272 rapes; 538,368 robberies; and 861,103 aggravated assaults in counties without nondiscretionary laws. The estimated coefficients suggest that if these counties had been subject to state concealed-

Table 4.1 The effect of nondiscretionary concealed-handgun laws on crime rates: National, County-Level, Cross-Sectional, Time-Series Evidence

	Percent change in various crime rates for changes in explanatory variables								
Change in explanatory variable	Violent crime	Murder	Rape	Aggravated assault	Robbery	Property crime	Burglary	Larceny	Auto theft
Nondiscretionary law adopted	-4.9%* (1%)	-7.7%* (2%)	-5.3%* (1%)	-7.01%* (1%)	-2.2%*** (.3%)	2.7%* (1%)	.05% (.02%)	3.3%* (1%)	7.1%* (1%)
Arrest rate for the crime category (e.g., violent crime, murder, etc.) increased by 100 percentage points	-0.48%* (9%)	-1.39%* (7%)	-0.81%* (4%)	-0.896%* (9%)	-0.57%* (4%)	-0.76%* (10%)	-2.4%* (11%)	-0.18%* (4%)	-0.18%* (3%)
Population per square mile increased by 1,000	6%* (5%)	-2% (1%)	-2% (1%)	0.58% (.4%)	31.6%* (17%)	0.48% (1%)	-7%* (9%)	3.7%* (4%)	48%* (36%)
Real per-capita personal income increased by $1,000	0.79%* (1%)	1.63%* (2%)	-0.59%*** (1%)	0.47% (1%)	0.47% (1%)	-1.02%* (3%)	-1.84%* (4%)	-1.23%* (2%)	1.5%* (2%)

Real per-capita unemployment Ins. increased by $100	−2.2%* (.07%)	−4.6%** (1%)	−4.7%* (1%)	−1.9%* (.05%)	0.7% (.01%)	3.8%* (2%)	6.0%* (3%)	1.9%* (.08%)	2.1%* (.06%)
Real per-capita income maintenance increased by $100	−0.7% (.3%)	2.5%** (1%)	−1.7% (.7%)	1.39% (.7%)	−3.2%* (1%)	1.9%* (2%)	3.9%* (4%)	0.2% (.1%)	3.3%* (2%)
Real per-capita retirement payments per person over 65 increased by $1,000	−0.197% (.5%)	−1.3% (3%)	−0.24% (4%)	−0.68% (2%)	−0.55% (1%)	−0.87% (4%)	−1.06% (7%)	−0.63% (2%)	−0.93% (2%)
Population increased by 100,000	0.86% (1%)	−0.34%* (.4%)	−2.94% (3%)	0.45%* (.06%)	−0.61%*** (.06%)	−2.18%* (6%)	−2.14%* (5%)	−3.10%* (6%)	−0.04%* (.05%)

Note: The percentage reported in parentheses is the percent of a standard deviation change in the endogenous variable that can be explained by one-standard-deviation change in the exogenous variable. Year and county dummies are not shown, and the results for demographic variables are shown in appendix. All regressions use weighted least squares, where the weighting is each county's population. Entire sample used for all counties over the 1977–1992 period.

*The result is statistically significant at the 1 percent level for a two-tailed t-test.

**The result is statistically significant at the 5 percent level for a two-tailed t-test.

***The result is statistically significant at the 10 percent level for a two-tailed t-test.

handgun laws and had thus been forced to issue handgun permits, murders in the United States would have declined by about 1,400.

Given the concern raised about increased accidental deaths from concealed weapons, it is interesting to note that the entire number of accidental handgun deaths in the United States in 1988 was only 200 (the last year for which these data are available for the entire United States).[6] Of this total, 22 accidental deaths were in states with concealed-handgun laws, while 178 occurred in states without these laws. The reduction in murders is as much as eight times greater than the total number of accidental deaths in concealed-handgun states. We will revisit the impact that concealed-handgun laws have on accidental deaths in chapter 5, but if these initial results are accurate, the net effect of allowing concealed handguns is clearly to save lives, even in the implausible case that concealed handguns were somehow responsible for all accidental handgun deaths.[7]

As with murders, the results indicate that the number of rapes in states without nondiscretionary laws would have declined by 4,200, aggravated assaults by 60,000, and robberies by 12,000.[8]

On the other hand, property-crime rates increased after nondiscretionary laws were implemented. If states without concealed-handgun laws had passed such laws, there would have been 247,000 more property crimes in 1992 (a 2.7 percent increase). The increase is small compared to the changes that we observed for murder, rape, and aggravated assault, though it is about the same size as the change for robbery. Criminals respond to the threat of being shot while committing such crimes as robbery by choosing to commit less risky crimes that involve minimal contact with the victim.[9]

It is possible to put a rough dollar value on the losses from crime in the United States and thus on the potential gains from nondiscretionary laws. A recent National Institute of Justice study estimates the costs to victims of different types of crime by measuring lost productivity; out-of-pocket expenses, such as those for medical bills and property losses; and losses from fear, pain, suffering, and lost quality of life.[10] While the use of jury awards to measure losses such as fear, pain, suffering, and lost quality of life may be questioned, the estimates provide us with one method of comparing the reduction in violent crimes with the increase in property crimes.

By combining the estimated reduction in crime from table 4.1 with the National Institute of Justice's estimates of what these crimes would have cost victims had they occurred, table 4.2 reports the gain from allowing concealed handguns to be $5.7 billion in 1992 dollars. The reduction in violent crimes represents a gain of $6.2 billion ($4.2 billion from

Table 4.2 The effect of nondiscretionary concealed-handgun laws on victims' costs: What if all states had adopted nondiscretionary laws?

Crime category	Change in number of crimes if states without nondiscretionary laws in 1992 had adopted them			Change in victims' costs if states without nondiscretionary laws in 1992 had adopted them		
	Estimates using county-level data	Estimates using county-level data and state time trends	Estimates using state-level data	Estimates using county-level data	Estimates using county-level data and state time trends	Estimates using state-level data
Murder	−1,410	−1,840	−1,590	−$4.2 billion	−5.57 billion	−$4.8 billion
Rape	−4,200	−3,700	−4,800	−$374 million	−$334 million	−$431 million
Aggravated assault	−60,400	−61,100	−93,900	−$1.4 billion	−$1.4 billion	−$2.2 billion
Robbery	−11,900	−10,990	−62,900	−$98 million	−$90 million	−$518 million
Burglary	1,100	−112,700	−180,800	$1.5 million	−$162 million	−$261 million
Larceny	191,700	−93,300	−180,300	$73 million	−$35 million	−$69 million
Auto theft	89,900	−41,500	−11,100	$343 million	−$2 million	−$42 million
Total change in victims' costs				−$5.7 billion	−$7.6 billion	−$8.3 billion

Note: Estimates of the costs of crime are in 1992 dollars, from the National Institute of Justice's study.

murder, $1.4 billion from aggravated assault, $374 million from rape, and $98 million from robbery), while the increase in property crimes represents a loss of $417 million ($343 million from auto theft, $73 million from larceny, and $1.5 million from burglary). However, while $5.7 billion is substantial, to put it into perspective, it equals only about 1.23 percent of the total losses to victims from these crime categories. These estimates are probably most sensitive to the value of life used (in the National Institute of Justice Study this was set at $1.84 million in 1992 dollars). Higher estimated values of life would obviously increase the net gains from the passage of concealed-handgun laws, while lower values would reduce the gains. To the extent that people are taking greater risks regarding crime because of any increased sense of safety produced by concealed-handgun laws,[11] the preceding numbers underestimate the total savings from allowing concealed handguns.

The arrest rate produces the most consistent effect on crime. Higher arrest rates are associated with lower crime rates for all categories of crime. Variation in the probability of arrest accounts for 3 to 11 percent of the variation in the various crime rates.[12] Again, the way to think about this is that the typical observed change in the arrest rate explains up to about 11 percent of the typical change in the crime rate. The crime most responsive to the arrest rate is burglary (11 percent), followed by property crimes (10 percent); aggravated assault and violent crimes more generally (9 percent); murder (7 percent); rape, robbery, and larceny (4 percent); and auto theft (3 percent).

For property crimes, the variation in the percentage of the population that is black, male, and between 10 and 19 years of age explains 22 percent of the ups and downs in the property-crime rate.[13] For violent crimes, the same number is 5 percent (see appendix 5). Other patterns also show up in the data. Not surprisingly, a higher percentage of young females is positively and significantly associated with the occurrence of a greater number of rapes.[14] Population density appears to be most important in explaining robbery, burglary, and auto theft rates, with the typical variation in population density explaining 36 percent of the typical change across observations in auto theft.

Perhaps most surprising is the relatively small, even if frequently significant, effect of a county's per-capita income on crime rates. Changes in real per-capita income account for no more than 4 percent of the changes in crime, and in seven of the specifications it explains at most 2 percent of the change. It is *not* safer to live in a high-income neighborhood if other characteristics (for example, demographics) are the same. Generally, high-income areas experience more violent crimes but fewer property crimes. The two notable exceptions to this rule are rape and auto theft: high-income areas experience fewer rapes and more auto theft. If the race, sex, and age variables are replaced with separate variables showing the percentage of the population that is black and white, 50 percent of the variation in the murder rate is explained by variations in the percentage of the population that is black. Yet because of the high rates at which blacks are arrested and incarcerated or are victims of crimes (for example, 38 percent of all murder victims in 1992 were black; see table 1.1), this is not unexpected.

One general caveat should be made in evaluating the coefficients involving the demographic variables. Given the very small portions of the total populations that are in some of these narrow categories (this is particularly true for minority populations), the effect on the crime rate from a one-percentage-point increase in the percentage of the population in that category greatly overstates the true importance of that age, sex, or race grouping. The assumption of a one-percentage-point change is arbitrary and is only provided to give the reader a rough idea of what these coefficients mean. For a better understanding of the impact of these variables, relatively more weight should be placed on the second number, which shows how much of the variation in the various crime rates can be explained by the normal changes in each explanatory variable.[15]

We can take another look at the sensitivity of the results from table 4.1 and examine the impact of different subsets of the following variables: the nondiscretionary law, the nondiscretionary law and the arrest rates, and the nondiscretionary law and the variables that account for the national changes in crime rates across years. Each specification yields results that show even more significant effects from the nondiscretionary law, though when results exclude variables that measure how crime rates differ across counties, they are likely to tell us more about which states adopt these laws than about the impact of these laws on crime.[16] The low-crime states are the most likely to pass these laws, and their crime rates become even lower after their passage. I will attempt to account for this fact later in chapter 6.

In further attempts to test the sensitivity of the results to the various control variables used, I reestimated the specifications in table 4.1 without using either the percentages of the populations that fall into the different sex, race, and age categories or the measures of income; this tended to produce similar though somewhat more significant results with respect to concealed-handgun laws. The estimated gains from passing concealed-handgun laws were also larger.

While these regressions account for nationwide changes in crime rates on average over time, one concern is that individual states are likely to have their own unique time trends. The question here is whether the states adopting nondiscretionary concealed-handgun laws experienced falling crime rates over the entire time period. This cannot be true for all states as a whole, because as figure 3.5 shows, violent crimes have definitely not been diminishing during the entire period. However, if this downward trend existed for the states that adopted nondiscretionary laws, the variables shown in table 4.1 could indicate that the average crime rate was lower after the laws were passed, even though the drop in the average level was due merely to a continuation of a downward trend that began before the law took effect. To address this issue, I reestimated the specifications shown in table 4.1 by including state dummy variables that were each interacted with a time-trend variable.[17] This makes it possible to account not only for the national changes in crime rates with the individual year variables but also for any differences in state-specific trends.

When these individual state time trends were included, all results indicated that the concealed-handgun laws lowered crime, though the coefficients were not statistically significant for aggravated assault and larceny. Under this specification, the passage of nondiscretionary concealed-handgun laws in states that did not have them in 1992 would have reduced murders in that year by 1,839; rapes by 3,727; aggravated assaults by 10,990; robberies by 61,064; burglaries by 112,665; larcenies by 93,274; and auto thefts by 41,512. The total value of this reduction in crime in 1992 dollars would have been $7.6 billion. With the exceptions of aggravated assault and burglary, violent-crime rates still experienced larger drops from the adoption of concealed-handgun laws than did property crimes.

Despite the concerns over the aggregation issues discussed earlier, economists have relied on state-level data in analyzing crime primarily because of the difficulty and extra time required to assemble county-level data. As shown in tables 2.2–2.4, the large within-state heterogeneity raises significant concerns about relying too heavily on state-level data.

To provide a comparison with other crime studies relying on state-level data, table 4.3 reestimates the specifications reported in table 4.1 using state-level rather than county-level data. While the results in these two tables are generally similar, two differences immediately manifest themselves: (1) the specifications now imply that nondiscretionary concealed-handgun laws lower all types of crime, and (2) concealed-handgun laws explain much more of the variation in crime rates, while arrest rates (with the exception of robbery) explain much less of the variation.[18] While concealed-handgun laws lower both violent- and property-crime rates, the rates for violent crimes are still much more sensitive to

Table 4.3 Aggregating the data: state-level, cross-sectional, time-series evidence

Change in explanatory variable	Percent change in various crime rates for changes in explanatory variables								
	Violent crime	Murder	Rape	Aggravated assault	Robbery	Property crime	Burglary	Larceny	Auto theft
Nondiscretionary law adopted	−10.1% (5.8%)	−8.62%** (5%)	−6.07%** (4.7%)	−10.9%* (6.5%)	−14.21%* (5.7%)	−4.19%** (4.8%)	−0.88% (.43%)	−8.25%* (7.6%)	−3.14% (3.8%)
Arrest rate for the crime category increased by 100 percentage points	−8.02%* (1.5%)	−7.3%* (5.3%)	−2.05%*** (.69%)	−15.3%* (3.9%)	−10.5%* (14.4%)	−59.9% (8.1%)	−14.5%* (6.5%)	−71.5%* (7.6%)	−65.7%* (10.4%)

Note: Except for the use of state dummies in place of county dummies, the control variables are the same as those used in table 4.1 including year dummies, though they are not all reported. The percent reported in parentheses is the percent of a standard deviation change in the endogenous variable that can be explained by a one-standard-deviation change in the exogenous variable. All regressions use weighted least squares, where the weighting is according to each state's population. Entire sample used over the 1977 to 1992 period.

*The result is statistically significant at the 1 percent level for a two-tailed t-test.
**The result is statistically significant at the 5 percent level for a two-tailed t-test.
***The result is statistically significant at the 10 percent level for a two-tailed t-test.

the introduction of concealed handguns, falling two-and-one-half times more than those for property crimes.

Suppose we rely on the state-level results rather than the county-level estimates. We would then conclude that if all states had adopted nondiscretionary concealed-handgun laws in 1992, about 1,600 fewer murders and 4,800 fewer rapes would have been committed.[19] Overall, table 4.3 allows us to calculate that the estimated monetary gain from reductions in crime produced by nondiscretionary concealed-handgun laws was $8.3 billion in 1992 dollars (again, see table 4.2 for the precise breakdown). Yet, at least in the case of property crimes, the concealed-handgun law coefficients are sensitive to whether the regressions are run at the state or county level. This suggests that aggregating observations into units as large as states is a bad idea.[20]

DIFFERENTIAL EFFECTS ACROSS COUNTIES, BETWEEN MEN AND WOMEN, AND BY RACE AND INCOME

Let us now return to other issues concerning the county-level data. Criminal deterrence is unlikely to have the same impact across all counties. For instance, increasing the number of arrests can have different effects on crime in different areas, depending on the stigma attached to arrest. In areas where crime is rampant, the stigma of being arrested may be small, so that the impact of a change in arrest rates is correspondingly small.[21] To test this, the specifications shown in table 4.1 were reestimated by breaking down the sample into two groups: (1) counties with above-median crime rates and (2) counties with below-median crime rates. Each set of data was reexamined separately.

As table 4.4 shows, concealed-handgun laws do indeed affect high- and low-crime counties similarly. The coefficient signs are consistently the same for both low- and high-crime counties, though for two of the crime categories—rape and aggravated assault—concealed-handgun laws have statistically significant effects only in the relatively high-crime counties. For most violent crimes—such as murder, rape, and aggravated assault—concealed-weapons laws have much greater deterrent effects in high-crime counties. In contrast, for robbery, property crimes, auto theft, burglary, and larceny, the effect appears to be greatest in low-crime counties.

Table 4.4 also shows that the deterrent effect of arrests is significantly different, at least at the 5 percent level, between high- and low-crime counties for eight of the nine crime categories (the one exception being violent crimes). The results further reject the hypothesis that arrests would be associated with greater stigma in low-crime areas. Additional

Table 4.4 Aggregating the data: Do law-enforcement and nondiscretionary laws have the same effects in high- and low-crime areas?

Change in explanatory variable	Percent change in various crime rates for changes in explanatory variables								
	Violent crime	Murder	Rape	Aggravated assault	Robbery	Property crime	Burglary	Larceny	Auto theft
	Sample where county crime rates are above the median								
Nondiscretionary law adopted	−6.0%*	−9.9%*	−7.2%*	−4.5%*	−3.4%*	1.6%*	0.4%	3.0%*	5.2%*
Arrest rate for the crime category increased by 100 percentage points	−5.2%*	−12.3%*	−3.3%*	−6.3%*	−29.4%*	−53.5%*	−56.5%*	−59.6%*	−13.3%*
	Sample where county crime rates are below the median								
Nondiscretionary law adopted	−3.7%**	−4.4%**	−3.0%	−0.3%	−7.9%*	8.8%*	3%**	8.7%*	7.2%*
Arrest rate for the crime category increased by 100 percentage points	−5.2%*	−4.9%*	−6.6%*	−6.8%*	−3.7%*	−13.5%*	−27.1%*	−10%*	−1.4%*

Note: The control variables are the same as those used in table 4.1, including year and county dummies, though they are not reported. All regressions use weighted least squares, where the weighting is each county's population. Entire sample used over the 1977 to 1992 period.

*The result is statistically significant at the 1 percent level for a two–tailed t-test.

**The result is statistically significant at the 5 percent level for a two–tailed t-test.

***The result is statistically significant at the 10 percent level for a two–tailed t-test.

arrests in low- and high-crime counties generate extremely similar changes in the aggregate category of violent crime, but the arrest-rate coefficient for murder is almost three times greater in high-crime counties than in low-crime counties. If these results suggest any conclusion, it is that for most crimes, tougher measures have more of an impact in high-crime areas.

The effect of gun ownership by women deserves a special comment. Despite the relatively small number of women who obtain concealed-handgun permits, the concealed-handgun coefficient for explaining rapes in the first three sets of results is consistently similar in size to the effect that this variable has on other violent crime. January 1996 data for Washington and Oregon reveal that women constituted 18.6 and 22.9 percent, respectively, of those with concealed-handgun permits.[22] The set of women who were the most likely targets of rape probably chose to carry concealed handguns at much higher rates than women in general. The preceding results show that rapists are particularly deterred by handguns. As mentioned earlier, the National Crime Victimization Survey data show that providing a woman with a gun has a much greater effect on her ability to defend herself against a crime than providing a gun to a man. Thus even if few women carry handguns, the change in the "cost" of attacking women could still be as great as the change in the "cost" of attacking men, despite the much higher number of men who are becoming armed. To phrase this differently, if one more woman carries a handgun, the extra protection for women in general is greater than the extra protection for men if one more man carries a handgun.[23]

These results raise a possible concern as to whether women have the right incentive to carry concealed handguns. Despite the fact that women who carry concealed handguns make other women so much safer, it is possible that women might decide not to carry them because they see their own personal gain as much smaller than the total benefit to all women that carrying a concealed handgun produces. While the problem is particularly pronounced for women, people in general often take into account only the benefits that they individually receive from carrying a gun and not the crime-reduction benefits that they are generating for others.[24]

As mentioned in chapter 2, an important concern is that passing a nondiscretionary concealed-handgun law should not affect all counties equally. In particular, when states had discretionary laws, counties with the highest populations were also those that most severely restricted people's ability to carry concealed weapons. Adopting nondiscretionary laws therefore produced the greatest change in the number of permits in the more populous counties. Thus, a significant advantage of using this county data is that it allows us to take advantage of county-level variation in the impact of nondiscretionary concealed-handgun laws. To test this variation across counties, figures 4.1 and 4.2 repeat all the specifications in table 4.1 but examine instead whether the effect of the nondiscretionary law varies with county population or population density. (The simplest way to do this is to multiply the nondiscretionary-law variable by either the county population or population density.) While all the other coefficients remain virtually unchanged, this new interaction implies the same crime-reducing effects from the nondiscretionary law as reported earlier. In all but one case the coefficients are more significant and larger.

The coefficients are consistent with the hypothesis that the new laws induce the greatest changes in the largest counties, which have a much greater response in both directions to changes in the laws. Violent crimes fall more and property crimes rise more in the largest counties. The figures indicate how these effects vary for counties of different sizes. For example, when counties with almost 600,000 people (two standard deviations above the mean population) pass a concealed-handgun law, the murder rate falls by 12 percent. That is 7.4 times more than it was reduced for the average county (75,773 people).

Although the law-enforcement officials that I talked to continually mentioned population as being the key variable, I also reexamined whether the laws had different effects in more densely populated counties. Given the close relationship between county population and population density, it is not too surprising to find that the impact of concealed handguns in more densely populated areas is similar to their impact in more populous counties. The most densely populated areas are the ones most helped by concealed-handgun laws. Passing a concealed-handgun law lowers the murder rate in counties with about 3,000 people per square mile (the levels found in Fairfax, Virginia; Orleans, Louisiana, which contains New Orleans; and Ramsey, Minnesota, which contains St. Paul) by 8.5 percent, 12 times more than it lowers murders in the average county. The only real difference between the results for population and population density occur for the burglary rate, where concealed-handgun laws are associated with a small reduction in burglaries for the most densely populated areas.

Figures 4.3 and 4.4 provide a similar breakdown by income and by the percentage of the population that is black. Higher-income areas and counties with relatively more blacks both have particularly large drops in crime associated with concealed-handgun laws. Counties with a 37 percent black population experienced 11 percent declines in both murder and aggravated assaults. The differences with respect to income were not as large.[25]

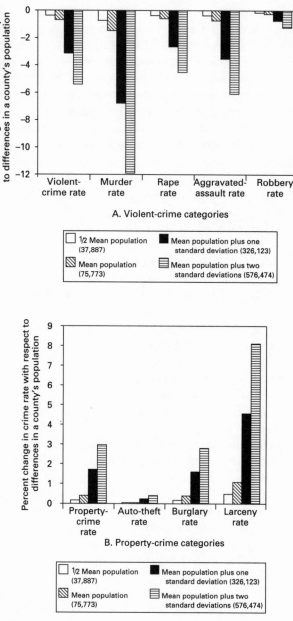

Figure 4.1. Do larger changes in crime rates from nondiscretionary concealed-handgun laws occur in more populous counties?

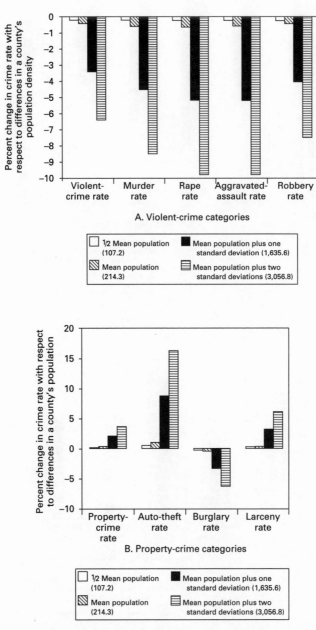

Figure 4.2. Do larger changes in crime rates from nondiscretionary concealed-handgun laws occur in more densely populated counties?

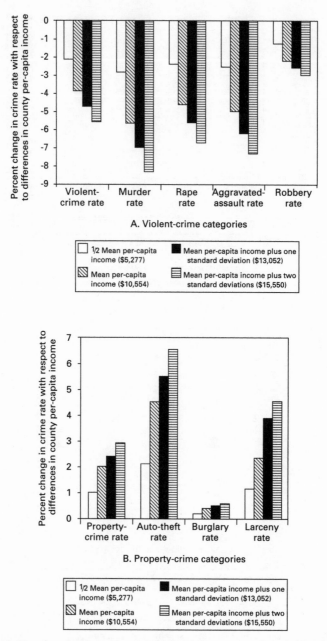

Figure 4.3. How does the change in crime from nondiscretionary concealed-handgun laws vary with county per-capita income?

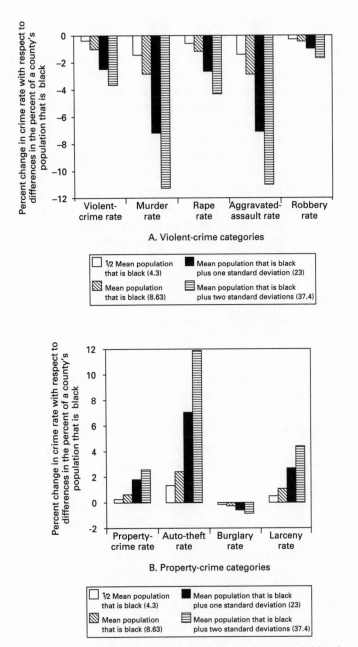

Figure 4.4. How does the change in crime from nondiscretionary concealed-handgun laws vary with the percent of a county's population that is black?

With the extremely high rates of murder and other crimes committed against blacks, it is understandable why so many blacks are concerned about gun control. University of Florida criminologist Gary Kleck says, "Blacks are more likely to have been victims of crime or to live in neighborhoods where there's a lot of crime involving guns. So, generally, blacks are more pro-control than whites are." Nationally, polls indicate that 83 percent of blacks support police permits for all gun purchases.[26] While many blacks want to make guns harder to get, the irony is that blacks benefit more than other groups from concealed-handgun laws. Allowing potential victims a means for self-defense is more important in crime-prone neighborhoods. Even more strikingly, the history of gun control in the United States has often been a series of attempts to disarm blacks.[27] In explaining the urgency of adopting the U.S. Constitution's Fourteenth Amendment, Duke University Law Professor William Van Alstyne writes,

> It was, after all, the defenselessness of the Negroes (denied legal rights to keep and bear arms by state law) from attack by night riders—even to protect their own lives, their own families, and their own homes—that made it imperative that they, as citizens, could no longer be kept defenseless by a regime of state law denying them the common right to keep and bear arms.[28]

Indeed, even in the 1960s much of the increased regulation of firearms stemmed from the fear generated by Black Panthers who openly carried guns.

Alexis Herman, the current Secretary of Labor, experienced firsthand the physical risks of growing up black in Alabama. Describing her difficult confirmation hearings, an Associated Press story included the following story:

> Anyone who thought the frustrations of waiting for confirmation would discourage her knew nothing about the lessons Herman learned from her father. They forgot that he sued to integrate the Democratic Party in Alabama, and later became the state's first black ward leader. They never heard about the night he put a pistol in his young daughter's hands and stepped out of the car to confront the Ku Klux Klan.
>
> "He taught me that you have to face adversity. He taught me to stand by my principles," Herman said in the interview. "He also taught me how to work within the system for change."
>
> Herman said her father never raised his voice, but he always kept a small silver pistol under the driver's seat of his DeSoto as he drove from community meeting to community meeting around Mobile. She always sat close by his side, unless the pistol was out. "The only way that I ever

knew trouble was around was that the gun would come out from under the driver's seat and he'd put it by his side," she said.

As they left the home of a minister one Christmas Eve, the pistol was on the car seat. She was 5. "It was a dark road, a dirt road to get back to the main highway," she recalled. "We were driven off the road by another car, and they were Klansmen."

She hid on the floor and her father pressed the pistol's white handle into her palm. "He told me, 'If anybody opens this door, I want you to pull this trigger.'" He locked the door behind him and walked ahead to keep them away from the car. She crouched in the dark, listening until the shouts and scuffling died down.

Eventually, the minister came to the car to drive Herman home. Her father, who had been beaten, rode in another car.[29]

Recently, after testifying before the Illinois state House of Representatives on whether to pass a concealed-handgun bill, I was approached by a black representative from Chicago who supported the bill.[30] He told me that, at least for Illinois, he was not surprised by my finding that areas with large minority populations gained the most from these laws. Noting the high rate at which young, black males are stopped by police and the fact that it is currently a felony to possess a concealed handgun, he said that an honest, law-abiding, young, black male would be "nuts" to carry a concealed handgun in Illinois. He mentioned a case that had occurred just a week earlier: Alonzo Spellman—a black professional football player for the Chicago Bears—had been arrested in Chicago after a routine traffic violation revealed that he had a handgun in his car.[31] Noting the inability of the police to protect people in heavily black areas when "bad guys" already had illegal guns, the representative said he believed that the current power imbalance between law-abiding people and criminals was greatest in black areas.

Perhaps it is not too surprising that blacks and those living in urban areas gain the most from being able to defend themselves with concealed handguns, since the absence of police appears most acute in black, central-city neighborhoods. Until 1983, the American Housing Survey annually asked sixty thousand households whether their neighborhoods had adequate police protection. Black, central-city residents were about twice as likely as whites generally to report that they did not have adequate protection, and six times more likely to say that they had considered moving because of an insufficient police presence in their neighborhoods.[32]

These results should at least give pause to the recent rush in California to pass city ordinances and state laws banning low-cost, "Saturday night specials." Indeed, the results have implications for many gun-control rules that raise gun prices. Law-abiding minorities in the most crime-prone areas produced the greatest crime reductions from being able to defend themselves. Unfortunately, however unintentionally, California's new laws risk disarming precisely these poor minorities.

USING OTHER CRIME RATES TO EXPLAIN THE CHANGES IN THE CRIME RATES BEING STUDIED

Other questions still exist regarding the specifications employed here. Admittedly, although arrest rates and average differences in individual counties are controlled for, more can be done to account for the changing environments that determine the level of crime. One method is to use changes in other crime rates to help us understand why the crime rates that we are studying are changing over time. Table 4.5 reruns the specifications used to generate figure 4.1A but includes either the burglary or robbery rates as proxies for other changes in the criminal justice system. Robbery and burglary are the violent- and property-crime categories that are the least related to changes in concealed-handgun laws, but they still tend to move up and down together with all the other types of crimes.[33]

Some evidence that burglary or robbery rates will measure other changes in the criminal justice system or other omitted factors that explain changing crime rates can be seen in their correlations with other crime categories. Indeed, the robbery and burglary rates are very highly correlated with the other crime rates.[34] The two sets of specifications reported in table 4.5 closely bound the earlier estimates, and the estimates continue to imply that the introduction of concealed-handgun laws coincided with similarly large drops in violent crimes and increases in property crimes. These results differ from the preceding results in that the nondiscretionary laws are not significant related to robberies. The estimates on the other control variables also remain essentially unchanged.[35]

CRIME: CHANGES IN LEVELS VERSUS CHANGES IN TRENDS

The preceding results in this chapter examined whether the average crime rate fell after the nondiscretionary laws went into effect. If changes in the law affect behavior with a lag, changes in the trend are probably more relevant; therefore, a more important question is, How has the crime trend changed with the change in laws? Examining whether there is a change in levels or a change in whether the crime rate is rising or falling could yield very different results. For example, if the crime rate

Table 4.5 Using crime rates that are relatively unrelated to changes in nondiscretionary laws as a method of controlling for other changes in the legal environment: controlling for robbery and burglary rates

Change in the explanatory variable	Percent change in various crime rates for changes in explanatory variables								
	Violent crime	Murder	Rape	Aggravated assault	Robbery	Property crime	Burglary	Larceny	Auto theft
	Controlling for robbery rates								
Nondiscretionary law adopted multiplied by county population (evaluated at mean county population)	-2.6%*	-4.3%*	-1.9%*	-2.6%*	—	1.4%*	0.08%	1.3%*	3.7%*
	1%	1.1%	0.4%	0.4%		0.5%	0.04%	0.4%	0.5%
Arrest rate for the crime category increased by 100 percentage points	-0.038*	-0.13*	-0.07*	-0.08*	—	-0.06*	-0.20*	-0.015*	-0.014*
	7%	7%	4%	8%		8%	9%	3%	2%

Table 4.5 Continued

Change in the explanatory variable	Percent change in various crime rates for changes in explanatory variables								
	Violent crime	Murder	Rape	Aggravated assault	Robbery	Property crime	Burglary	Larceny	Auto theft
					Controlling for burglary rates				
Nondiscretionary law adopted multiplied by *county population (evaluated at mean county population)	-2.4%* 1%	-4.3%* 1.1%	-2.0%* 0.4%	-2.6%* 0.4%	0.4% 0.04%	1.8%* 0.7%	—	1.4%* 0.4%	3.6%* 0.5%
Arrest rate for the crime category increased by 100 percentage points	-0.026%* 5%	-0.13%* 6%	-0.05%* 3%	-0.05%* 5%	-0.043%* 3%	-0.05%* 6%	—	-0.01%* 2%	-0.01%* 2%

Note: While not all the coefficient estimates are reported, all the control variables are the same as those used in table 4.1, including year and county dummies. All regressions use weighted least squares, where the weighting is each county's population. Net violent and property-crime rates are respectively net of robbery and burglary rates to avoid producing any artificial collinearity. Likewise, the arrest rates for those values omit the portion of the corresponding arrest rates due to arrests for robbery and burglary. While not reported, the coefficients for the robbery and burglary rates were extremely statistically significant and positive. Entire sample used over the 1977 to 1992 period.

*The result is statistically significant at the 1 percent level for a two-tailed t-test.

was rising right up until the law was adopted but falling thereafter, some values that appeared while crime rate was rising could equal some that appeared as it was falling. In other words, deceptively similar levels can represent dramatically different trends over time.

I used several methods to examine changes in the trends exhibited over time in crime rates. First, I reestimated the regressions in table 4.1, using year-to-year changes on all explanatory variables (see table 4.6). These regressions were run using both a variable that equals 1 when a nondiscretionary law is in effect as well as the change in that variable (called "differencing" the variable) to see if the initial passage of the law had an impact. The results consistently indicate that the law lowered the rates of violent crime, rape, and aggravated assault. Nondiscretionary laws discourage murder in both specifications, but the effect is only statistically significant when the nondiscretionary variable is also differenced. The property-crime results are in line with those of earlier tables, showing that nondiscretionary laws produce increases in property crime. Violent crimes decreased by an average of about 2 percent annually, whereas property crimes increased by an average of about 5 percent.

As one might expect, the nondiscretionary laws affected crime immediately, with an additional change spread out over time. Why would the entire effect not be immediate? An obvious explanation is that not everyone who would eventually obtain a permit to carry a concealed handgun did so right away. For instance, as shown by the data in table 4.7, the number of permits granted in Florida, Oregon, and Pennsylvania was still increasing substantially long after the nondiscretionary law was put into effect. Florida's law was passed in 1987, Oregon's in 1990, and Pennsylvania's in 1989.

Reestimating the regression results from table 4.1 to account for different time trends in the crime rates before and after the passage of the law provides consistent strong evidence that the deterrent impact of concealed handguns increases with time. For most violent crimes, the time trend prior to the passage of the law indicates that crime was rising. The results using the simple time trends for these violent-crime categories are reported in table 4.8. Figures 4.5 through 4.9 illustrate how the violent-crime rate varies before and after the implementation of nondiscretionary concealed-handgun laws when both the linear and squared time trends are employed. Comparing the slopes of the crime trends before and after the enactment of the laws shows that the trends become more negative to a degree that is statistically significant after the laws were passed.[36]

These results answer another possible objection: whether the findings are simply a result of so-called crime cycles. Crime rates rise or fall over

Table 4.6 Results of rerunning the regressions on differences

Exogenous variables	Endogenous variables in terms of first differences of the natural logarithm of the crime rate								
	Δln(violent-crime rate)	Δln(Murder rate)	Δln(Rape rate)	Δln(Aggravated-assault rate)	Δln(robbery rate)	Δln(property-crime rate)	Δln(Burglary rate)	Δln(Larceny rate)	Δln(Auto-theft rate)
	All variables except for the nondiscretionary dummy differenced								
Nondiscretionary law adopted	−2.2%***	−2.6%	−5.2%*	−4.6%*	−3.3%****	5.2%*	3.5%*	5.2%*	12.8%*
First differences in the arrest rate for the crime category	−0.05%*	−0.15%*	−0.09%*	−0.09%*	−0.06%*	−0.08%*	−0.24%*	−0.02%*	−0.02%*
	All variables differenced								
First differences in the dummy for nondiscretionary law adopted	−2.7%*	−3.6%***	−3.9%*	−5.4%*	−0.7%	4.8%*	0.7%	6.2%*	24.2%*
First differences in the arrest rate for the crime category	−0.05%*	−0.15%*	−0.09%*	−0.09%*	−0.06%*	−0.08%*	−24%*	−0.02%*	−0.02%*

Note: The variables for income; population; race, sex, and age of the population; and density are all in terms of first differences. While not all the coefficient estimates are reported, all the control variables used in Table 4.1 are used here, including year and county dummies. All regressions use weighted least squares, where the weighting is each county's population. Entire sample used over the 1977 to 1992 period.

*The result is statistically significant at the 1 percent level for a two-tailed t-test.

***The result is statistically significant at the 10 percent level for a two-tailed t-test.

****The result is statistically significant at the 11 percent level for a two-tailed t-test.

Table 4.7 Permits granted by state: Florida, Oregon, and Pennsylvania

Year	Florida	Oregon	Pennsylvania
1987	17,000[a]	N.A.	N.A.
1988	33,451	N.A.	267,335[c]
1989	51,335	N.A.	314,925
1990	65,636	N.A.	360,649
1991	67,043	N.A.	399,428
1992	75,578	22,197[b]	360,919
1993	95,187	32,049	426,011
1994	134,008	43,216	492,421
1995	163,757	65,394	571,208
1996	192,016	78,258	N.A.

[a]Estimate of the number of concealed-handgun permits issued immediately before Florida's law went into effect from David McDowall, Colin Loftin, and Brian Wiersema, "Easing Concealed Firearms Laws: Effects on Homicide in Three States," *Journal of Criminal Law and Criminology*, 86 (Fall 1995): 194.
[b]December 31, 1991.
[c]Number of permits issued under discretionary law.

time. If concealed-handgun laws were adopted at the peaks of these cycles (say, because concern over crime is great), the ensuing decline in crime might have occurred anyway without any help from the new laws. To deal with this, I controlled not only for national crime patterns but also for individual county patterns by employing burglary or robbery rates to explain the movement in the other crime rates. I even tried to control for individual state trends. Yet the simplest way of concisely illustrating that my results are not merely a product of the "normal" ups and downs in crime rates is to look again at the graphs in figures 4.5–4.9. With the exception of aggravated assault, the drops not only begin right when the laws pass but also take the crime rates well below what they had been before the passage of the laws. It is difficult to believe that, on the average, state legislatures could have timed the passage of these laws so accurately as to coincide with the peaks of crime waves; nor can the resulting declines be explained simply as reversions to normal levels.

WAS THE IMPACT OF NONDISCRETIONARY CONCEALED-HANDGUN LAWS THE SAME EVERYWHERE?

Just as we found that the impact of nondiscretionary laws changed over time, we expect to find differences across states. The reason is the same in both cases: deterrence increases with the number of permits. While the information obtained from state government officials only pertained to why permits were issued at different rates across counties within a

Table 4.8 Change in time trends for crime rates before and after the adoption of nondiscretionary laws

	Percent change in various crime rates for change in explanatory variable								
	Violent crime	Murder	Rape	Aggravated assault	Robbery	Property crime	Auto theft	Burglary	Larceny
Change in the crime rate from the difference in the annual change in crime rates in the years before and after the change in the law (annual rate after the law − annual rate before the law)	−0.9%*	−3%*	−1.4%*	−0.5%*	−2.7%*	−0.6%*	−0.3%**	−1.5%*	−0.1%

Note: The control variables are the same as those used in table 4.1, including year and county dummies, though they are not reported, because the coefficient estimates are very similar to those reported earlier. All regressions use weighted least squares, where the weighting is each county's population. Entire sample used over the 1977 to 1992 period.
*The result is statistically significant at the 1 percent level for a two-tailed t-test.
**The result is statistically significant at the 5 percent level for a two-tailed t-test.

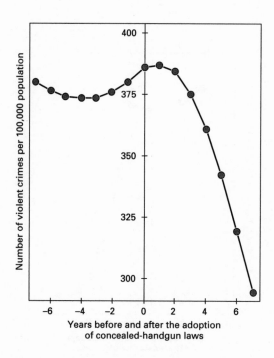

Figure 4.5. The effect of concealed-handgun laws on violent crimes

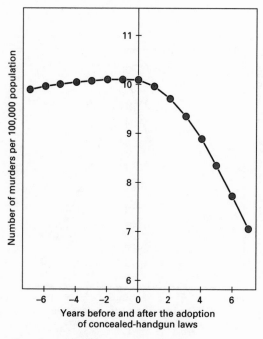

Figure 4.6. The effect of concealed-handgun laws on murders

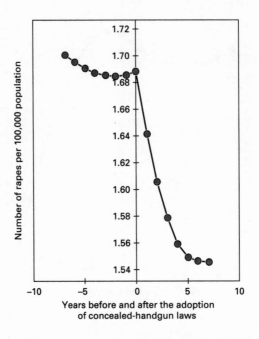

Figure 4.7. The effect of concealed-handgun laws on rapes

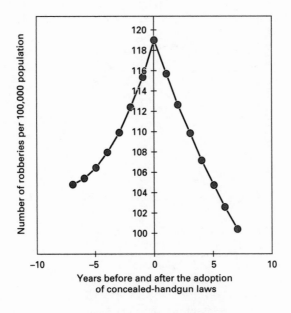

Figure 4.8. The effect of concealed-handgun laws on robbery rates

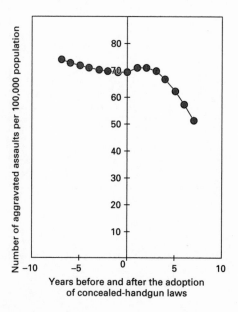

Figure 4.9. The effect of concealed-handgun laws on aggravated assaults

given state, the rate at which new permits are issued at the state level may also vary based upon population and population density. If this is true, then it should be possible to explain the differential effect that non-discretionary laws have on crime in each of the states that passed such laws in the same way that we examined differences across counties.

Table 4.9 reexamines my earlier regressions, where I took into account that concealed-handgun laws have different effects across counties, depending upon how lenient officials had been in issuing permits under a previously discretionary system. The one change from earlier tables is that a different coefficient is used for the counties in each of the ten states that changed their laws during the 1977 to 1992 period. At least for violent crimes, the results indicate a very consistent effect of nondiscretionary concealed-handgun laws across states. Nine of the ten states experienced declines in violent-crime rates as a result of these laws, and eight of the ten states experienced declines in murder rates; in the states where violent crimes, murders, or robberies rose, the increases were very small. In fact, the largest increases were smaller than the smallest declines in the states where those crime rates fell.

Generally, the states with the largest decreases in any one category tended to have relatively large decreases across all the violent-crime categories, although the "leader" in each category varied across all the

Table 4.9 State-specific impact of nondiscretionary concealed-handgun laws

	Violent crime	Murder	Rape	Aggravated assault	Robbery	Property crime	Auto theft	Burglary	Larceny
Florida	-4%	-10%	-8%	-4%	0.3%	1%	2%	0.3%	2%
Georgia	0.2	-2	0.5	-0.2	0	1	1	1	1
Idaho	-3	-1	0.1	-3	-7	-1	-3	-3	-1
Maine	-17	-5	1	-24	-8	1	-4	-2	2
Mississippi	-3	0.6	3	-8	0	-0.2	3	2	-1
Montana	-10	-5	-10	-12	-6	-4	-5	5	-4
Oregon	-3	-1	-1	-3	-4	-2	3	-4	-2
Pennsylvania	-1	-3	-1	1	-2	1	3	-1	3
Virginia	-2	1	-1	-2	-2	-1	-2	-2	-1
West Virginia	-1	-11	-5	-1	1	3	0	4	2
Summary of the coefficients' signs									
Negative	9	8	6	9	6	5	4	5	5
Positive	1	2	4	1	4	5	6	5	5

Note: The table uses arrest rates adjusted for counties wherein the adoption of nondiscretionary concealed-handgun laws was most likely to represent a real change from past practice by multiplying the nondiscretionary-law variables by the population in each county. The percents are evaluated at the mean county population.

violent-crime categories.[37] Likewise, the states with relatively small crime decreases (for example, Georgia, Oregon, Pennsylvania, and Virginia) tended to exhibit little change across all the categories.

Property crimes, on the other hand, exhibited no clear pattern. Property crimes fell in five states and increased in five states, and the size of any decrease or increase was quite small and unsystematic.

Ideally, any comparison across states would be based on changes in the number of permits issued rather than simply the enactment of the nondiscretionary law. States with the largest increases in permits should show the largest decreases in crime rates. Unfortunately, only a few states have recorded time-series data on the number of permits issued. I will use such data in chapter 5. For the moment, it is still useful to see whether the patterns in crime-rate changes found earlier across counties are also found across states. In particular, we would like to know whether the largest declines occurred in states with the largest or most dense populations, which we believed had the greatest increase in permits. The justification for the county-level differences was very strong because it was based on conversations with individual state officials, but those officials were not asked to make judgments across states (nor was it likely that they could do so). Further, there is much more heterogeneity across counties, and a greater number of observations. The relationship posited earlier for county populations also seems particularly tenuous when dealing with state-level data because a state with a large population could be made up of a large number of counties with small populations.

With this list of reservations in mind, let us look at the results we get by using state-level density data. Table 4.10 provides the results with respect to population density, and we find that, just as in the case of counties, larger declines in crime were recorded in the most densely populated states. The differences are quite large: the most densely populated states experienced decreases in violent crimes that were about three times greater than the decreases in states with the average density. The results were similar when state populations were taken into account.

OTHER GUN-CONTROL LAWS AND DIFFERENT TYPES OF CONCEALED-HANDGUN LAWS

Two common restrictions on handguns arise from (1) increased sentencing penalties for crimes involving the use of a gun and (2) waiting periods required before a citizen can obtain a permit for a gun. How did these two types of laws affect crime rates? Could it be that these laws—rather than concealed-handgun laws—explain the deterrent effects? To answer this question, I reestimated the regressions in tables 4.1 and 4.3 by

Table 4.10 Effects of concealed-handgun laws across states related to differences in state population density

State population density	Violent crimes	Murder	Rape	Aggravated assault	Robbery	Property crimes	Auto theft	Burglary	Larceny
1/2 Mean 179 per square mile	-2.7%	-3.2%	-5%	-1%	-7%	-1%	3%	-5%	1%
Mean 358 per square mile	-5.4	-6.3	-10	-2	-14	-1	6	-10	2
Plus 1 standard deviation 778 per square mile	-11.8	-13.7	-21	-4	-29	-3	12	-22	4
Plus 2 standard deviations 1,197 per square mile	-18.2	-21.1	-32	-6	-45	-5	19	-33	7

Note: The regressions used for this table multiplied the variable for whether the law was enacted by that state's population density. The control variables used to generate these estimates are the same as those used in table 4.1, including year and county dummies, though they are not reported, because the coefficient estimates are very similar to those reported earlier. All regressions use weighted least squares, where the weighting is each state's population.

(1) adding a variable to control for state laws that increase sentencing penalties when crimes involve guns and (2) adding variables to measure the impact of waiting periods.[38] It is not clear whether adding an extra day to a waiting period had much of an effect; therefore, I included a variable for when the waiting period went into effect along with variables for the length of the waiting period in days and the length in days squared to pick up any differential impact from longer lengths. In both sets of regressions, the variable for nondiscretionary concealed-handgun laws remains generally consistent with the earlier results.[39] While the coefficients for arrest rates are not reported here, they also remain very similar to those shown previously.

So what about these other gun laws? The pattern that emerges from table 4.11 is much more ambiguous. The results for county-level data suggest that harsher sentences for the use of deadly weapons reduce violent crimes, especially crimes of aggravated assault and robbery. While the same county-level data frequently imply an impact on murder, rape, aggravated assault, and robbery, the effects are quite inconsistent. For example, simply requiring the waiting period appears to raise murder and rape rates but lower the rates for aggravated assault and robbery. The lengths of waiting periods also result in inconsistent patterns: longer periods at first lower and then raise the murder and rape rates, with the reverse occurring for aggravated assault. Using state- level data fails to confirm any statistically significant effects for the violent-crime categories. First, it reveals no statistically significant or economically consistent relationship between either the presence of waiting periods or their length and violent-crime rates. The directions of the effects also differ from those found using county data. Taken together, the results make it very difficult to argue that waiting periods (particularly long ones) have an overall beneficial effect on crime rates. In addition, one other finding is clear: laws involving sentence length and waiting periods do not alter my earlier findings with respect to nondiscretionary laws; that is, the earlier results for nondiscretionary laws cannot merely be reflecting the impact of other gun laws.

THE IMPORTANCE OF THE TYPES OF CONCEALED-HANDGUN LAWS ADOPTED: TRAINING AND AGE REQUIREMENTS

Finally, we need to consider how concealed-handgun laws vary across states and whether the exact rules matter much. Several obvious differences exist: whether a training period is required, and if so, how long that period is; whether any minimum age limits are imposed; the number of

Table 4.11 Controlling for other gun laws

Exogenous variables	Violent crime	Murder	Rape	Aggravated assault	Robbery	Property crime	Burglary	Larceny	Auto theft
				County-level Regressions					
Nondiscretionary law adopted	−4.2%*	−8.7%*	−6%*	−5.5%*	−2%	3.6%*	1%	4.5%*	8.2%*
Enhanced sentencing law adopted	−4%	−0.3%	1.1%	−1.5%***	−2.9%***	−0.001%	−2%	1.2%***	−1.8%**
Waiting law adopted	2.3%	23%*	25%*	−9.4%**	−9%***	2%	2%	−0.3%	−8%**
Percent change in crime by increasing the waiting period by one day: linear effect	−0.08%	−9.4%*	−13.6%*	6.5%*	−11%*	−1.5%***	−4.5%*	1.2%	−1%
Percent change in crime by increasing the waiting period by one day: squared effect	−0.08%	0.55%*	0.8%*	−0.5%*	0.73%*	0.019%	0.23%*	−0.17%*	0.099%

State-level regressions

Nondiscretionary law adopted	-10.1%*	-8.1%**	-5.7%***	-10.2%*	-13.3%*	-3.4%	-7.6%*	-2.2%	-1%
Enhanced sentencing law adopted	3.5%	3%	3%	-2.8%	1%	3%***	0.5%	3.7%**	2%
Waiting law adopted	10%	6.8%	22%*	2.6%	15%	3.3%	6.5%	2.3%	-3.1%
Percent change in crime by increasing the waiting period by one day: linear effect	-3%	-3%	-10%*	-0.65%	-10%**	-0.95%	-2.2%	-0.53%	-2.4%
Percent change in crime by increasing the wating period by one day: squared effect	0.12%	-0.13%	0.59%*	-0.041%	0.59%**	-0.021%	0.05%	-0.06%	-0.25%

Note: The control variables are the same as those used in table 4.1, including year and county dummies, though they are not reported, because the coefficient estimates are very similar to those reported earlier. All regressions use weighted least squares, where the weighting is each county's population.

*The result is statistically significant at the 1 percent level for a two-tailed t-test.

**The result is statistically significant at the 5 percent level for a two-tailed t-test.

***The result is statistically significant at the 10 percent level for a two-tailed t-test.

years for which the permit is valid; where people are allowed to carry the gun (for example, whether schools, bars, and government buildings are excluded); residency requirements; and how much the permit costs. Six of these characteristics are reported in table 4.12 for the thirty-one states with nondiscretionary laws.

A major issue in legislative debates on concealed-handgun laws is whether citizens will receive sufficient training to cope with situations that can require difficult, split-second decisions. Steve Grabowski, president of the Nebraska state chapter of the Fraternal Order of Police, notes that "police training is much more extensive than that required for concealed-handgun permits. The few hours of firearms instruction won't prepare a citizen to use the gun efficiently in a stress situation, which is a challenge even for professionals."[40] Others respond that significantly more training is required to use a gun offensively, as a police officer may be called on to do, than defensively. Law-abiding citizens appear reticent to use their guns and, as noted earlier, in the majority of cases simply brandishing the gun is sufficient to deter an attack.

Reestimating the earlier regressions, I included measures for whether a training period was required, for the length of the training period, and for the age limit.[41] The presence or length of the training periods typically show no effect on crime, and although the effects are significant for robbery, the size of the effect is very small. On the other hand, age limits display quite different and statistically significant coefficients for different crimes. The 21-year-old age limit appears to lower murder rates, but it tends to reduce the decline in rape and overall violent-crime rates that is normally associated with nondiscretionary concealed-handgun laws. Because of these different effects, it is difficult to draw firm conclusions regarding the effect of age limits.

RECENT DATA ON CRIME RATES

After I originally put the data together for this study, and indeed after I had written virtually all of this book, additional county-level data became available for 1993 and 1994 from the FBI's *Uniform Crime Reports.* These data allow us to evaluate the impact of the Brady law, which went into effect in 1994. Four additonal states (Alaska, Arizona, Tennessee, and Wyoming) also had right-to-carry laws in effect for at least part of the year. The new information allows us to double-check whether the results shown earlier were mere aberrations.

Table 4.13 reexamines the results from tables 4.1, 4.8, and 4.11 with these new data, and the findings are generally very similar to those already reported. The results in section A that correspond to table 4.1 imply an even larger drop in murder rates related to the passage of concealed-handgun laws (10 percent versus 7.7 percent previously), though

Table 4.12 Current characteristics of different nondiscretionary concealed-handgun laws

State with nondiscretionary law	Last significant modification	Permit duration (years)	Training length (hours)	Age requirement	Initial fee	Renewal fee	Issuing agency
Alabama	1936	1	None	21	$15–25	$6	Sheriff
Alaska	1994	5	12	21	$123	$57	Dept. of Public Safety
Arizona	1995	4	16	21	$50	?	Dept. of Public Safety
Arkansas	1995	4	5	21	$100	?	State Police
Connecticut	1986	5	5	21	$35	$35	State Police
Florida	1995	3	5	21	$85	$70	Dept. of State
Georgia	1996	5	None	21	$32		Judge of Probate Court
Idaho	1996	4	7	21	$56	$24	Sheriff
Indiana	1980	4	None	18	$25	$15	Chief of Police or Sheriff
Kentucky	1996	3	8 hrs Classroom + firing-range training	21	$60	$60	Sheriff
Louisiana	1996	4	9[a]	21	$100	?	Dept. of Public Safety

Table 4.12 Continued

State with nondiscretionary law	Last significant modification	Permit duration (years)	Training length (hours)	Age requirement	Initial fee	Renewal fee	Issuing agency
Maine	1985	4	5	21	$35	$20	Chief of Police or Sheriff
Mississippi	1990	4	None	21	$100	$50	Dept. of Public Safety
Montana	1991	4	None	18	$50	$25	Sheriff
Nevada	1995	5		21	$60	$25	Sheriff
New Hampshire	1923	2	None	21	$4		Chief of Police
North Carolina	1995	4	5	21	$90		Sheriff
North Dakota	1985	3	None	21	$25	$80	Bureau of Criminal Investigation
Oklahoma	1995	4	8	23	$125	$125	State Bureau of Criminal Investigation
Oregon	1993	4	5	21	$65	$50	Sheriff
Pennsylvania	1995	5	None	21	$17.50	$17.50	Chief of Police or Sheriff
South Carolina	1996	4		21	$50	$50	State Law Enforcement Division

South Dakota	1986	4	None	18	$6		Chief of Police or Sheriff
Tennessee	1996	4		21	$100		Dept. of Public Safety
Texas	1995	4	10–15	21	$140[b]	Set by department	Dept. of Public Safety
Utah	1995	2		21	$64	$5	Dept. of Public Safety
Vermont (unregulated)	None	None	None	None	None	None	None
Virginia	1995	2	5	21	<$50	<$50	Clerk of Circuit Court
Washington	1995	5	None	21	$36+ $24 FBI fee	$33	Judge; Chief of Police, or Sheriff
West Virginia	1996	5	5	18	$50	$50	Sheriff
Wyoming	1994	5	–5	21	$50	$50	Attorney General

[a]This training period is waived for those who receive a permit directly from their local sheriff.
[b]The fee is reduced to $70 for those who are over 60 years of age.

Table 4.13 Earlier results reexamined using additional data for 1993 and 1994

Change in explanatory variable	Percent change in various crime rates for changes in explanatory variables				
	Violent crime	Murder	Rape	Aggravated assault	Robbery
Section A: Nondiscretionary law adopted	−4.4%*	−10.0%*	−3.0%*	−5.7%*	0.6%
Section B: The difference in the annual change in crime rates in the years before and after the change in the law (annual rate after the law minus annual rate before the law)	−0.5%*	−2.9%*	−1.7%*	−0.3%*	−2.2%*
Section C: Brady law adopted	3%	−2.3%	3.9%**	3.7%**	−3.9%

Note: This table uses county-level, violent-crime data from the Uniform Crime Report that were not available until the rest of the book was written. Here I was not able to control for all the variables used in table 4.1. All regressions use weighted least squares, where the weighting is each county's population. Section C also controls for the other variables that were included in Table 4.11 to account for changes in other gun laws. Section A corresponds to the regressions in table 4.1, section B to those in table 4.8, and section C to those in table 4.11, except that a dummy variable for the Brady law was added for those states that did not previously have at least a five-day waiting period.
*The result is statistically significant at the 1 percent level for a two-tailed t-test.
**The result is statistically significant at the 10 percent level for a two-tailed t-test.

the declines in the rates for overall violent crime as well as rape and aggravated assault are smaller. Robbery is also no longer statistically significant, and the point estimate is even positive. As noted earlier, given the inverted **V** shape of crime-rate trends over time, comparing the average crime rates before and after the passage of these laws is not enough, since crime rates that are rising before the law and falling afterward can produce similar average crime rates in the two periods. To deal with this, section B of table 4.13 corresponds to the results reported earlier in table 4.8. The estimates are again quite similar to those reported earlier. The effect on rape is larger than those previously reported, while the effects for aggravated assault and robbery are somewhat smaller. All the results indicate that concealed-handgun laws reduce crime, and all the findings are statistically significant.

Finally, section C of table 4.13 provides some very interesting estimates of the Brady law's impact by using a variable that equals 1 only for those states that did not previously have at least a five-day waiting period. The claims about the criminals who have been denied access to guns as a result of this law are not necessarily evidence that the Brady law lowers crime rates. Unfortunately, these claims tell us nothing about whether criminals are ultimately able to obtain guns illegally. In addition, to the extent that law-abiding citizens find it more difficult to obtain guns, they may be less able to defend themselves. For example, a woman who is being stalked may no longer be able to obtain a gun quickly to scare off an attacker. Numerous newspaper accounts tell of women who were attempting to buy guns because of threats by former lovers and were murdered or raped during the required waiting period.[42]

The evidence from 1994 indicates that the Brady law has been associated with significant increases in rapes and aggravated assaults, and the declines in murder and robbery have been statistically insignificant. All the other gun-control laws examined in table 4.11 were also controlled for here, but because their estimated impacts were essentially unchanged, they are not reported.

What Happens to Neighboring Counties in Adjacent States When Nondiscretionary Handgun Laws are Adopted?

> If you put more resources in one place, it will displace some of the crime.
>
> Al L'Ecuyer, West Boylston
> (Massachusetts) Police Chief[43]

Up to this point we have asked what happens to crime rates in places that have adopted nondiscretionary laws. If these laws do discourage criminals, however, they may react in several ways. We already have discussed two: criminals could stop committing crimes, or they could commit other, less dangerous crimes like those involving property, where the probability of contact with armed victims is low. Yet as the epigraph for this section notes, a third possibility is that criminals may commit crimes in other areas where potential victims are not armed. A fourth outcome is also possible: eliminating crime in one area can help eliminate crime in other areas as well. This last outcome may occur if criminals had been using the county that adopted the law as a staging area. Crime-prone, poverty-stricken areas of cities may find that some of their crime spills over to adjacent areas.

This section seeks to test what effect concealed-handgun laws and higher arrest rates have on crime rates in adjacent counties in neighboring states. Since concealed-handgun laws are almost always passed at the state level, comparing adjacent counties in neighboring states allows us to examine the differential effect of concealed-handgun laws. Evidence that changes in a state's laws coincide with changes in crime rates in neighboring states will support the claim that the laws affect criminals. If these laws do not affect criminals, neighboring states should experience no changes in their crime rates.

Although any findings that nondiscretionary concealed-handgun laws cause criminals to leave the jurisdictions that adopt these laws would provide additional evidence of deterrence, such findings would also imply that simply looking at the direct effect of concealed-handgun laws on crime overestimates the total gain to society from these laws. In the extreme, if the entire reduction in crime from concealed-handgun laws was simply transferred to other areas, society as a whole would be no better off with these laws, even if individual jurisdictions benefited. While the evidence would confirm the importance of deterrence, adopting such a law in a single state might have a greater deterrent impact than if the entire nation adopted the law. The deterrent effect of adopting nondiscretionary concealed-handgun laws in additional states could also decline as more states adopted the laws.

To investigate these issues, I reran the regressions reported in table 4.1, using only those counties that were within fifty miles of counties in neighboring states. In addition to the variable that examines whether your own state has a nondiscretionary concealed-handgun law, I added three new variables. One variable averages the dummy variables for whether adjacent counties in neighboring counties have such laws. A second variable examines what happens when your county and your neighboring county adopt these laws. Finally, the neighboring counties' arrest rates are added, though I do not bother reporting them, because the evidence indicates that only the arrest rates in your own county, not your neighboring counties, matter in determining your crime rate.

The results reported in table 4.14 confirm that deterrent effects do spill over into neighboring areas. For all the violent-crime categories, adopting a concealed-handgun law reduces the number of violent crimes in your county, but these results also show that criminals who commit murder, rape, and robbery apparently move to adjacent states without the laws. The one violent-crime category that does not fit this pattern is aggravated assault: adopting a nondiscretionary concealed-handgun law lowers the number of aggravated assaults in neighboring counties. With respect to the benefits of all counties adopting the laws, the last column

Table 4.14 Estimates of the impact of nondiscretionary concealed-handgun laws on neighboring counties

Type of crime	Percent change in own crime rate		
	Own county has nondiscretionary law	Average neighbor has nondiscretionary law	Average neighbor and own county have nondis-cretionary law
Violent crime	−5.5%	0	−5.7%
Murder	−7.6%	3.5%	−4.1%
Rape	−6.2%	6%	0
Robbery	−4%	2.8%	−1.1%
Aggravated assault	−7.4%	−3.3%	−10.7%
Property crime	1%	1%	2%
Auto theft	−1.3%	2%	3.4%
Burglary	1%	4.7%	−1%
Larceny	9%	−2%	10.8%

shows that all categories of violent crime are reduced the most when all counties adopt such laws. The results imply that murder rates decline by over 8 percent and aggravated assaults by around 21 percent when a county and its neighbors adopt concealed-handgun laws.

As a final test, I generated the figures showing crime trends before and after a neighbor's adoption of the law by the method previously used, in addition to the time trends for before and after one's own adoption of the concealed-handgun laws. The use of an additional squared term allows us to see if the effect on crime is not linear. Figures 4.10–4.13 provide a graphic display of the findings for the different violent-crime categories, though the results for the individual violent-crime categories are equally dramatic. In all violent-crime categories, the adoption of concealed-handgun laws produces an immediate and large increase in violent-crime rates in neighboring counties, and in all the categories except aggravated assaults the spillover increases over time just as the counties with the nondiscretionary law see their own crime rates continue to fall. The symmetry and timing between the reduction in counties with non-discretionary laws and increases in neighboring counties without the laws is striking.

Overall, these results provide strong additional evidence for the deterrent effect of nondiscretionary concealed-handgun laws. They imply that the earlier estimate of the total social benefit from these laws may have overestimated the initial benefits, but underestimated the long-term

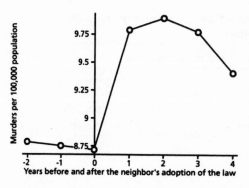

Figure 4.10. Impact on murder rate from a neighbor's adoption of nondiscretionary concealed-handgun law

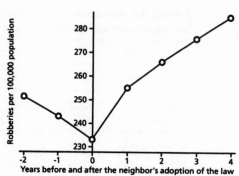

Figure 4.11. Impact on robbery rate from a neighbor's adoption of nondiscretionary concealed-handgun law

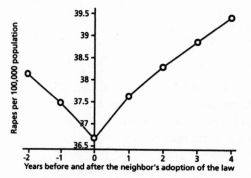

Figure 4.12. Impact on rape rate from a neighbor's adoption of nondiscretionary concealed-handgun law

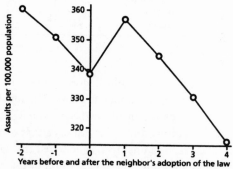

Figure 4.13. Impact on aggravated assault rate from a neighbor's adoption of nondiscretionary concealed-handgun law

benefits as more states adopt these laws. In the long run, the negative spillover effect subsides, and the adoption of these laws in all neighboring states has the greatest deterrent effect on crime.

CONCLUSIONS

The empirical work provides strong evidence that concealed-handgun laws reduce violent crime and that higher arrest rates deter all types of crime. The results confirm what law-enforcement officials have said— that nondiscretionary laws cause a greatest change in the number of permits issued for concealed handguns in the most populous, urbanized counties. This provides additional support for the claim that the greatest declines in crime rates are related to the greatest increases in concealed-handgun permits. The impact of concealed-handgun laws varies with a county's level of crime, its population and population density, its per-capita income, and the percentage of the population that is black. Despite the opposition to these laws in large, urban, densely populated areas, those are the areas that benefit the most from the laws. Minorities and women tend to be the ones with the most to gain from being allowed to protect themselves.

Some of the broader issues concerning criminal deterrence discussed in chapter 1 were evaluated, and the hypotheses used produced information about the locations where increased police efforts had the most significant deterrent effects on crime. Splitting the data set into high- and low-crime counties shows that arrest rates do not affect crime rates equally in all counties: the greatest return to increasing arrest rates is in the most crime-prone areas.

The results also confirm some of the potential aggregation problems with state-level data. The county-level data explain about six times more variation in violent-crime rates and eight times more variation in property-crime rates than do state-level data. Generally, the effect of concealed-handgun laws on crime appeared much greater when state-level regressions were estimated. However, one conclusion is clear: the very different results for state- and county-level data should make us very cautious in aggregating crime data. The differences in county characteristics show that dramatically greater differences exist among counties within any state than among different states. Whether increased arrest rates are concentrated in the highest-crime counties in a state or spread out equally across all counties makes a big difference in their impact on crime. Likewise, it is a mistake to think that concealed-handgun laws change crime rates in all counties in a state equally. The data should definitely remain as disaggregated as possible.

The three sets of estimates that rely on county-level data, state-level data, or county-level data that accounts for how the law affected different counties have their own strengths and weaknesses. While using county-level data avoids the aggregation problems present with state-level data, the initial county-level regressions rely heavily on variation in state laws and thus are limited to comparing the variation in these fifty jurisdictions. If weight is thus given to any of the results, it would appear that the greatest weight should be given to the county-level regressions that interact the nondiscretionary-law variable with measures of how liberally different counties issued permits under the preexisting discretionary systems. These regressions not only avoid the aggregation problems but also take fullest advantage of the relationship between county-level variations in crime rates and the impact of nondiscretionary laws. They provide the strongest evidence that concealed-handgun laws reduce all types of crime. Despite these different approaches, one result is clear: the results are remarkably consistent with respect to the deterrent effect of nondiscretionary concealed-handgun laws on violent crime. Two of these three sets of estimates imply that concealed-handgun laws also result in lower property-crime rates, although these rates decline less than the rates for violent crimes.

This study represents a significant change in the general approach to crime studies. This is the first study to use cross-sectional time-series evidence at both the county and state levels. Instead of simply using either cross-sectional state- or city-level data, this study has made use of the much larger variations in arrest rates and crime rates between rural and urban areas, and it has been possible to control for whether the lower crime rates resulted from the gun laws themselves or from other differences in these areas (for example, low crime rates) that lead to the adoption of these laws.

Five

The Victims and the Benefits from Protection

CONCEALED-HANDGUN LAWS, THE METHOD OF MURDER, AND THE CHOICE OF MURDER VICTIMS

Do laws allowing individuals to carry concealed handguns cause criminals to change the methods they use to commit murders? For example, the number of murders perpetrated with guns may rise after such laws are passed, even though the total number of murders falls. While concealed-handgun laws raise the risk of committing murders with guns, murderers may also find it relatively more dangerous to kill using other methods once people start carrying concealed handguns, and they may therefore choose to use guns to put themselves on a more even basis with their potential prey. Using data on the methods of murder from the Mortality Detail Records provided by the U.S. Department of Health and Human Services, I reran the murder-rate regression from table 4.1 on counties with populations over 100,000 during the period from 1982 to 1991. I then separated murders committed with guns from all other murders. Table 5.1 shows that carrying concealed handguns appears to have been associated with approximately equal drops in both categories of murders. Carrying concealed handguns appears to make all types of murders relatively less attractive.

We may also wonder whether concealed-handgun laws have any effect on the types of people who are likely to be murdered. The *Supplementary Homicide Reports* of the FBI's *Uniform Crime Reports* contain annual, state-level data from 1977 to 1992 on the percent of victims by sex, race, and age, as well as information on the whether the victims and the offenders knew each other (whether they were members of the same family, knew each other but were not members of the same family, were strangers, or no relationship was known).[1] Table 5.2, which uses the same setup as in table 4.1, is intended to explain these characteristics of the victims. The regressions indicate no statistically significant relationship between the concealed-handgun law and a victim's sex, race, relationships with offenders, or age (the last is not shown). However, while they are not quite

Table 5.1 Do concealed-handgun laws influence whether murders are committed with or without guns? Murder methods for counties with more than 100,000 people from 1982 to 1991

Exogenous variables	ln(Total murders)	ln(Murder with guns)	ln(murders by nongun methods)
Nondiscretionary law adopted	−9.7%*	−9.0%**	−8.9%**
Arrest rate for murder increased by 100 percentage points	−0.15%*	−0.10%*	−0.14%*

Note: While not all the coefficient estimates are reported, all the control variables are the same as those used in table 4.1, including the year and county dummies. All regressions use weighted least squares, where the weighting is each county's population. The first column uses the UCR numbers for counties with more than 100,000 people. The second column uses the numbers on total gun deaths available from the Mortality Detail Records, and the third column takes the difference between the UCR numbers for total murders and Mortality Detail Records of gun deaths. Endogenous variables are in murders per 100,000 population.
*The result is statistically significant at the 1 percent level for a two-tailed t-test.
**The result is statistically significant at the 10 percent level for a two-tailed t-test.

statistically significant, two of the estimates appear important and imply that in states with concealed-handgun laws victims know their nonfamily offenders 2.6 percentage points more frequently than not, and that the number of victims for whom it was not possible to determine whether a relationship existed declined by 2.9 percentage points.

This raises the question of whether the possible presence of concealed handguns causes criminals to prefer committing crimes against people they know, since presumably they would be more likely to know if an acquaintance carried a concealed handgun. The principal relationship between age and concealed handguns is that the concealed weapon deters crime against adults more than against young people—because only adults can legally carry concealed handguns—but the effect is statistically insignificant.[2] Some of the benefits from allowing adults to carry concealed handguns may be conferred on younger people whom these adults protect. In addition, when criminals who attack adults leave states that pass concealed-handgun laws, there might also be fewer criminals left to attack the children. The earlier evidence from figures 4.10–4.13 indicates that concealed-handgun laws actually drive criminals away, leaving fewer criminals to attack either adults or those under eighteen. Younger people may also benefit from concealed-carry laws simply because criminals cannot always easily determine who is eligible to carry a concealed handgun. Attackers may find seventeen-year-olds difficult to distinguish from eighteen-year-olds.

Table 5.2 Changes in characteristics of murder victims: annual, state-level data from the Uniform Crime Reports, Supplementary Homicide Reports, from 1977 to 1992

| | Percent change in various endogenous variables for changes in explanatory variables | | | | | | | | | |
| | By victim's sex | | | By victim's race | | | By victim's relationship to offender | | | |
Change in explanatory variable	Percent of Male Victims	Percent of Female Victims	Percent of victims, sex unknown	Percent of victims that are white	Percent of victims that are black	Percent of victims that are Hispanic	Percent of victims where the offender is known to victim but is not in family	Percent of victims where the offender is in the family	Percent of victims where the offender is a stranger	Percent victims where the relationship is unknown
Nondiscretionary law adopted	0.39	−0.44	0.05	0.01	0.70	−0.87	2.58	−0.25	0.54	−2.88
Arrest rate for murder increased by 100 percentage points	0.068	−0.14	0.07	−2.02**	1.32**	0.33	1.74**	−1.45*	0.79	−1.08

To interpret this table, the first coefficient (0.39) implies that the percent of male victims increases by 0.39 percentage points if a state adopts a nondiscretionary concealed-handgun law. While not all the coefficient estimates are reported, all the control variables are the same as those used in table 2.3, including the year and state dummies. All regressions use weighted least squares, where the weighting is each state's population.

*The result is statistically significant at the 1 percent level for a two-tailed t-test.

**The result is statistically significant at the 5 percent level for a two-tailed t-test.

The arrest rates for murder produce more interesting results. The percent of white victims and the percent of victims killed by family members both declined when arrest rates were increased, while the percent of black victims and the percent killed by non–family members whom they knew both increased. The results imply that higher arrest rates have a much greater deterrent effect on murders involving whites and family members. One explanation is that whites with higher incomes face a greater increase in expected penalties for any given increase in the probability of arrest.

MASS PUBLIC SHOOTINGS

Chapter 1 noted the understandable fear that people have of mass public shootings like the one on the Long Island Railroad or at the top of the Empire State Building. To record the number of mass public shootings by state from 1977 to 1992, a search was done of news-article databases (Nexis) for the same period examined in the rest of this study. A mass public shooting is defined as one that occurred in a public place and involved two or more people either killed or injured by the shooting. The crimes excluded involved gang activity; drug dealing; a holdup or a robbery; drive-by shootings that explicitly or implicitly involved gang activity, organized crime, or professional hits; and serial killings, or killings that took place over the span of more than one day. The places where public shootings occurred included such sites as schools, churches, businesses, bars, streets, government buildings, public transit facilities, places of employment, parks, health care facilities, malls, and restaurants.

Unlike my earlier data, these data are available only at the state level. Table 5.3 shows the mean rate at which such killings occurred both before and after the adoption of the nondiscretionary concealed-handgun laws in the ten states that changed their laws during the 1977 to 1992 period and, more broadly, for all states that either did or did not have such laws during the period. In each case the before-and-after means are quite statistically significantly different at least at the 1 percent level,[3] with the rates being dramatically lower when nondiscretionary concealed-handgun laws were in effect. For those states from which data are available before and after the passage of such laws, the mean per-capita death rate from mass shootings in those states plummets by 69 percent.[4]

To make sure that these differences were not due to some other factor, I reestimated the specifications used earlier to explain murder rates for the state-level regressions with time trends before and after the adoption of the nondiscretionary concealed-handgun laws. The variable being ex-

Table 5.3 Mass shooting deaths and injuries

	Mean death and injury rate per year for years in which the states do not have nondiscretionary concealed-handgun laws (1)	Mean death and injury rate per year for years in which the states do have nondiscretionary concealed-handgun laws (2)
	A. Comparing the before-and-after mean mass shooting deaths and injuries for states that changed their concealed-handgun laws during the 1977–1992 period[1]	
Number of mass shooting deaths and injuries for the ten states that changed their laws during the 1977–1992 period	1.63	1.19
Mass shooting deaths and injuries per 100,000 population for the ten states that changed their laws during the 1977–1992 period	0.039	0.012
	B. Comparing the mean mass shooting deaths and injuries for all states with nondiscretionary concealed-handgun laws and those without such laws[2]	
Number of mass shooting deaths and injuries	2.09	0.89
Mass shooting deaths and injuries per 100,000 population	0.041	0.037

[1]Column 1 for section A has 128 observations; column 2 has 32 observations.
[2]Column 1 for section B has 656 observations; column 2 has 160 observations.

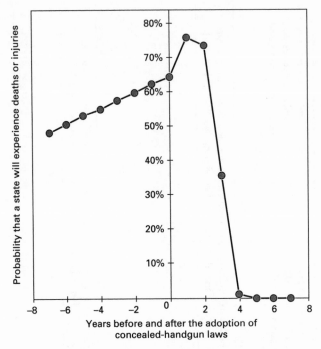

Figure 5.1. Probability that the ten states that adopted concealed-handgun laws during the 1977–1992 period experienced deaths or injuries from a shooting spree in a public place

plained is now the total number of deaths or injuries due to mass public shootings in a state.[5]

Figure 5.1 shows that although the total number of deaths and injuries from mass public shootings actually rises slightly immediately after a nondiscretionary concealed-handgun law is implemented, it quickly falls after that, with the rate reaching zero five years after the law is enacted.[6] Why there is an initial increase is not immediately obvious, though during this early period relatively few people have concealed-handgun permits. Perhaps those planning such shootings do them sooner than they otherwise would have, before too many citizens acquire concealed-handgun permits. One additional qualification should also be made. While nondiscretionary concealed-handgun laws reduced deaths and injuries from mass public shootings to zero after five years in the ten states that changed their laws during the 1977 to 1992 period, a look at the mean death and injury rates from mass public shootings in the eight states that passed such laws before 1977 shows that these rates were quite low but definitely not zero. This tempers the conclusion here and implies that while deaths and injuries from mass public shootings fall dramatically after nondiscretionary concealed-handgun laws are passed, it is unlikely that the true rate will drop to zero for the average state that adopts these laws.

COUNTY DATA FOR ARIZONA, PENNSYLVANIA, AND OREGON, AND STATE DATA FOR FLORIDA

One problem with the preceding results was the use of county population as a proxy for how restrictive counties were in allowing concealed-handgun permits before the passage of nondiscretionary laws. Since I am still going to control county-specific levels of crime with county dummies, a better measure would have been to use the actual change in the number of gun permits before and after the adoption of a concealed-handgun law. The per-capita number of permits provides a more direct measure of the expected costs that criminals face in attacking people. Knowing the number of permits also allows us to calculate the benefit from issuing an additional permit.

Fortunately, the information on the number of permits issued by county is available for three states: Arizona, Oregon, and Pennsylvania. Florida also provides yearly permit data at the state level. Arizona and Oregon also provided additional information on the conviction rate and the mean prison-sentence length. However, for Oregon, because the sentence-length variable is not directly comparable over time, it is interacted with all the individual year variables, so that we can still retain any cross-sectional information in the data. One difficulty with the Arizona sentence-length and conviction data is that they are available only from 1990 to 1995, and since the nondiscretionary concealed-handgun law did not take effect until July 1994, we cannot control for all the other variables that we control for in the other regressions.

Unlike Oregon and Pennsylvania, Arizona did not allow private citizens to carry concealed handguns prior to July 1994 (and permits were not actually issued until the end of the year), so the value of concealed-handgun permits equals zero for this earlier period. Unfortunately, however, because Arizona changed its law so recently, I cannot control for all the variables that I controlled for in the other regressions. Florida's data are even more limited, but they allow the study of the simple relationship between crime and permits at the state level for a relatively long period of time.

The results in table 5.4 for Pennsylvania and table 5.5 for Oregon provide a couple of consistent patterns.[7] The most economically and statistically important relationship involves the arrest rate: higher arrest rates consistently imply lower crime rates, and in twelve of the sixteen regres-

Table 5.4 Crime and county data on concealed–handgun permits: Pennsylvania counties with populations greater than 200,000

						Crimes per 100,000 population			
Percent change in the crime rate	Violent crime	Murder	Rape	Aggravated assault	Robbery	Property crime	Auto theft	Burglary	Larceny
Due to a 1 percent change in the number of right-to-carry pistol permits/population over 21 between 1988 and each year since the law was implemented	−5.3%**	−26.7%*	−5.7%**	−4.8%**	1.2%	−0.12%	1.5%	−1.4%	0.7%
Due to a 1 percent change in the arrest rate for the crime category	−0.79%*	−0.37%*	−0.08%	−0.76%*	−0.84%*	−0.41%**	−0.065%	−1.1%*	0.13%

Note: While not all the coefficient estimates are reported, all the control variables are the same as those used in table 4.1, including year and county dummies. All regressions use weighted least squares, where the weighting is each county's population. The nondiscretionary-law-times-county-population variable that was used in the earlier regressions instead of the variable for change in right-to-carry permits was tried here and produced very similar results. I also tried controlling for either the robbery or burglary rates, but I obtained very similar results.
*The result is statistically significant at the 1 percent level for a two-tailed t-test.
**The result is statistically significant at the 10 percent level for a two-tailed t-test.

Table 5.5 Crime and county data on concealed-handgun permits: Oregon data

Percent change in the crime rate	Crimes per 100,000 population						
	Murder	Rape	Aggravated assault	Robbery	Auto theft	Burglary	Larceny
Due to a 1 percent change in the number of right-to-carry pistol permits/population over 21 between 1988 and each year since the law was implemented	−37%****	−6.7%	−4.8%	−4.7%	12%	2.7%	−9%**
Due to a 1 percent change in the arrest rate for the crime category	−0.34%*	−1%*	−0.4%*	−0.4%*	−.04%	−0.7%*	−0.9%*
Due to a 1 percent change in the conviction rate for the crime category	−0.2%*	−0.09%*	−1.5%***	−0.19%*	−0.37%*	−0.27%*	−0.86%*

Note: While not all the coefficient estimates are reported, all the control variables are the same as those used in table 4.1, including year and county dummies. I also controlled for sentence length, but the different reporting practices used by Oregon over this period make its use somewhat problematic. To deal with this problem, the sentence-length variable was interacted with year-dummy variables. Thus, while the variable is not consistent over time, it is still valuable in distinguishing penalties across counties at a particular point in time. The categories for violent and property crimes are eliminated because the mean sentence-length data supplied by Oregon did not allow us to use these two categories. All regressions use weighted least squares, where the weighting is each county's population.

*The result is statistically significant at the 1 percent level for a two-tailed t-test.

**The result is statistically significant at the 5 percent level for a two-tailed t-test.

***The result is statistically significant at the 10 percent level for a two-tailed t-test.

****The result is statistically significant at the 11 percent level for a two-tailed t-test.

sions the effect is statistically significant. Five cases for Pennsylvania (violent crime, murder, aggravated assault, robbery, and burglary) show that arrest rates explain more than 15 percent of the change in crime rates.[8] Automobile theft is the only crime for which the arrest rate is insignificant in both tables.

For Pennsylvania, murder and rape are the only crimes for which percapita concealed-handgun permits explain a greater percentage of the variation in crime rates than does the arrest rate. However, increased concealed-handgun licensing explains more than 10 percent of the variation in murder, rape, aggravated assault, and burglary rates. Violent crimes, with the exception of robbery, show that greater numbers of concealed-handgun permits lower violent crime rates, while property crimes exhibit very little relationship. The portion of the variation for property crimes that is explained by concealed-handgun licensing is only about one-tenth as large as the variation for violent crimes that is explained by such licensing, which is not too surprising, given the much more direct impact that concealed handguns have on violent crime.[9] The regressions for Oregon weakly imply a similar relationship between concealed-handgun use and crime, but the effect is only strongly statistically significant for larceny; it is weakly significant for murder.

The Oregon data also show that higher conviction rates consistently result in significantly lower crime rates. The change in conviction rates explains 4 to 20 percent of the change in the corresponding crime rates;[10] however, for five of the seven crime categories, increases in conviction rates appear to produce a smaller deterrent effect than increases in arrest rates.[11] The greatest differences between the deterrent effects of arrest and conviction rates produce an interesting pattern. For rape, increasing the arrest rate by 1 percent produces more than ten times the deterrent effect of increasing the conviction rate for those who have been arrested by 1 percent. For auto theft, arrest seems more important than conviction: a 1 percent increase in the arrest rate reduces crime by about ten times more than the same increase in convictions. These results are consistent with the assumption that arrests produce large penalties in terms of shame or negative reputation.[12] In fact, the existing evidence shows that the reputational penalties from arrest and conviction can dwarf the legally imposed penalties.[13] This is some of the first evidence that the reputational penalties from arrests alone provide significant deterrence for some crimes.

One possible explanation for these results is that Oregon simultaneously passed both the nondiscretionary concealed-handgun law and a waiting period. The statistics in table 4.11 suggest that the long waiting period imposed by the Oregon law (fifteen days) increased murder by 5 percent, rape by 2 percent, and robbery by 6 percent. At least in the case of murder, which is weakly statistically significant in any case, the estimates from tables 4.11 and 5.5 together indicate that if Oregon had not adopted its waiting period, the drop in murder resulting from the concealed-handgun law would have been statistically significant at the 5 percent level.

The results for sentence length are not shown, but the t-statistics are frequently near zero, and the coefficients indicate no clear pattern. One possible explanation for this result is that all the changes in sentencing rules produced a great deal of noise in this variable, not only over time but also across counties. For example, after 1989, whether a crime was prosecuted under the pre- or post-1989 rules depended on when the crime took place. If the average time between when the offense occurred and when the prosecution took place differed across counties, the recorded sentence length could vary even if the actual time served was the same.

Florida's state-level data showing the changes in crime rates and changes in the number of concealed-handgun permits are quite suggestive (see figure 5.2). Cuba's Mariel Boat Lift created a sudden upsurge in Florida's murder rate from 1980 through 1982. By 1983 the murder rate had return to its pre-Mariel level, and it remained relatively constant or exhibited a slight upward trend until the state adopted its nondiscretionary concealed-handgun law in 1987. Murder-rate data are not available for 1988 because of changes in the reporting process, but the available evidence indicates that the murder rate began to drop when the law was adopted, and the size of the drop corresponded with the number of concealed-handgun permits outstanding. Ironically, the first post-1987 upward movement in murder rates occurred in 1992, when Florida began to require a waiting period and background check before issuing permits.

Finally, a very limited data set for Arizona produces no significant relationship between the change in concealed-handgun permits and the various measures of crime rates. In fact, the coefficient signs themselves indicate no consistent pattern; the fourteen coefficients are equally divided between negative and positive signs, though six of the specifications imply that the variation in the number of concealed-handgun permits explains at least 8 percent of the variation in the corresponding crime rates.[14] This is likely to occur for several reasons. The sample is extremely small (only 64–89 observations, depending on which specification), and we have only a year and a half over which to observe the effect of the law. In addition, if Arizona holds true to the pattern observed in other states, the impact of these laws is smallest right after the law passes.

The results involving either the mean sentence length for those sen-

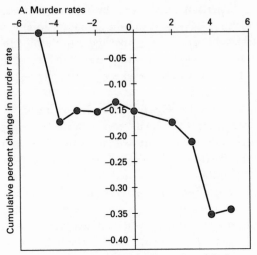

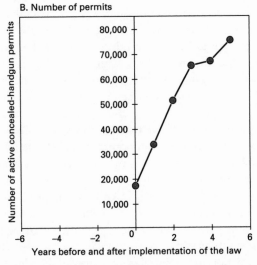

Figure 5.2A. Cumulative percent change in Florida's murder rate

Figure 5.2B. Concealed-handgun permits after implementation of the law in Florida

tenced in a particular year or the actual time served for those ending their sentences also imply no consistent relationship between sentence length and crime rates. While the coefficients are negative in eleven of the fourteen specifications, they provide weak evidence of the deterrent effect of longer prison terms: only two coefficients are negative and statistically significant.

The Brady law also went into effect during this period.[15] Using the Arizona data to investigate the impact of the Brady law indicates that its only discernible effect was in the category of aggravated assault, where the statistics imply that it increased the number of aggravated assaults by 24 percent and the number of rapes by 3 percent. Yet it is important to remember that the data for Arizona covered only a very short period of time when this law was in effect, and other factors influencing crime could not be taken into account. While I do not believe that the Brady law was responsible for this large increase in assaults, I at least take this as evidence that the law did not reduce aggravated assaults and as confirmation of the belief that relying on this small sample for Arizona is problematic.

Overall, Pennsylvania's results provide more evidence that concealed-handgun ownership reduces violent crime, murder, rape, aggravated assault, and burglary. For Oregon, the evidence implies that murder and larceny decrease. While the Oregon data imply that the effect of handgun permits on murder is only marginally statistically significant, the point estimate is extremely large economically, implying that a doubling of permits reduces murder rates by 37 percent. The other coefficients for Pennsylvania and Oregon imply no significant relationship between the change in concealed-handgun ownership and crime rates. The evidence from the small sample for Arizona implies no relationship between crime and concealed-handgun ownership. All the results also support the claim that higher arrest and conviction rates deter crime, although—perhaps partly because of the relatively poor quality of the data—no systematic effect appears to arise from longer prison sentences.

PUTTING DOLLAR VALUES ON THE CRIME-REDUCTION BENEFITS AND PRIVATE COSTS OF ADDITIONAL CONCEALED-HANDGUN PERMITS

By combining evidence that additional concealed handguns reduce crime with the monetary estimates of victim losses from crime produced by the National Institute of Justice, it is possible to attach a monetary value to the benefits of additional concealed-handgun permits. While the results for Arizona imply no real savings from reduced crime, the estimates for

Pennsylvania indicate that potential costs to victims are reduced by $5,079 for each additional concealed-handgun permit, and for Oregon, the savings are $3,439 per permit. As noted in the discussion of table 4.2, the results are largely driven by the effect of concealed handguns in lowering murder rates (with savings of $4,986 for Pennsylvania and $3,202 for Oregon).[16]

These estimated gains appear to far exceed the private costs of owning a concealed handgun. The purchase price of handguns ranges from $100 or less for the least-expensive .25-caliber pistols to over $700 for the newest, ultracompact, 9-millimeter models.[17] The permit-filing fees can range from $19 every five years in Pennsylvania to a first-time, $65 fee with subsequent five-year renewals at $50 in Oregon, which also requires several hours of supervised safety training. Assuming a 5 percent real interest rate and the ability to amortize payments over ten years, purchasing a $300 handgun and paying the licensing fees every five years in Pennsylvania implies a yearly cost of only $43, excluding the time costs incurred. The estimated expenses are higher for Oregon, because of the higher fees and the costs in time and money of obtaining certified safety instruction. Even if these annual costs double, however, they are still quite small compared to the social benefits. While ammunition purchases and additional annual training would increase annualized costs, the long life span of guns and their resale value work to reduce the above estimates.

The results imply that handgun permits are being issued at much lower than optimal rates, perhaps because of the important externalities not directly captured by the handgun owners themselves. While the crime-reducing benefits of concealed handguns are shared by all those who are spared being attacked, the costs of providing this protection are borne exclusively by permit holders.

ACCIDENTAL DEATHS AND SUICIDES

Even if nondiscretionary handgun permits reduce murder rates, we are still left with the question of what happens to the rates for accidental death. As more people carry handguns, accidents may be more likely. Earlier, we saw that the number of murders prevented exceeded the entire number of accidental deaths. In the case of suicide, the nondiscretionary laws increase the probability that a gun will be available when an individual feels particularly depressed; thus, they could conceivably lead to an increase in the number of suicides. While only a small portion of accidental deaths are attributable to guns (see appendix 4), the question remains whether concealed-handgun laws affect the total number of deaths through their effect on accidental deaths.

To get a more precise answer to this question, I used county-level data from 1982 to 1991 in table 5.6 to test whether allowing concealed handguns increased accidental deaths. Data are available from the Mortality Detail Records (provided by the U.S. Department of Health and Human Services) for all counties from 1982 to 1988 and for counties with populations over 100,000 from 1989 to 1991. The specifications are identical to those shown in all the previous tables, with the exceptions that they no longer include variables related to arrest or conviction rates and that the variables to be explained are either measures of the number of accidental deaths from handguns or measures of accidental deaths from all other nonhandgun sources.

While there is some evidence that the racial composition of the population and the level of welfare payments affect accident rates, the impact of nondiscretionary concealed-handgun laws is consistently both quite small economically and insignificant statistically. The first estimate in column 1 implies that accidental deaths from handguns rose by about 0.5 percent when concealed-handgun laws were passed. With only 200 accidental handgun deaths nationwide during 1988 (22 accidental handgun deaths occurred in states with nondiscretionary laws), the implication is that enacting concealed-handgun laws in states that currently do not have them would increase the number of deaths by less than one (.851 deaths). Redoing these tests by adding together accidental handgun deaths and deaths from "unknown" types of guns produces similar results.

With 186 million people living in states without concealed-handgun laws in 1992,[18] the third specification implies that implementing such laws across those remaining states would have resulted in about nine more accidental handgun deaths.[19] Combining this finding with earlier estimates from table 4.1, we find that if the rest of the country had adopted concealed-handgun laws in 1992, the net reduction in total deaths would have been approximately 1,405 to 1,583.

One caveat should be added to these numbers, however: both columns 2 and 4 indicate that accidental deaths from nonhandgun sources increased by more than accidental deaths from handguns after the nondiscretionary concealed-handgun laws were implemented. To the extent that the former category increased because of uncontrolled factors that also increase accidental deaths from handguns, the results presented here are biased toward finding that concealed-handgun laws have increased accidental deaths from handguns.

Finally, I examined similar specifications using data on suicide rates. The possibility exists that if a person becomes depressed while away from home, the presence of a concealed handgun might encourage that person

Table 5.6 Did nondiscretionary concealed-handgun laws increase the number of accidental deaths? (1982–91 county-level data)

	Deaths per 100,000 population			
	Ordinary least squares, natural logarithm of endogenous variable		Tobit	
Change in explanatory variable	Accidental deaths from handguns	Accidental deaths from nonhandgun sources	Accidental deaths from handguns	Accidental deaths from nonhandgun sources
Nondiscretionary law adopted	0.48%	9.9%**	0.574 more deaths	1.331 more deaths
Percent change in crime (for Tobit number of deaths per 100,000) for an increase in population of one person per square mile	−0.07%*	0.09%*	−0.004%	−0.016%
Percent change in crime (for Tobit number of deaths per 100,000) for an increase in $1,000 of real per-capita personal income	2.67%	−5.7%*	4.4%	−9%*

Note: While not all the coefficient estimates are reported, all the control variables are the same as those used in table 4.1, including year and county dummies. Absolute t-statistics are in parentheses. All regressions weight the data by each county's population.
*The result is statistically significant at the 1 percent level for a two-tailed t-test.
**The result is statistically significant at the 10 percent level for a two-tailed t-test.

to act impulsively, whereas an enforced delay might ultimately prevent a suicide. If anything, the results implied a statistically insignificant and small increase in suicides (less than one-tenth of 1 percent). Hence it is reasonable to conclude that no relationship exists between concealed-handgun laws and suicide rates.

TOTAL GUN OWNERSHIP AND CRIME

Traditionally, people have tried to use cross-county comparisons of gun ownership and crime rates to determine whether gun ownership enhances or detracts from safety.[20] Worldwide, there is no relationship between gun ownership and crime rates. Many countries, such as Switzerland, Finland, New Zealand, and Israel, have high gun-ownership rates and low crime rates, while many other countries have both low gun-ownership rates and either high or low crime rates. For example, in 1995 Switzerland's murder rate was 40 percent lower than Germany's despite having a three-times higher gun-ownership rate. Yet, making a reliable comparison across countries is an arduous task simply because it is difficult to obtain gun-ownership data both over time and across countries, and to control for all the other differences across the legal systems and cultures across countries. International comparisons are also risky because polls underreport ownership in countries where gun ownership is illegal, and they are conducted by different polling organizations that ask questions in widely differing ways. How crime is measured also varies across countries.

Fortunately, more consistent data are available to investigate the relationship between total gun ownership in the United States and crime. In chapter 3 I presented poll data from general-election surveys that offer consistent polling across states, showing how gun ownership varied across states for 1988 and 1996. There is broad variation in gun ownership across states, and the crime rates also vary across states and over time. Even with rather few observations, however, these data suggest that we may be able to answer an obvious question: Is the crime rate higher in states with more guns?

To test the relationship between gun ownership and crime, I attempted to examine the relationship between the percentage of the adult population owning guns and the crime rate after accounting for the arrest rate, real personal income, population per square mile, regional dummy variables (for the Northeast, Midwest, and South), the percentage of blacks among each state's population, and a variable to pick up the average change in crime rates between 1988 and 1995. This last variable was also intended to help pick up any differences in the results that arise from the slightly different poll methods in the two years. Ideally, one

Table 5.7 The relationship between state crime rates and the general election poll data on the percent of the state's adult population owning guns

Crime rates	Percent change in the crime rate from a 1 percentage point increase in a state's gun-ownership rate	Estimated change in victim costs from a 1 percent increase in the number of guns nationwide
Violent crime	−4.1*	
Murder	−3.3*	$2.7 billion
Rape	0	
Aggravated assault	−4.3*	$44 million
Robbery	−4.3*	$200 million
Property crime	−1.5**	
Burglary	−1.6*	$54 million
Larceny	−1.3	$38 million
Auto theft	−3.2*	$17 million
Total savings		$3.1 billion

Note: While the other coefficient values are not reported here, these regression results control for the arrest rate, real personal income, population per square mile, regional dummy variables (for the Northeast, Midwest, South, and the intercept picking up the West), the percent of the state's population that is black, and a year-dummy variable for 1996 to pick up the average change in crime rate between the years. All regressions use weighted least squares, where the regressions are weighted by the state populations.
*The result is statistically significant at the 1 percent level for a two-tailed t-test.
**The result is statistically significant at the 5 percent level for a two-tailed t-test.

would want to construct the same type of cross-sectional, time-series data set over many years and states that was used in the earlier discussions; unfortunately, however, such extensive poll data on gun ownership are not available. Because we lack the most recent data for the above-named variables, all the variables except for the percentage of the state's adult population that owns guns is for 1995.

As table 5.7 shows, a strong negative relationship exists between gun ownership and all of the crime rates except for rape, and the results are statistically significant for seven of the nine categories. Indeed, the effect of gun ownership on crime is quite large: a 1 percent increase in gun ownership reduces violent crime by 4.1 percent. The estimates from the National Institute of Justice of the costs to victims of crime imply that increasing gun ownership nationwide by 1 percent would reduce victim costs by $3.1 billion, though we must bear in mind that these conclusions are based on a relatively small sample. Similar estimates for accidental gun deaths or suicides reveal no significant relationships.

CONCLUSION

Nondiscretionary concealed-handgun laws have equal deterrent effects on murders committed both with and without guns. Despite differences in the rates at which women and men carry guns, no difference exists in the total benefit they derive in terms of reduced murder rates. The evidence strongly rejects claims that criminals will be more likely to use firearms when their potential victims are armed. Furthermore, the increased presence of concealed handguns under nondiscretionary laws does not raise the number of accidental deaths or suicides from handguns.

As in other countries, people who engage in mass public shootings are deterred by the possibility that law-abiding citizens may be carrying guns. Such people may be deranged, but they still appear to care whether they will themselves be shot as they attempt to kill others. The results presented here are dramatic: states that adopted nondiscretionary laws during the 1977–1992 period virtually eliminated mass public shootings after four or five years. These results raise serious concerns over state and federal laws banning *all* guns from schools and the surrounding area. At least permitting school employees access to guns would seem to make schools less vulnerable to mass shootings.

One prominent concern about leniency in permitting people to carry concealed handguns is that the number of accidental deaths might rise, but I can find no statistically significant evidence that this occurs. Even the largest estimate of nine more accidental deaths per year is extremely small in comparison to the number of lives saved from fewer murders.

The evidence for Pennsylvania and Oregon also provides the first estimates of the annual social benefits that accrue from private expenditures on crime reduction. Each additional concealed-handgun permit reduces total losses to victims by between three and five thousand dollars. The results imply that handgun permits are being obtained at much lower than optimal rates in two of the three states for which I had the relevant data, perhaps because the individual owners bear all the costs of owning their handguns but receive only a small fraction of the total benefits. The evidence implies that concealed handguns are the most cost-effective method of reducing crime that has been analyzed by economists; they provide a higher return than increased law enforcement or incarceration, other private security devices, or social programs like early educational intervention.[21]

The general-election exit-poll data may also be used to calculate the change in total costs to crime victims when more people own guns. These preliminary estimates are quite dramatic, indicating that, nationwide, each 1 percent increase in the number of people owning guns reduces victim costs by over 3 billion dollars.

The data continue to supply strong evidence supporting the economic notion of deterrence. Higher arrest and conviction rates consistently and dramatically reduce the crime rate. Consistent with other recent work,[22] the results imply that increasing the arrest rate, independent of the probability of eventual conviction, imposes a significant penalty on criminals. Perhaps the most surprising result is that the deterrent effect of a 1 percent increase in arrest rates is much larger than the same increase in the probability of conviction. It was also surprising that while longer prison terms usually implied lower crime rates, the results were normally not statistically significant.

Six

What Determines Arrest
Rates and the Passage of
Concealed-Handgun Laws?

The regressions used in previous chapters took both the arrest rate and the passage of nondiscretionary concealed-handgun laws as given. This chapter deals with the unavoidably complicated issue of determining whether the variables I am using to explain the crime rate are in themselves determined by other variables. Essentially, the findings here confirm the deterrence effect of concealed-handgun laws and arrest rates.

Following the work of Isaac Ehrlich, I now let the arrest rate depend on crime rates as well as on population measures and the resources invested in police.[1] The following crime and police measures were used: the lagged crime rates; measures of police employment and payroll per capita, per violent crime, and per property crime at the state level (these three measures of employment are also broken down by whether police officers have the power to make arrests). The population measures were as follows: income; unemployment insurance payments; the percentages of county population by age, sex, and race (already used in table 4.1); and county and year dummy variables.[2] In an attempt to account for political influences, I further included the percentage of a state's population belonging to the National Rifle Association, along with the percentage voting for the Republican presidential candidate.[3]

Because presidential candidates and political issues vary from election to election, the variables for the percentage voting Republican are not perfectly comparable across years. To account for these differences across elections, I used the variable for the percentage voting Republican in a presidential election for the years closest to that election. Thus, the percent of the vote obtained in 1980 was multiplied by the individual year variables for the years from 1979 to 1982, the percent of the vote obtained in 1984 was multiplied by the individual year variables for the years from 1983 to 1986, and so on through the 1992 election. A second set of regressions explaining the arrest rate also includes the change in the log of the crime rates as a proxy for the difficulties that police forces may face in adjusting to changing circumstances.[4] The time period studied in all these regressions, however, is more limited than in the previous tables because the state-level data on police employment and payroll available from the U.S. Department of Justices' Expenditure and Employment data set for the criminal justice system covered only the years from 1982 to 1992.

Aside from the concern over what determines the arrest rate, we want to answer another question: Why did some states adopt nondiscretionary concealed-handgun laws while others did not? As noted earlier, if states adopted such laws because crime rates were either rising or expected to rise, our preceding regression estimates (using ordinary least-squares) will underestimate the drop in crime. Similarly, if such laws were adopted because crime rates were falling, the bias is in the opposite direction—the regression will overestimate the drop in crime. Thus, in order to explain whether a county was likely to be in a state that had adopted concealed-handgun laws, I used the rates for both violent crime and property crime, along with the change in those crime rates.[5] To control for general political differences that might affect the chances for the passage of these laws, I also included the percentage of a state's population that belonged to the National Rifle Association; the Republican presidential candidate's percentage of the statewide vote; the percentage of blacks and whites in a state's population; the total population in the state; regional dummy variables for whether the state is in the South, Northeast, or Midwest; and year dummy variables.

The regressions reported here are different from those reported earlier because they allow us to let the crime rate depend on the variables for the concealed-handgun law and the arrest rate, as well as other variables, but the variables for the concealed-handgun law and the arrest rate are in turn dependent on other variables.[6] While these estimates use the same set of control variables employed in the preceding tables, the results differ from all my previous estimates in one important respect: nondiscretionary concealed-handgun laws are associated with large, significant declines in all nine crime categories. I tried estimating a specification that mimicked the regressions in Ehrlich's study. Five of the nine crime categories implied that a change of one standard deviation in the predicted value of the nondiscretionary-law variable explains at least 10 percent of a change of one standard deviation in the corresponding crime rates. Nondiscretionary concealed-handgun laws explain 11 percent of the variation in violent crime, 7.5 percent of the variation in murder, 6 percent for rape, 10 percent for aggravated assault, and 5 percent for robbery. In fact, concealed-handgun laws explain a greater percentage of the change in murder rates than do arrest rates.

A second approach examined what happened to the results when the arrest rate was determined not only by past crime rates but also by the change in the crime rate in the previous year. The concern here is that rapid changes in crime rates make it more difficult for police agencies to maintain the arrest rates they had in the past. With the exception of robbery, the new set of estimates using the change in crime rates to explain arrest rates indicated that the effect of concealed-handgun laws was usually more statistically significant but economically smaller. For example, in the new set of estimates, concealed-handgun laws explained 3.9 percent of the variation in murder rates compared to 7.5 percent for the preceding estimates. While these results imply that even crimes involving relatively little contact between victims and criminals experienced declines, nondiscretionary concealed-handgun laws reduced violent crimes by more than they reduced property crimes.

Both sets of estimates provide strong evidence that higher arrest rates reduce crime rates. Among violent crimes, rape consistently appears to be the most sensitive to higher arrest rates. Among property crimes, larceny is the most sensitive to higher arrest rates.

The estimates explaining which states adopt concealed-handgun laws show that the states adopting these laws are relatively Republican with large National Rifle Association memberships and low but rising rates of violent crime and property crime. The set of regressions used to explain the arrest rate shows that arrest rates are lower in high-income, sparsely populated, Republican areas where crime rates are increasing. This evidence calls into question claims that police forces are not catching criminals in high-crime, densely populated areas.

I reestimated the state-level data using similar specifications. The coefficients on the variables for both arrest rates and concealed-handgun laws remained consistently negative and statistically significant. The state-level data again implied a much stronger effect from the passage of concealed-handgun laws and a much weaker effect from higher arrest rates. In order to use the longer data series available for the nonpolice employment and payroll variables, I even reestimated the regressions without those variables. This produced similar results.[7]

Finally, using the predicted values for the arrest rates allows us to investigate the significance of another weakness of the data. The arrest-rate data suffers not only from some missing observations but also from some instances where it is undefined when the crime rate in a county equals zero. This last issue is problematic only for murders and rapes in low-population counties. In these cases, both the numerator and denominator in the arrest rate equal zero, and it is not clear whether I should count this as an arrest rate equal to 100 or 0 percent, neither of which is correct, as it is truly undefined. The previously reported evidence arising from regressions that were run only on the larger counties (population over 10,000) sheds some light on this question, since these counties have fewer observations with undefined arrest rates. In addition, if the earlier reported evidence that adopting nondiscretionary concealed-handgun laws changed the number of permits the least in the lower-population counties, one would expect relatively little change in counties with missing observations.

The analysis presented in this section allowed us to try another, more appropriate approach to deal with this issue.[8] I created predicted arrest rates for these observations using the regressions that explain the arrest rate, and then I reestimated the regressions with the new, larger samples. While the coefficient for murder declined, implying a 5 percent drop when nondiscretionary laws are adopted, the coefficient for rape increased, implying a drop of more than 10 percent. Only very small changes appeared in the other estimates. All coefficients were statistically significant. The effect of arrest rates also remained negative and statistically significant. As one final test to deal with the problems that arise from using the arrest rates, I reestimated the regressions using only the predicted values for the nondiscretionary-law variable. In this case the coefficients were always negative and statistically significant, and they indicate that these laws produce an even larger negative effect on crime than the effect shown in the results already reported.

CONCLUSION

Explicitly accounting for the factors that influence a state's decision to adopt a nondiscretionary concealed-handgun law and that determine the arrest rate only serves to strengthen the earlier results: with this approach, both concealed-handgun laws and arrest rates explain much larger percentages of the changes in the crime rate than they did earlier. Several other facts are clear. Nondiscretionary laws have so far been adopted by relatively low-crime states in which the crime rate is rising. These states have also tended to vote Republican and to have high percentages of their populations enrolled in the National Rifle Association.

For studies that use the number of police officers as a proxy for the level of law enforcement, these results suggest some caution. Property-crime rates appear to have no systematic relationship to the number of police officers either with or without the power to make arrests. For violent crime, the presence of more police officers *with* arrest powers lowers the arrest rate, while a greater number of police officers *without* arrest powers raises the arrest rate.

Neither of these results alone is particularly troubling, because increasing the number of police officers could reduce the crime rate enough so that the arrest rate could fall even if the officers did not slack off. Theoretically, the relationship between the number of police officers and the arrest rate could go either way. Yet in the case of violent crimes, the drop in arrest rates associated with more police officers is too large to be explained by a drop in the crime rate. In fact, the direct relationship between the number of police officers and violent crime implies a positive relationship. There are many possible explanations for this. Quite plausibly, the presence of more police officers encourages people to come forward to report crime. Another possibility is that relatively large police forces tend to be unionized and have managed to require less work from their officers. The bottom line is that using the number of police officers directly as a proxy for the level of law enforcement is at best a risky proposition. We must control for many other factors before we know exactly what we are measuring.

Seven

**The Political and
Academic Debate**

The Political Process

When my original study was released, many commentators were ready to attack it. Anyone who had shown any interest in looking at the article was given a copy while I was in the process of revising it for the _Journal of Legal Studies,_ although I quickly learned that it was not common practice to circulate studies to groups on both sides of the gun debate. Few comments were offered privately, but once the paper began to receive national press coverage, the attacks came very quickly.

Before the press coverage started, it was extremely difficult to get even a proponent of gun control to provide critical comments on the paper when I presented it at the Cato Institute in early August 1996. I approached twenty-two pro-control people before Jens Ludwig, a young assistant professor at Georgetown University, accepted my request to comment on the paper.

One of the more interesting experiences occurred when I asked Susan Glick, of the Violence Policy Center, to participate.[1] Glick, whom I called during June 1996, was one of the last people that I approached. She was unwilling to comment on my talk at Cato because she didn't want to "help give any publicity to the paper." Glick said that her appearance might help bring media attention to the paper that it wouldn't otherwise have gotten. When I pointed out that C-SPAN was likely to cover the event, she said she didn't care because "we can get good media whenever we want." When I asked her if I could at least send her a copy of the paper because I would appreciate any comments that she might have, she said, "Forget it, there is no way that I am going to look at it. Don't send it."[2]

However, when the publicity broke on the story with an article in _USA Today_ on August 2, she was among the many people who left telephone messages immediately asking for a copy of the paper. In her case, the media were calling, and she "need[ed] [my] paper to be able to criticize it." Because of all the commotion that day, I was unable to get back to her right away. ABC National Television News was doing a story on my study for that day, and when at around 3:00 P.M. the ABC reporter doing the story, Barry Serafin, called saying that certain objections had been raised about my paper, he mentioned that one of those who had criticized it was Ms. Glick. After talking to Mr. Serafin, I gave Glick a call to ask her if she still wanted a copy of my paper. She said that she wanted it sent to her right away and wondered if I could fax it to her. I then noted that her request seemed strange because I had just gotten off the telephone with Mr. Serafin at ABC News, who had told me that she had been very critical of the study, saying that it was "flawed." I asked how she could have said that there were flaws in the paper without even having looked at it yet. At that point Ms. Glick hung up the telephone.[3]

Many of the attacks from groups like Handgun Control, Inc. and the Violence Policy Center focused on claims that my study had been paid for by gun manufacturers or that the *Journal of Legal Studies* was not a peer-reviewed journal and that I had chosen to publish the study in a "student-edited journal" to avoid the close scrutiny that such a review would provide.[4] These attacks were completely false, and I believe that those making the charges knew them to be false. At least they had been told by all the relevant parties here at the University of Chicago and at the Olin Foundation that the funding issues were false, and the questions about publishing in a "student-edited journal" or one that was not peer-reviewed were well known to be false because of the prominence of the journal. Some statements involved claims that my work was inferior to an earlier study by three criminologists at the University of Maryland who had examined five counties.

Other statements, like those in the *Los Angeles Times,* tried to discredit the scholarliness of the study by claiming that "in academic circles, meanwhile, scholars found it curious that he would publicize his findings before they were subjected to peer review."[5] In fact, the paper was reviewed and accepted months before media stories started discussing it in August 1996.

The attacks claiming that this work had been paid for by gun manufacturers have been unrelenting. Congressman Charles Schumer (D–N.Y.) wrote as follows in the *Wall Street Journal:* "I'd like to point out one other 'association.' The Associated Press reports that Prof. Lott's fellowship at the University of Chicago is funded by the Olin Foundation, which is 'associated with the Olin Corporation,' one of the nation's largest gun manufacturers. Maybe that's a coincidence, too. But it's also a fact."[6] Others were even more direct. In a letter that the Violence Policy Center mass-mailed to newspapers around the country, M. Kristen Rand, the Center's federal policy director, wrote,

Lott's work was, in essence, funded by the firearms industry—the primary beneficiary of increased handgun sales. Lott is the John M. Olin fellow at the University of Chicago law school, a position founded by the Olin Foundation. The foundation was established by John Olin of the Olin Corp., manufacturer of Winchester ammunition and maker of the infamous "Black Talon" bullet. Lott's study of concealed handgun laws is the product of gun-industry funding. . . . (See, as one of many examples, "Gun Industry Paid," *Omaha World Herald,* March 10, 1997, p. 8.)[7]

Dan Kotowski, executive director of the Illinois Council Against Handgun Violence, said that "the study was biased because it was funded by the parent company of Winchester, Inc., a firearms manufacturer."[8] Kotowski is also quoted as saying that the claimed link between Winchester and my study's conclusions was "enough to call into question the study's legitimacy. It's more than a coincidence."[9] Similar claims have been made by employees of Handgun Control, Inc. and other gun-control organizations.

Indeed, gun-control groups that were unwilling to comment publicly on my study at the Cato Institute forum had time to arrange press conferences that were held exactly at the time that I was presenting my paper in Washington. Their claims were widely reported by the press in the initial news reports on my findings. A typical story stated that "Lott's academic position is funded by a grant from the Olin Foundation, which is associated with the Olin Corp. Olin's Winchester division manufactures rifles and bullets,"[10] and it was covered in newspapers from the *Chicago Tribune* to the *Houston Chronicle* and the *Des Moines Register,* as well as in "highbrow" publications like *The National Journal.* The Associated Press released a partial correction stating that the Olin Foundation and Olin Corporation are separate organizations and that the Winchester subsidiary of the Olin Corporation makes ammunition, not guns, but a Nexis search of news stories revealed that only one newspaper in the entire country that had published the original report carried the Associated Press correction.[11]

Congressman Schumer's letter did produce a strong response from William Simon, the Olin Foundation's president and former U.S. Secretary of the Treasury, in the *Wall Street Journal* for September 6, 1996:

An Insult to Our Foundation
As president of the John M. Olin Foundation, I take great umbrage at Rep. Charles Schumer's scurrilous charge (Letters to the Editor, Sept. 4) that our foundation underwrites bogus research to advance the interests of companies that manufacture guns and ammunition. He asserts (falsely) that the John M. Olin Foundation is "associated" with the Olin Corp. and (falsely again) that the Olin Corp. is one of the nation's largest gun manu-

facturers. Mr. Schumer then suggests on the basis of these premises that Prof. John Lott's article on gun-control legislation (editorial page, Aug. 28) must have been fabricated because his research fellowship at the University of Chicago was funded by the John M. Olin Foundation.

This is an outrageous slander against our foundation, the Olin Corp., and the scholarly integrity of Prof. Lott. Mr. Schumer would have known that his charges were false if he had taken a little time to check his facts before rushing into print. Others have taken the trouble to do so. For example, Stephen Chapman of the *Chicago Tribune* looked into the charges surrounding Mr. Lott's study, and published an informative story in the Aug. 15 issue of that paper, which concluded that, in conducting his research, Prof. Lott was not influenced either by the John M. Olin Foundation or by the Olin Corp. Anyone wishing to comment on this controversy ought first to consult Mr. Chapman's article and, more importantly, should follow his example of sifting the facts before reaching a conclusion. For readers of the Journal, here are the key facts.

The John M. Olin Foundation, of which I have been president for nearly 20 years, is an independent foundation whose purpose is to support individuals and institutions working to strengthen the free enterprise system. We support academic programs at the finest institutions in the nation, including the University of Chicago, Harvard, Yale, Stanford, Columbia, the University of Virginia, and many others. We do not tell scholars what to write or what to say.

The foundation was created by the personal fortune of the late John M. Olin, and is not associated with the Olin Corp. The Olin Corp. has never sought to influence our deliberations. Our trustees have never taken into account the corporate interests of the Olin Corp. or any other company when reviewing grant proposals. We are as independent of the Olin Corp. as the Ford Foundation is of the Ford Motor Co.

The John M. Olin Foundation has supported for many years a program in law and economics at the University of Chicago Law School. This program is administered and directed by a committee of faculty members in the law school. This committee, after reviewing many applications in a very competitive process, awarded a research fellowship to Mr. Lott. We at the foundation had no knowledge of who applied for these fellowships, nor did we ever suggest that Mr. Lott should be awarded one of them. We did not commission his study, nor, indeed, did we even know of it until last month, when Mr. Lott presented his findings at a conference sponsored by a Washington think tank.

As a general rule, criticism of research studies should be based on factual grounds rather than on careless and irresponsible charges about the motives of the researcher. Mr. Lott's study should be evaluated on its own merits without imputing motives to him that do not exist. I urge Mr. Schumer to check his facts more carefully in the future.

Finally, it was incorrectly reported in the *Journal* (Sept. 5) that the John M. Olin Foundation is 'headed by members of the family that founded the Olin Corp.' This is untrue. The trustees and officers of the foundation have been selected by virtue of their devotion to John Olin's principles, not by virtue of family connections. Of our seven board members, only one is a member of the Olin family. None of our officers is a member of the Olin family—neither myself as president, nor our secretary-treasurer, nor our executive director.

This letter, I think, clarifies the funding issue, and I would only like to add that while the faculty at the Law School chose to award me this fellowship, even they did not inquire into the specific research I planned to undertake.[12] The judgment was made solely on the quality and quantity of my past research, and while much of my work has dealt with crime, this was my first project involving gun control. No one other than myself had any idea what research I was planning to do. However, even if one somehow believed that Olin were trying to buy research, it must be getting a very poor return on its money. Given the hundreds of people at the different universities who have received the same type of fellowship, I have been the only one to work on the issue of gun control.

Unfortunately, as the quote from Ms. Rand's letter and statements by many other gun-control advocates—made long after Simon's explanation—indicates, the facts about funding did little to curtail the comments of those spreading the false rumors.[13]

After these attacks on my funding, the gun-control organizations brought up new issues. For example, during the spring of 1997 the Violence Policy Center sent out a press release entitled "Who Is John Lott?" that claimed, among other things, "Lott believes that some crime is good for society, that wealthy criminals should not be punished as harshly as poor convicts." I had in fact been arguing that "individuals guilty of the same crime should face the same expected level of punishment" and that with limited resources to fight crime, it is not possible to eliminate all of it.[14] I would have thought that most people would recognize these silly assertions for what they were, but they were picked up and republished by publications such as the *New Republic*.[15]

The aversion to honest public debate has been demonstrated to me over and over again since my study first received attention. Recently, for example, Randy Roth, a visiting colleague at the University of Chicago Law School, asked me to appear on a radio program that he does from the University of Hawaii on a public radio station. I had almost completely stopped doing radio interviews a few months before because they were too much of an interruption to my work, but Randy, whom I have known only very briefly from lunch-table conversation, seemed like a very interesting person, and I thought that it would be fun to do the show with him. I can only trust that he doesn't normally have as much trouble as he had this time in getting an opposing viewpoint for his program. In a note that Randy shared with me, he described a conversation that he had with Brandon Stone, of the Honolulu Police Department, whom he had been trying for a while to get to participate. Randy wrote as follows on March 3, 1997:

Brandon called to say he had not changed his mind—he will not participate in any gun-control radio show involving John Lott. Furthermore, he said he had discussed this with all the others who are active in this area (the Hawaii Firearms Coalition, I think he called it), and that they have "banded together"—none will participate in such a show.

He said he didn't want to "impugn" John's character . . . [and] then he went on to talk about all the money involved in this issue, the fact that [the] Olin Corp. is in the firearm business and financing John's chair, etc. He said John's study had been given to the media before experts first could discredit it, implying that this "tactic" was used because the study could not withstand the scrutiny of objective scholars.

He said the ideas promoted by John's study are "fringe ideas" and that they are "dangerous." When I pointed out that such ideas not only have been publicly debated in other states, but that some of those states actually have enacted legislation, he basically just said that Hawaii is a special place and other states have sometimes been adversely affected by unfair tactics by the pro-gun lobby.

I kept coming back to my belief that public debate is good and that my show would give him an opportunity to point out anything about John's study that he believes to be incorrect, irrelevant, distorted, or whatever. He kept saying that public debate does more harm than good when others misuse the forum. When he specifically mentions the firearm industry ("follow the money" was his suggestion, to understand what John's study is all about), I reminded him of John's association with the University of Chicago and his outstanding reputation, both for scholarship and integrity. He then said he realized John was "my friend," as though I couldn't be expected to be objective. He also said that John was "out of his field" in this area.

My hunch is that it's going to be extremely difficult finding a studio guest with the credentials and ability to do a good job on the pro–gun-control side.

After talking with Randy and in an attempt to create a balanced program, I also telephoned Mr. Stone. While we did not get into the detail that he went into with Randy, I did try to address his concerns over my funding and my own background in criminal justice as chief economist at the U.S. Sentencing Commission during the late 1980s. Stone also expressed his concerns to me that Hawaiians would not be best served by our debating the issue and that Hawaiians had already made up their minds on this topic. I said that he seemed like an articulate person and that it would be good to have a lively discussion on the subject, but he said that the program "could only do more harm than good" and that any pro—gun-control participation would only lend "credibility" to the discussion.[16]

Before I did my original study, I would never have expected it to receive the attention that it did. None of the refereed journal articles that I have produced has received so much attention. Many people have told me that it was politically naive. That may be, but this much is clear: I never would have guessed how much people fear discussion of these issues. I never would have known how much effort goes into deliberately ignoring certain findings in order to deny them news coverage. Nor would I have seen, after news coverage did occur, how much energy goes into attacking the integrity of those who present such findings, with such slight reference—or no reference at all—to the actual merits of the research. I was also surprised by the absolute confidence shown by gun-control advocates that they could garner extensive news coverage whenever they wanted.

CRITICISMS OF THE ORIGINAL STUDY

A second line of attack came from academic, quasi-academic, and gun-control advocacy groups concerning the competence with which the study was conducted. Many of these objections were dealt with somewhere in the original study, which admittedly is very long. Yet it should have been easy enough for critics—especially academics—to check.

The attacks have been fairly harsh, especially by the standards of academic discourse. For example,

> "They highlight things that support their hypothesis while they ignore things contrary to their hypothesis," said Daniel Webster, an assistant professor at Johns Hopkins University Center for Gun Policy and Research.
>
> "We think the study falls far short of any reasonable standard of good social science research in making [their] case," said economist Daniel

Nagin of Carnegie-Mellon University, who has analyzed Lott's data with colleague Dan Black.[17]

I have made the data I used available to all academics who have requested them, and so far professors at twenty-four universities have taken advantage of that. Of those who have made the effort to use the extensive data set, Dan Black and Daniel Nagin have been the only ones to publicly criticize the study.

The response from some academics, particularly those at the Johns Hopkins Center for Gun Policy and Research, has been highly unusual in many ways. For instance, who has ever heard of academics mounting an attack on a scholarly study by engaging in a systematic letter-writing campaign to local newspapers around the country?[18] One letter from a citizen to the *Springfield (Illinois) State Journal-Register* noted, "Dear Editor: Golly, I'm impressed that the staff at Johns Hopkins University reads our local *State Journal-Register.* I wonder if they subscribe to it."[19]

The rest of this chapter briefly reviews the critiques and then provides my responses to their concerns. I discuss a number of issues below that represent criticisms raised in a variety of published or unpublished research papers as well as in the popular press:

1 *Is the scale of the effect realistic?*

Large reductions in violence are quite unlikely because they would be out of proportion to the small scale of the change in carrying firearms that the legislation produced. (Franklin Zimring and Gordon Hawkins, "Concealed-Handgun Permits: The Case of the Counterfeit Deterrent," *The Responsive Community* [Spring 1997]: 59, cited hereafter as Zimring and Hawkins, "Counterfeit Deterrent")

In some states, like Pennsylvania, almost 5 percent of the population has concealed-handgun permits. In others, like Florida, the portion is about 2 percent and growing quickly. The question here is whether these percentages of the population are sufficient to generate 8 percent reductions in murders or 5 percent reductions in rapes. One important point to take into account is that applicants for permits do not constitute a random sample of the population. Applicants are likely to be those most at risk. The relevant comparison is not between the percentage of the population being attacked and the percentage of the entire population holding permits, but between the percentage of the population most vulnerable to attack and the percentage of that population holding permits.

Let us consider some numbers from the sample to see how believable these results are. The yearly murder rate for the average county is 5.65 murders per 100,000 people, that is, .00565 percent of the people in the average county are murdered each year. An 8 percent change in this murder rate amounts to a reduction of 0.0005 percent. Obviously, even if only 2 percent of the population have handgun permits, that 2 percent is a huge number relative to the 0.0005 percent reduction in the murder rate. Even the largest category of violent crimes, aggravated assault, involves 180 cases per 100,000 people in the average county per year (that is, 0.18 percent of the people are victims of this crime in the typical year). A 7 percent change in this number implies that the assault rate declines from 0.18 percent of the population to 0.167 percent of the population. Again, this 0.013 percent change in the assault rate is quite small compared to the observed changes in the number of concealed-handgun permits.

Even if those who carry concealed handguns face exactly the same risk of being attacked as everyone else, a 2 percent increase in the portion of the population carrying concealed handguns seems comparable to the percentage-point reductions in crime. Bearing in mind that those carrying guns are most likely to be at risk, the drop in crime rates correlated with the presence of these guns even begins to seem relatively small. Assuming that just 2 percent of the population carries concealed handguns, the drop in the murder rate only requires that 0.025 percent of those with concealed-handgun permits successfully ward off a life-threatening attack to achieve the 0.0005 percent reduction in the murder rate. The analogous percentage for aggravated assaults is only 0.65 percent. In other words, if less than seven-tenths of one percent of those with concealed handguns successfully ward off an assault, that would account for the observed drop in the assault rate.

2 *The importance of "crime cycles"*

Crime rates tend to be cyclical with somewhat predictable declines following several years of increases. . . . Shall-issue laws, as well as a number of other measures intended to reduce crime, tend to be enacted during periods of rising crime. Therefore, the reductions in violent crime . . . attribute[d] to the implementation of shall-issue laws may be due to the variety of other crime-fighting measures, or to a commonly observed downward drift in crime levels towards some long-term average. (Daniel W. Webster, "The Claims That Right-to-Carry Laws Reduce Violent Crime Are Unsubstantiated," The Johns Hopkins Center for Gun Policy and Research, copy obtained March 6, 1997, p. 1; cited hereafter as Webster, "Claims")

Despite claims to the contrary, the regressions do control for national and state crime trends in several different ways. At the national level, I use a separate variable for each year, a technique that allows me to account for the changes in average national crime rates from one year to another. Any national cycles in crime rates should be accounted for by this method. At the state level, some of the estimates use a separate time trend for each state, and the results with this method generally yielded even larger drops in violent-crime rates associated with nondiscretionary (shall-issue) laws.

To illustrate that the results are not merely due to the "normal" ups and downs for crime, we can look again at the diagrams in chapter 4 showing crime patterns before and after the adoption of the nondiscretionary laws. The declines not only begin right when the concealed-handgun laws pass, but the crime rates end up well below their levels prior to the law. Even if laws to combat crime are passed when crime is rising, why would one believe that they happened to be passed right at the peak of any crime cycle?

As to the concern that other changes in law enforcement may have been occurring at the same time, the estimates account for changes in other gun-control laws and changes in law enforcement as measured by arrest and conviction rates as well as by prison terms. No previous study of crime has attempted to control for as many different factors that might explain changes in the crime rate.

3 *Did I assume that there was an immediate and constant effect from these laws and that the effect should be the same everywhere?*

The "statistical models assumed: (1) an immediate and constant effect of shall-issue laws, and (2) similar effects across different states and counties." (Webster, "Claims," p. 2; see also Dan Black and Daniel Nagin, "Do 'Right-to-Carry' Laws Deter Violent Crime?" *Journal of Legal Studies* 27 [January 1998], p. 213.)

One of the central arguments both in the original paper and in this book is that the size of the deterrent effect is related to the number of permits issued, and it takes many years before states reach their long-run level of permits. Again, the figures in chapter 4 illustrate this quite clearly.

I did not expect the number of permits to change equally across either counties or states. A major reason for the larger effect on crime in the more urban counties was that in rural areas, permit requests already were being approved; hence it was in urban areas that the number of permitted concealed handguns increased the most.

A week later, in response to a column that I published in the *Omaha World-Herald*,[20] Mr. Webster modified this claim somewhat:

> Lott claims that his analysis did not assume an immediate and constant effect, but that is contrary to his published article, in which the *vast majority* of the statistical models assume such an effect. (Daniel W. Webster, "Concealed-Gun Research Flawed," *Omaha World-Herald,* March 12, 1997; emphasis added.)

When one does research, it is most appropriate to take the simplest specifications first and then gradually make things more complicated. The simplest way of doing this is to examine the mean crime rates before and after the change in a law. Then one would examine the trends that existed before and after the law. This is the pattern that I followed in my earlier work, and I have followed the same pattern here. The bottom line should be, How did the different ways of examining the data affect the results? What occurs here is that (1) the average crime rate falls after the nondiscretionary concealed-handgun laws are adopted; (2) violent-crime rates were rising until these laws were adopted, and they fell dramatically after that; and (3) the magnitude of the drops, both across counties and states and over time, corresponds to the number of permits issued.

4   *When were these concealed-handgun laws adopted in different states?*

> Lott and Mustard also use incorrect dates of shall-issue law implementation in their analyses. For example, they claim that Virginia adopted its shall-issue law in 1988. . . . Some populous counties in Virginia continued to issue very few permits until 1995 (after the study period), when the state eliminated this discretion. Lott and Mustard identify 1985 as the year in which Maine liberalized its concealed-carry policy. It is unclear why they chose 1985 as the year of policy intervention, because the state changed its concealed-carry law in 1981, 1983, 1985, 1989, and 1991. (Webster, "Claims," p. 3; see also Daniel W. Webster, "Concealed-Gun Research Flawed," *Omaha World-Herald,* March 12, 1997; cited hereafter as Webster, "Flawed.")

I do think that Virginia's 1988 law clearly attempted to take away local discretion in issuing permits, and, indeed, all but three counties clearly complied with the intent of the law. However, to satisfy any skeptics, I examined whether reclassifying Virginia affected the results: it did not. The 1988 law read as follows:

> The court, after consulting the law-enforcement authorities of the county or city and receiving a report from the Central Criminal Records Exchange, *shall issue* such permit if the applicant is of good character, has demonstrated

a need to carry such concealed weapon, which need may include but is not limited to lawful defense and security, is physically and mentally competent to carry such weapon, and is not prohibited by law from receiving, possessing, or transporting such weapon [emphasis added].[21]

As with Virginia, I relied on a study by Clayton Cramer and David Kopel to determine when Maine changed its law to a nondiscretionary law. Maine enacted a series of changes in its law in 1981, 1983, 1985, and 1991. The 1985 law did not completely eliminate discretion, but it provided the foundation for what they then considered to be a switch to a de facto shall-issue regime, which was upheld in a number of important state court decisions.[22] The bottom line, however (again, as with Virginia), is that reclassifying Maine (or even eliminating it from the data set) does not change the results much.

5 *Should robbery be the crime most affected by the adoption of the nondiscretionary law?*

Shall-issue laws were adopted principally to deter predatory street crime, the most common example of which is robbery by a stranger. But [the] results indicate that shall-issue laws had little or no effect on robbery rates. Instead the strongest deterrent effects estimated were for rape, aggravated assault, and murder. (Webster, "Claims," p. 3)

Is it credible that laws that allow citizens to carry guns in public appear to have almost no effect on robberies, most of which occur in public spaces, yet do reduce the number of rapes, most of which occur outside of public spaces within someone's home. (Jens Ludwig, speaking on *Morning Edition,* National Public Radio, 10:00 A.M. ET December 10, 1996.)

I have two responses. First, as anyone who has carefully read this book will know, it is simply not true that the results show "little or no effect on robbery rates." Whether the effect was greater for robbery or other violent crimes depends on whether one simply compares the mean crime rates before and after the laws (in which case the effect is relatively small for robbery) or compares the slopes before and after the law (in which case the effect for robbery is the largest).

Second, it is not clear that robbery should exhibit the largest impacts, primarily because the term *robbery* encompasses many crimes that are not street robberies. For instance, we do not expect bank or residential robberies to decrease; in fact, they could even rise. Allowing law-abiding citizens to carry concealed handguns makes street robberies more difficult, and thus may make other crimes like residential robbery *relatively* more attractive. Yet not only is it possible that these two different components of robbery could move in opposite directions, but to rank some of these different crimes, one requires information on how sensitive different types of criminals are to the increased threat.

Making claims about what will happen to different types of violent crimes is much more difficult than predicting the relative differences between, say, crimes that involve no contact with victims and crimes that do. Even here, however, some of these questions cannot be settled *a priori.* For example, when violent crimes decline, more people may feel free to walk around in neighborhoods, which implies that they are more likely to observe the illegal actions of strangers.[23] Criminals who commit violent crimes are also likely to commit some property crimes, and anything that can make an area unattractive to them will reduce both types of crime.

6　*Do concealed-handgun laws cause criminals to substitute property crimes for rape?*

> Lott and Mustard argue that criminals, in response to shall-issue laws, substitute property crimes unlikely to involve contact with victims. But their theory and findings do not comport with any credible criminological theory because theft is the motive for only a small fraction of the violent crimes for which Lott and Mustard find shall-issue effects. It is difficult to rationalize why a criminal would, for example, steal a car because he felt deterred from raping or assaulting someone. (Webster, "Claims," p. 4. See also Jens Ludwig, "Do Permissive Concealed-Carry Laws Reduce Violent Crime?" Georgetown University working paper, October 8, 1996, p. 19, hereafter cited as Ludwig, "Permissive Concealed-Carry Laws.")

No one believes that hard-core rapists who are committing their crimes only for sexual gratification will turn into auto thieves, though some thefts do also involve aggravated assault, rape, or murder.[24] Indeed, 16 percent of murders in Chicago from 1990 to 1995 occurred in the process of a robbery.[25] What is most likely to happen, however, is that robbers will try to obtain money by other means such as auto theft or larceny. Although it is not unusual for rape victims to be robbed, the decline in rape most likely reflects the would-be rapist's fear of being shot.

I am also not completely clear on what Webster means when he says that "theft is the motive for only a small fraction of violent crimes," since robbery accounted for as much as 34 percent of all violent crimes committed during the sample between 1977 and 1992 (and this excludes robberies that were committed when other more serious crimes like murder or rape occurred in connection with the robbery).

7 *Comparing crime rates for two to three years before nondiscretionary laws go into*
   effect with crime rates for two to three years after the passage of such laws

> If right-to-carry laws have an immediate, substantial impact on the crime
> rates, the coefficients on the right-to-carry laws immediately after the en-
> actment of the law should be substantially different from those immedi-
> ately preceding the law's enactment. To test formally for the impact of
> right-to-carry laws, we see if the sum of the coefficients for two to three
> years prior to adoption is significantly different from the sum for two and
> three years following adoption. . . . Only in the murder equation do our
> findings agree with Lott and Mustard. In contrast to Lott and Mustard, we
> find evidence that robberies and larcenies are reduced when right-to-carry
> laws are passed and no evidence of an impact on rape and aggravated as-
> saults. (Dan Black and Daniel Nagin, "Do 'Right-to-Carry' Laws Deter Vi-
> olent Crime?" Carnegie-Mellon University working paper, October 16,
> 1996, p. 7)

Instead of the approach used earlier in this book (a simple time trend and
time trend squared for the number of years before and after the
concealed-handgun laws) Black and Nagin use ten different variables to
examine these trends. Separate variables were used for the first year after
the law, the second year after the law, the third year after the law, the
fourth year after the law, and five or more years after the law. Similarly,
five different variables were used to measure the effects for the five years
leading up to the adoption of the law. They then compare the average
coefficient values for the variables measuring the effects two to three
years before the law with the average effect for the variables two to three
years after the law.

A quick glance at figures 7.1 to 7.5, which plot their results, will explain their findings. Generally, the pattern is very similar to what we reported earlier. In addition, as crime is rising right up until the law is
adopted and falling thereafter, it is not surprising that some values when
the crime rate is going down are equal to those when it was going up. It
is the slopes of the lines and not simply their levels that matter. But more
generally, why choose to compare only two to three years before and
after to look for changes created by the law. Why not use all the data
available?

Examining the entire period before the law versus the entire period
after produces the significant results that I reported earlier in the book.
Alternatively, one could have chosen to analyze the differences in crime
rates between the year before the law went into effect and the year after,
but one would hope that if deviations are made from any simple rule,
some rationale for doing so would be given.

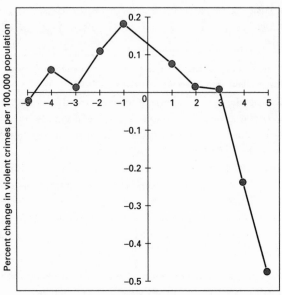

Figure 7.1. Average year-dummy effects for violent crimes, using Black's and Nagin's "full sample"

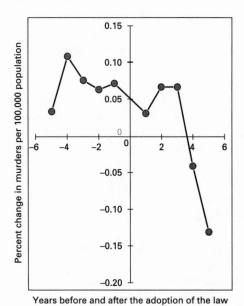

Figure 7.2. The effect of concealed-handgun laws on murder, using Black's and Nagin's "full sample"

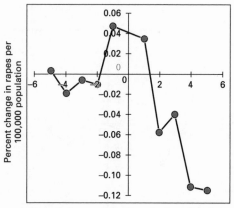

Figure 7.3. The effect of concealed-handgun laws on rapes, using Black's and Nagin's "full sample"

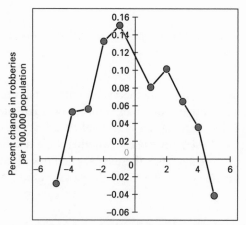

Figure 7.4. The effect of concealed-handgun laws on robbery, using Black's and Nagin's "full sample"

They claim that their results differ from ours because they find a statistically significant decline. This is puzzling; it is difficult to see why their results would be viewed as inconsistent with my argument. I had indeed also found some evidence that larcenies were reduced by nondiscretionary laws (for example, see the results using the state-level data or the results using two-stage least squares), but I chose to emphasize those results implying the smallest possible positive benefits from concealed-handgun laws.

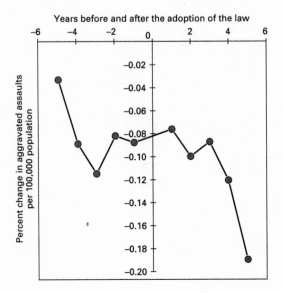

Figure 7.5. The effect of concealed-handgun laws on aggravated assaults, using Black's and Nagin's "full sample"

The bottom line—even using their choice of the dates that they deem most appropriate—is that murder and robbery rates fall after the passage of the laws and that none of the other violent-crime categories experienced an increase. Looking further at whether violent-crime rates were rising or falling before and after these laws, one finds that violent-crime rates were almost always rising prior to the passage of the law and always falling after it.

8 *The impact of including Florida in the sample*

Our concern is particularly severe for the state of Florida. With the Mariel boat lift of 1980 and the thriving drug trade, Florida's crime rates are quite volatile. Moreover, four years after the passage of the right-to-carry law in 1987, Florida passed several gun-related measures, including background checks of handgun buyers and a waiting period for handgun purchases. To test the sensitivity of the results to the inclusion of Florida, we reestimated the model . . . without Florida. Only in the robbery equation can we reject the hypothesis that the crime rate two and three years after adoptions is different than the crime rate two and three years prior to adoption. (Dan Black and Daniel Nagin, "Do 'Right-to-Carry' Laws Deter Violent Crime?" Carnegie-Mellon University working paper, October 16, 1996, p. 9)

In fact, Nagin and Black said they found that virtually all of the claimed benefits of carry laws were attributable to changes in the crime rate in just one state: Florida. (Richard Morin, "Unconventional Wisdom: New facts and Hot Stats from the Social Sciences," *Washington Post,* March 23, 1997, p. C5)

This particular suggestion—that we should throw out the data for Florida because the drop in violent crimes is so large that it affects the results—is very ironic. Handgun Control, Inc. and other gun-control groups continue, as of this writing, to cite the 1995 University of Maryland study, which claimed that if evidence existed of a detrimental impact of concealed handguns, it was for Florida.[26] If the Maryland study is to be believed, the inclusion of Florida must have biased my results in the opposite direction.[27]

More important, as we shall see below, the reasons given by Black and Nagin for dropping Florida from the sample are simply not valid. Furthermore, the impact of excluding Florida is different from what they claim. Figure 7.6 shows the murder rate in Florida from the early 1980s until 1992. The Mariel boat lift did dramatically raise violent-crime rates like murder, but these rates had returned to their pre-Mariel levels by 1982. For murder, the rate was extremely stable until the nondiscretionary concealed-handgun law passed there in 1987, when it began to drop dramatically.

The claim that Florida should be removed from the data because a

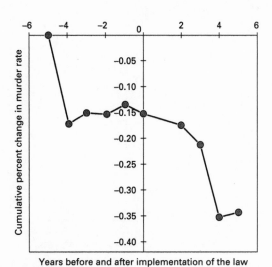

Figure 7.6. Florida's murder rates

waiting period and a background check went into effect in 1992 is even weaker. If this were a valid reason for exclusion, why not exclude other states with these laws as well? Why only remove Florida? Seventeen other states had waiting periods in 1992. A more valid response would be to try to account for the impact of these other laws—as I did in chapter 4. Indeed, accounting for these other laws slightly strengthens the evidence that concealed handguns deter crime.

The graph for Florida in figure 7.6 produces other interesting results. The murder rate declined in each consecutive year following the implementation of the concealed-handgun law until 1992, the first year that these other, much-touted, gun-control laws went into effect. I am not claiming that these laws caused murder rates to rise, but this graph surely makes it more difficult to argue that laws restricting the ability of law-abiding citizens to obtain guns would reduce crime.

While Black's and Nagin's explanations for dropping Florida from the data set are invalid, there is some justification for concern that results are being driven by a few unusual observations. Figure 7.7 shows the relationship between violent-crime rates and concealed-handgun laws when

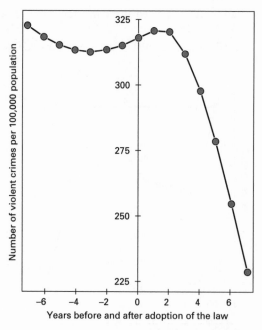

Figure 7.7. The effect of concealed-handgun laws on violent crimes, excluding Florida

Florida is excluded. A careful comparison of this graph with that of figure 4.5, which includes Florida, reveals only a few very small differences.

As a more systematic response to this concern, I excluded Florida and reestimated all the regressions shown in this book. Indeed, there were eight regressions out of the more than one thousand discussed in which the exclusion of Florida did cause the coefficient for the nondiscretionary variable to lose its statistical significance, although it remained negative. The rest of the regression estimates either remained unchanged or (especially for aggravated assault and robbery) became larger and more statistically significant.

Black and Nagin seem to feel that their role in this debate is to see if they can find some specification using any combination of the data that weakens the results.[28] But traditional statistical tests of significance are based on the assumption that the researcher is not deliberately choosing which results to present. Even if a result is statistically significant at the 1 percent level, one would expect that one out of every one hundred regressions would not yield a statistically significant result; in other words, out of one thousand regressions, one would expect to find at least ten for which the impact of nondiscretionary concealed-handgun laws was not statistically significant.

> Lott's claims that Florida's concealed-carry law was responsible for lower murder rates in that state is questionable. Florida did not experience reductions in murders and rapes until four or five years after the law was liberalized. Lott attributes this "delayed effect" to the cumulative influence of increases in carrying permits. Other research attributes Florida's declines in murders in the 1990s to laws requiring background checks and waiting periods for handgun purchases that were implemented several years after gun-carrying laws were liberalized. (Webster, "Flawed")

Much of Webster's comment echoes the issues raised previously by Black and Nagin—indeed, I assume that he is referring to their piece when he mentions "other research." However, while I have tested whether other gun-control laws might explain these declines in crime (see table 4.11), Black and Nagin did not do so, but merely appealed to "other research" to support their affirmation. The preceding quotation seems to imply that my argument involved some sort of "tipping" point: as the number of permits rose, the murder rate eventually declined. As figure 7.6 illustrates, however, Florida's decline in murder rates corresponded closely with the rise in concealed-handgun permits: no lag appears in the decline; rather, the decline begins as soon as the law goes into effect.

9 *The impact of including Maine in the sample*

One should also be wary of the impact that Maine has on Lott's graphs. . . .
When Maine was removed from the analyses, the suggested delayed
[effects of the law] on robberies and aggravated assaults vanished. (Webster, "Flawed")

This comment is curious not only because Mr. Webster does not cite a
study to justify this claim but also because he has never asked for the
data to examine these questions himself. Thus it is difficult to know how
he arrived at this conclusion. A more direct response, however, is simply
to show how the graphs change when Maine is excluded from the
sample. As figures 7.8 and 7.9 show, the exclusion of Maine has very little
effect.

10 *How much does the impact of these laws vary across states?*

[Dan Black and Dan Nagin] found the annual murder rate did go down in
six of the ten states—but it went up in the other four, including a 100
percent increase in West Virginia. Rape dropped in five states—but increased in the other five. And the robbery rate went down in six states—
but went up in four. "That's curious," Black said. If concealed weapons
laws were really so beneficial, their impact should not be so "wildly"
different from state to state. (Richard Morin, "Unconventional Wisdom:
New Facts and Hot Stats from the Social Sciences," *Washington Post,* March
23, 1997, p. C5)

Unfortunately, Black's and Nagin's evidence was not based on statewide
crime rates but on the crime rates for counties with over 100,000 people.

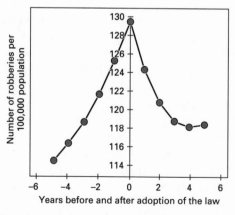

Figure 7.8. The effect of concealed-handgun laws on robbery rates, excluding Maine

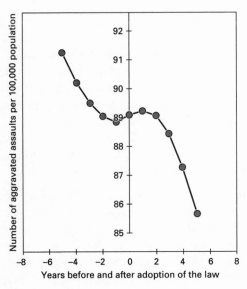

Figure 7.9. The effect of concealed-handgun laws on aggravated assaults, excluding Maine

This fact is important, for instance, in West Virginia, where it means that *only one single county*—Kanawha—was examined. The other fifty-four counties in West Virginia, which include 89 percent of the state's population, were excluded from their estimates. They used only one county for three of the ten states, and only three counties for another state. In fact, Black and Nagin managed to eliminate 85 percent of all counties in the nation in their analysis.

As shown in table 4.9 (see chapter 4), my estimates using all the counties certainly did not yield "wildly" different estimates across states. Violent-crime rates fell in nine of the ten states enacting new nondiscretionary concealed-handgun laws between 1977 and 1992. The differences that did exist across states can be explained by differences in the rates at which concealed-handgun permits were issued. Table 4.10 also provides evidence that the states that issued more permits experienced greater reductions in crime.

11 *Do the coefficient estimates for the demographic variables make sense?*

Perhaps even more surprising are the coefficient estimates for measures of a county's population that is black, female, and between the ages of 40 and 49 or over the age of 65. [Lott and Mustard find] evidence to suggest that these variables have a statistically significant, positive correlation with murder rates . . . and that black females ages 40 to 49 have a statistically significant positive correlation with the aggravated assault rate. . . . There remain two competing explanations for [these] findings. First, middle-aged and elderly African-American women could be actively [engaged] in the commission of car thefts, assaults, and murders across the United States. The more likely explanation is that [their results] are misspecified and, as a result, their coefficient estimates are biased. (Ludwig, "Permissive Concealed-Carry Laws," pp. 20–21. See also Albert W. Alschuler, "Two Guns, Four Guns, Six Guns, More: Does Arming the Pubic Reduce Crime?" *Valparaiso University Law Review* 31 (Spring 1997): 367.)

No, black females ages 40 to 49 are not responsible for a crime wave. Other results in the regressions that were not mentioned in this quotation indicate that the greater the percentage of women between the ages of 10 and 29, the greater the rape rate—but these estimates do not imply that young women are going out and committing rapes. To show that crime rates are higher where greater percentages of the population are of a certain demographic age group does not imply that the people in that group are committing the crimes. The positive relationship may exist because these people are relatively easy or attractive victims.

If such an objection were valid, it should also apply to my finding that in areas where personal incomes are high, auto-theft rates are also high. Should we infer from this that high-income individuals are more likely to steal cars? Presumably not. What is most likely is that wealthy individuals own cars that are attractive targets for auto thieves.

It is also important to note that the different demographic variables are very highly correlated with each other. The percentage of the population that is male and within a particular race and age grouping is very similar to the percentage that is female within that race and age group. Similar high correlations exist within racial groups across age groups. With thirty-six different demographic categories, determining whether an effect is specifically related to an individual category or simply arises because that category is correlated (whether negatively or positively) with another demographic group is difficult and not the object of this book. What I have tried to do is "overcontrol" for all possible demographic factors to make sure that any effects attributed to the right-to-carry law are not arising because I have accidentally left out some other factor.

12 *Can we compare counties with discretionary and nondiscretionary concealed-handgun laws?*

Many counties with very permissive permit systems can be found in states with no shall-issue laws, such as Louisiana and California. For example, in

El Dorado county in California, 1,289 concealed-carry permits were issued in 1995. With a population of 148,600, this implies that 0.87 percent of this county's population received concealed-carry permits in one year alone. In contrast, a total of 186,000 people in Florida had concealed-carry permits in 1996 out of a total state population of 13,958,000; that is, 1.33 percent of the population was licensed to carry concealed [guns]. Yet under [the] classification scheme used in most of their results, El Dorado county would not be classified as shall-issue, while every county in Florida would be so classified. (Jens Ludwig, "Permissive Concealed-Carry Laws," pp. 20–21.)

The simplest question that we are asking is, What happens to the crime rate when nondiscretionary laws are passed allowing law-abiding citizens to carry concealed handguns? The key here is the *change* in the leniency of the laws. The regressions have individual variables for each county that allow us to account for differences in the mean crime rate. The purpose of all the other variables is to explain why crime rates differ from this average. Under discretionary laws some counties are extremely liberal in granting permits—essentially behaving as if they had nondiscretionary laws. In the regressions, differences between counties with discretionary laws (including differences in how liberally they issued concealed-handgun permits) are already being partly "picked up" by these individual county variables. For my test to work, it is only necessary for nondiscretionary laws *on average* to increase the number of concealed-handgun permits.

True, the amount of change in the number of permits does vary across counties. As this book has documented, law officials in discretionary states across the country have said that the more rural counties with relatively low populations were much more liberal in granting permits under discretionary laws. Since no usable statistics are available regarding how easily permits are granted, I tested whether nondiscretionary laws changed the crime rates the most in counties with the largest or densest populations. The results confirmed that this was the case (see figure 4.1).

We also tried another approach to deal with this question. A few states did keep good records on the number of concealed-handgun permits issued at either the county or the state level. We reported earlier the results for Pennsylvania and Oregon (see tables 5.4 and 5.5 in chapter 5). Despite the small samples, we accounted for all the variables controlled for in the larger regressions, and the results confirmed that murder rates decline as the number of a permits issued in a county rises.

13 *Should changes in the arrest rate be accounted for when explaining changes in the crime rate?*

> The use of arrest rates as an explanatory variable is itself quite problematic. . . . Since the arrest rate is calculated as the number of arrests for a particular crime divided by the number of crimes committed, unobserved determinants of the crime rate will by construction also influence the arrest rate. When the arrest rate is included as an explanatory variable in a regression equation, this leads to the statistical problem known as "endogeneity," or "simultaneity bias." (Jens Ludwig, "Permissive Concealed-Carry Laws," pp. 7–8)

True, there is an endogeneity "problem." However, on theoretical grounds, the inclusion of the arrest rate is highly desirable. There is strong reason to believe that crime rates depend on the probability of punishment. In addition, to exclude variables that obviously should be included in the analysis would create even more important potential bias problems. Furthermore, the endogeneity problem was dealt with in the original paper: it was precisely our awareness of that problem that led us to use two-stage least squares to estimate the set of regressions, which is the recognized method of dealing with such a problem. As reported in chapter 6, the two-stage least-squares estimate provided even stronger evidence that concealed handguns deter crime.

The simplest point to make, however, is that excluding the arrest rate does not alter the findings regarding concealed handguns. Reestimating the regressions in tables 4.1 and 4.3 for the same samples and control variables produces virtually identical results. Ironically, two of my strongest critics, Dan Black and Dan Nagin, also tried excluding the arrest rates, and they admitted in early drafts of their paper that their results agreed with ours: "The inclusion of the arrest-rate variable has very little impact on the coefficient estimates of the right-to-carry laws."[29]

14 *Are the graphs in this book misleading?*

> Lott rebuts many of the criticisms of his study by pointing to his simple but misleading graphs. The graphs are visually compelling yet very deceptive. What is not obvious to the casual observer of the graphs is that each data point represents an aggregate average for states that liberalized their gun-carrying laws, but the states that make up the average are not the same each year. Lott examined 10 states he claims adopted "shall-issue" concealed-gun-carrying laws during his sample period. For many of the states studied, data were available for only one to three years after the laws were implemented. (Webster, "Flawed")

The graphs presented in the paper do indeed represent the average changes in crime rates before and after the implementation of these laws. The graphs consistently show that violent-crime rates are rising before these laws go into effect and falling afterward. Since some states only adopted nondiscretionary, "shall-issue" laws toward the end of the sample period, it was not possible to examine all the states for the same number of years after the laws were implemented. I disagree that this is "misleading" or "deceptive." The results were by no means generated by the aggregation itself, and anybody doubting the meaning of the graph can examine the regression results. Since the regressions already control for each county's average crime rate, any changes refer to deviations from that county's average crime rate.[30]

Ian Ayres and Steven Levitt use similar graphs and find similar results when they look at the deterrent effect of Lojack antitheft devices on cars (these are radio tracking devices that can be activated by police when a car is stolen).[31] In many ways, the theoretical deterrent effect of these devices is the same as that of concealed handguns: because the device is small and easy to hide, a criminal cannot easily know whether a car has the tracking device until the police arrive.

Future studies will be able to track these changes in crime over longer periods of time because more states will have had right-to-carry laws for longer periods of time. Such studies will ultimately help to test my findings. I have used all the data that was available at the time that David Mustard and I put this data set together. With 54,000 observations and hundreds of variables available over the 1977 to 1994 period, it is also by far the largest data set that has ever been put together for any study of crime, let alone for the study of gun control.[32] I find it ironic that my study is attacked for not having enough data when these same researchers have praised previous studies that relied on much shorter time periods for a single state or a few counties. For example, Mr. Webster expresses no such criticism when referring to a study conducted by the University of Maryland. Yet that study analyzed merely five counties and covered a shorter period of time after the law was enacted.[33]

15 *Should concealed-handgun laws have differential effects on the murder rates of youths and adults?*

> Ludwig points out that in many states only adults may carry concealed weapons. So, according to Lott's deterrence theory, adults should be safer than young people. But this hasn't happened, Ludwig says. (Kathleen Schalch describing Jens Ludwig's arguments on *Morning Edition,* National Public Radio, 10:00 A.M. ET Tuesday, December 10, 1996.)

As noted in chapter 4, I tested the hypothesis that murder rates would be lower for adults than for adolescents under nondiscretionary concealed-handgun laws, and reported the results in the original paper. However, the results did not bear out this possibility. Concealed-handgun laws reduce murder rates for both adults and for adolescents. One explanation may simply be that young people also benefited from the carrying of concealed handguns by adults. Several plausible scenarios may explain this. First, criminals may well tend to leave an area where law-abiding adults carry concealed handguns, and since all age groups live in the same neighborhood, this lowers crime rates for all population groups. Second, when gun-carrying adults are physically present, they may able to protect some youngsters in threatening situations.

Could some other factor be lowering the juvenile murder rate—something that is unrelated to concealed handguns? Perhaps, despite all the factors accounted for, the results of any research may be affected by unknown factors. But it is wrong to conclude, as Ludwig does, that "these findings are not consistent with the hypothesis that shall-issue laws decrease crime through a deterrence effect."[34]

16 *Are changes in the characteristics of victims consistent with the theory?*

> Lott and Mustard offer data on the character of victims in homicide cases. They report (astonishingly) that the proportion of stranger killings increases following the enactment of right-to-carry laws, while the proportion of intrafamily killings declines. That right-to-carry laws deter intrafamily homicides more than they deter stranger homicides is inconceivable. (Albert W. Alschuler, "Two Guns, Four Guns, Six Guns, More: Does Arming the Public Reduce Crime?" *Valparaiso University Law Review* 31 (1997): 369)

> Josh Sugarmann of the Violence Prevention Center noted that most murders are committed by people who know each other. "Concealed-weapons laws are not passed to protect people from people they know," Sugarmann said. (Doug Finke, "Sides Stick to Their Guns, Concealed-Carry Bill Set for Showdown in General Assembly," *Springfield State Journal-Register,* March 31, 1997, p. 1)

As noted in the first chapter, the category of acquaintance murder is extremely broad (encompassing shootings of cab drivers, gang members, drug dealers or buyers, and prostitutes or their clients). For the Chicago data that we discussed, the number of acquaintance murders involving friends was actually only a small percentage of the total number of acquaintance murders. If the breakdown found for Chicago provides even the remotest proxy for the national data, it is not particularly surprising that the relative share of acquaintance murders involving friends should rise, because we expect that many of the murders in this category are unlikely to be affected by law-abiding citizens carrying concealed handguns. Family members may also find that concealed handguns protect them from other estranged family members. A wife seeking a divorce may find that a concealed handgun provides her protection against a husband who is unwilling to let go of the relationship, and attacks by such people do not always take place in a home. Surely there are many cases of spousal abuse where women fear for their lives and find that a handgun provides them with a significant degree of protection.

A recent case involving a woman who used a handgun to protect herself from an abusive husband created an important new legal precedent in California: for the first time, women are now allowed to use self-defense before they suffer serious blows. The *San Francisco Examiner* reported as follows:

> [Fay] Johnson, a 47-year-old mother of four, said that on July 2, 1995, she feared her 62-year-old husband, Clarence, would beat her as he always did after a weekend of drinking and hanging out with his motorcycle buddies.
>
> She had overspent her budget on supplies for a Fourth of July barbecue and didn't have dinner ready, and the house was not clean—so when she heard her husband's motorcycle pull into the driveway, she decided to take matters into her own hands.
>
> Johnson said she grabbed a loaded gun . . . [and fired,] hitting her husband five times. He survived and testified against her. She was arrested and spent 21 months in prison until her acquittal.
>
> "I regret being in jail, but I just wouldn't tolerate it anymore," said Johnson, a friendly, articulate woman who is celebrating her freedom with her children and six grandchildren. "It would have been suicide."
>
> Johnson said she had endured nearly 25 years of mental and physical abuse at the hands of her husband, whose usual form of punishment was slamming her head into a wall. The beatings got so bad, she said, that she had to be hospitalized twice and tried getting counseling until he found out and forced her to stop. She said the pressure of the abuse had culminated that fateful day.[35]

Pointing to women who use handguns to protect themselves from abusive husbands or boyfriends in no way proves that the primary effects of concealed-handgun laws will involve such uses of guns, but these cases should keep us from concluding that significant benefits for these women are "inconceivable."

With reference to Alschuler's discussion, however, two points must be made clear. First, the diverse breakdown of these groupings makes it difficult to predict on theoretical grounds how the number of murders among family members, acquaintances, strangers, or unknown cases should necessarily change relative to each other. Second, as Alschuler himself has noted, these estimates are suggestive; they are not statistically significant, in that we cannot say with much certainty how concealed-handgun laws have affected the proportions of victims across the categories mentioned above.

An additional response should be made to Sugarmann's claims. Even if one accepts the claim that nondiscretionary concealed-handgun laws do not reduce the number of murders against people who know each other (and I do not concede this), what about other types of murders, such as those arising from street robbery? For Chicago during the period from 1990 to 1995, 16 percent of all murders involved nonacquaintance robbery. Moreover, one must ask about nonfriend acquaintance murders (excluding prostitution, gang, and drug cases), murders by complete strangers, and at least some of those murders still classified as mysteries (an additional 22 to 46 percent of all murders). Since permitted handguns are virtually never used in crimes against others and they do not produce accidental deaths, should not the reduction of these other types of murders still be deemed important?[36]

17 *Do nondiscretionary concealed-handgun laws only affect crimes that occur in public places?*

> Handguns were freely available for home and business use in all the "shall-issue" jurisdictions prior to the new laws. The new carrying privilege would thus not affect home or business self-defense but should have most of its preventive impact on street crime and offenses occurring in other public places. But the study contains no qualitative analysis of different patterns within crime categories to corroborate the right-to-carry prevention hypothesis. (Zimring and Hawkins, "Counterfeit Deterrent," p. 54)

Contrary to the claim of Zimring and Hawkins, concealed handguns may very well affect crime in homes and businesses in several ways. First, being allowed to carry a concealed gun outside is likely to increase the number of guns owned by law-abiding citizens. Since these guns will be kept at least part of the time in the home, this should have a deterrent effect on crimes committed at home and also at one's business. Second, as some of the evidence suggests, nondiscretionary laws could even increase the number of crimes that occur in the home as criminals turn away from other crimes, like street robbery, for which the risks that criminals face have gone up. These two effects would thus work in opposite directions. Finally, to the extent that nondiscretionary handgun laws drive criminals out of a certain geographical area, rates for all types of crimes could fall.

Aggregation of the crime categories makes it difficult to separate all the different substitution effects. Still, the results presented here are very consistent with the two primary dimensions that we focused on: whether there is contact between the criminal and the victim, and whether the crime occurs where law-abiding citizens could already legally carry a gun.

18 *Is it reasonable to make comparisons across states?*

> The sort of state that passes a "shall-issue" law in the 1980s is apt to be the same kind of place where ordinary citizens carrying concealed firearms might not be regarded as a major problem even before the law changed.... Idaho is not the same sort of place that New York is, and there seem to be systematic differences between states that change standards for concealed weapons and those that do not. (Zimring and Hawkins, "Counterfeit Deterrent," pp. 50–51)

The observed drop in crime rates in states that have enacted nondiscretionary concealed-handgun laws does not by itself imply that we will observe the same effect in other states that adopt such laws later. Several different issues arise here. First, the regressions used in this book have attempted to control for many differences that can explain the level of crime (for example, income, poverty, unemployment, population and population density, demographic characteristics, law enforcement, other gun laws). Admittedly, even my long list of variables does not pick up all the differences between states, which is the reason that a variable is added for each county or state to pick up the average differences in crime rates across places. Individual time trends are also allowed for each state.

Yet despite all these attempts to control for variables, some caution is still in order—especially when dealing with areas that are particularly extreme along dimensions that do not have obvious counterparts in areas with nondiscretionary laws. One obvious example would be New York City. While the regression results show that areas with the largest and most dense populations gain the most from nondiscretionary laws, there is always the possibility that the relationship changes for values of population and density that are different from those in places where we have been able to study the effects of these laws. To date, the fourth and fifth largest cities in the country have passed nondiscretionary laws (Houston and Philadelphia), and additional experience with large cities may help determine whether these laws would be equally useful in a city like New York. If one were skeptical about the effects in large cities, the laws should first be changed in Los Angeles and Chicago.

A second issue is whether there is something unique about states that have adopted nondiscretionary laws, and whether that characteristic caused them not only to adopt the laws but also reduced the potential problems resulting from adoption. For example, if local legislators in a few states had special information confirming that the citizens in their state were uniquely trustworthy with regard to concealed handguns, that might have led these few states to pass the laws and have little difficulty with them. It could then "falsely" appear that nondiscretionary laws are generally successful. Such an argument may have been plausible at one time, but its force has declined now that such large and varied areas are covered by these laws. Equally important is the fact that not all jurisdictions have willingly adopted these laws. Many urban areas, such as Atlanta and Philadelphia, fought strongly against them, but lost out to coalitions of rural and suburban representatives. Philadelphia's opposition was so strong that when Pennsylvania's nondiscretionary law was first passed, Philadelphia was partially exempted.

19 *Does my discussion provide a "theory" linking concealed-handgun ownership to reductions in crime? Do the data allow me to link the passage of these laws with the reduction in crime?*

> Two idiosyncratic aspects of the Lott and Mustard analysis deserve special mention. . . . In the first place, there is very little in the way of explicit theory advanced to explain where and when right-to-carry laws should operate as deterrents to the types of crime that can be frustrated by citizens carrying concealed handguns. . . . They have no data to measure the critical intermediate steps between passing the legislation and reductions in crime rates. This is the second important failing . . . that is not a recurrent feature in econometric studies. (Zimring and Hawkins, "Counterfeit Deterrent," pp. 52, 54)

This set of complaints is difficult to understand. The theory is obvious: A would-be criminal act is deterred by the risk of being shot. Many different tests described in this book support this theory. Not only does the drop in crime begin when nondiscretionary laws are adopted, but the extent of the decline is related to the number of permits issued in a state. Nondiscretionary laws reduce crime the most in areas with the greatest increases in the number of permits. As expected, crimes that involve criminals and victims in direct contact and crimes occurring in places where the victim was previously unable to carry a gun are the ones that consistently decrease the most.

20 What can we infer about causality?

Anyone who has taken a course in logical thinking has been exposed to the fallacy of arguing that because A happened (in this case, passage of a concealed-weapon law) and then B happened (the slowing of the rate of violent crime), A must surely have caused B. You can speculate that the passage of concealed-gun legislation caused a subsequent slowing of the rate of violent crime in various states, but you certainly can't prove it, despite the repeated claims that a University of Chicago law professor's "study" has offered "definitive scholarly proof." (Harold W. Andersen, "Gun Study Akin to Numbers Game," *Omaha World Herald*, April 3, 1997, p. 15)

An obvious danger arises in inferring causality because two events may coincide in time simply by chance, or some unknown factor may be the cause of both events. Random chance is a frequent concern with pure time-series data when there is just one change in a law. It is not hard to believe that when one is examining a single state, unrelated events A and B just happened to occur at the same time. Yet the data examined here involve many different states that changed their laws in many different years. The odds that one might falsely attribute the changes in the crime rate to changes in the concealed-handgun laws decline as one examines more experiences. The measures of statistical significance are in fact designed to tell us the likelihood that two events may have occurred randomly together.

The more serious possibility is that some other factor may have caused both the reduction in crime rates and the passage of the law to occur at the same time. For example, concern over crime might result in the passage of both concealed-handgun laws and tougher law-enforcement measures. Thus, if the arrest rate rose at the same time that the concealed-handgun law passed, not accounting for changes in the arrest rate might result in falsely attributing some of the reduction in crime rates to the concealed-handgun law. For a critic to attack the paper, the correct approach would have been to state what variables were not included in the analysis. Indeed, it is possible that the regressions do not control for some important factor. However, this study uses the most comprehensive set of control variables yet used in a study of crime, let alone any previous study on gun control. As noted in the introduction, the vast majority of gun-control studies do not take any other factors that may influence crime into account, and no previous study has included such variables as the arrest or conviction rate or sentence length.

Other pieces of evidence also help to tie together cause and effect. For example, the adoption of nondiscretionary concealed-handgun laws has not produced equal effects in all counties in a state. Since counties with easily identifiable characteristics (such as rural location and small population) tended to be much more liberal in granting permits prior to the change in the law, we would expect them to experience the smallest changes in crime rates, and this is in fact what we observe. States that were expected to issue the greatest number of new permits and did so after passing nondiscretionary laws observed the largest declines in crime. We know that the number of concealed-handgun permits in a state rises over time, so we expect to see a greater reduction in crime after a nondiscretionary law has been in effect for several years than right after it has passed. Again, this is what we observe. Finally, where data on the actual number of permits at the county level are available, we find that the number of murders declines as the number of permits increases.

The notion of statistical significance and the number of different specifications examined in this book are also important. Even if a relationship is false, it might be possible to find a few specifications out of a hundred that show a statistically significant relationship. Here we have presented over a thousand specifications that together provide an extremely consistent and statistically significant pattern about the relationship between nondiscretionary concealed-handgun laws and crime.

21 *Concerns about the arrest rates due to missing observations*

To control for variation in the probability of apprehension, the [Lott and Mustard] model specification includes the arrest ratio, which is the number of arrests per reported crime. Our replication analysis shows that the inclusion of this variable materially affects the size and composition of the estimation data set. Specifically, division by zero forces all counties with no reported crimes of a particular type in a given year to be dropped from the sample for that year. [Lott's and Mustard's] sample contains all counties, regardless of size, and this problem of dropping counties with no reported crimes is particularly severe in small counties with few crimes. The frequencies of missing data are 46.6% for homicide, 30.5% for rape, 12.2% for aggravated assault, and 29.5% for robbery. Thus, the [Lott and Mustard] model excludes observations based on the realization of the dependent variable, potentially creating a substantial selection bias. Our strategy for finessing the missing data problem is to analyze only counties maintaining populations of at least 100,000 during the period 1977 to 1992. . . . Compared to the sample [comprising] all counties, the missing data rate in the large-county sample is low: 3.82% for homicide, 1.08% for rape, 1.18% for assault, and 1.09% for robberies. (Dan Black and Daniel Nagin, "Do 'Right-to-Carry' Laws Deter Violent Crime?" *Journal of Legal Studies* 27 [January 1998], forthcoming)

The arguments made by Black and Nagin have changed over time, and some of their statements are not consistent.[37] In part because of the public nature of their attacks, I have tried to deal with all of the different attacks, so that those who have heard them may hear my responses. The problem described immediately above by Black and Nagin is indeed something one should be concerned about, but I had already dealt with the problem of missing observations in the original paper, and I discuss it again here at the end of chapter 6. My original paper and chapter 4 also reported the results when the arrest rate was removed entirely from the regressions. The discussion by Black and Nagin exaggerates the extent of the problem and, depending on the crime category being examined, quite amazingly proposes to solve the missing data problem by throwing out data for between 77 and 87 percent of the counties.

Black and Nagin present a very misleading picture of the trade-offs involved with the solution that examined the more populous counties.[38] The relevant comparison is between weighted numbers of missing observations, not the total number of missing observations, since the regressions are weighted by county population and the missing observations tend to be from relatively small counties, which are given a smaller weight.[39] When this is done, the benefits obtained by excluding all counties with fewer than 100,000 people become much more questionable. The most extreme case is for aggravated assault, where Black and Nagin eliminate 86 percent of the sample (a 29 percent drop in the weighted frequency) in order to reduce weighted missing values from 2.8 to 1.5 percent. Even for murder, 77 percent of the sample is dropped, so that the weighted missing data declines from 11.7 to 1.9 percent. The rape and robbery categories lie between these two cases, both in terms of the number of counties with fewer than 100,000 people and in terms of the change in the amount of weighted missing data.[40]

Why they choose to emphasize the cut-off that they did is neither explained nor obvious. The current cost-benefit ratio is rather lopsided. For example, eliminating counties with fewer than 20,000 people would have removed 70 percent of the missing arrest ratios for murder and lost only 20 percent of the observations (the weighted frequencies are 23 and 6 percent respectively). There is nothing wrong with seeing whether the estimates provide the same results over counties of various sizes, but if that is their true motivation for excluding portions of the data, it should be clearly stated.

Despite ignoring all these observations, it is only when they *also* remove the data for Florida that they weaken my results for murder and rape (though the results for aggravated assault and robbery are even larger and more statistically significant). Only eighty-six counties with more than 100,000 people adopted nondiscretionary concealed-handgun laws between 1977 and 1992, and twenty of these counties are in Florida. Yet after all this exclusion of data, Black and Nagin still find no evidence that allowing law-abiding citizens to carry concealed handguns increases crime, and two violent-crime categories show a statistically significant drop in crime. The difference between their approach and mine is rather stark: I did not select which observations to include; I used all the data for all the counties over the entire period for which observations were available.

22 *What can we learn about the deterrent effect of concealed handguns from this study?*

The regression study [that Lott and Mustard] report is an all-or-nothing proposition as far as knowledge of legal impact is concerned. If the model is wrong, if their bottom-line estimates of impact cannot withstand scrutiny, there is no intermediate knowledge of the law's effects on behavior that can help us sort out the manifold effects of such legislation. As soon as we find flaws in the major conclusions, the regression analyses tell us nothing. What we know from this study about the effects of "shall-carry" laws is, therefore, nothing at all. (Zimring and Hawkins, "Counterfeit Deterrent," p. 59)

Academics can reasonably differ about what factors account for changes in crime. Sociologists and criminologists, for example, have examined gun control without trying to control for changes in arrest or conviction rates. Others might be particularly concerned about the impact of drugs on crime. Economists such as myself try to include measures of deterrence, though I am also sympathetic to other concerns. In this book and my other research, my approach has not been to say that only one set of variables or even one specification can explain the crime rate. My attitude has been that if someone believes that a variable is important and has any plausible reason for including it, I have made an effort to include it. This book reports many different approaches and specifications—all of which support the conclusion that allowing law-abiding citizens to carry concealed handguns reduces crime. I believe that no other study on crime has used as extensive a data set as was used here, and no previous study has attempted to control for as many different specifications.

23 *Summarizing the concerns about the evidence that concealed-handgun laws deter crime*

> The gun lobby claims to have a new weapon in its arsenal this year—a study by economist John Lott. But the Lott study shoots blanks. In reviewing Lott's research and methodology, Carnegie-Mellon University Profs. Daniel Nagin and Dan Black, and Georgetown University's Prof. Jens Ludwig corrected for the many fatal flaws in Lott's original analysis and found no evidence of his claim that easing restrictions on carrying concealed handguns leads to a decrease in violent crime. Nagin, Black, and Ludwig recently concluded in a televised debate with Lott that "there is absolutely no credible evidence to support the idea that permissive concealed-carry laws reduce violent crime," and that "it would be a mistake to formulate policy based on the findings from Dr. Lott's study." (James Brady, "Concealed Handguns; Putting More Guns on Streets Won't Make America Safer," *Minneapolis Star Tribune,* March 21, 1997, p. 21A)

Unlike the authors of past papers on gun control such as Arthur Kellermann and the authors of the 1995 University of Maryland study, I immediately made my data available to all academics who requested it.[41] To date, my data have been supplied to academics at twenty-four universities, including Harvard, Stanford, the University of Pennsylvania, Emory, Vanderbilt, Louisiana State, Michigan State, Florida State, the University of Texas, the University of Houston, the University of Maryland, Georgetown, and the College of William and Mary.

James Brady's op-ed piece ignores the fact that some of these academics from Vanderbilt, Emory, and Texas paid their own way to attend the December 9, 1996, debate sponsored by his organization—Handgun Control. While Handgun Control insisted on rules that did not allow these academics to participate, I am sure that they would have spoken out to support the integrity of my original study.

Those who have attempted to replicate the findings in the original *Journal of Legal Studies* paper have been able to do so, and many have gone beyond this to provide additional support for the basic findings. For example, economists at Vanderbilt University have estimated over 10,000 regressions attempting to see whether the deterrent effects of nondiscretionary laws are at all sensitive to all possible combinations of the various data sets on demographics, income, population, arrest rates, and so on. Their results are quite consistent with those reported in this book.[42]

I have tried in this chapter to examine the critiques leveled against my work. In many cases, the concerns they describe were addressed in the original paper. In others, I believe that relatively simple responses exist to the complaints. However, even taking these critics at their worst, I still believe that a comment that I made at the December 9 discussion sponsored by Handgun Control still holds:

> Six months ago, who would have thought that Handgun Control would be rushing out studies to argue that allowing law-abiding citizens to carry concealed handguns would have no effect, or might have a delayed impact, in terms of dropping crimes? (*Morning Edition,* National Public Radio, 10:00 A.M. ET, December 10, 1996.

As more than 30 diners sat in Sam's St. John's Sea-
food [in Jacksonville, Florida] about 7:20 P.M., a
masked man entered the eatery and ordered everyone to the floor, said co-owner Sam Bajalia. The
man grabbed waitress Amy Norton from where she
and another waitress were huddled on the floor
and tried to get her to open the cash register.

At that point, [Oscar] Moore stood up and shot
him. Another diner . . . pulled out a .22-caliber der-
ringer and fired at the man as he ran out of the
restaurant. At least one shot hit the fleeing robber.

[The robber was later arrested when he sought
medical care for his wound.] . . .

"I'm glad they were here because if that girl
couldn't open the register, and he didn't get [any]
money, he might have started shooting," Bajalia
said.[1]

[It was] 1:30 A.M. when Angelic Nichole Hite, 26, the
night manager, and Victoria Elizabeth Shaver, 20,
the assistant manager at the Pizza Hut at 4450
Creedmoor Road, were leaving the restaurant with
Marty Lee Hite, 39, the manager's husband. He had
come to pick her up after work.

They saw a man wearing a ski mask, dark
clothes, gloves, and holding a pistol walking toward
them, and the Hites ran back inside the restaurant.
Shaver apparently had reached her car already. . . .
The couple couldn't close the door behind them because the robber ran up and wedged the barrel of
his handgun in the opening. As they struggled to
get the door closed, . . . the masked man twice said
he would kill them if they didn't open it.

Marty Hite, who carried a .38-caliber handgun,
pulled out his weapon and fired three times
through the opening, striking the robber in the ab-
domen and upper chest. The would-be bandit

staggered away, and the Hites locked the door and called police.

The Wake County district attorney will review the shooting, but Raleigh police did not file charges against the manager's husband. Police said it appeared the couple retreated as far as they could and feared for their lives, which would make it a justified shooting.[2]

Many factors influence crime, with arrest and conviction rates being the most important. However, nondiscretionary concealed-handgun laws are also important, and they are the most cost-effective means of reducing crime. The cost of hiring more police in order to change arrest and conviction rates is much higher, and the net benefits per dollar spent are only at most a quarter as large as the benefits from concealed-handgun laws.[3] Even private, medium-security prisons cost state governments about $34 a day per prisoner ($12,267 per year).[4] For concealed handguns, the permit fees are usually the largest costs borne by private citizens. The durability of guns allows owners to recoup their investments over many years. Using my yearly cost estimate of $43 per concealed handgun for Pennsylvanians, concealed handguns pay for themselves if they have only $\frac{1}{285}$ of the deterrent impact of an additional year in prison. This calculation even ignores the other costs of the legal system, such as prosecution and defense costs—criminals will expend greater effort to fight longer prison sentences in court. No other government policy appears to have anywhere near the same cost-benefit ratio as concealed-handgun laws.

Allowing citizens without criminal records or histories of significant mental illness to carry concealed handguns deters violent crimes and appears to produce an extremely small and statistically insignificant change in accidental deaths. If the rest of the country had adopted right-to-carry concealed-handgun provisions in 1992, about 1,500 murders and 4,000 rapes would have been avoided. On the other hand, consistent with the notion that criminals respond to incentives, county-level data provide some evidence that concealed-handgun laws are associated with increases in property crimes involving stealth and in crimes that involve minimal probability of contact between the criminal and the victim. Even though both the state-level data and the estimates that attempt to explain why the law and the arrest rates change indicate that crime in all the categories declines, the deterrent effect of nondiscretionary handgun laws is largest for violent crimes. Counties with the largest populations, where the deterrence of violent crimes is the greatest, are also the counties where the substitution of property crimes for violent crimes by criminals is the highest. The estimated annual gain in 1992 from allowing concealed handguns was over $5.74 billion.

Many commonly accepted notions are challenged by these findings. Urban areas tend to have the most restrictive gun-control rules and have fought the hardest against nondiscretionary concealed-handgun laws, yet they are the very places that benefit the most from nondiscretionary concealed-handgun laws. Not only do urban areas tend to gain in their fight against crime, but reductions in crime rates are greatest precisely in those urban areas that have the highest crime rates, largest and most dense populations, and greatest concentrations of minorities. To some this might not be too surprising. After all, law-abiding citizens in these areas must depend on themselves to a great extent for protection. Even if self-protection were accepted, concerns would still arise over whether these law-abiding citizens would use guns properly. This study provides a very strong answer: a few people do and will use permitted concealed handguns improperly, but the gains completely overwhelm these concerns.

Another surprise involves women and blacks. Both tend to be the strongest supporters of gun control, yet both obtain the largest benefits from nondiscretionary concealed-handgun laws in terms of reduced rates of murder and other crimes. Concealed handguns also appear to be the great equalizer among the sexes. Murder rates decline when either more women or more men carry concealed handguns, but the effect is especially pronounced for women. An additional woman carrying a concealed handgun reduces the murder rate for women by about three to four times more than an additional man carrying a concealed handgun reduces the murder rate for men. Providing a woman with a concealed handgun represents a much larger change in her ability to defend herself than it does for a man.

The benefits of concealed handguns are not limited to those who use them in self-defense. Because the guns may be concealed, criminals are unable to tell whether potential victims are carrying guns until they attack, thus making it less attractive for criminals to commit crimes that involve direct contact with victims. Citizens who have no intention of ever carrying concealed handguns in a sense get a "free ride" from the crime-fighting efforts of their fellow citizens. However, the "halo" effect created by these laws is apparently not limited to people who share the characteristics of those who carry the guns. The most obvious example is the drop in murders of children following the adoption of nondiscretionary laws. Arming older people not only may provide direct protection to these children, but also causes criminals to leave the area.

Nor is the "halo" effect limited to those who live in areas where people are allowed to carry guns. The violent-crime reduction from one's own state's adopting the law is in fact greatest when neighboring states also allow law-abiding citizens to carry concealed handguns. The evidence also indicates that the states with the most guns have the lowest crime rates. Urban areas may experience the most violent crime, but they also have the smallest number of guns. Blacks may be the racial group most vulnerable to violent crime, but they are also much less likely than whites to own guns.

These estimates make one wonder about all the attention given to other types of gun legislation. My estimates indicate that waiting periods and background checks appear to produce little if any crime deterrence. Yet President Clinton credits the Brady law with lowering crime because it has, according to him, been "taking guns out of the hands of criminals."[5] During the 1996 Democratic National Convention, Sarah Brady, after whose husband the bill was named, boasted that it "has helped keep more than 100,000 felons and other prohibited purchasers from buying handguns."[6] From 1994 until the Supreme Court's decision in 1997, backers of the Brady law focused almost exclusively on the value of background checks, the one part of the law that the Supreme Court specifically struck down.[7]

Actually, the downward crime trend started in 1991, well before the Brady law became effective in March 1994. With a national law that goes into effect only once, it is difficult to prove empirically that the law was what altered crime rates, because so many other events are likely to have occurred at that same time. One of the major advantages of the large data set examined in this book is that it includes data from many different states that have adopted nondiscretionary laws in many different years.

Others estimate a much smaller effect of the Brady law on gun sales. In 1996 the General Accounting Office reported that initial rejections based on background checks numbered about 60,000, of which over half were for purely technical reasons, mostly paperwork errors that were eventually corrected.[8] A much smaller number of rejections, 3,000, was due to convictions for violent crimes, and undoubtedly many of the people rejected proceeded to buy guns on the street. By the time the background-check provision was found unconstitutional, in June 1997, only four people had gone to jail for violations.

Presumably, no one would argue that rejected permits are meaningful by themselves. They merely proxy for what might happen to crime rates, provided that the law really stops criminals from getting guns. Do criminals simply get them from other sources? Or do the restrictions primarily inconvenience law-abiding citizens who want guns for self-defense? The results presented in this book are the first systematic national look at such gun laws, and if the national Uniform Crime Report data through 1994 or state waiting periods and background checks are any indication, the empirical evidence does not bode well for the Brady law. No statistically significant evidence has appeared that the Brady law has reduced crime, and there is some statistically significant evidence that rates for rape and aggravated assault have actually risen by about 4 percent relative to what they would have been without the law.

Yet research does not convince everybody. Perhaps the Supreme Court's June 1997 decision on the constitutionality of the Brady law's national background checks will shed light on how effective the Brady law was. The point of making the scope of the background check *national* was that without it, criminals would buy guns from jurisdictions without the checks and use them to commit crimes in the rest of the country. As these national standards are eliminated, and states and local jurisdictions discontinue their background checks,[9] will crime rates rise as quickly without this provision of the law as gun-control advocates claimed they fell because of it? My bet is no, they will not. If President Clinton and gun-control advocates are correct, a new crime wave should be evident by the time this book is published.

Since 1994, aside from required waiting periods, many new rules making gun ownership by law-abiding citizens more difficult have come into existence. There were 279,401 active, federal gun-dealer licenses in the nation when the new licensing regulations went fully into effect in April 1994. By the beginning of 1997 there were 124,286, a decline of 56 percent, and their number continues to fall.[10] This has undoubtedly made purchasing guns less convenient. Besides increasing licensing fees from $30 to $200 for first-time licenses and imposing renewal fees of $90, the 1994 Violent Crime Control and Law Enforcement Act imposed significant new regulatory requirements that were probably much more important in reducing the number of licensees.[11]

The Bureau of Alcohol, Tobacco, and Firearms (BATF) supports this decrease largely because it believes that it affects federal license holders who are illegally selling guns. The BATF's own (undoubtedly high) estimate is that about 1 percent of federal license holders illegally sell guns, and that this percentage has remained constant with the decline in licensed dealers.[12] If so, 155,115 licensees have lost their licenses in order to eliminate 1,551 illegal traffickers. Whether this lopsided trade-off justifies stiffer federal regulation is unclear, but other than simply pointing to the fact that crime continued on its downward course nationally during this period, no evidence has been offered. No attempt has been made to iso-late this effect from many other changes that occurred over the same period of time.[13]

Changes in the law will also continue to have an impact. Proposals are being made by the U.S. Department of Justice to "require owners of fire-arms 'arsenals' to provide notice to law enforcement," where the defini-tion of what constitutes an "arsenal" seems to be fairly subjective, and to "require gun owners to record the make, model, and serial number of their firearms as a condition of obtaining gun insurance." Other proposals would essentially make it impossible for private individuals to transfer firearms among themselves.

It is too early to conclude what overall impact these federal rules have had on gun ownership. Surely the adoption of the Brady law dramati-cally increased gun ownership as people rushed out to buy guns before the law went into effect,[14] and the evidence discussed in chapter 3 also indicates that gun ownership increased dramatically between 1988 and 1996. But without annual gun-ownership data, we cannot separate all the different factors that have altered the costs and benefits of gun own-ership.

Other changes are in store during the next couple of years that could affect some of the discussion in this book. The Clinton administration has been encouraging the development of devices for determining at a distance what items a person is carrying.[15] Such devices will enable police to see whether individuals are carrying guns and can help disarm crimi-nals,[16] but criminals who managed to acquire them could also use them to determine whether a potential victim would offer armed resistance. The ability to target unarmed citizens would lower the risks of commit-ting crime and reduce the external benefits produced by concealed hand-guns. Since both police and criminals might use them, the net effect on crime rates of their use is not immediately clear.

Yet governmental use of these detection devices is not a foregone con-clusion. Before granting the government the right to use such long-range devices, we must answer some novel questions regarding constitutional rights. For example, would the ability to take a picture of all the objects that a person is carrying amount to an invasion of privacy? Would it con-stitute an illegal search?[17]

What implications does this study have for banning guns altogether? This book has not examined evidence on what the crime rate would be if all guns could be eliminated from society—no data were present in the data set for areas where guns were completely absent for any period of time, but the findings do suggest how costly the transition to that gun-free goal would be. If outlawing guns would primarily affect their ownership by law-abiding citizens, this research indicates that at least in the short run, we would expect crime rates to rise. The discussion is very similar to the debate over nuclear disarmament. A world without nuclear weapons might be better off, but unilateral disarmament may not be the best way to accomplish that goal. The large stock of guns in the United States, as well as the ease with which illegal items such as drugs find their way across borders implies that not only might the transition to a gun-free world be costly (if not impossible), but the transition might also take a long time.

Further, not everyone will benefit equally from the abolition of guns. For example, criminals will still maintain a large strength advantage over many of their victims (such as women and the elderly). To the extent that guns are an equalizer, their elimination will strengthen criminals relative to physically weak victims. As we have seen in discussing international crime data, eliminating guns alters criminals' behavior in other ways, such as reducing their fear of breaking into homes while the residents are there.

All these discussions, of course, ignore the issues that led the founding fathers to put the Second Amendment in the Constitution in the first place—important issues that are beyond the scope of this book.[18] They believed that an armed citizenry is the ultimate bulwark against tyrannical government. Possibly our trust in government has risen so much that we no longer fear what future governments might do. Having just fought a war for their independence against a government that had tried to confiscate their guns, the founding fathers felt very strongly about this issue.

WHAT CAN WE CONCLUDE?

How much confidence do I have in these results? The largest previous study on gun control produced findings similar to those reported here but examined only 170 cities within a single year. This book has examined over 54,000 observations (across 3,000 counties for eighteen years) and has controlled for a range of other factors never accounted for in previous crime studies. I have attempted to answer numerous questions. For example, do higher arrest or conviction rates reduce crime? What about changes in other handgun laws, such as penalizing the use of a gun in the commission of a crime, or the well-known waiting periods? Do income, poverty, unemployment, drug prices, or demographic changes matter? All these factors were found to influence crime rates, but no previous gun study had accounted for changing criminal penalties, and this study is the first to look at more than a few of any of these other considerations.

Preventing law-abiding citizens from carrying handguns does not end violence; it merely makes victims more vulnerable to attack. While people have strong views on either side of this debate, and one study is unlikely to end this discussion, the size and strength of my deterrence results and the lack of evidence that holders of permits for concealed handguns commit crimes should at least give pause to those who oppose concealed handguns. In the final analysis, one concern unites us all: Will allowing law-abiding citizens to carry concealed handguns save lives? The answer is yes, it will.

THE FEAR OF GUNS

A real fear about guns exists these days. Recently, I was picked up by a taxicab driver who told me that his wife had taken his gun and destroyed it. He had owned the gun for over twenty-five years and had served in the military, but his wife hadn't talked to him before she destroyed it. With all the news coverage on the shootings, accidental gun deaths, and murders committed with guns, his wife was simply terrified about keeping the gun in the home any longer. He hadn't tried to replace it, simply because his wife's opposition was so "emotional" and "strong" that it simply didn't make any sense to argue with her. Having served in the military, the cab driver had no problem with guns, but his wife had always refused to touch the weapon. In fact, he wasn't even sure how it had been possible for her to touch the gun long enough to get it removed from the house. The driver was concerned about crime and had kept the gun around the home for self-protection, and he had made that argument to her. But he described how his wife was fearful that there would be an accident with the gun.

His story reminded me of my own wife's feelings about guns. Before I had started this research, my home had been a "gun-free zone." More than banning real guns, however, my wife had insisted that our children not even play with toy guns because she didn't want her children growing up to be comfortable even around toy guns. I had never felt strongly enough about the issue to argue with her; indeed, it had never occurred to me even to bother arguing with her. I understood the cab driver's reaction to his wife's throwing out his gun—you pick your fights in a relationship; you simply don't bother arguing about something that you don't really care a lot about when your partner feels so intensely about the issue. However, since my research into this area we have indeed purchased a gun.

Unfortunately, the cab driver's experience is not that unusual. A researcher at the University of Chicago Medical School called me about the harassment that her husband—a police officer and federally licensed firearms dealer—was facing from the city council in Muncie, Indiana.

Her husband sold only about ten to twelve guns a year to other police officers, and she said that with the high licensing fees, he was losing money doing this. He simply did it as a service for the other police officers. In any case, the city council was claiming that he had not filled out the proper forms notifying them that he was a dealer. He denies this and faces fines and a possible loss of his license. The city council was apparently concerned about accidental gun deaths that might arise from the guns that he sold.

The wife of a fellow economist recently went to a doctor's office at the University of Chicago hospital, where she was asked to fill out the typical forms about past medical history. One question asked whether she owned a gun. When the doctor saw that she had answered yes, the doctor warned her about the dangers of having a gun in the home and said that she hoped that she had it locked up. The wife countered: "Wouldn't that defeat the whole point of having a gun?" The doctor then said, "Yes I guess it would, but I'm required to tell you that."

Sharon Stone, the movie actress, made headlines by publicly announcing her decision to give up her guns "even though she once saved her life by pointing a loaded shotgun at a crazed stalker" after three telephone calls to 911 failed to get the police to arrive. She decided that with all the recent violence and accidents involving guns she was afraid of having guns in her home.[1] Another reaction is the suspension from school of sixth-graders for accidentally having a squirt gun in their backpacks.[2]

President Clinton puts forward a program to spend $15 million to buy guns from people living in cities. Andrew Cuomo, the secretary of housing and urban development, warns that "reducing guns reduces crime. We know that. Reducing guns also reduces the number of accidents that occur. . . . It reduces the number of suicides through guns."[3]

Newsweek recently devoted a special issue to guns and violence.[4] Despite thirty-four pages on the topic, the notion of defensive gun use was not mentioned even once. ABC's *Nightline* has had guests advising people not to use firearms for self-defense and instead suggesting, "We would recommend and possibly assist with a review of the security of the building and if necessary recommend further security to attend the house if they require it."[5] Yet we are not indoors all the time, and even being inside does not guarantee protection.

With all the news coverage of only the bad things that happen with guns and the constant drumbeat of claims from the Clinton administration, I can understand the public's reaction to guns.[6]

The news is also filled with brutal crimes against women, but none of the mainstream media mention the possibility of women getting guns to defend themselves. The assumption that the police will always be available to protect us collides directly with the horrible event that is being covered on the news. What should people do when the police are not able to be there? By contrast, when bad events happen with guns the question that is normally asked is: Are more gun controls needed? No one asks: Did banning guns from certain areas make the law-abiding citizens more vulnerable?

The following sections will examine new data on concealed-handgun laws and ask whether many of the new proposed reforms ranging from safe-storage laws to one-gun-a-month rules will save lives. I then respond to the criticisms made after my book was published.

UPDATING THE BASIC RESULTS

I started this research several years ago with data from 1977 to 1992, all the county data that were available at that time. When the book was first published, I had updated the data through 1994. It is now possible to expand the data even further, through 1996. This is quite important, since so many states very recently have passed right-to-carry laws. During 1994, Alaska, Arizona, Tennessee, and Wyoming enacted new right-to-carry laws, and during 1995, Arkansas, Nevada, North Carolina, Oklahoma, Texas, and Utah followed suit.[7] Between 1977 and 1996 a total of twenty states had changed their laws and had them in effect for at least one full year.[8]

Some commentators complained that even though my study was by far the largest statistical crime study ever, there was simply not enough data to properly evaluate the impact of the laws. Others suspected that the findings were simply a result of studying relatively unusual states.[9] Another criticism was that poverty was not properly accounted for.[10]

While the methods I used in the book were by far the most comprehensive that I know of, I have continued to look into other methods. By putting together an entirely new data set—using city-level information—it is possible to go beyond my previous efforts to control for policing-policy variables such as arrest and conviction rates, number of police per-capita, expenditures on police per capita, and a proxy for the so-called broken-windows policing policy. The city-level data that I have now compiled include direct information on whether a city has adopted community policing, problem-oriented policing, and/or the broken-windows approach.

One of the commentators on my book suggested that in addition to year-to-year changes in the national crime rate as well as state and county crime trends, another way to account for crime cycles is by measuring whether the crime rates are falling faster in right-to-carry states than in other states in their region rather than compared to just the nation as a whole. While it is impossible to use a separate variable for each year for each individual state, because that would falsely appear to explain all the year-to-year changes in average crime rates in a state, it is possible to group states together. This new set of estimates would account not only for whether the crime rates in concealed-handgun states are falling relative to the national crime rate but now also for whether they are falling relative to the crime rates in their region. To do this, the country is divided into five regions (Northeast, South, Midwest, Rocky Mountains, and Pacific) and variables are added to measure the year-to-year changes in crime by region. [11] All county- and city-level regressions will employ these additional control variables.

Some have criticized my earlier work for not doing enough to account for poverty rates. As a response, I have incorporated in this section of the book state-level measures of poverty and unemployment rates in addition to all the county-level variables that accounted for these factors earlier in this book. The execution rates for murders in each state are now included in estimates to explain the murder rate. Finally, new data on the number of permits granted in different states make it easier to link crime rates to the number of permits granted.

REVIEWING THE BASIC RESULTS

The central question is, How did crime rates change before and after the right-to-carry laws went into effect? The test used earlier in this book examined the difference in the time trends before and after the laws were enacted.[12] With the extended data and the additional variables for the year-to-year changes in crime by region (so-called regional fixed year effects), state poverty, unemployment, and death-penalty execution rates, table 9.1 shows that this pattern closely resembles the pattern found earlier in the book: violent-crime rates were rising consistently before the right-to-carry laws and falling thereafter.[13] The change in these before-and-after trends was always extremely significant—at least at the 0.1 percent level. Compared to the results for tables 4.8 or 4.13, the effects were larger for overall violent crimes, rape, robbery, and aggravated assaults and smaller for murder. For each additional year that the laws were in effect, murders fell by an additional 1.5 percent, while rape, robbery, and aggravated assaults all fell by about by 3 percent each year. The other variables continued to produce results similar to those that were found earlier.[14]

While no previous crime study accounts for year-to-year changes in regional crime rates, it is possible to go even beyond that and combine

Table 9.1 Reexamining the change in time trends before and after the adoption of nondiscretionary laws, using additional data for 1995 and 1996

	Percent change in various crime rates for changes in explanatory variables							
	Violent crime	Murder	Rape	Robbery	Aggravated assault	Property crime	Burglary	Larceny	Auto theft
Change in the crime rate from the difference in the annual change in crime rates in the years before and after the adoption of the right-to-carry law (annual rate of change after the law − annual rate of change before the law)	−2.3%*	−1.5%*	−3.2%*	−2.9%*	−3.0%*	−1.6%*	−2.5%*	−0.9%*	−2.1%*

Note: This table uses county-level violent and property-crime data from the Uniform Crime Report that were not available when I originally wrote the book. All regressions use weighted least squares, where the weighting is each county's population. The regressions correspond to those in tables 4.8 and 4.13. The one difference from the earlier estimates is that these regressions now also allow the regional fixed effects to vary by year.

different approaches. Including not only the factors accounted for in table 9.1 but also individual state time trends produces similar results. The annual declines in crime from right-to-carry laws are greater for murder (2.2 percent), rape (3.9 percent), and robbery rates (4.9 percent), while the impact on aggravated assaults (0.8 percent) and the property crime rates (0.9 percent) is smaller.

Figures 9.1–9.5 illustrate how the violent-crime rates vary before and

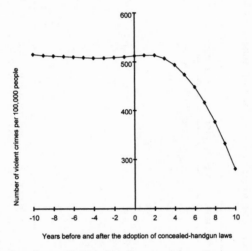

Figure 9.1. The effect of concealed-handgun laws on violent crimes

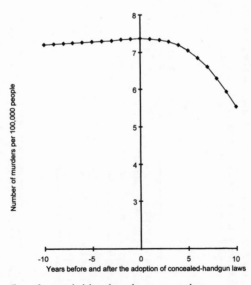

Figure 9.2. The effect of concealed-handgun laws on murders

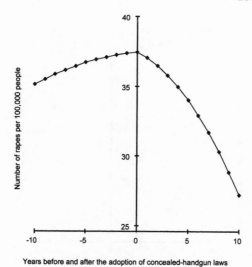

Figure 9.3. The effect of concealed-handgun laws on rapes

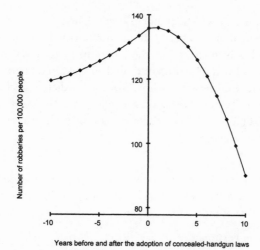

Figure 9.4. The effect of concealed-handgun laws on robberies

after the implementation of right-to-carry laws when both the linear and squared time trends are employed. Despite expanding the data through 1996 so that the legal changes in ten additional states could be examined, the results are similar to those previously shown in figures 4.5–4.9.[15] As in the earlier results, the longer the laws are in effect, the larger the decline in violent crime. The most dramatic results are again for rape and

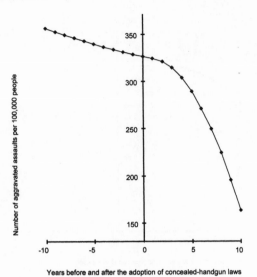

Figure 9.5. The effect of concealed-handgun laws on aggravated assaults

robbery rates, which were rising before the right-to-carry law was passed and falling thereafter. Robbery rates continue rising during the first full year that the law is in effect, but the rate of increase slows and begins to fall by the second year. It is this continued increase in robbery rates which keeps the violent crimes as a whole from immediately declining. While aggravated assaults were falling on average before the right-to-carry law was adopted, figure 9.5 shows that the rate of decline accelerated after the law went into effect.

What Determines the Number of Permits Issued and What Is the Net Benefit from Issuing Another Permit?

The Number of Permits

The relationship between the percentage of the population with permits and the changes in crime rates is central to much of the debate over the right to carry. My previous work was based on the number of permits issued for counties in Oregon and Pennsylvania as well as on discussions with various government officials on what types of counties issued the most permits. The comparison across states assumed that what created the difference in permit rates across counties also applied across states. Some more state-level data have now become available on permit rates, but such data are still relatively scarce. In addition to Florida, Oregon, and Pennsylvania, I have also acquired some annual permit-rate data up to 1996 for Alaska, Arizona, Oklahoma, South Carolina, Texas, Utah, and Wyoming, though these states had these rules in effect for no more than a few years.

While these data are limited, they allow us to examine what factors determine permitting rates, which in turn lets us link the permitting rate to changes in crime. Permit prices, the amount of training required to get a permit, the length of time that permitting rules have been in effect, and the crime rate are all important factors in determining how many people will get permits. Permitting fees and prices charged for training courses are expected to reduce the number of permits issued, but another important cost of getting a permit is the time spent meeting the requirements. This is not to say that there are not also benefits from training (that is a separate issue), but in the narrow issue of how many permits will be issued, there is no doubt that longer training requirements discourage some people from getting permits.

What permitting rules are in place largely depends upon when the laws were first enacted. States that adopted right-to-carry laws more recently tend to have more restrictive licensing requirements. For example, the three states (Alaska, Arizona, and Texas) requiring at least ten hours of training adopted their rules during the last few years of the sample, and Arizona is the only right-to-carry state that requires additional training when permits are renewed. Six of the eight states with permitting fees of at least $100 have also enacted the law during the last few years. This raises the concern that the drops in crime from the passage of right-to-carry laws may be smaller in the states that have most recently adopted these laws simply because they have issued fewer permits.

Based on state-level data, table 9.2 shows the impact of permit fees, training requirements, and how long (in years) the law has been in effect. Because the evidence indicates that the number of new permits is likely to trail off over time, the estimates include both the number of years the law has been in effect and the number of years squared. Fees and training requirements were first investigated without square terms. Notice that only a small fraction of the population gets permits, ranging from less than 1 percent to 6 percent. With that in mind, the regression results show that for each $10 increase in fees, the population getting permits is reduced by about one half of a percentage point. And requiring five hours of training (rather than none) reduces the number of permits by about two-thirds of a percentage point. In a typical state without any fees or training requirements, the percentage of the population with permits would grow from about 3 percent to a little less than 6 percent after a decade.

Table 9.2 What determines the rate at which people obtain permits?

	$10 increase in permit fee	5-hour increase in training requirement	5 years after the law has passed, assuming no fee or training requirement	10 years after the law has passed, assuming no fee or training requirement
Percentage of the state population with permits	−.5%*	−.6%*	4.8%*	6.1%*

*The result is significant at the 1 percent level for a two-tailed t-test.

I also ran more complicated specifications including squared terms for fees and training requirements. They give similar results: fees discourage people from obtaining permits over almost the entire range (until fees go over $130, which is near the highest fee in the sample—$140 for Texas). Anecdotal evidence from newspapers indicates that yet another factor is important: the fear of an attack. Thus, crime and multiple-victim public shootings increase gun sales and concealed-handgun permits.[16] Other variables, such as violent-crime rates, murder rates, the number of multiple-victim public shootings, or the death rate from those attacks, are also important for determining how many people get permits, but they do not alter the impact of the previously mentioned variables. Each additional multiple-victim public shooting increases a state's number of permits by about two-tenths of a percentage point, and each additional person who is killed in such a shooting (per 1 million people living in a state) increases handgun permits by one-tenth of a percentage point.

The Crime Rate and the Estimated Number of Concealed Handguns

The above estimates allow us to revisit the impact of permits and crime rates. While the time-series data on permits issued in different states are relatively short, we do have detailed information on the factors that help determine the number of permits (the fees, training requirements, and how long the law has been in effect). The results from the specification shown in table 9.2 were used to construct "predicted values." Constructing a predicted percentage of a state's population with permits allows us to do more than relying on how crime rates change over time or on the anecdotal evidence I obtained from surveying different state permitting agencies.

These new results using state-level data, shown in table 9.3, indicate that violent-crime rates fell across the board as more permits were issued, with the largest drop occurring for robberies. These results correspond closely to the diagrams reported in figures 4.6–4.9 and 7.1–7.4, which indicate that robberies and rapes are most dramatically affected by the number of years that right-to-carry laws are in effect. The coefficients imply that for every 1,000 additional people with permits, there are 0.3 fewer murders, 2.4 fewer rapes, 21 fewer robberies, and 14.1 fewer aggravated assaults.[17] On the other hand, with the exception of burglary, property crime remained statistically unchanged as more people obtained permits.

Would society benefit from more people getting permits? As already noted, obtaining a permit costs money and takes time. Carrying around a gun is also inconvenient, and many states impose penalties if the gun does not remain concealed.[18] On the positive side, permit holders benefit from having the gun for protection and might also come to the rescue of others. But perhaps just as important are the benefits to general crime deterrence produced by concealed-carry laws, for they also help protect others indirectly, as criminals do not know which people can defend themselves until they attack. This raises the real risk that too few people will get permits, as permit holders personally bear all these costs but produce large benefits for others.

Whether too few permits are being issued depends on how the crime rate changes as more and more permits are issued and whether it is the permit holder or the general public who primarily reaps the benefit from more concealed carry.

The impact of increasing the number of permits on crime is shown in table 9.3, column 1. However, the impact does not need to be constant as more people get permits. Indeed, there may well exist what economists call "diminishing returns"—that is, the crime-reducing benefits from another person getting a permit falls as more people get permits. The reason behind this is twofold: first, those most at risk could be the first to get permits; second, once one adult in a public setting (e.g., a store) has a concealed handgun, the additional benefit from a second or third person being armed should be relatively smaller.

But it is also conceivable that the probability that a victim can defend herself must rise above a certain threshold before it does much to discourage criminals. For instance, if only a few women brandish guns, a would-be rapist may believe that a defensive use is simply an exception and go after another woman. Perhaps if a large enough percentage of women defend themselves, the would-be rapist would decide that the risk to himself is too high.

Table 9.3 Using the predicted percent of the population with permits to explain the changes in different crime rates for state data

	One-percentage-point change in the share of the state population with permits (1)	Pattern when a quadratic term is added for the percent of the population with permits (2)	Number by which total crimes are reduced when an additional 1 percent of the population obtains permits in 1996, using the estimates from column 1 for states that had a right-to-carry law in effect by that year (3)
Violent crime	−7%*	Drop reaches its maximum when 23% of the population has permits	
Murder	−4%***	Drop reaches its maximum when 8% of the population has permits	432 lives saved
Rape	−7%*	Drop is increasing at an increasing rate as more people get permits	3,862 fewer rapes
Robbery	−13.6%*	Drop tapers off, but so slowly that it is still falling when 100 percent of the population has permits	35,014 fewer robberies

Aggravated assault	−5%**	Drop reaches its maximum when 6 percent of the population has permits
Property crime	−2.6%***	Drop continues at a constant rate
Burglary	−10%*	Drop is increasing at an increasing rate as more people get permits
Larceny	−.6%	No significant pattern
Auto theft	−3%	Drop reaches its maximum when 3 percent of the population has permits

28,562 fewer aggravated assaults
144,227 fewer burglaries
27,922 fewer larcenies
21,254 fewer auto thefts

Note: Using the National Institute of Justice estimates of what crime costs victims to estimate the net savings from 1 percent more of the population obtaining permits (or of each additional permit) in 1998 dollars, the cost is reduced by $3.45 billion ($2,516 per permit).

*The result is significant at the 1 percent level for a two-tailed t-test.

**The result is significant at the 5 percent level for a two-tailed t-test.

***The result is significant at the 15 percent level for a two-tailed t-test.

One can test for diminishing returns from more permits by using a squared term for the percentage of the population with permits. The results (shown in column 2) indicate that right-to-carry states experience additional drops in all the violent-crime categories when more permits are issued. For murder, rape, and robbery, all states experience further reductions in crime from issuing more permits, though diminishing returns appear for murder and aggravated assault. (Only one state—Pennsylvania—approaches the number of permits beyond which there would be little further reduction in aggravated assaults from issuing more permits.) An important word of caution is in order here. These particular estimates of the percentage of the population that minimizes crime are rather speculative, because they represent predictions outside the range for which observed permit levels are available. (We thus cannot use these results to predict with confidence what would happen if a state got up to, say, 8 percent having permits.) Still, there is little doubt that issuing additional permits beyond what we have today lowers crime.

Chapter 5 employed county-level permit data from Oregon and Pennsylvania and used the estimated victimization costs from the National Institute of Justice to determine the net benefit to society from issuing an additional permit. Similar estimates can be made for the thirty-one states issuing permits in 1996: each one-percentage-point increase in the population obtaining permits is associated with a $3.45 billion annual net saving to crime victims (in 1998 dollars). Each additional permit produces a total societal benefit of $2,500 per year. While this estimate is smaller than my earlier figures for Oregon and Pennsylvania, the total benefits greatly exceed the total costs of getting a permit. In other words, the numbers suggest that not enough permits are being issued.

The results also indicate that permitting fees are highly detrimental. For each $10 increase in fees, the percentage of the population with permits falls by one half of one percentage point. For the thirty-one states with right-to-carry laws, this increases victimization costs by $1.7 billion. The large effect from higher permitting fees might be due to the poorest and most vulnerable being especially discouraged from obtaining a permit. Blacks living in higher-crime urban areas benefit disproportionately from concealed-handgun permits. High fees are more likely to deter individuals from carrying guns when those individuals are poor. When fees are high, there may be a smaller crime-reduction benefit from right-to-carry laws even if the same percentage of the population were to obtain permits.

To test this, I reestimated the relationship between predicted permits and crime by also including the direct impact of permit fees on the crime rate.[19] The regressions for violent crime, murder, robbery, and aggravated assault all indicate that, holding constant the percentage of the population with permits, higher fees greatly reduce the benefit from right-to-carry laws. For example, the drop in robberies from one percent of the population having permits is about two percentage points smaller when the fee is raised from $10 to $50.

UPDATING THE EVIDENCE ON WHO BENEFITS FROM PERMITS

While the preceding results relied on state-level data, we know from previous work (already presented in this book) that different parts of states obtained greatly varying benefits from issuing permits. This finding is confirmed with the new, updated data. But I will here discuss a somewhat different specification, linking the changes in crime more closely to the issuing of more permits. The percentage of the population with permits is interacted with the percentage of the adult population in a county that is over sixty-four years of age, the population density per square mile, the percentage that is black, the percentage that is female, and per-capita personal income. The earlier interactions in chapter 4, reported with county population, are skipped over here because they again produce results that are extremely similar to the regressions with an interaction for population density.[20]

The results reported in figures 9.6–9.9 are all quite statistically significant and imply the same pattern reported earlier when using the data through 1992. The benefits of right-to-carry laws are not uniform across counties. Counties with a high portion of elderly people, blacks, and females—the most vulnerable victims—all benefit disproportionately more from concealed-handgun laws. So do those living in counties that are densely populated.

Certain crime patterns do emerge. For example, in counties with many elderly people (23 percent of the population over age sixty-four) right-to-carry laws have a large deterrent effect against aggravated assaults and robberies but seem to have a relatively small effect on rapes. In contrast, counties with few elderly individuals (7 percent of their population over sixty-four years of age) have only about a third of the drop in violent crime that counties with many elderly people have. Heavily black areas benefit the most through reductions in robberies and rapes, while areas where women make up a larger share of the population and those living in the wealthiest areas obtain the largest benefits from drops in aggravated assaults and rapes. The benefit for blacks is very large. Increasing the percentage of the black population in a county from half the mean (4.4 percent) to two standard deviations above the mean (37 per-

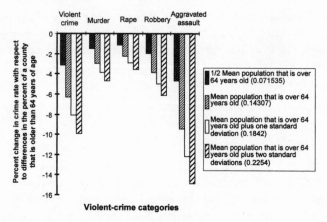

Figure 9.6. How does the change in crime from nondiscretionary concealed-handgun laws occur in counties with relatively more people over age sixty-four?

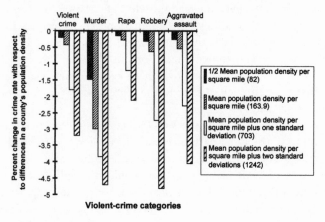

Figure 9.7. How does the change in crime from nondiscretionary concealed-handgun laws occur in the most densely populated counties?

cent) increases the reduction in violent crime from right-to-carry laws from about one percentage point to over seven percentage points.

Unlike the earlier data presented in chapter 4, which represented crime through 1992, not all the states adopting right-to-carry laws during 1993–1996 moved from a discretionary to a nondiscretionary law. Some states had previously prohibited the carrying of concealed handguns. This is important because one of the reasons that I examined the interactions of population or population density with right-to-carry laws was that state government officials had told me that under a discretionary system lower-population counties had already tended to be more liberal

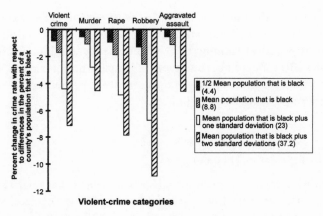

Figure 9.8. How does the change in crime from nondiscretionary concealed-handgun laws vary with the percentage of a county's population that is black?

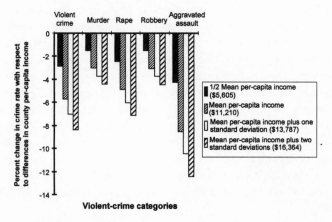

Figure 9.9. How does the change in crime from nondiscretionary concealed-handgun laws vary with county per-capita income?

in granting permits. Higher-population counties were thus expected to experience the largest increase in issuing permits and thus the largest drops in violent crime after a nondiscretionary system was adopted. In fact, I find that the more populous counties in states changing from discretionary to nondiscretionary laws had a statistically bigger relative drop in violent-crime rates than states that changed from banning concealed handguns to nondiscretionary laws.

These updated results confirm my earlier findings that those who are relatively weaker physically (women and the elderly) and those who are most likely to be crime victims (blacks and those living in urban areas) tend to benefit the most from the passage of right-to-carry laws. Taken together, these results indicate that legislators should be sensitive not only to the costs of running the permitting program, but also to how the rules affect the number and types of people who get permits. Focusing only on setting fees to recoup the costs of the permitting system will end up being financially short sighted.

How Sensitive Are the Results to Different Specifications?

While I have tried to control for all sorts of factors that might explain changes in crime over time, it is indeed possible to get overzealous and account for *too many* variables. Including variables that do not really affect crime can actually create problems similar to excluding factors that should be included. Take a simple example of explaining how the stock market, say the Dow Jones industrials, changes over time. Obvious variables to include would be the interest rate and the expected growth in the economy, but many other variables—many of dubious importance— could possibly also be included. The problem arises when such variables are correlated to changes in stock prices merely by chance. An extreme case would be including the prices of various grocery store products. A store might sell thousands of items, and one—say, the price of peanut butter—might happen to be highly correlated with the stock prices over the particular period examined. We know that peanut butter has little to do with explaining overall stock prices, but if it just accidentally happens to move up and down with the movements in the stock market, other variables (like the interest rate) may no longer prove to be statistically significant.

There are ways to protect against this "dubious variable" problem. One is to expand the sample period. If no true causal relationship exists between the two variables, the probability that this coincidence will continue to occur during future years is low. And this is exactly what I have done as more data have become available: first by looking at data through 1992, then extending them to 1994, and now up until 1996. Another approach guarding against the "dubious variable" problem is to replicate the same test in many different places. Again, this is exactly what I have done here: I have studied the impact of right-to-carry laws in different states at different times. As charged by many a critic, it is still conceivable that some other factor just happened to occur also when an individual state passed the law, but the probability of mere coincidence falls as the experiences of more and more states are examined. It is also possible that adding variables that don't belong can cause you to get a more significant result for other factors than is warranted.

Generally, excluding variables that should be included is a more significant problem than including variables that should not be included, and in general I have tried to err on the side of including whatever possible factors can be included. Indeed, a strong case can be made that one must be careful not to include too many variables like state time trends, which can be endlessly added on and have little theoretical justification. Still, I do not consider any of these variables to be similar to the price of peanut butter at the local grocery store in the previous discussion, but obviously some researchers might believe that some variables should not be included. One way to investigate this issue is to include only those variables that different investigators view as relevant. In the early stages of my research, when I presented my original research as a working paper at seminars, I asked participants for other factors that should be included, and some of their comments were very helpful. I also tried in vain to ask pro-gun-control researchers what variables they wanted me to include in the regressions, but (as discussed in chapter 7) they did not make any suggestions when my initial research was circulated for comments. What comments they made after the publicity broke claimed that I had not controlled for factors that I had indeed accounted for.

Since the original research immediately received a lot of attention, I have let my critics decide for themselves what variables should be included by simply giving them complete access to the data. I know from personal communication that some critics (such as Black and Nagin) did indeed examine numerous different specifications.[21]

A more systematic, if time-consuming, approach is to try all possible combinations of these so-called control variables—factors which may be interesting but are included so that we can be sure of the importance of some other "focus" variables.[22] In my regressions to explain crime rates there are at least nine groups of control variables—population density, waiting periods and background checks, penalties for using guns in the commission of a crime, per-capita income, per-capita unemployment insurance payments, per-capita income maintenance payments, retirement payments per person for those over sixty-five, state poverty rate, and state unemployment rate.[23] To run all possible combinations of these nine groups of control variables requires 512 regressions. The regressions for murder rates also require a tenth control variable for the death-penalty execution rate and thus results in 1,024 combinations of control variables. Given the nine different crime categories, this amounts to 5,120 regressions.

This approach is decidedly biased toward not finding a consistent effect of the right-to-carry laws, because it includes many combinations of control variables that no researcher thinks are correct specifications. Indeed, even the strongest, best-accepted empirical relationships usually fail this test.[24] Since different people will have different preferences for what variables should be included, this massive set of results makes sense only if one knows what variables produce what results. If a range of conflicting estimates are then produced, people can judge for themselves what they think the "true" range of the estimates is.

Two sets of variables have been primarily used to test the impact of right-to-carry laws: crime trends before and after the adoption of right-to-carry laws and the percentage of people with permits. Yet another division is possible by focusing on counties with a large number of people to avoid the difficulty that low-population counties frequently have zero murder or rape rates and thus have "undefined" arrest rates.[25] Eliminating counties with fewer than 20,000 people removes about 70 percent of the missing arrest ratios for murder while sacrificing 20 percent of the observations (the population-weighted frequencies are 23 and 6 percent, respectively). Dropping out more populous counties reduces the sample size but has virtually no impact on further reducing the frequency of missing arrest rates. Even if I limit the estimates to the full sample and counties with more than 20,000 people, combining that with the two other types of specifications now results in 20,480 regressions. Because of all the concerns over possible crime trends, all estimates include variables to account for the average differences across counties and years as well as by year within region as well as the thirty-six demographic variables.[26]

Figures 9.10–9.13 present the range of estimates associated with these different combinations of variables and specifications, both in terms of their extreme bounds and their median value. What immediately stands out when one examines all these estimates is how extremely consistent the violent-crime results are. For example, take figure 9.10. A one-percentage-point change in people with permits lowers violent-crime rates by 4.5–7.2 percent. Indeed, all the estimates (over two thousand of them) for overall violent crime, murder, rape, robbery, and aggravated assault indicate that increases in permits reduce crime. All the combinations of the other ten sets of control variables imply that a one-percentage-point increase in the population holding permits reduces murder rates by 2–3.9 percent annually. Compared to the state-level data, the benefits from right-to-carry laws are much smaller for robbery and much larger for aggravated assaults.

Figure 9.11 uses the simple before-and-after trends to examine the impact of the right-to-carry laws, and the results for the violent-crime rates

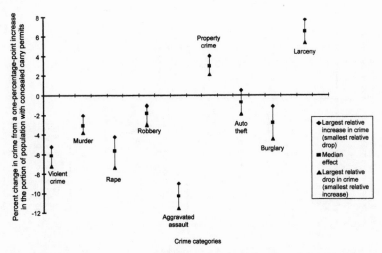

Figure 9.10. Sensitivity of the relationship between the percentage of the population with permits and annual changes in crime rates: data for all counties

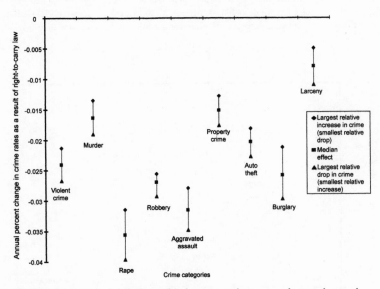

Figure 9.11. Sensitivity of the relationship between right-to-carry laws and annual changes in crime rates: data for all counties

are generally consistent with those shown in figure 9.10. Again, all the violent-crime-rate regressions show the same direction of impact from the concealed-handgun law. The median estimated declines in violent-crime rates are quite similar to those initially reported in table 9. 1. For each additional year that the right-to-carry laws are in effect, violent

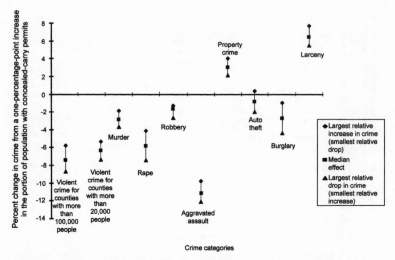

Figure 9.12. Sensitivity of the relationship between the percentage of the population with permits and annual changes in crime rates: data for counties with either more than 20,000 people or more than 100,000 people (all individual crime categories—that is, all categories except "violent crime"—are for counties with more than 20,000 people)

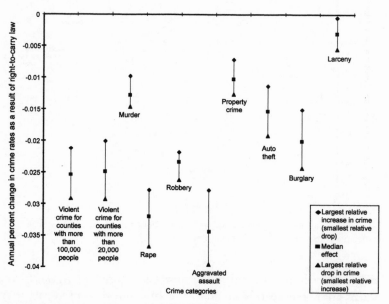

Figure 9.13. Sensitivity of the relationship between right-to-carry laws and annual changes in crime rates: data for counties with either more than 20,000 people or more than 100,000 people (all individual crime categories—that is, all categories except "violent crime"—are for counties with more than 20,000 people)

crimes decline by 2.4 percent, murders by 1.6 percent, rapes and aggravated assaults by over 3 percent, and robberies by 2.7 percent.

With the notable exception of burglaries, which consistently decline, figures 9.10 and 9.11 provide mixed evidence for whether right-to-carry laws increase or decrease other property crimes. Even when one focuses on estimates of one type, such as those using the percentage of the population with permits, the county- and state-level data yield inconsistent results. Yet while the net effect of right-to-carry laws on larceny and auto theft is not clear, one conclusion can be drawn: the passage of right-to-carry laws has a consistently larger deterrent effect against violent crimes than property crimes and may even be associated with increases in property crimes.

Figures 9.12 and 9.13 limit the sample to the more populous counties and continue reaching very similar results. For counties with more than 20,000 people, the estimate ranges are always of the same sign and have magnitudes similar to those results which examined all the counties. Both figures also looked at the sensitivity of the overall violent-crime rate for counties over 100,000. The range of estimates was again very similar, though they implied a slightly larger benefit than for the more populous counties. For example, figure 9.12 shows that in counties with more than 20,000 people violent crime declines by between 5.4 and 7.4 percentage points for each additional 1 percent of the population with permits, while the analogous drop for counties with more than 100,000 people is between 5.8 and 8.7 percentage points.

A total of 13,312 regressions for the various violent-crime categories are reported in this section. The evidence clearly indicates that right-to-carry laws are always associated with reductions in violent crime, and 89 percent of the results are statistically significant at least at the 1 percent level. The results are not sensitive to including particular control variables and always show that the benefits from these laws increase over time as more people obtain permits. The 8,192 regressions for property crime imply a less consistent relationship between right-to-carry laws and property crime, but even when drops in property crime are observed, the declines are smaller than the decrease in violent crime.

While limiting the sample size to only larger-population counties provides one possible method of dealing with "undefined" arrest rates, it has a serious drawback—information is lost by throwing out those counties with fewer than 20,000 people. Another approach is to control for either the violent- or property-crime arrest rate depending upon whether the crime rate being studied is that of violent or property crime. Even if a county has zero murders or rapes in a particular year, virtually all counties have at least some violent or property crime, thus eliminating the "undefined" arrest rate problem and still allowing us to account for county-level changes over time in the effectiveness of law enforcement. This approach also helps mitigate any spurious relationship between crime and arrest rates that might arise because the arrest rate is a function of the crime rate. Reestimating the 4,096 regressions in figure 9.10 for murder, rape, robbery, aggravated assault, auto theft, burglary, and larceny with this new measure of arrest rates again produces very similar results.

City Crime Data

County data, rather than city data, allow the entire country to be examined. This is important, since, obviously, not everyone lives in cities. Such data further allow us to deal with differences in how permits are issued, such as the discretion states grant to local law enforcement. Relying on county data allows a detailed analysis of many important factors, such as arrest and conviction rates, the number of police, expenditures on police, (sometimes) prison sentences, and proxies for policing policies like the so-called broken-windows strategy (according to which police focus on less serious property crimes as a means of reducing overall violent crime). Yet a drawback with county data is that policing policies cannot be dealt with well, for such policy decisions are made at the level of individual police departments—not at the county level.[27] With a few exceptions such as San Francisco, Philadelphia, and New York, where county and city boundaries coincide, only city-level data can be used to study these issues.

The focus of my research is guns and crime, but I had to make sure that I accounted for whatever policing policies are being employed.[28] Three policing strategies dominate the discussion: community-oriented policing, problem-oriented policing, and the broken-windows approach. While community-oriented policing is said to involve local community organizations directly in the policing effort, problem-oriented policing is sometimes viewed as a less intrusive version of the broken-windows policy. Problem-oriented policing began as directing patrols on the basis of identified crime patterns but nowadays involves the police in everything from cleaning housing projects and surveying their tenants to helping citizens design parking garages to reduce auto theft.[29] An extensive Westlaw database search was conducted to categorize which cities adopted which policing strategies as well as their adoption and rescission dates.[30]

Other recent research of mine demonstrates the importance of racial and gender hiring decrees on the effectiveness of police departments.[31] When hiring rules are changed so as to create equal pass rates on hiring exams across different racial groups—typically by replacing intelligence tests with what some claim are arbitrary psychological tests—the evidence indicates that the quality of new hires falls across the board. And the longer these new hiring policies are in place, the more detrimental the effect on police departments. As with the right-to-carry laws, simple before-and-after trends were included to measure the changing impact of these rules over time.

Let us return to the main focus, guns and crime. To examine the impact of right-to-carry laws, the following list of variables has been accounted for: city population, arrest rate by type of crime, unemployment rate, percentage of families headed by females, family poverty rate, median family income, per-capita income, percentage of the population living below poverty, percentage of the population that is white, percentage that is black, percentage that is Hispanic, percentage that is female, percentage that is less than five years of age, percentage that is between five and seventeen, percentage that is between eighteen and twenty-five, percentage that is between twenty-six and sixty-four, percentage that is sixty-five and older, median population age, percentage of the population over age twenty-five with a high school diploma, percentage of the population over age twenty-five with a college degree, and other types of gun-control laws (waiting periods, background checks, and additional penalties for using guns in the commission of a crime). As with the earlier county- and state-level data, variables are included to measure the length of state waiting periods, as well as the change in average crime rates from state waiting periods, background checks, penalties for using a gun in the commission of crime, and whether the federal Brady law altered existing state rules. Again, all estimates include variables to account for the average differences across counties and years as well as by year within region.

Table 9.4 provides strong evidence that even when detailed information on policing policies is taken into account, passing concealed-handgun laws deters violent crime. The benefit in terms of reduced murder rates is particularly large, with a drop of 2.7 percent each additional year that the right-to-carry law is in effect. The drop experienced for rapes is 1.5 percent per year. The one violent crime for which the decline is not statistically significant is aggravated assault. On the other hand, property crimes increase after the adoption of right-to-carry laws, confirming some of the earlier findings.

Consent decrees—which mandate police hiring rules that ensure equal pass rates by race and sex—significantly and adversely affect all crime categories but rape. For each additional year that the consent decree is in effect, overall violent crimes rise by 2.4 percent and property crimes rise by 1.9 percent.

Table 9.4 Accounting for policing policies using city-level data

	Percent change in various crime rates for changes in explanatory variables							
	Violent crime	Murder	Rape	Robbery	Aggravated assault	Property crime	Burglary	Larceny	Auto theft
Change in the crime rate from the difference in the annual change in crime rates in the years before and after the adoption of a right-to-carry law (annual rate of change after the law − annual rate of change before the law)	−1.2%**	−2.7%*	−1.5%**	−1.0%*	−0.6%	0.92%**	1.0%*	0.7%**	1.2%**
Change in the crime rate after imposition of a consent decree regarding the hiring of police officers	2.4%*	0.4%***	−0.27%	3.5%*	1.4%*	1.9%*	2.4%*	2.0%*	0.5%**
Change in the average crime rate after implementation of community policing	−3.3%[a]	2.2%	−4.9%[a]	−1.7%[b]	−2.5%[b]	1.6%[a]	−1.2%[c]	2.5%[a]	7.7%[a]

Change in the average crime rate after implementation of problem-orientated policing	2.4%	−4.1%	−4.5%	3.6%	2.6%	1.8%	−1.8%	−2.7%[c]	24.9%[a]
Change in the average crime rate after implementation of broken-window policing	−0.8%	6.7%[c]	−10.1%[a]	−3.8%	2.3%	−6.4%[a]	−5.6%[a]	−12.3%[a]	18.2%[a]
Average crime rate after adoption of one-gun-a-month purchase rule	9.3%	14.7%[d]	6.8%	7.9%[d]	15.8%[c]	−0.6%	2.7%	−4.9%	11%
Change in the average crime rate in a state after a neighboring state adopts a one-a-month rule	9.6%[a]	18.4%[a]	11.9%	4.1%	17.2%[a]	13%[a]	10.6%[b]	14.3%[c]	11%[c]

[a]The result is significant at the 1 percent level for a two-tailed t-test.
[b]The result is significant at the 5 percent level for a two-tailed t-test.
[c]The result is significant at the 10 percent level for a two-tailed t-test.
[d]The result is significant at the 12 percent level for a two-tailed t-test.
*The F-test is significant at the 1 percent level.
**The F-test is significant at the 5 percent level.
***The F-test is significant at the 10 percent level.

The evidence for the before-and-after average crime rates for the different types of policing policies is more mixed, and my research does not attempt to deal with issues of why the different rules were adopted to begin with.[32] In ten cases, the policing policies produce significant reductions in crime, but in six cases there are significant increases in crime. Including cases that are not statistically significant still produces no consistent pattern: the policing policies are associated with declines in crime in fifteen cases and increases in twelve cases. A possible explanation for such results might be that adopting new policing policies reallocates resources within the police department, causing some crime rates to go down while others go up. Indeed, each of the three policing policies is associated with increases in some categories of crime and decreases in others. It is difficult to pick out many patterns, but community policing reduces violent crimes at the expense of increased property crimes.

REVISITING MULTIPLE-VICTIM PUBLIC SHOOTINGS

> Student eyewitnesses and shooting victims of the Pearl High School (Mississippi) rampage used phrases like "unreal" and "like a horror movie" as they testified Wednesday about seeing Luke Woodham methodically point his deer rifle at them and pull the trigger at least six times. . . . The day's most vivid testimony came from a gutsy hero of the day. Assistant principal Joel Myrick heard the initial shot and watched Woodham choosing his victims. When Woodham appeared headed for a science wing where early classes were already under way, Myrick ran for his pickup and grabbed his .45-caliber pistol. He rounded the school building in time to see Woodham leaving the school and getting into his mother's white Chevy Corsica. He watched its back tires smoke from Woodham's failure to remove the parking brake. Then he ordered him to stop. "I had my pistol's sights on him. I could see the whites of his knuckles" on the steering wheel, Myrick said. He reached into the car and opened the driver-side door, then ordered Woodham to lie on the ground. "I put my foot on his back area and pointed my pistol at him," Myrick testified.[33]

Multiple-victim public shootings were not a central issue in the gun debate when I originally finished writing this book in the spring of 1997. My results on multiple-victim public shootings, presented in chapter 5, were obtained long before the first public school attacks occurred in October 1997. Since that time, two of the eight public school shootings (Pearl, Mississippi, and Edinboro, Pennsylvania) were stopped only when citizens with guns interceded.[34] In the Pearl, Mississippi, case, Myrick stopped the killer from proceeding to the nearby junior high school and continuing his attack there. These two cases also involved the fewest people harmed in any of the attacks. The armed citizens managed to stop the attackers well before the police even had arrived at the scene—4½ minutes before in the Pearl, Mississippi, case and 11 minutes before in Edinboro.

In a third instance, at Columbine High School in Littleton, Colorado, an armed guard was able to delay the attackers and allow many students to escape the building, even though he was assigned to the school because he had failed to pass his shooting proficiency test. The use of homemade grenades, however, prevented the guard from fighting longer. There is some irony in Dylan Klebold, one of the two killers, strongly opposing the proposed right-to-carry law that was being considered in Colorado at the time of the massacre.[35] In the attack on the Jewish community center in Los Angeles in which five people were wounded, the attacker had apparently "scouted three of the West Coast's most prominent Jewish institutions—the Museum of Tolerance, the Skirball Cultural Center and the University of Judaism—but found security too tight."[36]

It is remarkable how little public discussion there has been on the topic of allowing people to defend themselves. It has only been since 1995 that we have had a federal law banning guns by people other than police within one thousand feet of a school.[37]

Together with my colleague William Landes, I compiled data on all the multiple-victim public shootings occurring in the United States from 1977 to 1995, during which time fourteen states adopted right-to-carry laws. As with earlier numbers reported in this book, the incidents we considered were cases with at least two people killed or injured in a public place. We excluded gang wars or shootings that were by-products of another crime, such as robbery. The United States averaged twenty-one such shootings annually, with an average of 1.8 people killed and 2.7 wounded in each incident.

What can stop these attacks? We examined a range of different gun laws, including waiting periods, as well the frequency and level of punishment. However, while arrest and conviction rates, prison sentences, and the death penalty reduce murders generally, they have no significant effect on public shootings. There is a simple reason for this: Those who commit these crimes usually die in the attack. They are killed in the attack or, as in the Colorado shooting, they commit suicide. The normal penalties simply do not apply.

In the deranged minds of the attackers, their goal is to kill and injure as many people as possible. Some appear to do it for the publicity, which

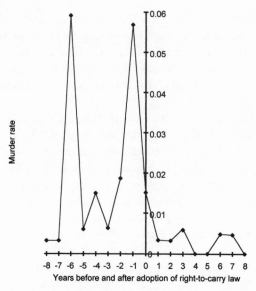

Figure 9.14. Murders from multiple-victim public shootings per 100,000 people: data from 1977 to 1995

is related to the harm inflicted. Some may do it only because they value harming others. The best way to prevent these attacks might therefore be to limit the carnage they can cause if they do attack. We find only one policy that effectively accomplishes this: the passage of right-to-carry laws.

When different states passed right-to-carry laws during the nineteen years we studied, the number of multiple-victim public shootings declined by a whopping 84 percent. Deaths from all these shootings plummeted by 90 percent, and injuries by 82 percent. Figure 9.14 demonstrates how the raw number of attacks changes before and after the passage of right-to-carry laws. The extensive research that we have done indicates that these results hold up very well when the long list of factors discussed in this book is taken into account. The very few attacks that still occur in states after enactment of right-to-carry laws tend to occur in particular places where concealed handguns are forbidden, such as schools.

The reason why the deterrent effect on multiple-victim public attacks is greater than on attacks on individual victims is fairly straightforward. Say the probability that a victim has a permitted concealed handgun is 5 percent. That will raise the expected costs to the criminal and produce some deterrence. Yet if one hundred adults are present on a train or in a restaurant, even if the probability that any one of them will be able to offer a defense is only 5 percent, the probability that at least someone there has a permitted concealed handgun is near 100 percent.[38] The results for multiple-victim public shootings are consistent with the central findings of this book: as the probability that victims are going to be able to defend themselves increases, the level of deterrence increases.

Concealed-handgun laws also have an important advantage over uniformed police, for would-be attackers can aim their initial assault at a single officer, or alternatively wait until he leaves the area. With concealed carrying by ordinary citizens, it is not known who is armed until the criminal actually attacks. Concealed-handgun laws might therefore also require fewer people carrying weapons. Some school systems (such as Baltimore) have recognized this problem and made nonuniformed police officers "part of the faculty at each school."[39]

Despite all the debate about criminals behaving irrationally, reducing their ability to accomplish their warped goals reduces their willingness to attack. Yet even if mass murder is the only goal, the possibility of a law-abiding citizen carrying a concealed handgun in a restaurant or on a train is apparently enough to convince many would-be killers that they will not be successful. Unfortunately, without concealed carry, ordinary citizens are sitting ducks, waiting to be victimized.

OTHER GUN-CONTROL LAWS

> "Gun control? It's the best thing you can do for crooks and gangsters," Gravano said. "I want you to have nothing. If I'm a bad guy, I'm always gonna have a gun. Safety locks? You will pull the trigger with a lock on, and I'll pull the trigger. We'll see who wins."[40]
> Sammy "the Bull" Gravano, the Mafia turncoat, when asked about gun control

The last year has seen a big push for new gun-control laws. Unfortunately, the discussion focuses on only the possible benefits and ignores any costs. Waiting periods may allow for a "cooling-off period," but they may also make it difficult for people to obtain a gun quickly for self-defense. Gun locks may prevent accidental gun deaths involving young children, but they may also make it difficult for people to use a gun quickly for self-defense.[41] The exaggerated stories about accidental gun deaths, particularly those involving young children, might scare people into not owning guns for protection, even though guns offer by far the most effective means of defending oneself and one's family.

Some laws, such as the Brady law, may prevent some criminals from buying guns through legal channels, such as regular gun stores. Nevertheless, such laws are not going to prevent criminals from obtaining guns through other means, including theft. Just as the government has had difficulty in stopping gangs from getting drugs to sell, it is dubious that the government would succeed in stopping criminals from acquiring guns to defend their drug turf.

Similar points can be made about one-gun-a-month rules. The cost that they impose upon the law abiding may be small. Yet there is still a security issue here: someone being threatened might immediately want to store guns at several places so that one is always easily within reach. The one-gun-a-month rule makes that impossible. Besides this issue, the rule is primarily an inconvenience for those who buy guns as gifts or who want to take their families hunting.

The enactment dates for the safe-storage laws and one-gun-a-month rules are shown in table 9.5.[42] For the implementation dates of safe-storage laws, I relied primarily on an article published in the *Journal of the American Medical Association,* though this contained only laws passed up

Table 9.5 Enactment dates of other gun control laws

State	Date law went into effect*
Safe-storage laws:[a]	
Florida	10/1/89
Iowa	4/5/90
Connecticut	10/1/90
Nevada	10/1/91
California	1/1/92
New Jersey	1/17/92
Wisconsin	4/16/92
Hawaii	6/29/92
Virginia	7/1/92
Maryland	10/1/92
Minnesota	8/1/93
North Carolina	12/1/93
Delaware	10/1/94
Rhode Island	9/15/95
Texas	1/1/96
One-gun-a-month laws:[b]	
South Carolina	1976
Virginia	7/93
Maryland	10/1/96

[a]Source for the dates of enactment of safe-storage laws through the end of 1993 is Peter Cummings, David C. Grossman, Frederick P. Rivara, and Thomas D. Koepsell, "State Gun Safe Storage Laws and Child Mortality Due to Firearms," *Journal of the American Medical Association,* 278 (October 1, 1997): 1084–86. The other dates were obtained from the Handgun Control Web site at http://www.hand-guncontrol.org/caplaws.htm.
[b]Data were obtained through a Nexis/Lexis search. Lynn Waltz, "Virginia Law Cuts Gun Pipeline to Capital's Criminals, *Norfolk Virginian-Pilot,* September 8, 1996, p. A7.

through the end of 1993.[43] Handgun Control's Web site provided information on the three states that passed laws after this date. The laws share certain common features, such as making it a crime to store firearms in a way that a reasonable person would know allows a child to gain use of a weapon. The primary differences involve exactly what penalties are imposed and the age at which a child's access becomes allowed. While Connecticut, California, and Florida classify such violations as felonies, other states classify them as misdemeanors. The age at which children's access is permitted also varies across states, ranging from twelve in Virginia to eighteen in North Carolina and Delaware. Most state rules protect owners from liability if firearms are stored in a locked box, secured with a trigger lock, or obtained through unlawful entry.

The state-level estimates are shown in table 9.6. Only the right-to-carry laws are associated with significant reductions in crime rates. Among the violent-crime categories, the Brady law is only significantly related to rape, which increased by 3.6 percent after the law passed. (While the coefficients indicate that the law resulted in more murders and robberies but fewer aggravated assaults and as a consequence fewer overall violent crimes, none of those effects are even close to being statistically significant.) Only the impact of the Brady law on rape rates is consistent with the earlier results that we found for the data up through 1994.

Safe-storage rules also seem to cause some real problems. Passage of these laws is significantly related to almost 9 percent more rapes and robberies and 5.6 percent more burglaries. In terms of total crime in 1996, the presence of the law in just these fifteen states was associated with 3,600 more rapes, 22,500 more robberies, and 64,000 more burglaries. These increases might reflect the increased difficulty victims have in reaching a gun to protect themselves. However, a contributing factor might be the horror stories that often accompany the passage of these laws, reducing people's desire to own a gun in the first place. The increase in burglaries is particularly notable. Burglars appeared to be less afraid of entering homes after these laws were passed. Additional state data would be required to answer the question of whether "hot burglaries"—burglaries occurring while the residents are in the dwelling—increased and whether burglars spent less time casing dwellings after these laws were passed. Evidence of these other changes would help confirm that these laws have emboldened criminals.

On the other side of this question is the number of accidental gun deaths that will be prevented. The General Accounting Office reported in 1991 that mechanical safety locks are unreliable in preventing children over six years of age from using a gun,[44] but there is still the question of

Table 9.6 Evaluating other gun-control laws using state-level data

	Percent change in various crime rates for changes in explanatory variables								
	Violent crime	Murder	Rape	Robbery	Aggravated assault	Property crime	Burglary	Larceny	Auto theft
Change in the crime rate from the difference in the annual change in crime rates in the years before and after the adoption of the right-to-carry law (annual rate of change after the law – annual rate of change before the law)	−2.0%*	−3.2%*	−1.4%*	−3.8%*	−2.3%*	−1.3%*	−2.9%*	−0.8%***	0.06%
Change in the average crime rate after the adoption of Brady law	−2.4%	3.6%	3.6%ᵃ	0.02%	−4.2%	−0.6%	0.7%	−0.6%	2.5%
Change in the average crime rate after the adoption of safe-storage rules	0.04%	1.3%	8.9%ᵃ	8.9%ᵃ	−4.4%	2.5%	5.6%ᵇ	2.0%	−0.6%

how many of these children's lives might have been saved, and even if locks are unreliable for older children, some deaths may be prevented. Even if one believes that the high-end estimated benefits are correct, that as many as 31 of the 136 children under age fifteen who had died from accidental gunshots in 1996 would have been saved by nationwide safe-storage laws, table 9.6 implies some caution.[45] The effect for murders was not statistically significant, but it still provides the best estimate that we have and the size of the effect is still instructive. It indicates that in just these fifteen states, 109 lives would be lost from this law. If the entire country had these safe-storage laws, the total lost lives would have risen to 255.

Yet other research that I have done with John Whitley indicates that this is the most optimistic possible outcome from safe-storage laws. We find no support for the theory that safe-storage laws reduce either juvenile accidental gun deaths or suicides. Instead, these storage requirements appear to impair people's ability to use guns defensively. Because accidental shooters also tend to be the ones most likely to violate the new law, safe-storage laws increase violent and property crimes against low-risk citizens with no observable offsetting benefit in terms of reduced accidents or suicides. Just as important, we found that examining the simple before-and-after average effects of the law underestimates the increases in crime that result from safe-storage laws. When the before-and-after trends are accounted for, the group of fifteen states that adopted these laws faced an annual average increase of over 300 more murders, 3,860 more rapes, 24,650 more robberies, and over 25,000 more aggravated assaults during the first five full years after the passage of the safe-storage laws. Using the National Institute of Justice estimates of victim costs from crime indicates that the average annual costs borne by victims averaged over $2.6 billion.

The one-gun-a-month rule seems to have negative consequences, too. But only three states passed these laws during the twenty years studied, so there is always the issue of whether enough data exist and whether other factors might have played a role. Nevertheless, the passage of these laws was associated with more murders, more robberies, and more aggravated assaults, and the effects appear to be quite large.

One possible suspicion, however, is that the large effect of one-gun-a-month rules merely reflects some regional crime increases, increases that just happen to coincide with the adoption of these laws. To counter this potential problem, I again allowed year-to-year average differences to vary by region, as I had done for the county- and city-level data. The results for right-to-carry laws were essentially unchanged, and the pattern for other gun-control laws remained very similar, though some of the statistical significance declined. The Brady law was still associated with a statistically significant increase in rapes. Using the simple before-and-after averages, safe-storage laws were still associated with statistically significant increases in rape, robbery, and burglary. Indeed, not only did the coefficients remain significant at the 1 percent level, but the results actually implied slightly larger increases in these crime categories, with the effect from state storage laws on rape now increasing to 9 percent, on robbery to 9.9 percent, and on burglary to 6.8 percent.

THE POLITICAL AND ACADEMIC DEBATE CONTINUED

Attacking the Messenger

> *David Yassky* [member of the board of directors of Handgun Control, Inc.]: The people who fund your studies are gun manufacturers.
>
> *Lott:* That is a lie.
>
> *Yassky:* That is not a lie. That is not a lie.
>
> *Lott:* That is a lie.
>
> *Yassky:* It is paid for by gun manufacturers who manufacture firearms.
>
> From *Debates/Debates,* a nationally syndicated program on public television that was broadcast during the week of April 22, 1999

> *Michael Beard* [president of the Coalition to Stop Gun Violence]: Yes, and you're unbiased. You work for, what, the Olin Foundation, which manufactures firearms . . .
>
> *Lott:* No I don't. I work for the University of Chicago.
>
> *Beard:* Who pays your salary?
>
> *Lott:* The University of Chicago pays my salary.
>
> *Beard:* Through the Olin Foundation.
>
> *Lott:* No, that's not true.
>
> From *CNN Today,* June 18, 1999; 1:29 P.M. Eastern Time

Gun-control advocates all too frequently use these types of arguments in debates. Often callers on radio shows make similar claims. Even if the claim merely diverts the discussion away from whether guns save more lives than they cost, my guess is that the gun-control organizations view the personal attack as a success.[46] Unfortunately, no matter how many times I deny the charge or explain that no, I did not apply for money from the Olin Foundation; no, I was paid by the University of Chicago; no, the Olin Foundation and the Olin Corporation are separate entities; and no, it was the faculty at the University of Chicago who decided on my appointment and they asked no questions about my future research topics, many people still tune out after these charges are raised.

During 1999, numerous newspaper columns also made similar claims, for instance: "John R. Lott Jr., the latest darling of gun advocates everywhere. He's the Olin Fellow of Law and Economics at the University of Chicago School of Law. (That's 'Olin' as in Olin-Winchester, one of the world's leading manufacturers of ammunition)."[47] Or "They fail to mention that Lott is a John M. Olin fellow. This Olin Foundation is funded through the Olin Corp., the parent company of Winchester Ammunition. Winchester makes more money as the sale of handguns goes up."[48] Letter writers to newspapers have also chimed in: "It was particularly helpful that he exposed Professor John R. Lott Jr. as an intellectually dishonest toady of the bullet manufacturing industry."[49] Even after being given facts to the contrary, some state legislators have continued making claims like "The Lott study's been thrown out. . . . It's a joke. . . . Professor Lott is funded by the Olin Corporation which is funded by Winchester."[50] And, of course, Internet news-group discussions are filled with such assertions.[51] Others bring up the topic only to point out that while others believe it to be important, they do not personally believe that it is relevant.[52]

Gun-control groups have repeatedly attacked me rather than my findings and distorted the research I have done in other areas. State legislators in Michigan, Missouri, Nebraska, and Maryland have begun calling me up to ask whether it is true that I don't think that police departments should hire black or female police officers. Handgun Control and the Violence Policy Center spread claims such as "Lott has argued that the hiring of more women and minorities in law enforcement has actually increased crime rates."[53] They have made this claim on their Web sites, in debates, and on radio programs.[54] In fact, I had stated that this would be the wrong conclusion to reach. The paper argued: "But it would be a serious mistake not to realize that this simple relationship is masking that the new rules reduce the quality of new hires from other groups."[55] The affirmative action rules which changed the testing standards lowered the quality of new police hires across the board, and that was showing itself in the simple relationship between minority hires and crime.[56]

On the upside, many have come to my defense. One academic review of my book noted, "The personal (and, to those who know him, completely unfounded) attacks on John Lott's integrity were made with such ferocity and in so many media outlets nationwide that one can only conclude that Lott was, with apologies to our gracious First Lady, the target of a vast left-wing conspiracy to discredit his politically incorrect findings."[57] Another academic review wrote: "the ease with which gun-control advocates could get misleading and even false claims published by the press raises important public choice questions. Many of these claims were highly personal and vicious, including outright lies about alleged funding of Lott's research by the firearms industry . . . , about the outlet for his then forthcoming work . . . , about Lott's fringe ideas . . . , and about his lack of qualifications. . . . Most academics probably would have withdrawn back into the sheltered halls of their universities rather than expose themselves to the vicious public attacks that John Lott faced."[58] Other academics have written that "gun control groups attempted to discredit his work by smearing him with accusations that they had to know were patently false"[59] and about the "vicious campaign of lies and distortions."[60] Publications for police officer associations have also been very supportive.[61]

Once in a while, I have come to feel that there is a well-organized campaign to impugn my findings, especially on days when I have done radio talk shows for stations based in different parts of the country and callers state word for word the exact same charge that I have been paid to do my research by gun makers. Originally, I had thought that these personal attacks would fade away after a year or so, but they have now continued for three years, so unfortunately they will probably continue. The most disconcerting aspect of this, especially for my family, has been the numerous physical threats, including an instance of a note on our apartment door.[62]

Yet the gun-control organizations still realized that they had to do more to counter my work. In December 1996, Handgun Control had organized a debate that was broadcast on C-SPAN between myself and three critics: Dan Black, Dan Nagin, and Jens Ludwig. However, none of the researchers that they invited were able to claim that concealed-handgun laws increased crime. I can only imagine that this put Handgun Control in a bind. It is hard to oppose legislation or a referendum by arguing that concealed-handgun laws do no harm. Not being able to find support from the researchers that they work closely with, Handgun Control finally came out with its own numbers in a press release on January 18, 1999, arguing that between 1992 and 1997 violent-crime rates were falling more quickly in the states that most restricted concealed handguns than in the states with more liberal rules.

Their claim was widely and uncritically reported in publications from Newsweek to USA Today, as well as during the spring 1999 campaign to pass a concealed-handgun law in Missouri.[63] Press coverage and Handgun Control itself usually referred to this contention as coming from the FBI.[64]

Handgun Control examined the change in violent crime between only two years, 1992 and 1997, and strangely enough they chose to classify states according to what their laws were in 1997, at the end of the period. This odd classification makes a considerable difference, for some states' right-to-carry laws did not even go into effect until late 1996, with few permits issued until 1997. It makes no sense to attribute the increase in crime to a law for the five years before the law goes into effect. A third of the states with right-to-carry laws did not enact them until after late 1995. Of course, the way any trained researcher would approach the question is to separate the change in crime rates before and after the different states changed their laws. That is only common sense. Only changes in crime after the law goes into effect can be attributed to the passage of the law.

Given the evidence in this book, I would also argue that since one is examining the change in crime rates it is important to separate out those states that have had changes in permits and those that have not. If a state has had its right-to-carry law in place for decades, it is extremely unlikely that it will be experiencing any additional growth in permits and thus it should not be expecting any additional changes in its crime rates from this law. Handgun Control also did not account for any other factors that could have influenced crime. Nor did they even classify states consistently across their own press releases issued within months of each other.[65]

During the Missouri campaign, many reporters called me up to comment about the "FBI numbers" on crime rates.[66] When I would point out that the claim was actually based on a report produced by Handgun Control, they said that they didn't know what to do with the conflicting claims. Editorials and news stories in the *St. Louis Post-Dispatch* and the *Kansas City Star* normally just accepted the Handgun Control assertion as established truth.

After repeatedly encountering this response from reporters, I started suggesting to reporters that they ask some local academic (a statistician, criminologist, or economist) to evaluate the two conflicting claims. One reporter with the *St. Louis Post-Dispatch*, Kim Bell, expressed the concern that they might run into a professor with a preconceived bias and that would make the test unfair. I told her that I was willing to take that risk, but that if she were concerned about that problem, she could always approach a few different academics. Others who refused to take me up on this challenge included Bill Freivogel, deputy editor at the *Post-Dispatch*, and Rich Hood, an editor at the *Kansas City Star.* Rather, their newspapers simply presented Handgun Control's claims as fact.

Criticisms of the Book

Some reviewers clearly have not even bothered to read my book, or at least it didn't matter to them whether they read it. A review in the *British Journal of Criminology* claimed that "there is nothing in Lott's study to connect this more general information to the specific county-based data on the issuing of concealed-carry permits," "Lott is dealing with a time frame entirely prior to the introduction of the non-discretionary concealed-carry laws in most of the states which now have them," and "he has pre-occupied himself exclusively with 'good guns' owned by 'good people.'"[67] Another book review, in the *New England Journal of Medicine,* starts off by falsely claiming that I "approvingly" quote Archie Bunker's suggestion to stop airplane hijacking by arming "all the passengers."[68]

As of this writing (September 1999), Handgun Control's Web site still continues to assert the same "major criticisms" of my research—"where are the robbery effects?" "auto theft as a substitute for rape," "Lott fails to account for other initiatives—including other gun control laws," "Lott fails to account for cyclical changes in crime rates"—and the same claims about misclassifying state laws.[69] Ironically, they also continue citing the McDowall et. al. (1995) study that we discussed in chapter 2, which examined a total of only five counties picked from three states, attempted to account for no other factors that might be changing over the same period of time, and examined only murders with guns.[70]

Time magazine reported that "Other critics raise questions about whether Lott massaged the numbers. One arcane quarrel: for statistical purposes, Lott dropped from his study sample any counties that had no reported murders or assaults for a given year."[71] It also said that "the book does not account for fluctuating factors like poverty levels and policing techniques." After the story on my book ran, I called up the reporter, Romesh Ratnesar, and said that I knew that he had read the book carefully, so I was surprised that he would write these claims as if they were true. I, as well as critics like Black and Nagin, had looked at the evidence once arrest rates were excluded so as to include those counties with zero arrest rates. What was particularly disappointing was that I had spent the time to obtain all the data that were available. The county-level data were used for all the years and for all the counties for which they were available, both when I did the original paper and when I wrote the book. As to the other claim, I had measures of poverty and policing techniques like the broken-window strategy included.

While I appreciated that the *Time* magazine piece was published, claims that "the book does not account" for these factors are clearly wrong. Ratnesar agreed that these issues were dealt with in the book, but that his role was not to serve as a "referee" between the two sides. His job was to report what the claims were.[72]

I keep on being amazed at the absolute faith that so many news media people place in the gun-control organizations and the "facts" issued by them. Take another example: Molly Ivins, a syndicated columnist, asserted that "[Lott] himself admits, he didn't look at any other causative factors—no other variables, as they say."[73] She also argued that "Lott's study supposedly showed that when 10 Western states passed 'right-to-carry' laws between 1985 and 1992, they had less violent crime" and that "according to the author's research, getting rid of black women older than 40 would do more to stop murder than anything else we could try." Syndicated columnist Tom Teepen wrote a very similar column a year earlier in which he also claimed that this book "failed to consider other anti-crime variables in making its cause-and-effect claims, a fundamental gaffe."[74]

I did get a chance to talk with Mr. Teepen, and he told me that he wrote his review without even reading the book. He apparently relied on conversations that he had with people at Handgun Control and the Violence Policy Center. When I talked to Cynthia Tucker, an editor at the *Atlanta Journal-Constitution,* where Mr. Teepen is based, about having a letter responding to the charges Mr. Teepen made, she found it "unbelievable" that he would have written the review without first looking at the book. She grudgingly said that if it were true, they would publish as a response a short letter, but that she would have to check into it first. Needless to say, the newspaper published my letter the following Sunday.[75] In contrast, unfortunately, Ms. Ivins never returned my telephone calls or responded to my E-mail messages and never corrected her claims.[76]

Undoubtedly, some of the claims constitute simple mistakes, but more than a few reflect columnists and others being too quick to accept whatever gun-control groups tell them. I will spare the reader the long list of other false claims reported in the press.[77] Yet, obviously, many people, particularly those with gun-control organizations, continually make statements that they know are false—safe in the knowledge that only a tiny fraction of readers or listeners ever check the assertions. Unfortunately, the gun-control organizations risk losing significant credibility only with the few who read the book.[78]

Other critiques by academics and the media—some old, some new—require more in-depth discussions. The rest of this section reviews the critiques and then provides my responses.

1 *How do we know that these findings are not a result of the normal ups and downs in crime rates?*

The central problem is that crime moves in waves, yet Lott's analysis does not include variables that can explain these cycles. (David Hemenway, "Book Review of *More Guns, Less Crime,*" *New England Journal of Medicine,* December 31, 1998)

Jens Ludwig, assistant professor of public policy at Georgetown University, argued that Lott's data don't prove "anything about what laws do to crime." He noted that crime rates, including homicide, are cyclical: They rise and fall every five to 10 years or so in response to forces that are not well understood. Ludwig suggested that this pattern explains the apparent effectiveness of concealed weapons laws. Imagine, he said, a state where the murder cycle is on the upswing and approaching its peak and public concern is correspondingly high. Then a particularly ghastly mass shooting occurs. Panicked legislators respond by passing a law that allows equally panicked citizens to carry concealed weapons. A year or two later, the murder rate goes down, as Lott's study found. (Richard Morin, "Guns and Gun Massacres: A Contrary View," *Washington Post*, May 30, 1999, p. B5)

Lott's variables are not good predictors of crime waves. Nor does he provide for any effect of history in the way he models crime. For example, the year 1982 could as well follow 1991 as 1981 in his analyses. (David Hemenway, "More Guns, Less Crime," *New England Journal of Medicine*, May 20, 1999)

Even my most determined critics concede one point: violent-crime rates fell at the point in time that the right-to-carry laws went into effect. The real question is: Why did the crime rates fall? Do these laws simply happen to get passed right when crime rates hit their peaks? Why don't we observe this coincidence of timing for other gun-control laws?

It is logically possible that such coincidental timing could take place. But there is more evidence besides decreases in crime after right-to-carry laws are adopted. First, the size of the drop is closely related to the number of permits issued (as indicated in the first edition and confirmed by the additional data shown here). Second, the new evidence presented here goes even further: it is not just the number of permits, but also the type of people who obtain permits that is important. For example, high fees discourage the poor, the very people who are most vulnerable to crime, from getting permits. Third, if it is merely coincidental timing, why do violent-crime rates start rising in adjacent counties in states without right-to-carry laws exactly when states which have adopted right-to-carry laws are experiencing a drop in violent crime?

Finally, as the period of time studied gets progressively longer, the results are less likely to be due to crime cycles, since any possible crime "cycles" involve crime not only going down but also "up." If crime happened to hit a peak, say, every ten years, and right-to-carry laws tended to be passed right at the peak, then the reported effect of the law would spuriously show a negative impact right after the enactment. However, five years after that an equally large positive spurious effect on crime would have to show up. Instead, my results reveal permanent reductions in crime that only become larger with time, as more people acquire concealed-carry permits.

Furthermore, my study accounted for possible crime cycles in many ways: individual year variables accounted for average national changes in crime rates, and different approaches in chapter 4 controlled for individual state and county time trends and did not take away the effects of concealed carry. To the contrary, they resulted in similar or even stronger estimates for the deterrence effect. Other estimates used robbery or burglary rates to help account for any left-out factors in explaining other crime rates. Since crime rates generally tend to move together, this method also allows one to detect individual county trends. In updating the book, I have included estimates that account for the separate average year-to-year changes in five different regions in the country. Despite all these additional controls the deterrence effect continues to show up strongly.

It is simply false to claim, "nor does he provide for any effect of history," as I have variables that account for "changes" in crime rates from previous years. I have variables that measure explicitly the number of years that the law has been in effect as well as the number of years until it goes into effect. In addition, I have used individual state linear time trends that explicitly allow crime rates to change systematically over time.

Earlier discussions in chapter 7 on crime cycles (pp. 130–31) and causality (pp. 152–54) also explain why these concerns are misplaced.

2   *Does it make sense to control for nonlinear time trends for each state?*

> The results suggest that the Lott and Mustard model, which includes only a single national trend, does not adequately capture local time trends in crime rates. To test for this possibility, we generalized the Lott and Mustard model to include state-specific trends in an effort to control for these unobserved factors. . . . we report the results for models with a quadratic time trend. The only significant impact estimate is for assaults, and its sign is positive, not negative. (Dan Black and Dan Nagin, "Do Right-to-Carry Laws Deter Violent Crime?" *Journal of Legal Studies,* January 1998, p. 218)

Much more was controlled for than "a single national trend" in my study (e.g., as just mentioned above, state and county trends as well as other crime rates). While it is reasonable to include individual linear state trends or nonlinear trends for regions, including nonlinear trends for individual states makes no sense. The approach by Black and Nagin is particularly noteworthy because it is the one case in which an academic study has claimed that a statistically significant, even if small, increase in any type of violent crime (aggravated assault) occurs after the law.

Consider a hypothetical case in which the crime rate for each and every state follows the pattern that Black and Nagin found in their earlier paper and that I showed in this book (discussed in chapter 7, pp. 136–37): crime rates were rising up until the law went into effect and falling thereafter. Allowing a separate quadratic time trend for each state results in the time trend picking up both the upward path before the law and the downward path thereafter. If the different state crime patterns all peaked in the year in which their state law went into effect, the state-specific quadratic trends would account for all the impact of the law. A variable measuring the average crime rates before and after the law would then no longer reflect whether the law raised or lowered the crime rate.[79] This is analogous to the "dubious variable" problem discussed earlier. If enough state-specific trends are included, there will be nothing left for the other variables to explain.

If shall-issue laws deter crime, we would expect crime rates to rise until the law was passed and then to rise more slowly or to fall. The effect should increase over time as more permits are issued and more criminals adjust to the increased risks that they face. But the quadratic specification used by Black and Nagin replicates that pattern, state by state. Their results show not that the effect from the quadratic curve is insignificant, but that the deviation of the law's effect from a quadratic curve over time is generally insignificant.

To see this more clearly, take the hypothetical case illustrated in figure 9.15, in which a state faced rising crime rates.[80] The figure shows imaginary data for crime in a state that passed its shall-issue law in 1991. (The dots in the figure display what the crime rate was in different years.) The pattern would clearly support the hypothesis that concealed-handgun laws deter violent crime, but the pattern can easily be fitted with a quadratic curve, as demonstrated with the curved line. There is no systematic drop left over for any measure of the right-to-carry law to detect— in terms of the figure, the difference between the dots and the curved line shows no particular pattern.

Phrased differently, the deterrence hypothesis implies a state-specific time pattern in crime rates (because different states did or did not pass shall-issue laws, or passed them at different dates). All Black and Nagin have shown is that they can fit such a state-specific pattern with a state-specific quadratic time trend, and do this well enough that the residuals no longer show a pattern.

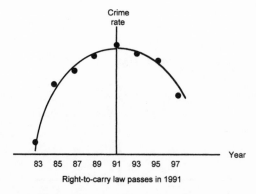

Figure 9.15. Fitting a nonlinear trend to individual states

3   *Should one expect an immediate and constant effect from right-to-carry laws with the same effect everywhere?*

While he includes a chapter that contains replies to his critics, unfortunately he doesn't directly respond to the key Black and Nagin finding that formal statistical tests reject his methods. The closest he gets to addressing this point is to acknowledge "the more serious possibility is that some other factor may have caused both the reduction in crime rates and the passage of the law to occur at the same time," but then goes on to say that he has "presented over a thousand [statistical model] specifications" that reveal "an extremely consistent pattern" that right-to-carry laws reduce crime. Another view would be that a thousand versions of a demonstrably invalid analytical approach produce boxes full of invalid results. (Jens Ludwig, "Guns and Numbers," *Washington Monthly,* June 1998, p. 51)[81]

We applied a number of specification tests suggested by James J. Heckman and V. Joseph Hotz. The results are available from us on request. The specifics of the findings, however, are less important than the overall conclusion that is implied. The results show that commonly the model either overestimates or underestimates the crime rate of adopting states in the years prior to adoption. (Dan Black and Dan Nagin, "Do Right-to-Carry Laws Deter Violent Crime?" *Journal of Legal Studies,* January 1998, p. 218)

Black and Nagin actually spent only a few brief sentences on this issue at the very end of their paper. Nevertheless, I did respond to this general point in the original book. Their test is based upon the claim that I believe "that [right-to-carry] laws have an impact on crime rates that is constant over time."[82] True, when one looks at the simple before-and-after average crime rates, as in the first test presented in table 4.1 and

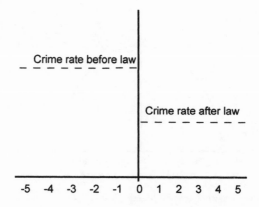

Years before and after implementation of the law

Figure 9.16. What was the crime pattern being assumed in the simple test provided in table 4.1?

a corresponding table in my original work with Mustard, this was the assumption that was being made.[83] Figure 9.16 illustrates the crime pattern assumed by that test. But I emphasized that looking at the before-and-after averages was not a very good way to test the impact of the right-to-carry laws (e.g., see p. 90), and I presented better, more complicated specifications which showed even larger benefits from these laws. Black and Nagin's test confirms the very criticisms that I was making of these initial simplifying assumptions.

Looking at the before-and-after averages merely provides a simplified starting point. If criminals respond to the risk of meeting a potential victim who is carrying a concealed handgun, the deterrent effect of a concealed-handgun law should be related to the number of concealed handguns being carried and that should rise gradually over time. It was precisely because of these concerns that I included a variable for the number of years since the law had been in effect. As consistently demonstrated in figure 1 in my original paper as well as the figures in this book (e.g., pp. 77–79), these estimated time trends confirm that crime rates were rising before the law went into effect and falling afterward, with the effect increasing as more years went by.

As already discussed in the book, I did not expect the impact to be the same across all states, for obviously all states cannot be expected to issue permits at the same rate (see the response to point 3 on pp. 131–32). Indeed, this is one of the reasons why I examined whether the drops in crime rates were greatest in urban, high-population areas.

On this issue David Friedman, a professor at the University of Santa Clara Law School, wrote that "The simplifying assumptions used in one of the regressions reported in the Lott and Mustard paper (Table 3) are not true—something that should be obvious to anyone who has read Lott and Mustard's original article, which included a variety of other regressions designed to deal with the complications assumed away in that one. Black and Nagin simply applied tests of the specification to demonstrate that they were not true."[84] Similar points have also been raised in academic reviews of the book: "Another tactic was to criticize one part of the research by raising issues that Lott actually raised and addressed in another part of the study. Those criticisms that were not uninformed or misleading were generally irrelevant since taking them into account did not change his empirical results. Nonetheless, they were widely cited by an unquestioning press."[85]

4   *Can changes in illegal drug use explain the results?*

> Even though Lott's fixed effects regressions will correct for some of the unobserved differences between the two groups of states [shall-issue and non-shall-issue states], we worry in particular that the crack induced crime jump in the mid-1980s in the states that did not pass shall issue laws may account for the apparent crime-reducing effects of the concealed-handgun laws. The omission of crack-related explanatory variables may have spuriously correlated lower crime with the passage of shall issue laws instead of correctly relating higher crime to the introduction of crack. The adoption of shall issue laws by six states in the 1980s may be associated with an unexpected crime rate increase in states that did not pass the laws rather than a concealed-gun-induced decrease in state that did. Two testable conclusions flow from our crack hypothesis: 1) Lott's results may not be robust to changes in specification that more fully capture differences in states that adopt or shun shall issue laws and 2) Lott's results may become weaker as additional years of data are added (because crack-related crime seems to have been declining sharply, giving the nonadopting states a relatively better crime performance in the last five years). (Ian Ayres and John J. Donohue III, "Nondiscretionary Concealed Weapons Laws: A Case Study of Statistics, Standards of Proof, and Public Policy," *American Law and Economics Review* 1, nos. 1–2 [Fall 1999]: 464–65)

Their concern over cocaine- or crack-induced crime is surely a legitimate one, and it must be examined for the research to be convincing. Indeed, if the accessibility of cocaine or crack were primarily a problem in non-right-to-carry areas, they might experience a relative increase in crime, particularly for murder. Using the simplest approach—of using variables to account for national changes in crime between years—would not detect the differences in time trends then between shall-issue and non-shall-issue states. Still, the original tests in this book did address this problem in many different ways.

While it is difficult to directly measure the violence-inducing influence of cocaine or crack, I do attempt to measure directly the relative accessibility of cocaine in different markets. For example, the book and the original paper reported that including price data for cocaine (pp. 279–80, n. 8) did not alter the results. Using yearly county-level pricing data also has the advantage of detecting cost and not demand differences between counties, thus measuring the differences in availability across counties.[86] The simplest regressions did use only national year dummy variables, but other attempts were made to account for differences in time trends by including either individual state or county trends. Ayres and Donohue argue that the differences in time trends between states with right-to-carry laws and those without such laws are really due to the crack cocaine market. If the differences in trends that Ayres and Donohue describe actually exist, these state or county trends (particularly the county-level ones) should account for this. However, including these trends actually strengthens the results, which is the opposite of what Ayres and Donohue predict.

The spillover effects on neighboring counties strongly undermine their critique. Earlier we examined the crime rates for counties within either fifty or one hundred miles of each other on either side of a state border (the reported results are based on counties whose county centers are within fifty miles of each other). Neighboring counties without right-to-carry laws directly on the other side of the border experienced an increase in violent crime precisely when the counties adopting the law were experiencing a drop. But that is not all. The size of the spillover is larger if the neighboring counties are closely matched to each other in population density. In other words, criminals in more urban areas (as measured by population density) are more likely to move across the border if the neighboring county is also urban. Ayres and Donohue argue that different parts of the country may have experienced different impacts from the crack epidemic. Yet if you have two urban counties next to each other, how can the Ayres and Donohue discussion explain why one urban county would face a crime increase from drugs when the neighboring urban county is experiencing a drop? Such an isolation would be particularly surprising given that these counties are known to be closely tied to each other in terms of criminals moving between them.

The timing of changes in right-to-carry laws also makes their argument less plausible. Ayres and Donohue do not explain why the local changes in the cocaine market just happen to coincide with the passage of right-to-carry laws, which have occurred at very different times in different states.

Other points are relevant to this issue. While the violent-crime rates fell across the entire state, the biggest drops occurred in the most crime-prone, heavily urbanized areas. Even if states that tend to adopt right-to-carry laws also "tend to be Republican and have high NRA membership and low crime rates" and thus to be less typical of the states where crack is a problem, there still exist high-crime counties within the state that do not fit the overall state profile. Indeed, it is those densely populated, high-crime counties that experience the biggest drops in violent crime. Finally, using the data up through 1996 produces similar results. Since so many states adopted right-to-carry laws at different times during the 1990s, it is not clear how cocaine or crack can account for the particular pattern claimed by Ayres and Donohue. Indeed, if anything, since the use of cocaine appears to have gradually spread to more rural states over time and subsided in areas where it had originally been a problem, the differences in trend that they are concerned about may have even been the reverse of what they conjecture.

5   *Do right-to-carry laws significantly reduce the robbery rate?*

Was there substitution from violent crime to property crime? Lott found that the laws were associated with an increase in property crime. . . . Lott argues that this change occurred because criminals respond to the threat of being shot while committing such crimes as robbery by choosing to commit less risky crimes that involve minimal contact with the victim. Unfortunately for this argument, the law was not associated with a significant decrease in robberies. In fact, when data for 1993 and 1994 was included, it was associated with a small (not statistically significant) increase in robberies. The law was associated with a significant reduction in assaults, but there does not seem to be any reason why criminals might substitute auto theft for assault. (Tim Lambert, "Do More Guns Cause Less Crime?" from his posting on his Web site at the School of Computer Science and Engineering, University of New South Wales [http://www.cse.unsw.EDU.AU/~lambert/guns/lott/])

Q. What's your take on John Lott's study and subsequent book that concludes concealed weapon laws lower the crime rate? (Lott's book is titled "More Guns, Less Crime," University of Chicago Press, 1998.)

A. His basic premise in his study is that these laws encourage private citizens to carry guns and therefore discourage criminal attacks, like homicides and rapes. Think for a second. Most murders and rapes occur in homes. So where would you see the greatest impact if his premise were true? You would see it in armed robbery. But there's no effect on armed robbery. His study is flawed, but it's costing us enormous problems. People are citing it everywhere. (Quote in the St. Paul, Minnesota, newspaper the *Pioneer Planet,* August 3, 1998, from an interview with Bob Walker, president of Handgun Control, Inc.)

Both the preceding quotes and many other criticisms are based on not recognizing that a law can be associated with reduced crime even when the average crime rate in the period after the law is the same as or higher than the average crime rate before the law.[87] For example, look at the four diagrams in figure 9.17. The first two diagrams show dramatic changes in crime rates from the law, but very different before-and-after average crime rates. In the first diagram (17*a*), the average crime rate after the law is lower than the average crime rate before it, while the reverse is true in the second diagram. The second diagram (17*b*) corresponds to an example in which the simple variable measuring the average effect from the law would have falsely indicated that the law actually "increased" the average crime rate, while in actual fact the crime rate was rising right up

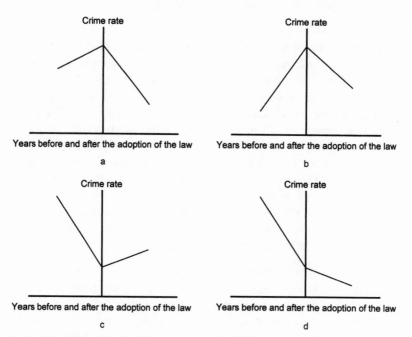

Figure 9.17. Why looking at only the before-and-after average crime rates is so misleading

until the law passed and falling thereafter. If I had another figure where the inverted V shape was perfectly symmetrical, the before-and-after averages would have been the same. (With this in mind, it would be useful to reexamine the earlier estimates for robbery shown in figures 4.8 and 7.4.)

The third diagram (17c) illustrates the importance of looking at more than simple before-and-after averages in another way. A simple variable measuring the before-and-after averages would indicate that the average crime rate "fell" after the law was adopted, yet once one graphs out the before-and-after trends it is clear that this average effect is quite misleading—the crime rate was falling until the law went into effect and rising thereafter. Finally, the fourth diagram (17d) shows a case in which the average crime rate is obviously lower after the law than beforehand but the drop is merely a continuation of an existing trend. Indeed, if anything, the rate of decline in crime rates appears to have slowed down after the law. Looking at the simple before-and-after averages provides a very misleading picture of the changing trends in crime rates.

6 *Is the way criminals learn about victims' ability to defend themselves inconsistent with the results?*

Zimring and Hawkins observe that there are two potential transmission mechanisms by which potential criminals respond to the passage of a shall issue law. The first, which they term the announcement effect, changes the conduct of potential criminals because the publicity attendant to the enactment of the law makes them fear the prospect of encountering an armed victim. The second, which they call the crime hazard model, implies that potential criminals will respond to the actual increased risk they face from the increased arming of the citizenry. Lott adheres to the standard economist's view that the latter mechanism is the more important of the two—but he doesn't fully probe its implications. Recidivists and individuals closely tied to criminal enterprises are likely to learn more quickly than non-repeat criminals about the actual probability of encountering a concealed weapon in a particular situation. Therefore, we suspect that shall issue laws are more likely to deter recidivists. . . . Thus, if Lott's theory were true, we would also suspect that the proportion of crime committed by recidivists should be decreasing and that crime categories with higher proportions of recidivism—and robbery is likely in this category—should exhibit the highest reductions. Once again, though, the lack of a strong observed effect for robbery raises tensions between the theoretical predictions and Lott's evidence. (Ian Ayres and John J. Do-

nohue III, "Nondiscretionary Concealed Weapons Laws: A Case Study of
Statistics, Standards of Proof, and Public Policy," *American Law and Economics
Review* 1, nos. 1–2 [Fall 1999]: 458–59)

I have always viewed both the mentioned mechanisms as plausible. Yet
the question of emphasis is an empirical issue. Was there a once-and-for-
all drop in violent crimes when the law passed? Did the drop in violent
crimes increase over time as more people obtained permits? Or was there
some combination of these two influences? The data strongly suggest
that criminals respond more to the actual increased risk, rather than the
announcement per se. Indeed, all the data support this conclusion: table
4.6, the before- and after-law time trends, the county-level permit data
for Oregon and Pennsylvania, and the new results focusing on the predicted percentage of the population with permits. The deterrence effect
is closely related to the percentage of the population with permits.

I have no problem with Ayres and Donohue's hypothesis that criminals who keep on committing a particular crime will learn the new risks
faster than will criminals who only commit crimes occasionally.[88] However, that hypothesis will be difficult to evaluate, for data on the number
and types of crimes committed by criminals are known to be notoriously
suspect, as they come from surveys of criminals themselves. Some of the
criminals appear to be bragging to surveyors and claim many thousands
of crimes each year. But one thing is clear from these surveys: criminals
often commit many different types of crimes, and hence it is generally
incorrect to say that criminals only learn from one type of crime. In any
case, even if Ayres and Donohue believe that robbers are more likely to
learn from their crimes, the estimated deterrent effect on robbery turns
out to be very large when the before-and-after trends are compared.[89]

It is interesting that one set of critiques attacks me for allegedly assuming a once-and-for-all drop in crime from right-to-carry laws (see point
3 above), while at the same time I am attacked for assuming that the
drop can be related only to the number of permits issued.

7 *Have prominent "pro-gun" researchers questioned the findings in my book?*

To dispel the notion that Lott is simply being victimized by the "PC
crowd," it may be helpful to mention the reaction of Gary Kleck, a Florida
State criminologist known for his generally "pro-gun" views. . . . Kleck
argues in his recent book that it is "more likely [that] the declines in crime
coinciding with relaxation of carry laws were largely attributable to other
factors not controlled in the Lott and Mustard analysis." (Jens Ludwig,
"Guns and Numbers," *Washington Monthly*, June 1998, p. 51)

Even Gary Kleck, a researcher long praised by the NRA and identified as an authority on gun-violence prevention by Lott himself, has dismissed the findings. (Sarah Brady, "Q: Would New Requirements for Gun Buyers Save Lives? Yes: Stop Deadly, Unregulated Sales to Minors, at Gun Shows and on the Internet," *Insight*, June 21, 1999, p. 24)

The quote by Kleck has frequently been mentioned by Jim and Sarah Brady and other members of Handgun Control and the Violence Policy Center.[90] However, it is a rather selective reading of what he wrote. Their claim that Kleck "dismissed the findings" is hard to reconcile with Kleck's comment in the very same piece that my research "represents the most authoritative study" on these issues.[91]

Let me try to explain the meaning of Kleck's quote. I have talked to Gary on several occasions about what additional variables I should control for, but he has been unable to concretely suggest anything; it rather seemed to be more a "feeling" of his that there might be other factors out there. But the issue is more complicated than simply stating that something else should be accounted for: there must exist some left-out factor that just happened to be changing in all the twenty states that had enacted right-to-carry laws for at least a year between 1977 and 1996. Perhaps one can find some left-out national change in some specific year, yet this would not have much of an effect on the regression results.

Gary Kleck has long felt strongly that guns have no net effect on the crime rate. Why he has felt that way has never been clear to me (though I have asked), especially considering his own survey results, which indicate that citizens use guns to stop violent crime about 2.5 million times each year—a large order of magnitude bigger than the reported number of crimes committed with guns.[92] Thus, the couple of sentences that gun-control advocates refer to from what Gary has written about my research did not totally surprise me. Gary told me that he thought it was "quite amusing" that people from Handgun Control and other gun-control organizations were now starting to cite him as an expert. He also said that he thought that the quotes were being misused, and that he still stood by the blurb for my book—the blurb stating that my research represented "the most extensive, thorough, and sophisticated study we have on the effects of loosening gun control laws."

8 *Do concealed-handgun permit holders pose a risk to others?*

But Susan Glick, a researcher for the Violence Policy Center in Washington, a research group that focuses on gun laws found that many people issued concealed-weapons permits in Texas, a state with comparatively loose gun laws, had run afoul of the law. Some 15 people in Texas out of perhaps 200,000 who were issued permits to carry concealed weapons since 1996 have been charged with murder or attempted murder, Ms. Glick said. (Dirk Johnson, "Divided Missouri to Vote on a Right to Carry Concealed Guns," *New York Times,* April 2, 1999, p. A16)

In states with lax CCW [concealed carry weapon] laws, hundreds of licensees have committed crimes both before and after their licensure. For example, in Texas, which weakened its CCW law in 1996, the Department of Public Safety reported that felony and misdemeanor cases involving CCW permit holders rose 54.4% between 1996 and 1997. (Douglas Weil, "Carrying Concealed Guns Is Not the Solution," Intellectualcapital.com, March 26, 1998)

Antigun activists complain that no reliable data exists linking concealed weapons to crime because the gun lobby has been successful in hiding it. (James N. Thurman, "As More Carry Hidden Guns, Who's Safer?" *Christian Science Monitor,* September 1, 1999, p. 1; Thurman was responding to my statement that "The kinds of people who go through the criminal background check and undergo the training aren't the kinds of people who commit the crimes")

The types of people who obtain permits tend to be extremely law abiding. That holds true for Texas as well as other states. Texas issued over 192,000 permits during the first three years of its right-to-carry law, from January 1, 1996, to December 31, 1998. Arrests for crimes "involving a gun" are a particularly misleading statistic, because someone who uses a gun defensively is likely to be arrested except if the police officer was completely sure that the person behaved properly. By March 1999, an Associated Press report stated that "only 515 of the charges . . . resulted in convictions, though some were still pending. . . . the bulk of the convictions against licensed concealed-handgun holders were misdemeanors, including 185 for drunken driving and 21 for prostitution. Felonies included 31 convictions for aggravated assault, six for assault causing bodily injury and five for aggravated sexual assault. No licensed handgun holder in Texas has been convicted of murder."[93] Tela Goodwin Mange, a Texas Department of Public Safety spokeswoman, noted that "The fact there are so few incidents relative to the number of people who have concealed handguns is a positive thing."

Doug Weil is indeed correct that Texas experienced a 54 percent increase in arrests between 1996 and 1997, but he fails to mention that the number of permits also increased by 50 percent between those two years, thus making the rate at which permit holders were arrested virtually unchanged. Weil's statement also makes it appear that the law changed between the two years, but the Texas law actually went into effect January 1, 1996.

Texas's experience is probably best summarized by Glenn White, president of the Dallas Police Association: "I lobbied against the law in 1993 and 1995 because I thought it would lead to wholesale armed conflict. That hasn't happened. All the horror stories I thought would come to pass didn't happen. No bogeyman. I think it has worked out well, and that says good things about the citizens who have permits. I am a convert."[94]

The experience has been similar in other states. The vast majority of revocations involve misdemeanors. Even when gun-related violations occur, the vast majority involve cases like carrying a gun into a restricted area like an airport. There is no evidence that any of these violations amounted to anything more than forgetfulness. The *National Journal* reported recently that permit holders "turn out to be unusually law-abiding, safer even than off-duty cops."[95]

Here are the revocation data for other states:

Alaska. Of the permits issued from January 1, 1995, to August 17, 1999, .3 percent were revoked for any reason. None involved the firing of a gun.[96]

Arizona. Of the permits issued between the end of the fall of 1994 and July 31, 1999, .1 percent were revoked, though up to half of these were revocations for "administrative reasons" (such as people dying or saying that they no longer required the permit).[97]

Florida. Of the permits issued during October 1, 1987, to February 28, 1999, .2 percent were revoked for any reason. Of these, 113, or .02 percent, were revoked for any type of firearms-related violations, and almost all of these were nonthreatening.[98]

Indiana. Of the active permit holders, .16 percent had their permits revoked or suspended for any reason during 1998.[99]

North Carolina. Of the permits issued between December 1, 1995, and August 4, 1999, .3 percent were revoked for any reason. While no detailed records exist for what reasons prompted revocations, those who oversaw the collection of the statistics could not recall hearing of any case of improperly firing a gun.[100]

Oklahoma. Of the permits issued from 1996 to August 1999, .1 percent were revoked for any reason.[101] Even these small numbers exaggerate the risks posed by permit holders, for some of these permit holders had their licenses "revoked" simply because they died. The Oklahoma Supreme

Court also recently ruled that the state had improperly revoked some permits for reasons unrelated to one's fitness to carry a concealed handgun.

South Carolina. Of the permits issued from July 1996 to August 16, 1999, .4 percent were revoked for any reason. No violations involved a permit holder firing a gun. Sometimes the reason for the revocation was relatively trivial. For instance, one person lost his permit for not keeping his gun properly hidden—he was not wearing a shirt so the gun could be seen extending above his pants' waistband.

Utah. Of the permits issued between the summer of 1994 and July 1999, .4 percent were revoked for any reason. Of these revocations, 80 percent resulted from drunk driving. No violations involved the firing of a gun by a permit holder in Utah.[102]

Wyoming. Of the permits issued during fall 1994 to July 1999, .2 percent were revoked for any reason. James M. Wilson, the supervisor for the permitting program, stated that "Revocations did not include any cases of discharging of a firearm."[103]

9   *Are the CBS and Voter News Service polls accurately reflecting how gun ownership rates vary across states?*

Douglas Weil: But the most important information is that the Voter News Service, which conducted the 1996 poll has said the poll cannot be used in the manner Dr. Lott used it. It cannot be used to say anything about gun ownership in any state, and it cannot be used to compare gun ownership to the earlier 1988 voter poll. ("More Guns, Less Crime? A Debate between John Lott, Author of *More Guns, Less Crime,* and Douglas Weil, Research Director of Handgun Control, Inc.," an on-line debate sponsored by *Time* magazine, transcript from July 1, 1998)

Statistics from the CBS and Voter News Service exit polls (discussed in chapters 3 and 5) were originally "weighted" by these organizations to reflect the share of different racial, sex, and age groups in the national population. For example, white females between thirty and thirty-nine make up 6 percent of the population but may end up accounting for a larger percentage of those surveyed in a poll. If white females in that age group are overrepresented in the calculations made to determine what voters support, the poll will not accurately reflect how voters as a whole will vote in an election. To correct this, polls were adjusted so that different groups are weighted according to their actual shares of either the voting or the general population. It is therefore necessary for the researcher to use a state's demographics to adjust that state's poll results

himself, because the shares that different groups make of state populations differ from their shares of the national population. That is precisely
what I did.

There were also differences in how the 1988 and 1996 surveys were
phrased, and I already discussed those biases right at the beginning of
chapter 3. In the notes accompanying that discussion, I mentioned that
these biases do not appreciably affect changes in survey results between
these two years. The important point is that the changes in how the questions were worded should not alter the relative ranking of states or what
types of people are more likely to own guns. Regressions using data from
the two years used variables that account for the average difference across
years as well as the average differences across states to account for any
biases.

10 *Have I ignored the costs of gun violence?*

> He ignores the huge cost on medical systems that gun violence causes.
> (Steve Young of the Bell Campaign, an anti-gun group, as quoted in Frank
> Main, "Economist Says Guns Fight Crime," *Chicago Sun-Times,* July 8, 1999,
> p. 6)

The costs of crime include medical or other costs of crime like lost time
from a job or replacement costs for damage and replacement costs for
items taken or destroyed. I do not ignore such costs. But unlike my critics, neither do I ignore the crimes that are stopped because people are
able to defend themselves. The net effect is what is relevant, and that is
directly measured by what happens to the number of crimes. To the extent that people commit crimes with permitted concealed handguns, the
number of crimes will rise. To the extent that such handguns deter criminals, the number of crimes will decline. When criminals substitute
different types of crimes, the issue then is how the medical and other
costs of those different crimes compare. As to the costs of different
crimes, I relied on a study produced the National Institute of Justice,
rather than produce my own independent numbers.

An interesting contrast to my work is a recent paper published in the
Journal of the American Medical Association which claimed to show that there
were "$2.3 billion in lifetime medical costs for people shot in 1994." Jens
Ludwig, one of the authors of the study, argues that "cities such as Chicago could use the study in their lawsuits against the gun industry."[104]
But the correct question is not whether guns involve medical costs but
whether total medical costs are greater with or without guns. The logic
is akin to determining whether police should be allowed to carry guns

only by looking at the number of wrongful shootings, and not the times that guns are used to protect officers or deter criminals. Eliminating guns will not eliminate violence and the costs associated with those attacks. Indeed, from a historical perspective, murder rates were higher in England before guns were invented. Medical costs also include costs from suicides and attempted suicides, and the evidence discussed in chapter 5 indicates that suicides will still occur at pretty much the same rate even if guns are not present. For example, crashing one's car in an attempt to kill oneself can produce substantial medical costs, but even methods like overdosing on sleeping pills or slitting one's wrists with a knife involve medical costs.

11 *What happens to the evidence when Florida and counties with fewer than 100,000 people are removed from the sample?*

> Lott does not respond to Black and Nagin's finding that excluding Florida and small counties (with population less than 100,000) from his samples destroys the statistical significance of all of the violent-crime categories except assault. This suggests that Lott's results are not as robust as he claims. True, Lott's thesis is not embarrassed by varying degrees of deterrence across states (especially since he shows that this variance may be related to the number of permits issued). However, his thesis is shaken by the considerable number of state specific crime categories where concealed-handgun laws are associated with an increase in crime and where the overall significance of his results is undermined by the exclusion of Florida and small counties. (Ian Ayres and John J. Donohue III, "Nondiscretionary Concealed Weapons Laws: A Case Study of Statistics, Standards of Proof, and Public Policy," *American Law and Economics Review* 1, nos. 1–2 [Fall 1999]: 463)

I thought that I had dealt with this issue in the book. Dropping all counties with fewer than 100,000 people plus Florida reduces the significance in regressions that examine only the average crime rates before and after the law is adopted. Making these changes increases the impact of the law when one examines the before-and-after trends. As the careful reader might guess, the reason that the before-and-after average is not significant for some crimes is that dropping all these observations actually causes the changes to look more like the inverted V that we have so frequently discussed. Picking and choosing which observations to include, which single specification to report, and even which crime categories to report (Black and Nagin do not report the overall violent-crime rates) allows them to knock down the significance of two of the crime categories. (By any standards that I know, a t-statistic of 1.9 for robberies is still statistically significant at better than the 5 percent level, and their co-efficient still implies a drop in before-and-after averages of 4.6 percent.) Dropping 87 percent of the sample and reporting only the specifications examining the before-and-after averages may be Black and Nagin's pre-ferred sample and specification, but even these results imply significant benefits and no cost from passing right-to-carry laws. If they had re-ported the overall violent-crime rate, they would have shown that over-all violent crime fell after the right-to-carry laws were passed.

Table 9.7 provides uses the updated data to examine the importance of dropping out counties with fewer than 100,000 people as well as Flor-ida. The impact of the law is greater for overall violent-crime rates and aggravated assaults and smaller for the other three violent-crime catego-ries. Each additional year after the law goes into effect produces an addi-tional 3 percent drop in violent-crime rates.

When Black and Nagin break down the differences by individual states, they claim to find three crime categories in which one of the ten states had a statistically significant increase in crime rates (West Virginia for murder, Mississippi for rape, and Pennsylvania for robbery). But their re-sults do not show the variation across states, for they are derived from only a small subset of observations from those states. The West Virginia sample included only one of its fifty-five counties, as it was the only one with more than 100,000 people. The Mississippi data included just three of its eighty-two counties. The results reported earlier in table 4.9 provide the information on how the right-to-carry laws affected the crime rates across states.

12 *Are the results valid only when Maine and Florida are included?*

I will try to summarize the argument here. Ian Ayres and John Donohue are concerned about the inclusion of Maine and Florida for several rea-sons: (1) the results discussed by Black and Nagin, (2) the issue of whether the crack epidemic might have just happened to cause the relative crime rates to rise in non-right-to-carry states in the late 1980s, and (3) objec-tions to whether Cramer and Kopel were correct in classifying Maine as a right-to-carry state. To satisfy their concerns, Ayres and Donohue use sev-eral different approaches, such as dropping both Maine and Florida out of the sample. They also divide the shall-issue dummy variable into two sep-arate variables: a variable to measure the average before-and-after crime rates for those states that adopted their right-to carry laws before Decem-ber 1987 (Maine and Florida) and a similar variable to measure the average before-and-after crime rates for those states that adopted their crime rates after December 1987.

Table 9.7 What is the impact of removing both counties with fewer than 100,000 people and Florida from the sample?

	Percent change in various crime rates for changes in explanatory variables							
	Violent crime	Murder	Rape	Robbery	Aggravated assault	Property crime	Burglary	Larceny	Auto theft
Change in the crime rate from the difference in the annual change in crime rates in the years before and after the adoption of the right-to-carry law (annual rate of change after the law – annual rate of change before the law)	–3.3%*	–0.45%****	–2.6%**	–3.0%*	–4.7%*	–0.8%	–2.1%**	–0.24%	–1.8%**

*The F-test is significant at the 1 percent level.
**The F-test is significant at the 5 percent level.
***The F-test is significant at the 10 percent level.
****The F-test is significant at the 15 percent level.

Ayres and Donohue find that violent-crime rates consistently fall in states adopting right-to-carry laws after 1987, but the effect is often statistically insignificant. The drops in violent crime appear much larger and more significant for the earlier states. Indeed, as reported earlier in this book, Maine and Florida experience two of the three largest overall drops in violent crime (see table 4.9). Yet the focus on the before-and-after averages again obscures the benefits from right-to-carry laws.

The results presented in table 9.8 take the two approaches that I have been using: the estimated number of permits issued in a state and the differences between the trends in crime rates before and after the adoption of the right-to-carry laws. With the exception of rape, Maine and Florida experience greater drops in all violent-crime categories, but all the violent-crime rates decline for states adopting right-to-carry laws during the post-1987 period and all but two of these declines are statistically significant at least at the 10 percent level. The estimates using the percentage of the population with permits imply that there were no statistically different effects for the two sets of states for murder and rape.

13 *Was it proper to assume that more permits were issued in the more populous counties after right-to-carry laws were adopted?*

> Since the links between the issuance of permits and the crime reduction that Lott attributes to the shall issue laws is so crucial to establishing causality, more research on this issue is needed. Lott's county population proxies rely on his assumption that population density is a good predictor of the difficulty in obtaining permits under discretionary laws. However, if many states went directly from prohibiting concealed weapons to a nondiscretionary law (like Arizona), Lott's assumed relationship between permits and density would break down. (Ian Ayres and John J. Donohue III, "Nondiscretionary Concealed Weapons Laws: A Case Study of Statistics, Standards of Proof, and Public Policy," *American Law and Economics Review* 1, nos. 1–2 [Fall 1999]: 446)

The original tests shown in figures 4.1 and 4.2 were based upon conversations that I had had with state officials in nondiscretionary states. If the state officials' claims were correct that high-population counties had been much more restrictive in issuing permits than low-population counties, adoption of right-to-carry laws would have seen the biggest issuance of permits in these counties and thus the biggest drops in crime. The results confirmed this prediction. Obviously, this claim depends upon all the states switching from discretionary to nondiscretionary laws, and indeed all the states examined for the tests shown in these earlier figures did make that change. None of the states during 1977–1992

Table 9.8 Reexamining the claim that states adopting the law before and after December 1987 were differently affected by right-to-carry laws

	Percent change in various crime rates for changes in explanatory variables								
	Violent crime	Murder	Rape	Robbery	Aggravated assault	Property crime	Burglary	Larceny	Auto theft
States adopting law prior to December 1987: one-percentage-point change in the share of the state population with permits to carry concealed handguns	−15.8%[a]	−5.4%[b]	−3.9%[d]	−9.7%[a]	−19.1%[a]	−15.5%[a]	−6.1%[a]	−22.6%[a]	−8.9%[a]
States adopting law after December 1987: one-percentage-point change in the share of the state population with permits to carry concealed handguns	−4.1%[a]	−2.7%[a]	−5.0[a]	−1.0%	−7.8%[a]	4.8%[a]	−2.0%[a]	8.7%	0.34%
States adopting law prior to December 1987: change in the crime rate from the difference in the annual change in crime rates in the	−7.2%*	−9.2%*	−0.9%	−7.1%*	−5.7%*	−2.4%*	−1.1%	−4.1%*	−4.1%*

years before and after the adoption of the right-to-carry law (annual rate of change after the law – annual rate of change before the law)						−0.7%¸	−2.4%*	0.5%*	−1.4%*
States adopting law after December 1987: change in the crime rate from the difference in the annual change in crime rates in the years before and after the adoption of the right-to-carry law (annual rate of change after the law – annual rate of change before the law)	−1.7%*	−0.7%***	−3.3%*	−2.9%*	−2.4%*			

aThe result is significant at the 1 percent level for a two-tailed t-test.
bThe result is significant at the 5 percent level for a two-tailed t-test.
cThe result is significant at the 10 percent level for a two-tailed t-test.
dThe result is significant at the 12 percent level for a two-tailed t-test.
*The F-test is significant at the 1 percent level.
**The F-test is significant at the 5 percent level.
***The F-test is significant at the 10 percent level.
****The F-test is significant at the 15 percent level.

switched from not issuing any permits to nondiscretionary rules. Arizona made its change in late 1994.

The updated results in the epilogue have continued to remain conscious of this issue, and I found that the more populous counties in states that changed from discretionary to nondiscretionary laws had bigger relative drops in violent-crime rates than states that changed from banning concealed handguns to nondiscretionary laws.

14 *Did the passage of right-to-carry laws result in more guns being carried in public places?*

> Perhaps by "more guns," Lott means more guns carried in public places. However, surveys indicate that 5–11% of US adults admit to carrying guns, dwarfing the 1% or so of the population that obtained concealed-weapon permits. . . . And if those who got permits were merely legitimating what they were already doing before the new laws, it would mean there was no increase at all in carrying or in actual risks to criminals. One can always speculate that criminals' perceptions of risk outran reality, but that is all this is—a speculation. More likely, the declines in crime coinciding with relaxation of carry laws were largely attributable to other factors not controlled in the Lott and Mustard analysis. (Tim Lambert, "Do More Guns Cause Less Crime?" from his posting on his Web site at the School of Computer Science and Engineering, University of New South Wales [http://www.cse.unsw.EDU.AU/~lambert/guns/lott/])

The survey results mentioned by Lambert refer to all transportation or carrying of guns by Americans. They include not only carrying concealed handguns (whether legally or illegally) but also people who have guns with them to go hunting or who may simply be transporting guns between residences.[105] On the other hand, any survey that focused solely on the illegal carrying of concealed handguns prior to the adoption of the law would find it difficult to get people to admit that they had been violating the law.

The 1 percent figure Lambert picks for carrying concealed handguns is also very misleadingly low. As I have shown in this book, permitting rates depend upon many factors (such as the level of fees and the amount of training required), but they also depend crucially on the number of years that the permitting rules have been in effect. The longer the amount of time that the rules are in effect, the more people who obtain permits. Not everyone who will eventually obtain a permit will apply for it immediately. With the large number of states that have only recently granted permits to people it is misleading to think that the current permit rate tells us the rate at which people in those states will be carrying concealed handguns even a few years from now.

Given how extremely law abiding these permit holders tend to be, it seems doubtful that most people carrying concealed handguns with permits were illegally carrying concealed handguns before the passage of the right-to-carry law. In many states, illegally carrying a concealed weapon would be the type of violation that would prevent people from ever even getting a permit. There is no evidence that these permit holders have violated this particular law. Yet even if as many as 10 percent of permit holders had previously been illegally carrying a concealed handgun, the coefficients from table 9.3 would still imply that for every 900 additional people with permits there are 0.3 fewer murders and 2.4 fewer rapes.

Finally, while the evidence linking the rate at which permits are issued and the drops in crime rates is important, it is only one portion of the evidence. For example, if there was no change in the number of people carrying concealed handguns, why did violent-crime rates in neighboring counties without the law increase at the same time that they were falling in neighboring counties with the right-to-carry law?

15 *Shouldn't permit holders be required to have the same type of training as police officers?*

> Proponents of [right-to-carry] legislation contend that citizens will be adequately trained to handle firearms responsibly, but this is rarely true. Police departments require officers to go through a great deal of safety and proficiency training before issued a gun—followed by regular refresher courses and qualifications throughout the officer's career. Citizens armed under the provisions of non-discretionary carry laws are not so highly trained, and frequently not trained at all, thereby further increasing the risk of injury and death with a firearm. (From the Web page of Handgun Control, Inc., entitled "Will the Real John Lott Please Stand Up?")

Police officers face a much more difficult job than citizens with concealed handguns. An officer cannot be satisfied if the criminal runs away after he brandishes a gun. Instead, police must act offensively, which is much more dangerous. Citizens are rarely put in situations that require the skill of pursuing an attacker.

There are both costs and benefits to training. Yet the question is ultimately an empirical one. Training requirements improve the deterrence effect for concealed-handgun laws, but the effects are small. What I do find is that longer training periods reduce the number of people obtaining permits, and the net effect of increased training is clearly to reduce the deterrent effect of adopting right-to-carry laws.

16 *Where does the academic debate stand?*

> In at least six articles published elsewhere, 10 academics found enough serious flaws in Lott's analysis to discount his findings completely. (David Hemenway, "Book Review of *More Guns, Less Crime,*" *New England Journal of Medicine,* December 31, 1998)

To date, I have shared my data with academics at forty-two different universities and researchers at two different policy think tanks. Everyone who tried was able to replicate my findings, and only three papers using the data have been critical of my general approach.[106] A more recent fourth piece might be viewed as mildly critical. Yet the vast majority of researchers concur that concealed handguns deter crime, and perhaps just as important, not even the critics claim to have found that they cost lives or increase crime. In the above quote, Hemenway is referring to only three studies that have examined the data. The other three pieces (to arrive at his total of six) basically merely cite these three critical papers.

Some authors—such as William Bartley and Mark Cohen or Carlisle Moody—use the original data and claim to have "found strong support for the hypothesis that the right-to-carry laws are associated with a decrease in the trend in violent crimes" or that their alternative specifications "confirm and reinforce the basic findings."[107] David Olson and Michael Maltz check the findings by using newly available county-level data from the Supplementary Homicide Report data in place of the FBI's Uniform Crime Report and obtain virtually the same drop in murders after the passage of the right-to-carry laws.[108] Others—including Florenz Plassmann and Nicolaus Tideman—contend that the reduction in murder rates is almost twice as large as I claimed. They conclude that their results "indicate that more guns generally lead to fewer rather than more murders, and that it would be wrong to dismiss right-to-carry laws on the ground that more guns mean more danger, without considering their discouraging effect on potential murders."[109]

Another paper by Florenz Plassman and Nicolaus Tideman examines the deterrent effects of right-to-carry laws both across states and over time. They find that all the states that adopted the laws between 1977 and 1992 experienced reductions in murder, rape, and robbery between the year the law was passed and the first, second and third full years that the law was in effect.[110] Other recent evidence by David Mustard suggests that right-to-carry laws help reduce the rate at which police are murdered.

The book reviews in economic journals have been favorable.[111] As one academic review claimed, "his empirical analysis sets a standard that will be difficult to match.... this has got to be the most extensive empirical study of crime deterrence that has been done to date.... The results are extremely robust, but they are also consistent with the theoretical principles."[112] Other academics from Northwestern University, the University of Texas, George Washington University, George Mason University, and Cardozo School of Law have also written supportive reviews.[113]

Yet, to me, the most remarkable thing about this debate is what goes unsaid. None of my academic critics has mentioned anything about the other gun-control laws that I have examined. Not a single academic has challenged my findings that the Brady law or state waiting periods or background checks caused some crime rates to increase. In fact, they have all avoided including these laws in their own research. Nonetheless, gun-control organizations, such as Handgun Control, to this day still attack me for supposedly not accounting for other gun-control laws in my research.

CONCLUSION

The noise came suddenly from behind early Tuesday—
feet rapidly pounding the pavement, voices cursing.
Before Jim Shaver could turn around, he was knocked to
the ground at East 13th Avenue and Mill Street, fighting
off punches from two young men. Police said the assail-
ants figured they'd found a drug dealer to rob, someone
who'd have both drugs and money. They couldn't have
been more wrong. Their victim was a 49-year-old nurse
on his way to work—a nurse with a concealed weapons
permit. The fists kept flying, even as Shaver told them—
twice, he said—that he had a gun. Fearing for his life,
Shaver pulled a .22-caliber revolver out of his coat
pocket and fired several shots. One of them hit 19-year-
old Damien Alexander Long in the right hip. Long's
alleged accomplice, Brandon Heath Durrett, 20, wasn't
injured. The pair ran off.[114]

A man who police said kidnapped a 2-year-old child and
robbed a disabled elderly woman of a medical monitor
was in jail Friday after he was captured and held at gun
point by a man with a license to carry a concealed handgun.... "I have never pulled a gun on anyone before,
and I wouldn't have pulled a gun on this man if he had
not run off with that little girl," [the man who stopped
the crime] said. "That mother was screaming for her
child. She was quite upset."[115]

Awe-struck Phoenix police declared Mr. Vertigan a hero and gave him $500 and a new pistol for catching a cop killer after running out of ammunition in a gunfight with three heavily armed men. Mr. Vertigan . . . came upon three armed Mexican drug-traffickers fatally ambushing a uniformed Phoenix policeman who was patrolling alone in Phoenix's tough Maryvale precinct. Firing 14 shots with his left hand during a slam-and-bump car chase that left the killers' license number imprinted on the front of his own car, Mr. Vertigan emptied his Glock 31 .357 Sig. He wounded the shooter, who was firing at him, and forced the getaway car to crash, slowing the shooter's partners long enough for pursuing police to seize them, as well as a pound of cocaine "eight balls" they were dealing from their white Lincoln. "I always felt that if my life was in danger or anyone around me was in immediate danger I never would hesitate to use that gun. Unfortunately, that day came," Mr. Vertigan said.[116]

A man who tried to commit an armed robbery at a Bensalem convenience store Friday morning was thwarted by a customer who pulled out his own gun and fired five shots at the crook. . . . Fearing he would be killed, police said, the customer began shooting at the suspect. . . . Police said the clerks were "a little shaken up" after the attempted robbery—but they guessed that the would-be robber was probably just as shocked. "I'll bet he never expected that to happen," said Fred Harran, Bensalem's deputy director of public safety.[117]

All these recent cases involved individuals with permitted concealed handguns. During 1999 concealed permit holders have prevented bank robberies, stopped what could have been a bloody attack by gang members at a teenage girl's high school graduation party, and stopped carjackings.[118] In the couple of months during which I was updating this book, armed citizens have helped capture murderers who had escaped prison, stopped hostage taking at a business which otherwise surely would have resulted in multiple deaths, and prevented robberies and rapes.[119] Residential attacks that were stopped by citizens with guns during 1999 were extremely common.[120]

One of the bigger puzzles to me has been the news coverage on guns. Admittedly, some of it is easy to explain. Suppose a media outlet has two stories to choose from: one in which there is a dead body on the ground and it is a sympathetic person like a victim, another in which a women brandishes a gun and the attacker runs away, no shots are fired, no dead bodies are on the ground, and no crime is actually consummated. It seems pretty obvious which story is going to get the news coverage. Yet if we really want to answer the question of which policies will save lives, we must take into consideration not only the newsworthy bad events but also the bad events that never happen because people are able to defend themselves. Unfortunately, the newsworthy bad events give people a warped impression of the costs and benefits from having guns around.

Even when defensive gun uses are mentioned in the press, those mentions do not focus on typical defensive gun uses. The news stories focus primarily on the extremely rare cases in which the attacker is killed, though a few times press stories do mention cases of a gun being used to seriously wound an attacker. News coverage of defensive gun uses in which a would-be victim simply brandished a gun are essentially unheard-of. I don't think one has to rely on a conspiracy explanation to understand why this type of news coverage occurs, for it is not that surprising that dead attackers are considered more newsworthy than prevented attacks in which nobody was harmed. Even so, it is still important to recognize how this coverage can color people's perspective on how guns are used defensively. Since most people probably are very reticent to take a life, if they believe that defensive gun use almost always results in the death of an attacker, they will become more uncomfortable with guns.

While these examples are easily understood, some other news coverage is not as obvious. Take the case of accidental gun deaths involving young children, which we discussed in chapter 1. My guess is that people believe these events to be much more frequent than they actually are. When I have given talks, I have sometimes asked the audience how many children under age five or ten die from accidental gun shots each year; the answers are frequently in the thousand-plus range. A few answers might mention only hundreds of deaths per year. No one comes close to the Centers for Disease Control numbers: seventeen accidental gun deaths for children under age five and forty-two for children under ten in 1996. The information that forty children under age five drown each year in five-gallon water buckets or that eighty drown in bathtubs always astounds the audience. People remember national news reports of young children dying from accidental handgun shots in the home. In contrast, when was the last time that you heard on the national news of a child drowning in a five-gallon water bucket?[121]

As a father of four boys, I can't imagine what life would be like if one of my sons died for any reason, including guns. But why so much more attention is given to guns when so many other risks pose a greater threat to our children is not immediately obvious to me. Indeed, it is difficult to think of anything other than guns that is as prevalent around American homes, and that is anywhere near as potentially dangerous, yet is responsible for as low an accidental death rate. With around 80 million people owning a total of 200–240 million guns, the vast majority of gun owners must be extremely careful or such gun accidents would be much more frequent.

I have asked some reporters why they think accidental gun deaths receive so much coverage, and the only answer seems to be that these events get coverage because they are so rare. Dog bites man is simply not newsworthy because it is so common, but man bites dog, well, that is news. Yet this explanation still troubles me, for there are other equally rare deaths involving children that get very little news coverage.

Another puzzle is the lack of coverage given to cases in which citizens with guns have prevented multiple-victim public shootings from occurring. Given the intense concern generated by these attacks, one would think that people would be interested in knowing how these attacks were stopped.

For a simple comparison, take the justified news coverage accorded the heroic actions of Dave Sanders, the Columbine High School teacher who helped protect some of the students and was killed in the process. By the Sunday morning five days after the incident, a Lexis-Nexis search (a type of on-line computer search that includes news media databases) indicates that over 250 of the slightly over 1,000 news stories around the country on this tragedy had mentioned this hero.

Contrast this with other school attacks in which the crimes were stopped well before the police were able to arrive. Take, for example, the October 1997 shooting spree at a high school in Pearl, Mississippi, described at the beginning of this section, which left two students dead. It was stopped by Joel Myrick, an assistant principal. He retrieved his permitted concealed handgun from his car and physically immobilized the shooter for about five minutes before police arrived.

A Lexis-Nexis search indicates that 687 articles appeared in the first month after the attack. Only 19 stories mentioned Myrick in any way. Only a little more than half of these mentioned he used a gun to stop the attack. Some stories simply stated Myrick was "credited by police with helping capture the boy" or that "Myrick disarmed the shooter." A later story reported by Dan Rather on CBS noted that "Myrick eventually subdued the young gunman." Such stories provide no explanation of how Myrick accomplished this feat.

The school-related shooting in Edinboro, Pennsylvania, which left one teacher dead, was stopped only after James Strand, the owner of a nearby restaurant, pointed a shotgun at the shooter when he was finishing reloading his gun. The police did not arrive until eleven minutes later. At least 596 news stories discussed this crime during the next month, yet only 35 mentioned Strand. Once again, the media ignored that a gun was used to stop the crime. The *New York Daily News* explained that Strand "persuaded [the killer] to surrender," while the *Atlanta Journal* wrote how he "chased [the killer] down and held him until police came." Saying that Strand "persuaded" the attacker makes it sound as if Strand were simply an effective speaker.

Neither Myrick nor Strand was killed during their heroics. That might explain why they were ignored to a greater degree than Dave Sanders in the Columbine attack. Yet one suspects a more politically correct explanation—especially when the media generally ignore defensive gun use. With five public-school-related shootings occurring during the 1997–1998 school year, one might have thought that the fact that two of them were stopped by guns would register in the public debate over such shootings.

The press's bias can be amply illustrated by other examples as well. Take the example of the July attack in Atlanta that left nine people dead. Mark Barton killed people working at two stock brokerages.[122] It did deserve the extensive news coverage that it received. Yet within the next week and a half there were three cases around Atlanta in which citizens with guns stopped similar attacks from occurring, and these incidents were given virtually no news coverage. They were an attack at a Lavonia, Georgia, store by a fired worker, an attack by a mental patient at an Atlanta hospital, and an Atlanta truckjacking.[123] The last two incidents were stopped by citizens with permitted concealed handguns, while the first was stopped by someone who had only been allowed to buy a gun hours before the attack because of Georgia's instant background check system. Meanwhile, a week after the Atlanta massacre, another attack, which left three people dead at a Birmingham, Alabama, business, again generated national television news coverage on all the networks and was the lead story on the CBS and NBC evening news.[124]

Again, I can see that bad events that never occur are not nearly as newsworthy as actual bad events. Yet multiple-victim attacks using methods other than guns are frequently ignored. On May 3, 1999, Steve Abrams drove his Cadillac into a crowded preschool playground because he "wanted to execute innocent children."[125] Two children died horrible deaths as one was mangled under the wheels and the other pinned to a tree by the car, and another five were badly injured. One woman's son was so badly mauled that "teachers and other parents stepped between [her] and the Cadillac to prevent her from seeing her son's battered body" even though he was still alive. Yet only one television network provided even a passing reference to this attack.[126] One very obvious news angle, it seems to me, would be to link this attack to the various public school attacks. Compare this news coverage with the attention generated by Buford Furrow's August 10, 1999, assault on a Jewish community center, which left five people wounded, three of them young boys.[127] Multiple-victim knife attacks have been ignored by the national media, and few people would realize that there were 1,884 bombing incidents in the United States in 1996, which left a total of 34 people dead and 365 people injured.[128]

The news coverage is also constantly framed as, Is more gun control the answer?[129] The question is never asked, Have increased regulations encouraged these attacks by making potential victims more vulnerable? Do these attacks demonstrate the importance of letting people be able to defend themselves?

We are constantly bombarded with pro-gun-control claims. While my research, when it is referred to in the press, is labeled as "controversial" or worse, the claims from the Clinton administration and Handgun Control, Inc., are reported without reference to any academics who might object to them. For years the Clinton administration has been placing public service ads claiming that "thirteen children die every day from guns," linking this claim with elementary school children's voices or pictures. But few of these thirteen deaths fit the image of innocent young children. Nine of these deaths per day involve "children" between seventeen and nineteen years old, primarily homicides involving gang members. Eleven of the deaths per day involved fifteen- to nineteen-year olds. This does not alleviate the sorrow created by these deaths or the 1.9 children under age fifteen that die from guns every day, but it strains credulity to have this number mentioned as evidence justifying the importance of trigger locks.

The Clinton administration has also been attempting to help out the city lawsuits against the gun makers by producing other research that will back up their claims that guns are being sold recklessly to criminals.[130] The administration claimed that around a third of the guns used in crimes were purchased legally with the intent of reselling them to criminals—so-called straw purchases. Yet the evidence was very indirect and purposely excluded most gun crimes from the sample to ensure a particular answer. The administration did not measure straw purchases, but simply assumed that guns legally purchased from a dealer and then used in the commission of a crime within three years must have involved straw purchases. These guns could have been stolen between the original sale and their use in a crime, but they would still be classified as straw purchases. To arrive at the percentages the administration reports, only guns that were both sold and used in the commission of a crime between the beginning of 1990 and the end of 1996 are examined.

Yet using this method the administration could have produced virtually any percentage it wanted. For example, accept its definition of a straw
purchase as guns that are both purchased and used within a three-year
period of time. If the administration had simply limited the sample to
guns that were purchased and used in the commission of a crime in a
three-year period from 1994 through 1996, it could have claimed that 100
percent of guns used in crimes were obtained through straw purchases.
In this case, all the guns they would have studied would fit their definition of a straw purchase.

Much of the debate today is framed so as to blame the greater accessibility of guns in America for the recent school violence. Gun-control
groups claim that today "guns are less regulated than toasters or teddy
bears."[131] The solutions range from banning gun possession for those under twenty-one to imprisoning adults whose guns are misused by minors
under eighteen.

Yet, to the contrary, gun availability has never before been as restricted
as it is now. As late as 1967, it was possible for a thirteen-year-old virtually
anywhere in the United States to walk into a hardware store and buy a
rifle. Relatively few states even had age restrictions for buying handguns
from a store. Buying a rifle through the mail was easy. Private transfers
of guns to juveniles were also unrestricted.

It was common for schools to have shooting clubs. Even in New York
City, virtually every public high school had a shooting club up until 1969.
It was common for high school students to take their guns with them
to school on the subways in the morning and turn them over to their
homeroom teacher or the gym coach so the heavy guns would simply
be out of the way. After school, students would pick up their guns when
it was time for practice. The federal government would even give students rifles and pay for their ammunition. Students regularly competed
in citywide shooting contests, with the winners being awarded university scholarships.

Contrast those days with regulations today. College or elementary students are now expelled from school for even accidentally bringing a water
pistol. Schools prohibit images of guns, knives, or other weapons on
shirts, on hats, or in pictures. Elementary school students have been suspended for carrying around a mere picture of a gun. High schools have
refused to publish yearbook pictures of students sitting on howitzers,
even when the picture shows graduating students who are joining the
military. School superintendents have lost their jobs for even raising the
question of whether someone at a school should have a gun for protection.[132]

Since the 1960s, the growth of federal gun control has been dramatic.

Before the Brady law in 1994, background checks and waiting periods were not required in most states. It was not a federal crime for those under eighteen to possess a handgun until 1994. The 1990s saw dramatically higher fees for registered dealers as well as many added paperwork requirements. Federal gun laws in 1930 amounted to only 3,571 words. They expanded to 19,907 words in 1960 and then more than quadrupled to 88,413 words today.[133]

The growth in state laws has kept pace. By 1997, California's gun-control statutes contained an incredible 158,643 words, nearly the length of the King James Version of the New Testament. And in 1999, at least four new gun laws have already been signed into law by the governor. Even a "gun-friendly" state government such as Texas has gun-control provisions containing over 41,000 words. None of this even begins to include the burgeoning local regulations on everything from licensing to mandatory gun locks.

But whose access has really been restricted by these laws? There is no academic study showing that waiting periods and background checks have reduced criminal access or resulted in less crime or youth violence. Indeed, for the Brady law, I have found that rape rates have increased. While the object is obviously to disarm criminals, the laws are primarily obeyed by good people. If the research in this book convinces me of anything, it is that disarming potential victims relative to criminals makes crime more attractive and more likely.

To restrict firearm access further and promote "safe zones" for our children, a 1995 federal law now bans guns within 1,000 feet of a school. Unfortunately, again, it is the law-abiding citizens who obey the law— not the criminals who are intent on harming our children. With the recent school attacks, even the most die-hard proponents of this law will be hard pressed to claim that this law has worked out the way that it was intended.

In Virginia, where rural areas have a long tradition of high school students going hunting in the morning, before school, the governor tried but failed to get the state legislature in 1999 to enact an exemption to the federal law allowing high school students to store their guns in their cars in the school parking lot. Indeed, one reason few students have been prosecuted for possessing a gun on school grounds is that many violations involve these very types of cases. Prosecutors find it crazy to send good kids to jail simply because they had a rifle locked in the trunk of their car while the car was parked in the school parking lot. The recent attempts in Congress to "put teeth" into the current laws through mandating prosecutions will take away this prosecutorial discretion and produce unintended results.

The horror with which people react to guns is inversely related to how accessible they are. It would appear that, at the very least, gun-control advocates face something of a dilemma. If guns are the problem, why was it that when guns were really accessible, even inside schools by students, we didn't have the problems that plague us now including the mass school shootings?

Rules that are passed to solve a problem can make the problem worse, which in turn generates calls for yet more regulations. The biggest problem with gun-control laws is that those who are intent on harming others, and especially those who plan to commit suicide, are the least likely to obey them. The issue is often disparagingly phrased as whether hunters are willing to be "inconvenienced," but this misses the real question: Will well-intended laws disarm potential victims and thus make it easier for criminals?

The experiences of other countries with gun control should also raise real concerns. For example, Australia banned a wide range of guns after Tasmania's horrible multiple-victim public shooting in 1996. But neither total crime nor total crime with guns has declined. In the first two years after the law, armed robberies had risen by 73 percent, unarmed robberies by 28 percent, assaults by 17 percent, and kidnappings by 38 percent.[134] Murders declined by 9 percent, but manslaughter rose by 32 percent. Another country that has recently banned guns is England, yet it now leads the United States by a wide margin in robberies and aggravated assaults, and although murder and rape is still higher in the United States, that difference has been shrinking.[135] It is seldom mentioned that other countries, like Brazil and Russia, with some of the toughest gun bans and restrictions in the world, have murder rates four times higher than what we have in the United States.

Another important source of regulation is the constant threat of legal action now faced by gun makers and those in anyway involved in handling guns. Colt has terminated a thousand field representatives and virtually stopped selling handguns to the civilian market.[136] Other gun makers have filed for bankruptcy protection.[137] Other businesses have also been affected. The *Wall Street Journal* notes that "In part to avoid becoming a target of new lawsuits," United Parcel Service is "tightening its rules for shipping handguns" and effectively tripling its prices.[138]

What seems missing from so much of the public debate is that regulations have both costs and benefits. Consider, then, the costs and benefits of some other recent gun-control proposals that have not already been addressed directly in this book:

Prison sentences for adults whose guns are misused by someone under 18. Parents are already civilly liable for any wrongful actions committed by their chil-

dren, but these recent federal proposals would institute a three-year minimum prison term for anyone whose gun is used improperly by any minor (not necessarily their own child), regardless of whether the gun
owner consented to or knew of the use. The rules are being created for
just one product when we would never think of applying them to other
products. This is draconian, to say the least—the equivalent of sending
Mom and Dad to prison because an auto thief kills someone while driving
the family car. What about other household products like the propane
tanks from barbecues or trailer homes used to make bombs? If the motivation is to prevent accidental deaths, why not apply this rule to items
that pose a much greater risk to children in the home? Criminal penalties
would surely motivate parents to store everything from medicines to
knives to water buckets more carefully. Most would consider such an
idea extreme, and it would only add to the grief or agony already suffered
by parents when their children are killed or hurt.

Age limits. Mr. Clinton proposes a federal ban on the possession of
handguns by anyone under twenty-one. Under a 1968 federal law,
twenty-one is already the minimum age to purchase a handgun, but setting the age to possess a handgun has been a state matter. While some
people between eighteen and twenty-one use guns improperly, others
face the risk of crime and would benefit from defending themselves. As
discussed earlier in this book (p. 86), laws allowing eighteen- to twenty-
one-year-olds to carry a concealed handgun reduce violent crime, just as
they do for citizens over twenty-one.

New rules for gun shows. The Clinton administration has provided no evidence that such shows are important in supplying criminals with guns.
Furthermore, it is simply false to claim that the rules for purchasing guns
at a gun show are any different from purchases elsewhere. Dealers at a
show must perform the same background checks and obey all the other
rules that they follow when they make sales at their stores. Private sales
are always unregulated whether they occur at a gun show or not.

If, as Mr. Clinton proposes, the government enacts new laws regulating private sales at gun shows, all someone would have to do is walk
outside the show and sell the gun there. To regulate private sales, the
government would have to register all guns. This is where the discussion
will soon be headed, as it is certain that gun-control advocates will
quickly point to the unenforceability of these new laws. Advocates of the
new rules must know that the proposed rules are doomed to failure and
should acknowledge openly whether they would advocate registration to
close the new "loopholes" they are creating. The other goal here is set
up fees and bureaucracy that will drive most gun shows out of business.

Background checks for buyers of bomb-making material. This will have little effect, simply because few items are likely to be covered. No one seriously discusses including fertilizer, used to make the bomb that killed 168 people in Oklahoma City in 1995, or propane tanks like the ones found after the Littleton massacre. There are simply too many common household items that can be used to make bombs.

Yet without academic evidence that existing regulations such as the Brady law and gun locks produce desirable results, it is surprising that we are now debating what new gun-control laws to pass. With that in mind, 294 academics from institutions as diverse as Harvard, Stanford, Northwestern, the University of Pennsylvania, and UCLA released an open letter to Congress during 1999 stating that the proposed new gun laws are "ill advised." They wrote that "With the 20,000 gun laws already on the books, we advise Congress, before enacting yet more new laws, to investigate whether many of the existing laws may have contributed to the problems we currently face." [139]

An effective as well as moving piece I recently read was written by Dale Anema, a father whose son was trapped for hours inside the Columbine High School building during the April 1999 attack. His agony while waiting to hear what happened to his son touches any parent's worst fears. Because he had witnessed this tragedy, he described his disbelief over the policy debate:

> Two pending gun bills are immediately dropped by the Colorado legislature. One is a proposal to make it easier for law-abiding citizens to carry concealed weapons; the other is a measure to prohibit municipalities from suing gun manufacturers. I wonder: If two crazy hoodlums can walk into a "gun-free" zone full of our kids, and police are totally incapable of defending the children, why would anyone want to make it harder for law-abiding adults to defend themselves and others? ... Of course, nobody on TV mentions that perhaps gun-free zones are potential magnets to crazed killers. [140]

Appendix One

How to Account for the Different
Factors That Affect Crime and
How to Evaluate the Importance
of the Results

The research in this book relies on what is known as *regression analysis,* a statistical technique that essentially lets us "fit a line" to a data set. Take a two-variable case involving arrest rates and crime rates. One could simply plot the data and draw the line somewhere in the middle, so that the deviations from the line would be small, but each person would probably draw the line a little differently. Regression analysis is largely a set of conventions for determining exactly how the line should be drawn. In the simplest and most common approach—ordinary least squares (OLS)—the line chosen minimizes the sum of the squared differences between the observations and the regression line. Where the relationship between only two variables is being examined, regression analysis is not much more sophisticated than determining the correlation.

The regression *coefficients* tell us the relationship between the two variables. The diagram in figure A1.1 indicates that increasing arrest rates decreases crime rates, and the slope of the line tells us how much crime rates will fall if we increase arrest rates by a certain amount. For example, in terms of figure A1, if the regression coefficient were equal to −1, lowering the arrest rate by one percentage point would produce a similar percentage-point increase in the crime rate. Obviously, many factors account for how crime changes over time. To deal with these, we use what is called *multiple regression analysis.* In such an analysis, as the name suggests, many explanatory (or exogenous) variables are used to explain how the endogenous (or dependent) variable moves. This allows us to determine whether a relationship exits between different variables after other effects have already been taken into consideration. Instead of merely drawing a line that best fits a two-dimensional plot of data points, as shown in figure A1.1, multiple regression analysis fits the best line through an

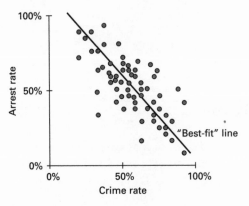

Figure A1.1. Fitting a regression line to a scatter diagram

n-dimensional data plot, where *n* is the number of variables being examined.

A more complicated regression technique is called *two-stage least squares.* We use this technique when two variables are both dependent on each other and we want to try to separate the influence of one variable from the influence of the other. In our case, this arises because crime rates influence whether the nondiscretionary concealed-handgun laws are adopted at the same time as the laws affect crime rates. Similar issues arise with arrest rates. Not only are crime rates influenced by arrest rates, but since an arrest rate is the number of arrests divided by the number of crimes, the reverse also holds true. As is evident from its name, the method of two-stage least squares is similar to the method of ordinary least squares in how it determines the line of best fit—by minimizing the sum of the squared differences from that line. Mathematically, however, the calculations are more complicated, and the computer has to go through the estimation in two stages.

The following is an awkward phrase used for presenting regression results: "a one-standard-deviation change in an explanatory variable explains a certain percentage of a one-standard-deviation change in the various crime rates." This is a typical way of evaluating the importance of statistical results. In the text I have adopted a less stilted, though less precise formulation: for example, "variations in the probability of arrest account for 3 to 11 percent of the variation in the various crime rates." As I will explain below, standard deviations are a measure of how much variation a given variable displays. While it is possible to say that a one-percentage-point change in an explanatory variable will affect the crime rate by a certain amount (and, for simplicity, many tables use such phrasing whenever possible), this approach has its limitations. The reason is that a 1 percent change in the explanatory variable may sometimes be very unlikely: some variables may typically change by only a fraction of a percent, so assuming a one-percentage-point change would imply a much larger impact than could possibly be accounted for by that factor. Likewise, if the typical change in an explanatory variable is much greater than 1 percent, assuming a one-percentage-point change would make its impact appear too small.

The convention described above—that is, measuring the percent of a one-standard-deviation change in the endogenous variable explained by a one-standard-deviation change in the explanatory variable—solves the problem by essentially normalizing both variables so that they are in the same units. Standard deviations are a way of measuring the typical change that occurs in a variable. For example, for symmetric distributions, 68 percent of the data is within one standard deviation of either side of the mean, and 95 percent of the data is within two standard deviations of the mean. Thus, by comparing a one-standard-deviation change in both variables, we are comparing equal percentages of the typical changes in both variables.[1]

The regressions in this book are also "weighted by the population" in the counties or states being studied. This is necessitated by the very high level of "noise" in a particular year's measure of crime rates for low-population areas. A county with only one thousand people may go through many years with no murders, but when even one murder occurs, the murder rate (the number of murders divided by the county's population) is extremely high. Presumably, no one would believe that this small county has suddenly become as dangerous as New York City. More populous areas experience much more stable crime rates over time. Because of this difficulty in consistently measuring the risk of murder in low-population counties, we do not want to put as much emphasis on any one year's observed murder rate, and this is exactly what weighting the regressions by county population does.

Several other general concerns may be anticipated in setting up the regression specification. What happens if concealed-handgun laws just happen to be adopted at the same time that there is a downward national trend in crime rates? The solution is to use separate variables for the different years in the sample: one variable equals 1 for all observations during 1978 and zero for all other times, another equals 1 for all observations during 1979 and zero otherwise, and so on. These "year-dummy" variables thus capture the change in crime from one year to another that can only be attributed to time itself. Thus if the murder rate declines nationally from 1991 to 1992, the year-dummy variables will measure the average decline in murder rates between those two years and allow us to ask if there was an additional drop, even after accounting for this national decline, in states that adopted nondiscretionary concealed-handgun laws.

A similar set of "dummy" variables is used for each county in the United States, and they measure deviations in the average crime rate across counties. Thus we avoid the possibility that our findings may show that nondiscretionary concealed-handgun laws appear to reduce crime rates simply because the counties with these laws happened to have low crime rates to begin with. Instead, our findings should show whether there is an additional drop in crime rates after the adoption of these laws.

The only way to properly account for these year and county effects, as well as the influences on crime from factors like arrest rates, poverty, and demographic changes, is to use a multiple-regression framework that allows us to directly control for these influences.

Unless we specifically state otherwise, the regressions reported in the tables attempt to explain the natural logarithms of the crime rates for the different categories of crime. Converting into "logs" is a conventional method of rescaling a variable so that a given absolute numerical change represents a given percentage change. (The familiar Richter scale for measuring earthquakes is an example of a base-10 logarithmic scale, where a tremor that registers 8 on the scale is ten times as powerful as one that registers 7, and one that registers 7 is ten times as powerful as one that registers 6.) The reason for using logarithms of the endogenous variable rather than their simple values is twofold. First, using logs avoids giving undue importance to a few, very large, "outlying" observations. Second, the regression coefficient can easily be interpreted as the percent change in the endogenous variable for every one-point change in the particular explanatory variable examined.

Finally, there is the issue of *statistical significance.* When we estimate coefficients in a regression, they take on some value, positive or negative. Even if we were to take two completely unrelated variables—say, sunspot activity and the number of gun permits—a regression would almost certainly yield a coefficient estimate other than zero. However, we cannot conclude that any positive or negative regression coefficient really implies a true relationship between the variables. We must have some measure of how certain the coefficient estimate is. The size of the coefficient does not really help here—even a large coefficient could have been generated by chance.

This is where statistical significance enters in. The measure of statistical significance is the conventional way of reporting how certain we can be that the impact is different from zero. If we say that the reported number is "positive and statistically significant at the 5 percent level," we mean that there is only a 5 percent chance that the coefficient happened to take on a positive value when the true relationship in fact was zero or negative.[2] To say that a number is statistically significant at the 1 percent level represents even greater certainty. The convention among many social scientists is usually not to affirm conclusions unless the level of significance reaches 10 percent or lower; thus, someone who says that a result is "not significant" most likely means that the level of significance failed to be as low as 10 percent.

These simple conventions are, however, fairly arbitrary, and it would be wrong to think that we learn nothing from a value that is significant at "only" the 11 percent level, while attaching a great deal of weight to one that is significant at the 10 percent level. The true connection between the significance level and what we learn involves a much more continuous relationship. We are more certain of a result when it is significant at the 10 percent level rather than at the 15 percent level, and we are more certain of a result at the 1 percent level than at the 5 percent level.

Appendix Two

Arrest rate: The number of arrests per crime.

Crime rate: The number of crimes per 100,000 people.

Cross-sectional data: Data that provide information across geographic areas (cities, counties, or states) within a single period of time.

Discretionary concealed-handgun law: Also known as a "may-issue" law; the term *discretionary* means that whether a person is ultimately allowed to obtain a concealed-handgun permit is up to the discretion of either the sheriff or judge who has the authority to grant the permit. The person applying for the permit must frequently show a "need" to carry the gun, though many rural jurisdictions automatically grant these requests.

Endogenous: A variable is endogenous when changes in the variable are assumed to caused by changes in other variables.

Exogenous: A variable is exogenous when its values are as given, and no attempt is made to explain how that variable's values change over time.

Externality: The costs of or benefits from one's actions may accrue to other people. External benefits occur when people cannot capture the beneficial effects that their actions produce. External costs arise when people are not made to bear the costs that their actions impose on others.

Nondiscretionary concealed-handgun law: Also known as a "shall-issue" or "do-issue" law; the term *nondiscretionary* means that once a person meets certain well-specified criteria for obtaining a concealed-handgun permit, no discretion is involved in granting the permit—it must be issued.

Pooled, cross-sectional, time-series data: Data that allow the researcher not only to compare differences across geographic areas, but also to see how these differences change across geographic areas over time.

Regression: A statistical technique that essentially lets us fit a line to a data set to determine the relationship between variables.

Statistical significance: A measure used to indicate how certain we can be that the impact of a variable is different from some value (usually whether it is different from zero).

Time-series data: Data that provide information about a particular place over time. For example, time-series data might examine the change in the crime rate for a city over many years.

Appendix Three

DESCRIPTION OF THE DATA

This appendix provides a detailed discussion of the variables used in this study and their sources. The number of arrests and offenses for each crime in every county from 1977 to 1992 were provided by the FBI's *Uniform Crime Reports (UCR)*. The UCR program is a nationwide, cooperative statistical effort by over 16,000 city, county, and state law-enforcement agencies to compile data on crimes that are reported to them. During 1993, law-enforcement agencies active in the UCR program represented over 245 million U.S. inhabitants, or 95 percent of the total population. The coverage amounted to 97 percent of the U.S. population living in Metropolitan Statistical Areas (MSAs) and 86 percent of the population in non-MSA cities and in rural counties.[1] The *Supplementary Homicide Reports* of the *UCR* supplied the data on the sex and race of victims and on whatever relationship might have existed between victim and offender.[2]

The regressions report results from a subset of the *UCR* data set, though we also ran the regressions with the entire data set. The main differences were that the effect of concealed-handgun laws on murder was greater than what is reported in this study, and the effects on rape and aggravated assault were smaller. Observations were eliminated because of changes in reporting practices or definitions of crimes; see *Crime in the United States* for the years 1977 to 1992. For example, from 1985 to 1994, Illinois operated under a unique, "gender-neutral" definition of sex offenses. Another example involves Cook County, Illinois, from 1981 to 1984, which experienced a large jump in reported crime because of a change in the way officers were trained to report crime.

The additional observations that were either never provided or were dropped from the data set include those from Arizona (1980), Florida (1988), Georgia (1980), Kentucky (1988), and Iowa (1991). Data for counties containing the following cities were also eliminated for the crime rates listed: violent crime and aggravated assault for Steubenville, Ohio (1977–89); violent crime and aggravated assault for Youngstown, Ohio (1977–87); violent crime, aggravated assault, and burglary for Mobile, Alabama

(1977–85); violent crime and aggravated assault for Oakland, California (1977–90); violent crime and aggravated assault for Milwaukee, Wisconsin (1977–85); all crime categories for Glendale, Arizona (1977–84); violent crime and aggravated assault for Jackson, Mississippi (1977 and 1982); violent crime and aggravated assault for Aurora, Colorado (1977 and 1982); violent crime and aggravated assault for Beaumont, Texas (1977 and 1982); violent crime and aggravated assault for Corpus Christi, Texas (1977 and 1982); violent crime and rape for Macon, Georgia (1977–81); violent crime, property crime, robbery, and larceny for Cleveland, Ohio (1977–81); violent crime and aggravated assault for Omaha, Nebraska (1977–81); all crime categories for Eau Claire, Wisconsin (1977–78); all crime categories for Green Bay, Wisconsin (1977); and all crime categories for Little Rock, Arkansas (1977–79).

The original *Uniform Crime Report* data set did not have arrest data for Hawaii in 1982. These missing observations were supplied to us by the Hawaii UCR program. In the original data set several observations included two observations for the same county and year identifiers. The incorrect observations were deleted from the data.

For all of the different crime rates, if the true rate was zero, we added 0.1 before we took the natural log of those values. It is not possible to take the natural log of zero, because any change from zero is an infinite percentage change. For the accident rates and the supplementary homicide data, if the true rate was zero, we added 0.01 before we took the natural logs of those values.[3]

The number of police in a state, the number of officers who have the power to make arrests, and police payrolls for each state by type of officer are available for 1982 to 1992 from the U.S. Department of Justice's *Expenditure and Employment Data for the Criminal Justice System.*

The data on age, sex, and racial distributions estimate the population in each county on July 1 of the respective years. The population is divided into five-year age segments, and race is categorized as white, black, and neither white nor black. The population data, with the exception of 1990 and 1992, were obtained from the U.S. Bureau of the Census.[4] The estimates use modified census data as anchor points and then employ an iterative proportional-fitting technique to estimate intercensal populations. The process ensures that the county-level estimates are consistent with estimates of July 1 national and state populations by age, sex, and race. The age distributions of large military installations, colleges, and institutions were estimated by a separate procedure. The counties for which special adjustments were made are listed in the report.[5] The 1990 and 1992 estimates have not yet been completed by the Bureau of the

Census and made available for distribution. We estimated the 1990 data by taking an average of the 1989 and 1991 data. We estimated the 1992 data by multiplying the 1991 populations by the 1990–91 growth rate of each county's population.

Data on income, unemployment, income maintenance, and retirement were obtained by the Regional Economic Information System (REIS). Income maintenance includes Supplemental Security Insurance (SSI), Aid to Families with Dependent Children (AFDC), and food stamps. Unemployment benefits include state unemployment insurance compensation, Unemployment for federal employees, unemployment for railroad employees, and unemployment for veterans. Retirement payments include old-age survivor and disability payments, federal civil employee retirement payments, military retirement payments, state and local government employee retirement payments, and workers compensation payments (both federal and state). Nominal values were converted to real values by using the consumer price index.[6] The index uses the average consumer price index for July 1983 as the base period. County codes for twenty-five observations did not match any of the county codes listed in the ICPSR codebook. Those observations were deleted from the sample.

Data concerning the number of concealed-weapons permits for each county were obtained from a variety of sources. Mike Woodward, of the Oregon Law Enforcement and Data System, provided the Oregon data for 1991 and after. The number of permits available for Oregon by county in 1989 was provided by the sheriff's departments of the individual counties. Cari Gerchick, Deputy County Attorney for Maricopa County in Arizona, provided us with the Arizona county-level conviction rates, prison-sentence lengths, and concealed-handgun permits from 1990 to 1995. The Pennsylvania data were obtained from Alan Krug. The National Rifle Association provided data on NRA membership by state from 1977 to 1992. The dates on which states enacted enhanced-sentencing provisions for crimes committed with deadly weapons were obtained from a study by Marvell and Moody.[7] The first year for which the enhanced-sentencing variable equals 1 is weighted by the portion of that first year during which the law was in effect.

For the Arizona regressions, the Brady-law variable is weighted for 1994 by the percentage of the year for which it was in effect (83 percent).

The Bureau of the Census provided data on the area in square miles of each county. Both the total number of unintentional-injury deaths and the number of those involving firearms were obtained from annual issues of *Accident Facts* and *The Vital Statistics of the United States.* The classification of types of weapons is from *International Statistical Classification of Diseases and Related Health Problems,* vol. 1, 10th ed. The handgun category includes guns for single-hand use, pistols, and revolvers. The total includes all other types of firearms.

The means and standard deviations of the variables are reported in appendix 4.

Appendix Four

Table A4.1 National Sample Means and Standard Deviations

Variable	Observations	Mean	Standard deviation
Gun ownership information:			
Nondiscretionary law dummy	50,056	0.16	0.368
Arrests rates (ratio of arrests to offenses)			
Index crimes[a]	45,108	27.43	126.73
Violent crimes	43,479	71.31	327.25
Property crimes	45,978	24.03	120.87
Murder	26,472	98.05	109.78
Rape	33,887	57.83	132.80
Aggravated assault	43,472	71.37	187.35
Robbery	34,966	61.62	189.50
Burglary	45,801	21.51	47.299
Larceny	45,776	25.57	263.71
Auto theft	43,616	44.82	307.54
Crime rates (per 100,000 people)			
Index crimes	46,999	2,984.99	3,368.85
Violent crimes	47,001	249.08	388.72
Property crimes	46,999	2,736.59	3,178.41
Murder	47,001	5.65	10.63
Murder rate with guns (from 1982 to 1991 in counties with more than 100,000 people)	12,759	3.92	6.48
Rape	47,001	18.78	32.39
Robbery	47,001	44.69	149.21
Aggravated assault	47,001	180.05	243.26
Burglary	47,001	811.8642	1,190.23
Larceny	47,000	1,764.37	2,036.03
Auto theft	47,000	160.42	284.60
Causes of accidental deaths and murders (per 100,000 people)			
Rate of accidental deaths from guns	23,278	0.151	1.216175

Table A4.1 Continued

Variable	Observations	Mean	Standard deviation
Rate of accidental deaths from causes other than guns	23,278	1.165152	4.342401
Rate of total accidental deaths	23,278	51.95	32.13482
Rate of murders (handguns)	23,278	0.44	1.930975
Rate of murders (other guns)	23,278	3.478	6.115275
Income data (all values in real 1983 dollars)			
Real per-capita personal income	50,011	10,554.21	2,498.07
Real per-capita unemployment insurance	50,011	67.58	53.10
Real per-capita income maintenance	50,011	157.23	97.61
Real per-capita retirement (over age 65)	49,998	12,328.5	4,397.49
Population characteristics			
County population	50,023	75,772.78	250,350.4
County population per square mile	50,023	214.33	1421.25
State population	50,056	6,199,949	5,342,068
State NRA membership (per 100,000 people)	50,056	1098.11	516.0701
Percent voting Republican in presidential election	50,056	52.89	8.41

ªIndex crimes represent the total of all violent and property crimes.

Table A4.2 Average percent of the total population in U.S. counties in each age, sex, and race cohort from 1977 to 1992 (50,023 observations)

	10–19 years of age	20–29 years of age	30–39 years of age	40–49 years of age	50–64 years of age	Over 65 years of age
Black male	0.9%	0.8%	0.5%	0.4%	0.4%	0.4%
Black female	0.9%	0.8%	0.6%	0.4%	0.5%	0.6%
White male	7.3%	6.8%	6.4%	4.9%	6.5%	5.4%
White female	6.8%	6.6%	6.3%	5.0%	6.9%	7.5%
Other male	0.2%	0.2%	0.2%	0.1%	0.1%	0.1%
Other female	0.2%	0.2%	0.2%	0.1%	0.1%	0.1%

Appendix Five

CONTINUATION OF THE RESULTS FROM
TABLE 4.2: THE EFFECT OF
DEMOGRAPHIC CHARACTERISTICS
ON CRIME

Table A5.1 The effect of demographic characteristics on crime

The following assume a 1 percent change in the portion of the population in each category	Violent-crime rate	Murder rate	Rape rate	Aggravated assault rate	Robbery rate	Property-crime rate	Burlgary rate	Larceny rate	Auto-theft rate
Percent of population that is black, male, and in the following age ranges:									
10–19	6%	11%	4%	9%***	11%***	13%*	7%**	17%*	5%
	(5%)	(8%)	(3%)	(7%)	(6%)	(22%)	(7%)	(25%)	(6%)
20–29	0%	7%	8%**	−5%*	−1%	−1%	−2%	−1%	1%
	(0%)	(4%)	(4%)	(3%)	(0%)	(2%)	(2%)	(1%)	(1%)
30–39	4%	11%**	−8%*	20%*	1%	4%	−1%	0%	15%*
	(2%)	(4%)	(3%)	(9%)	(0%)	(4%)	(0%)	(0%)	(11%)
40–49	−2%	−34%*	90%*	−37%*	−1%	−2%	−3%	19%*	−68%*
	(1%)	(9%)	(22%)	(11%)	(0%)	(1%)	(1%)	(10%)	(32%)
50–64	18%**	−35%*	−15%	29%*	−1%	−5%	9%	−13%***	6%
	(7%)	(11%)	(4%)	(10%)	(0%)	(4%)	(4%)	(9%)	(3%)
65 and over	12%	−14%	44%*	11%	17%	−4%	6%	−10%	−34%*
	(5%)	(4%)	(12%)	(4%)	(4%)	(3%)	(3%)	(6%)	(18%)
Percent of population that is black, female, and in the following age ranges:									
10–19	0%	4%	4%	−7%	−18%*	8%*	2%	16%*	−18%*
	(0%)	(3%)	(2%)	(6%)	(11%)	(14%)	(2%)	(23%)	(22%)
20–29	−10%*	−22%*	18%*	−19%*	−22%*	−10%*	−17%*	−1%	−25%*
	(7%)	(13%)	(9%)	(13%)	(11%)	(14%)	(13%)	(1%)	(26%)

Table A5.1 Continued

The following assume a 1 percent change in the portion of the population in each category	Violent-crime rate	Murder rate	Rape rate	Aggravated assault rate	Robbery rate	Property-crime rate	Burglary rate	Larceny rate	Auto-theft rate
30–39	12%*	−8%	15%*	9%*	38%*	13%*	27%*	9%*	17%*
	(7%)	(4%)	(6%)	(5%)	(14%)	(14%)	(16%)	(9%)	(14%)
40–49	1%	59%*	−74%*	27%*	−7%	6%	−5%	−3%	48%*
	(0%)	(19%)	(21%)	(10%)	(2%)	(4%)	(2%)	(2%)	(27%)
50–64	−21%*	20%***	10%	−5%	7%	−2%	−22%*	1%	12%
	(11%)	(9%)	(4%)	(3%)	(2%)	(2%)	(12%)	(1%)	(9%)
65 and older	−20%*	31%*	−52%*	−16%**	−37%*	−20%*	−39%*	−12%**	24%*
	(11%)	(14%)	(21%)	(8%)	(14%)	(22%)	(23%)	(12%)	(19%)
Percent of population that is white, male, and in the following age ranges:									
10–19	−1%	−3%	1%	4%**	0%	−1%	1%	0%	−6%*
	(1%)	(2%)	(0%)	(4%)	(0%)	(1%)	(1%)	(0%)	(8%)
20–29	1%	6%*	4%*	2%	4%*	0%	2%**	0%	−2%
	(1%)	(5%)	(3%)	(2%)	(3%)	(1%)	(2%)	(1%)	(3%)
30–39	−1%	−1%	−4%	7%*	−7%*	−5%*	−3%***	−6%*	−6%*
	(1%)	(5%)	(3%)	(6%)	(4%)	(8%)	(2%)	(8%)	(7%)
40–49	−1%	−2%	9%*	−4%	−11%*	−15%*	−10%*	−13%*	−10%*
	(0%)	(1%)	(4%)	(2%)	(5%)	(17%)	(7%)	(13%)	(8%)
50–64	−1%	−5%	4%	−9%*	−14%*	−13%*	7%*	−11%*	−27%*
	(0%)	(3%)	(2%)	(7%)	(8%)	(20%)	(6%)	(14%)	(31%)

65 and over								
−13%*	2%	4%	−17%*	4%	−14%*	−12%*	−14%*	−11%*
(15%)	(2%)	(4%)	(18%)	(3%)	(33%)	(15%)	(28%)	(19%)

Percent of population that is white, female, and in the following age ranges:

10–19								
2%	5%	7%*	−1%	6%**	8%*	8%*	9%*	9%*
(2%)	(3%)	(5%)	(1%)	(4%)	(15%)	(8%)	(14%)	(12%)
20–29								
1%	−4%***	6%*	4%**	1%	−1%	−4%*	3%**	−3%***
(1%)	(3%)	(4%)	(4%)	(1%)	(2%)	(5%)	(5%)	(4%)
30–39								
2%	4%	14%*	3%	−1%	4%*	2%	7%*	−10%*
(1%)	(3%)	(8%)	(4%)	(0%)	(6%)	(1%)	(9%)	(12%)
40–49								
−9%*	0%	−7%**	0%	−2%	6%*	−4%*	7%*	−2%
(5%)	(0%)	(3%)	(0%)	(1%)	(7%)	(2%)	(7%)	(2%)
50–64								
0%	1%	2%	8%*	3%	10%*	6%*	11%*	11%*
(0%)	(0%)	(1%)	(6%)	(2%)	(17%)	(6%)	(16%)	(13%)
65 and over								
6%*	−7%*	6%*	8%*	−9%*	2%**	5%*	4%*	−5%*
(9%)	(8%)	(7%)	(12%)	(9%)	(6%)	(8%)	(9%)	(10%)

Percent of population that is other males in the following age ranges:

10–19								
25%**	66%	56%*	19%	54%*	16%***	27%*	15%	60%*
(11%)	(23%)	(18%)	(7%)	(16%)	(13%)	(13%)	(11%)	(38%)
20–29								
−12%**	14%	−17%**	−6%	1%	8%*	0%	20%*	−41%
(4%)	(4%)	(4%)	(2%)	(0%)	(5%)	(0%)	(11%)	(18%)
30–39								
23%**	−30%	−19%	40%*	−10%	−18%***	−43%*	−4%	65%*
(6%)	(6%)	(4%)	(9%)	(2%)	(9%)	(12%)	(2%)	(24%)
40–49								
13%	−36%	−24%	−19%	78%*	3%	24%**	−23%***	46%*
(2%)	(5%)	(3%)	(3%)	(9%)	(1%)	(4%)	(7%)	(11%)
50–64								
−9%	−16%	24%	−28%	−40%**	−2%	27%**	−20%	−42%**
(2%)	(3%)	(4%)	(5%)	(6%)	(1%)	(6%)	(7%)	(13%)

Table A5.1 Continued

The following assume a 1 percent change in the portion of the population in each category	Violent-crime rate	Murder rate	Rape rate	Aggravated assault rate	Robbery rate	Property-crime rate	Burlgary rate	Larceny rate	Auto-theft rate
65 and over	35%** (6%)	−26% (3%)	87%* (10%)	102%* (15%)	−27% (3%)	−8% (2%)	19% (3%)	−23%*** (6%)	−18% (4%)
Percent of population that is other females in the following age ranges:									
10–19	−3% (1%)	−73%* (25%)	−11% (3%)	12% (5%)	−35%** (10%)	−18%** (14%)	−29%* (13%)	−23%** (16%)	−27%** (17%)
20–29	−13% (4%)	−33%*** (8%)	21%* (5%)	9% (3%)	−30% (6%)	−15%** (9%)	−32%** (11%)	−33%** (18%)	−56%* (26%)
30–39	−22%* (6%)	−11% (2%)	16% (3%)	−17% (4%)	−22% (4%)	−9% (4%)	27%* (8%)	−28%* (12%)	−75%* (28%)
40–49	−14% (2%)	57%** (8%)	8% (1%)	18% (3%)	−48%** (6%)	25%** (8%)	28%* (5%)	70% (20%)	−15% (4%)
50–64	−10% (2%)	44% (7%)	−66%* (10%)	−27% (5%)	37% (5%)	−5% (2%)	−49%* (11%)	16% (6%)	31%*** (9%)
65 and over	44%* (7%)	6% (1%)	−37%** (4%)	−44%* (6%)	−36%** (4%)	−11% (3%)	−14% (2%)	−5% (1%)	−59%* (13%)

*The result is statistically significant at the 1 percent level for a two-tailed t-test.
**The result is statistically significant at the 5 percent level for a two-tailed t-test.
***The result is statistically significant at the 10 percent level for a two-tailed t-test.

Notes

1. Gary Kleck, *Targeting Guns* (Hawthorne, NY: Aldine de Gruyter Publishers, 1997), and David B. Kopel, *Guns: Who Should Have Them?* (Amherst, NY: Prometheus Books, 1995), pp. 260–61, 300–1. The estimates on the number of guns are very sensitive to the rate at which guns are assumed to wear out. Higher depreciation rates produce a lower estimated current stock. About a third of all guns are handguns.

A recent poll by the *Dallas Morning News* indicated that "52 percent of the respondents said they or a member of their household own a gun. That response is consistent with Texas Polls dating to 1985 that found more than half of Texans surveyed own guns.

"In the latest poll, of those who said they owned a gun, 43 percent said they had two to five guns; 28 percent said they had one; and 19 percent said they had more than five guns. And of the gun owners polled, 65 percent said they had some type of shooting instruction." See Sylvia Moreno, "Concealed-Gun Law Alters Habits of Some Texans, Poll Finds Supporters, Foes Disagree About What That Means," *Dallas Morning News,* Nov. 3, 1996, p. 45A. The number of people owning guns is examined in more detail in chapter 3.

2. For example, in Chicago 59 percent of police officers report never having had to fire their guns. See Andrew Martin, "73% of Chicago Cops Have Been Attacked While Doing Their Job," *Chicago Tribune,* June 17, 1997, p. A3.

3. Dawn Lewis of Texans Against Gun Violence provided a typical reaction from gun-control advocates to the grand jury decision not to charge Gordon Hale. She said, "We are appalled. This law is doing what we expected, causing senseless death." Mark Potok, a Texan, said that the concealed-gun law saved his life. "I did what I thought I had to do," (*USA Today,* Mar. 22, 1996, p. 3A). For a more recent evaluation of the Texas experience, see "Few Problems Reported After Allowing Concealed Handguns, Officers Say," *Fort Worth Star-Telegram,* July 16, 1996. By the end of December 1996, more than 120,000 permits had been issued in Texas.

4. Japan Economic Newswire, "U.S. Jury Clears Man Who Shot Japanese Student," *Kyodo News Service,* May 24, 1993; and Lori Sharn, "Violence Shoots Holes in USA's Tourist Image," *USA Today,* Sept. 9, 1993, p. 2A.

5. Gary Kleck, *Point Blank: Guns and Violence in America* (Hawthorne, NY: Aldine de Gruyter Publishers, 1991).

6. John R. Lott, Jr., "Now That the Brady Law Is Law, You Are Not Any Safer Than Before," *Philadelphia Inquirer,* Feb. 1, 1994, p. A9. For a more detailed breakdown of police shootings in the larger U.S. cities, see William A. Geller and Michael S. Scott, *Deadly Force: What We Know* (Washington, DC: Police Executive Research Forum, 1992).

7. "Mexican Woman Who Killed Would-Be Rapist to Turn to Activism," *Associated Press Newswire,* Feb. 12, 1997, dateline Mexico City.

8. For many examples of how guns have prevented rapes from occurring, see Paxton Quigley, *Armed and Female* (New York: St. Martin's, 1989).

9. Newspaper stories abound. Examples of pizza deliverymen defending themselves can be found in the *Chicago Tribune,* May 22, 1997, p. 1; *Baltimore Sun,* Aug. 9, 1996, p. B1; *Tampa*

Tribune, Dec. 27, 1996, p. A1; and *Los Angeles Times,* Jan. 28, 1997, p. B1. Another recent example involved a pizza deliveryman in New Paltz, NY (*Middletown (New York) Times Herald Record,* Jan. 25, 1997). Examples of thwarted carjackings (*Little Rock Democrat-Gazette,* Aug. 3, 1996) and robberies at automatic teller machines (*York (Pennsylvania) Daily Record,* April 25, 1996) are also common.

For a case in which a gun was merely brandished to stop an armed street robbery, see the *Annapolis Capitol,* Aug. 7, 1996. Other examples of street robberies that were foiled by law-abiding citizens using concealed handguns include the case of Francisco Castellano, who was shot in the chest during an attempted street robbery by two perpetrators but was able to draw his own handgun and fire back. Castellano's actions caused the robbers to flee the scene (Corey Dada and Ivonne Perez, "Armed Robbery Botched as Restaurateur Shoots Back," *Miami Herald,* Aug. 3, 1996, p. B6.) The following story gives another example: "Curtis Smalls was standing outside the USF&G building when he was attacked by two thugs. They knocked him down, robbed, and stabbed him. Mr. Smalls pulled a .38-caliber revolver and shot both attackers, who were later charged with this attack and two other robberies and are suspects in at least 15 more robberies." This story was described in "Gun Laws Render Us Self-Defenseless," *Baltimore Sun,* Sept. 27, 1996. See also Charles Strouse, "Attacker Killed by His Victim," *Fort Lauderdale (Florida) Sun-Sentinel,* Sept. 16, 1997, p. 4B; Henry Pierson Curtis, "Bicyclist Kills Man Who Tried to Rob Him," *Orlando Sentinel,* Sept. 19, 1997, p. D3; and *Florence (Alabama) Times Daily,* Dec. 27, 1996, for other examples. Examples of foiled carjackings can be found in "Guns and Carjacking: This Is My Car," *Economist,* Sept. 20, 1997. Many other types of robberies have been foiled by people carrying concealed handguns. In at least one case, citizens carrying concealed handguns in Jacksonville, Florida may have saved a restaurant waitress from being shot ("Pistol-Packing Seniors in Florida Wound Robber," Reuter Information Service, Sept. 24, 1997, 6:15 P.M. EDT). For another example, see Clea Benson, "Wounded Barmaid Kills Gunman in Holdup," *Philadelphia Inquirer,* Jan. 23, 1997, p. R1.

10. Stories involving defensive uses of guns in the home are featured even more prominently. For example, four intruders forced their way into the home of two elderly women, struggled with them, and demanded their car keys. The attack stopped only after one of the women brandished her handgun ("Pistol-Packing Grandmas Honored by Sheriff," *Associated Press Newswire,* Feb. 16, 1997 2:30 P.M. EST, dateline Moses Lake, WA). In another case a twenty-three-year-old burglar "pummeled" a 92-year-old man and "ransack[ed]" his house. The burglar left only after the elderly man reached his gun ("Burglar Puts 92-Year-Old in the Gun Closet and Is Shot," *New York Times,* Sept. 7, 1995, p. A16). Although the defensive use of guns in the home is interesting, my focus in this book is on the effects of allowing citizens to carry concealed handguns.

11. Not all news stories of defensive uses involve shots being fired. For example, the *Arizona Republic* reported the following: "In January 1995, a permit-holder who lives in Scottsdale pulled a handgun from a shoulder holster and scared off two men armed with aluminum baseball bats who attempted to rob him near 77th Street and East McDowell Road. No shots were fired." ("In Arizona, High Numbers of Concealed-Weapon Permit Holders Are Found in the Suburbs," *Arizona Republic,* Mar. 17, 1996.)

12. "Mom Saves Self and Child with Handgun," *Atlanta Constitution,* Nov. 12, 1996, p. E2.

13. See *Los Angeles Times,* Jan. 28, 1997, p. B1. Similarly, Pete Shields, Handgun Control, Inc.'s founder, wrote that "the best defense against injury is to put up no defense—give them what they want or run. This may not be macho, but it can keep you alive." See Pete Shields, *Guns Don't Die, People Do* (New York: Arbor, 1981).

14. Problems exist with the National Crime Victimization Survey both because of its nonrepresentative sample (for example, it weights urban and minority populations too heavily) and because it fails to adjust for the fact that many people do not admit to a law-enforcement agency that they used a gun, even defensively; such problems make it

difficult to rely too heavily on these estimates. Unfortunately, this survey is the only source of evidence on the way the probability of significant injury varies with the level and type of resistance.

15. Lawrence Southwick, Jr., "Self-Defense with Guns: The Consequences," *Managerial and Decision Economics* (forthcoming), tables 5 and 6; see also Kleck, *Point Blank.*

16. For example, see David B. Kopel, *The Samurai, the Mountie, and the Cowboy* (Amherst, NY: Prometheus, 1992), p. 155; and John R. Lott, Jr., "Now That the Brady Law Is Law, You Are Not Any Safer Than Before," *Philadelphia Inquirer,* Feb. 1, 1994, p. A9.

17. James D. Wright and Peter Rossi, *Armed and Considered Dangerous: A Survey of Felons and Their Firearms* (Hawthorne, NY: Aldine de Gruyter Publishers, 1986).

Examples of anecdotes in which people successfully defend themselves from burglaries with guns are quite common. For example, see "Burglar Puts 92-Year-Old in the Gun Closet and Is Shot," *New York Times,* Sept. 7, 1995, p. A16. George F. Will, in "Are We 'a Nation of Cowards'?" *Newsweek,* Nov. 15, 1993, discusses more generally the benefits produced from an armed citizenry.

18. See Wright and Rossi, *Armed and Considered Dangerous,* p. 150.

19. Ibid., p. 151.

20. *Baltimore Sun,* Oct. 26, 1991; referred to in Don Kates and Dan Polsby, "Of Genocide and Disarmament," *Journal of Criminal Law and Criminology* 86 (Fall 1995): 252.

21. Rebecca Trounson, "Anxiety, Anger Surround Return of Young Survivors," *Los Angeles Times,* Mar. 14, 1997, p. A1.

22. It is possible that both terrorists and citizens are worse off because of the switch to bombings if shootings would have involved targeted attacks against fewer citizens.

23. David Firestone, "Political Memo: Gun Issue Gives Mayor Self-Defense on Crime," *New York Times,* Mar. 7, 1997, p. B1.

24. Using an on-line retrieval search, it is easy to find many news articles and letters to the editor that repeat this common claim. For example, one letter to the *Newark Star-Ledger* (Oct. 12, 1996) stated that "over half the firearm homicides are committed not by criminals but by friends, family members, and lovers—people with no criminal record."

25. The sum of these percentages does not equal precisely 100 percent because fractions of a percent were rounded to the nearest whole percent.

26. Captain James Mulvihill recently testified before the U.S. Senate that "the greater L. A. area suffers under the weight of more than 1,250 known street gangs, whose membership numbers approximately 150,000. These gangs are responsible for nearly 7,000 homicides over the last 10 years, and injury to thousands of other people." (Prepared testimony of Captain James Mulvihill, commander of the Safe Streets Bureau for Sheriff Block of Los Angeles County before the Senate Judiciary Committee, Apr. 23, 1997.)

27. I would like to thank Kathy O'Connell of the Illinois Criminal Justice Information Authority for taking the time to provide me with such a detailed breakdown of these data.

28. Many such murders also end up in the "undetermined relationship" category.

Probably the best known study of who kills whom is by Daly and Wilson. They examined nonaccidental homicide data for Detroit in 1972. In contrast to my emphasis here, however, they focused exclusively on trying to explain the composition of murders when relatives killed relatives. Of the total of 690 murders committed in Detroit in 1972, 243 (47.8 percent) involved unrelated acquaintances, 138 (27.2 percent) involved strangers, and 127 (25 percent) involved relatives. Of this last category, 32 (4.6 percent) involved blood relatives, and 80 (11.6 percent) victims were spouses (36 women killed by their husbands, and 44 men killed by their wives). The percentage of Chicago's murders involving relatives in 1972 was very similar (25.2 percent), though by the 1990–95 period the percentage of murders involving relatives had fallen to 12.6 percent (7.2 percent involving spouses). For the information about Detroit, see Martin Daly and Margo Wilson, *Homicide* (Hawthorne, NY: Aldine de Gruyter Publishers, 1988).

29. Kathy O'Connell of the Illinois Criminal Justice Information Authority provided these data.

30. See also Daniel D. Polsby, "From the Hip: The Intellectual Argument in Favor of Restrictive Gun Control Is Collapsing. So How Come the Political Strength of Its Advocates Is Increasing?" *National Review* (Mar. 24, 1997): 35–36.

31. In these seventy-five largest counties in 1988, 77 percent of murder arrestees and 78 percent of defendants in murder prosecutions had criminal histories, with over 13 percent of murders being committed by minors, who by definition cannot have criminal records. This implies that 89 percent of those arrested for murders must be adults with criminal records, with 90 percent of those being prosecuted. See Bureau of Justice Statistics Special Reports, "Murder in Large Urban Counties, 1988," (Washington, DC: U.S. Department of Justice, 1993), and "Murder in Families" (Washington, DC: U.S. Department of Justice, 1994); see also Don B. Kates and Dan Polsby, "The Background of Murders," Northwestern University Law School working paper (1997).

32. The average victim had 9.5 prior arraignments, while the average offender had 9.7. David M. Kennedy, Anne M. Piehl, and Anthony A. Braga, "Youth Violence in Boston: Gun Markets, Serious Youth Offenders, and a Use-Reduction Strategy," *Law and Contemporary Problems* 59 (Winter 1996): 147–96.

33. The relationship between age and sex and who commits murders holds across other countries such as Canada; see Daly and Wilson, *Homicide*, pp. 168–70.

34. James Q. Wilson and Richard J. Herrnstein, *Crime and Human Nature*, (New York: Simon and Schuster, 1985), p. 177. Wilson and Herrnstein also discuss in chapter 3 evidence linking criminality to physical characteristics. The surveys that they summarize find evidence that criminality is more likely among those who are shorter and more muscular.

35. Ibid., pp. 204–7; see also Michael K. Block and Vernon E. Gerety, "Some Experimental Evidence on the Differences between Student and Prisoner Reactions to Monetary Penalties," *Journal of Legal Studies* 24 (Jan. 1995): 123–138.

36. John J. DiIulio, Jr., "The Question of Black Crime," *The Public Interest* 117 (Fall 1994): 3–24; and "White Lies About Black Crime," *The Public Interest* 118 (Winter 1995): 30–44.

37. While there are many sources of misinformation on the deaths that arise from handguns, some stories attempt to clarify claims. For example, a *Nando Times* (www.nando.com) news story (Oct. 26, 1996) reported that "during a campaign visit here this week, President Clinton met with the widow of a police officer killed in the line of duty and later during a political rally cited his death as a reason to outlaw armor-piercing bullets. What he did not tell his audience, however, was that the officer died in an auto accident, not from gunfire. . . . Neither a bulletproof vest nor a ban on 'cop-killer bullets,' however, would have saved Officer Jerome Harrison Seaberry Sr., 35. He was responding to a radio call for backup on Christmas night last year when 'he lost control of his vehicle, going too fast . . . hit a tree head-on, and the vehicle burst into flames,' said Lake Charles Police Chief Sam Ivey. Armor-piercing bullets, Ivey said, 'had nothing to do with it.'"

38. National Center for Injury Prevention, *Injury Mortality Statistics* (Atlanta: Centers for Disease Control, 1999).

39. Editorial, "The Story of a Gun and a Kid," *Washington Times*, May 22, 1997, p. A18.

40. Joyce Price, "Heston Attacks Trigger-Lock Proposal: Actor Begins Role as NRA Executive," *Washington Times*, May 19, 1997, p. A4.

41. Currently, the impact of gun locks is difficult to test simply because no state requires them. Seven states (California, Connecticut, Florida, Hawaii, Minnesota, New Jersey, and North Carolina) and the District of Columbia have laws regarding proper storage, but these laws do not mandate a particular method of storage.

42. W. Kip Viscusi, "The Lulling Effect: The Impact of Child-Resistant Packaging on Aspirin and Analgesic Ingestions," *American Economic Review* (May, 1984): 324–27.

43. The Department of Justice's National Institute of Justice recently released a

government-funded study entitled "Guns in America: National Survey on Private Owner-ship and Use of Firearms," by Philip Cook and Jens Ludwig. The study used poll evidence from 2,568 adults in 1994 to claim that "20 percent of all gun-owning households had an unlocked, loaded gun at the time of the survey. The report cited the accidental deaths of 185 children under the age of 14, and many times that number of accidental shootings. For each death, there are several accidental shootings that cause serious injuries." Fifty percent of respondents were said to have stored an unloaded gun that was unlocked. The Justice Department's press release quoted Attorney General Janet Reno as claiming that "these results show how dangerous unlocked guns are to children. That's why we must pass the child-safety-lock provision in the President's Anti-Gang and Youth Violence Act of 1997, now before Congress. A locked gun can avoid a family tragedy." Ignoring prob-lems with the survey itself, several problems exist with these conclusions. First, the report does not show that those 20 percent of gun-owning households with "unlocked, loaded" guns were responsible for the 185 firearm deaths of children. We would be interested to know if the 20 percent of households included children. Second, the report only concen-trates on the costs, while ignoring any possible benefits. One question that might be useful in considering benefits is this: Where did those with unlocked, loaded guns tend to live? For example, were they more likely to live in urban, high-crime areas? (See De-partment of Justice, *PR Newswire,* May 5, 1997.)

Unfortunately, despite issuing press releases and talking to the press about their find-ings, neither the Department of Justice, nor professors Cook or Ludwig, nor the Police Foundation, which oversaw the government grant, have made any attempt to release their data at least by August 1997.

44. U.S. Department of Commerce, Bureau of the Census, *Statistical Abstract of the United States* (Washington, DC: U.S. Government Printing Office, 1995). A common claim I will discuss later is that "more than half of all firearm deaths occur in the home where the firearm is kept." As noted in the text, since one-half of all firearm deaths are suicides, this should come as no surprise.

45. Editorial, *Cincinnati Enquirer,* Jan. 23, 1996, p. A8. Others share this belief. "It's com-mon sense," says Doug Weil, research director at the Center to Prevent Handgun Vio-lence, in Washington. "The more guns people are carrying, the more likely it is that ordinary confrontations will escalate into violent confrontations" (William Tucker, "Maybe You Should Carry a Handgun," the *Weekly Standard,* Dec. 16, 1996, p. 30).

46. For these arguments, see P. J. Cook, "The Role of Firearms in Violent Crime," in M. E. Wolfgang and N. A. Werner, eds., *Criminal Violence* (Newbury, NJ: Sage Publishers, 1982); and Franklin Zimring, "The Medium Is the Message: Firearm Caliber as a Determi-nant of Death from Assault," *Journal of Legal Studies* 1 (1972): 97–124.

47. P. J. Cook, "The Technology of Personal Violence," *Crime and Justice: Annual Review of Research* 14 (1991): 57, 56 n. 4. Cook reported 82,000 defensive uses for an earlier period. The irony of Cook's position here is that his earlier work argued that the National Crime Victimization Survey radically underreports other violence-related events, including do-mestic violence, rapes, and gunshot woundings linked to criminal acts; see Gary Kleck, *Targeting Guns* (Hawthorne, NY: Aldine de Gruyter Publishers, 1997).

It is easy to find people who argue that concealed handguns will have no deterrent effect. H. Richard Uviller writes that "more handguns lawfully in civilian hands will not reduce deaths from bullets and cannot stop the predators from enforcing their criminal demands and expressing their lethal purposes with the most effective tool they can get their hands on." See H. Richard Uviller, *Virtual Justice: The Flawed Prosecution of Crime in America* (New Haven: Yale University Press, 1996), p. 95.

48. For instance, the University of Chicago's National Opinion Research Center states that reported gun-ownership rates are much lower in urban areas. In the nation's twelve largest cities, just 18 percent of all households report owning a gun. Women in rural areas

appear to own guns at about three times the rate that women in the twelve largest cities do. For a discussion about how these numbers vary between urban and rural areas generally or for women across areas, see James A. Davis and Tom W. Smith, *General Social Surveys, 1972–1993: Cumulative Codebook* (Chicago: National Opinion Research Center, 1993); and Tom W. Smith and Robert J. Smith, "Changes in Firearm Ownership Among Women, 1980–1994," *Journal of Criminal Law and Criminology* 86 (Fall 1995): 133–49. This issue is discussed further in chapter 3.

49. Gary Kleck provides an excellent discussion of the methodological weaknesses in the National Crime Victimization Survey. As an example, he writes, "Unfortunately, 88 percent of the violent crimes reported to the [National Crime Victimization Survey] in 1992 were committed away from the victim's home. Thus, by the time the self-protection question is asked, almost all the [respondents] who in fact had used a gun for self-protection know that they had already admitted that the incident occurred in a place where it would be a crime for them to have possessed a gun" (see Kleck, *Targeting Guns*).

50. Still another survey deals more directly with the number of lives potentially saved by defensive gun uses. It reports that potential victims believe that each year, 400,000 people "almost certainly" saved a life by using a gun, though even the researchers providing this estimate believe that the number is too high. See Gary Kleck and Marc Gertz, "Armed Resistance to Crime: The Prevalence and Nature of Self-Defense with a Gun," *Journal of Criminal Law and Criminology* 86 (Fall 1995): 150, 153, 180, 180–2; see also Gary Kleck, "Critique of Cook/Ludwig Paper," undated manuscript, Dept. of Criminology, Florida State University). Recent evidence confirms other numbers from Kleck's and Gertz's study. For example, Annest et al. estimate that 99,025 people sought medical treatment for nonfatal firearm woundings. When one considers that many criminals will not seek treatment for wounds and that not all wounds require medical treatment, Kleck's and Gertz's estimate of 200,000 woundings seems somewhat plausible, though even Kleck and Gertz believe that this is undoubtedly too high, given the very high level of marksmanship that this implies for those firing the guns. Even if the true number of times that criminals are wounded is much smaller, however, this still implies that criminals face a very real expected cost when they attack armed civilians. For discussions of the defensive use of guns, see J. L. Annest et al., "National Estimates of Nonfatal, Firearm-Related Injuries: Beyond the Tip of the Iceberg," *Journal of the American Medical Association* (June 14, 1995): 1749–54; and Lawrence Southwick, Jr., "Self-Defense with Guns: The Consequences," *Managerial and Decision Economics* (forthcoming).

51. Information from telephone call to Susan Harrell, Administrator, Bureau of License Issuance for the state of Florida in Tallahassee. David Kopel writes that "in Florida as a whole, 315,000 permits had been issued by December 31, 1995. Only five had been revoked because the permit holder committed a violent crime with a gun." See David Kopel, "The Untold Triumph of Concealed-Carry Permits," *Policy Review* 78 (July–Aug. 1996); see also Stan Schellpeper, "Case for a Handgun-Carry Law," *Omaha World-Herald*, Feb. 6, 1997, p. 27; and Clayton E. Cramer and David B. Kopel, "'Shall Issue': The New Wave of Concealed-Handgun Permit Laws," *Tennessee Law Review* 62 (Spring 1995): 679, 691. An expanded version of this last article is available from the Independence Institute, 14142 Denver West Parkway, Suite 185, Golden, Colorado, 80401-3134.

52. Cramer and Kopel, "New Wave of Concealed-Handgun Permit Laws," pp. 691–92.

53. Bob Barnhart, "Concealed-Handgun Licensing in Multnomah County," mimeo (Intelligence/Concealed Handgun Unit: Multnomah County, Oct. 1994).

54. See *Richmond Times Dispatch*, Jan. 16, 1997.

55. Schellpeper, "Case for a Handgun-Carry Law," p. 27.

56. "Packin' and More Peaceful," *Las Vegas Review-Journal*, Aug. 5, 1996, p. 6B.

57. Kentucky State Police Trooper Jan Wuchner is also quoted as saying that he has "heard nothing around the state related to crime with a gun committed by permit hold-

ers. There has been nothing like that that I've been informed of." See Terry Flynn, "Gun-Toting Kentuckians Hold Their Fire," *Cincinnati Enquirer,* June 16, 1997, p. A1.

58. Lee Anderson, "North Carolina's Guns," *Chattanooga Free Press,* May 31, 1997, p. A4.

59. Lawrence Messina, "Gun-Permit Seekers Not the Criminal Type," *Charleston Gazette,* July 28, 1997, p. C1.

60. This is the incident discussed in note 3 that occurred during the beginning of 1996 in Texas. As for citizens with concealed handgun permits coming to the aid of police officers see the end of note 68.

61. Peter Hermann, "Unarmed Resident Slain by Intruder; Victim's Rifle Taken by Authorities," *Baltimore Sun,* Sept. 19, 1996, p. B1.

62. Christi Parsons and Andrew Martin, "Bead Drawn on Gun Law," *Chicago Tribune,* May 22, 1997, p. 1; the article includes a long list of such cases, not all of which ended with the charges being dropped. For example,

> In Chicago, two motorists, both U.S. Marine Recruiters, were charged with felonies for allegedly having guns in their car when stopped by police for a minor traffic violation. State Rep. Joel Brunsvold (D–Milan) said a downstate woman who kept an assembled rifle in her car to shoot rodents on her farm was pulled over and charged with a felony, as if she had been planning a drive-by shooting. And in March, Chicago Bears defensive end Alonzo Spellman was charged with a felony after volunteering to a police officer during a traffic stop that he had a handgun inside his car.

63. Stephen Singular, *Talked to Death* (New York: Beech Tree Books, 1987), p. 142. In several other tragic cases people have carried concealed handguns because of death threats, only to be arrested by the police for carrying them; see, for example, Kristi Wright, "Executive Decision," *Omaha World-Herald,* June 8, 1997, p. 1E.

64. A recent case in Oklahoma illustrates how a gun allowed an elderly woman to defend herself:

> An 83-year-old woman proved her aim was good Tuesday morning as she shot a burglar trying to get inside her home. Della Mae Wiggins's home has been burglarized four times. She was beaten by a burglar in November. And she wasn't going to let it happen again. When she heard someone trying to break into her home at about 5 A.M., Wiggins said she grabbed a gun that had been loaded for nine years but never fired. She told police an intruder removed her window-unit air conditioner to enter her home. She said she warned the intruder she was armed. Then she pulled the trigger, hitting the intruder in the thigh. The man backed out the window and fled. (Robert Medley, "83-Year-Old Woman Shoots Fifth Burglar to Try to Victimize Her," *Oklahoma City Daily Oklahoman,* May 21, 1997.

This case also illustrates another point, because it involves a crime where the perpetrator would have been classified as knowing the intended victim. The attacker had just a few days earlier "mowed a lawn at a rental property for her."

65. Kristi O'Brien, "Concealed-Gun Legislation Bottled Up Again," *Copley News Service* (Apr. 15, 1997).

66. As Lon Cripps, the police chief in Langsberg, Montcalm County, Michigan, said in discussing concealed handguns, "There comes a time when you have to take responsibility for your own life. Police officers just aren't always going to be there" (*Detroit News,* June 14, 1996).

67. States where less than 10 percent of the members responded to the poll were excluded from the polling numbers reported by the National Association of Chiefs of Police.

68. Recent legislative testimony during 1997 provides similar evidence. In testifying before the Kansas House of Representatives on behalf of the Kansas State Lodge of the

Fraternal Order of Police, Joseph T. Gimar said, "We ... continue our support of the [right-to-carry] legislation with the belief that the citizens of Kansas will use it responsibly. ... I have gone to great lengths to speak to as many national [Fraternal Order of Police] members as possible, many in jurisdictions that have concealed-carry statutes, but [I] have been unable to find any that were in opposition to their statutes." (For this and other quotations by law-enforcement officers, see Gary K. Hayzlett, "Kansans Should Get to Carry and Conceal Arms," *Kansas City Star,* Mar. 21, 1997.)

Many stories involve armed citizens, some with licensed concealed handguns, who have come to the aid of police officers who are being attacked. For example,

> Shapiro was arrested April 9 after punching and kicking Howey police Officer David Kiss in the face and mouth during a State Road 48 traffic stop, which also involved his wife, Susan Jane Shapiro.
>
> The melee didn't break up until a Mission Inn employee who was passing by shot Mark Shapiro in the back of his left knee.
>
> The passer-by, Vincent McCarthy, 46, of Eustis, had a permit to carry his .25-caliber automatic pistol and will not be charged, Lake sheriff's authorities said.
>
> The Howey Town Council earlier this week commended McCarthy for coming to the aid of Kiss. (Linda Chong, "Man Gets House Arrest in Law Officer's Beating," *Orlando Sentinel Tribune,* May 16, 1992, p. 8)

69. Related stories can be found in the *Alva (Oklahoma) Review Courier,* Jan. 8, 1995; the *Tuscaloosa News,* Jan. 12, 1995; and the *Houston Post,* Jan. 22, 1994; see "Gun-Control Survey," *Law Enforcement Technology* (July–Aug. 1991), pp. 14–15.

Police officers are well aware that off-duty officers have often been able to thwart crimes because they were armed. News stories on such cases are easy to find; see, for example, Deborah Hastings, "Girl Killed in California During Stop for Ice Cream on Parents' Anniversary," *Associated Press,* June 18, 1997, dateline Los Angeles, 02:50 A.M. EDT).

70. See Richard Connelly, "Handgun Law's First Year Belies Fears of 'Blood in the Streets,'" *Texas Lawyer,* Dec. 9, 1996, p. 2.

71. See the *Florida Times-Union,* May 9, 1988, and *Palm Beach Post,* July 26, 1988.

72. Flynn, "Gun-Toting Kentuckians Hold Their Fire," p. A1.

73. However, other polls, such as one done by the Johns Hopkins Center for Gun Policy and Research, a group that I will discuss again in chapter 7, argue that people favor more restrictions on gun ownership and claim that 82 percent favored mandatory registration of all handguns (Larry Bivens, "Most Want Child-Proof Handguns, Poll Shows," *Detroit News,* Mar. 14, 1997, p. A5).

74. Tom Smith, "1996 National Gun-Policy Survey of the National Opinion Research Center: Research Findings," (Chicago: National Opinion Research Center, Mar. 1997), p. 21.

75. Ibid., pp. 8–9. The survey did include overwhelmingly positive responses to many questions on additional safety regulations for guns. I believe that many of these responses would have been significantly altered if the questions had been posed in terms of the trade-off between safety benefits and estimates of their costs, or if terms describing dangers to children had been eliminated (especially, as already noted in the text, since the number of children harmed by gun accidents is probably much smaller than most people believe).

76. Ibid., p. 13. The other major deciding factor for people's views on gun control appears to be whether they trust government. Those who do trust government are much more in favor of gun control.

77. Erika Schwarz (the first runner-up in the 1997 Miss America Pageant) decided to obtain a gun after a gunman stole her car when she pulled into her driveway. "It's about time they allow citizens to protect themselves. I don't advocate taking the law in your

own hand. But in a situation where you're cooped up in a car or house and somebody wants to harm you, this is a good law" (Guy Coates, "Beauty Gets Ready to Shoot Carjackers," *Chattanooga Free Press,* Aug. 14, 1997, p. B7). Similar stories are told by others who were motivated to obtain firearms training. A recent *Wall Street Journal* story discussed the reasons given by fourteen people who enrolled in a self-defense class run by Smith & Wesson: "The budget analyst had a knife held to her throat in a crowded Manhattan bar. Ms. Denman awoke 18 months ago in her rural home to find a masked, armed burglar at the foot of her bed. He'd kicked in her deadbolted door, and shot at her several times before fleeing. She dialed 911, and then waited 45 minutes for help to arrive." See Caitlin Kelly, "Gun Control," *Wall Street Journal,* Sept. 12, 1997, p. A20.

78. "Georgia Lawmakers Quietly Vote Themselves the Right to Carry Weapons," *Associated Press,* dateline Atlanta, Mar. 19, 1996, 11:09 P.M. EST.

79. According to Larry Mason of the Association of California Deputy District Attorneys, "The association is . . . glad prosecutors have been permitted to protect themselves and that they can continue to do so for their own peace of mind and well-being" (quoted in Greg Krikorian, "Lungren Rules Prosecutors Can Carry Guns to Offices," *Los Angeles Times,* July 25, 1997, p. B1).

The Fraternal Order of Police has also strongly supported legislation that would allow current or retired police officers to carry concealed handguns with them wherever they travel within the United States. (Prepared testimony of Bernard H. Teodorski, National Vice President, Fraternal Order of Police, before the House Committee on the Judiciary, Subcommittee on Crime (*Federal News Service,* July 22, 1997.)

80. *Los Angeles Times,* Jan. 4, 1996, p. E1; Louis Graham, "Officials, Celebs Become Gun-Toting Sheriff's Deputies in Long Tradition," *Memphis Commercial Appeal,* Oct. 3, 1994, pp. 1A, B7; and Clayton B. Cramer and David B. Kopel, "'Shall Issue': New Wave of Concealed-Handgun Permit Laws" (Independence Institute: Golden Colorado, Oct. 17, 1994).

81. See note 77 above.

82. See Adriel Bettelheim, "Campbell Gunning for Concealed-Weapon Proposal," *Denver Post,* June 8, 1997, p. A31.

83. Gary Marx and Janan Hanna, "Boy Called Unfit for Murder Trial," *Chicago Tribune,* Jan. 18, 1995, p. 3; and Joan Beck, "The Murder of Children," *St. Louis Post-Dispatch,* Oct. 24, 1994, p. B19.

84. Maggi Martin, "Symphony of Life Ended Too Quickly for Musician: Grieving Friends Say Man Stabbed in Lakewood Had Much to Give," *Cleveland Plain Dealer,* July 12, 1995, p. 1A.

85. John Stevenson, "Jurors Begin Deliberating Stroud's Fate," *Durham (North Carolina) Herald-Sun,* Feb. 9, 1995, p. C1.

86. In 1992, only three states did not allow insanity as a defense (Idaho, Montana, and Utah), but even in these states, insanity can be used in determining whether a person had intent.

87. See Dan Kahan and Martha Nussbaum, "Two Conceptions of Emotion in Criminal Law," *Columbia Law Review* 96 (Mar. 1996): 269–374.

88. *Model Penal Code* § 2100.3(1)(b) (1980).

89. See Kahan and Nussbaum, "Emotion in Criminal Law," *Columbia Law Review:* 315–17.

90. *Bullock v United States,* 122 F2d 214 (DC Cir 1941).

91. Kahan and Nussbaum, "Emotion in Criminal Law," *Columbia Law Review:* 325.

92. Anne Lamoy, "Murder Rate in KCK Lowest Since 1991," *Kansas City Star,* Jan. 1, 1997, p. C1.

93. John H. Kagel, Raymond C. Battalio, Howard Rachlin, and Leonard Green, "Demand Curves for Animal Consumers," *Quarterly Journal of Economics* 96 (Feb. 1981): 1–16; John H. Kagel, Raymond C. Battalio, Howard Rachlin, and Leonard Green, "Experimental Studies of Consumer Demand Behavior Using Laboratory Animals," *Economic Inquiry* 13

(Jan. 1975): 22–38; Raymond C. Battalio, John H. Kagel, and Owen R. Phillips, "Optimal Prices and Animal Consumers in Congested Markets," *Economic Inquiry* 24 (Apr. 1986): 181–93; Todd Sandler, "Optimal Prices and Animal Consumers in Congested Markets: A Comment," *Economic Inquiry* 25 (Oct. 1987): 715–20; Raymond C. Battalio, John H. Kagel, and Owen R. Phillips, "Optimal Prices and Animal Consumers in Congested Markets: A Reply," *Economic Inquiry* 25 (Oct. 1987): 721–22; and Raymond C. Battalio, John H. Kagel, Howard Rachlin, and Leonard Green, "Commodity Choice Behavior with Pigeons as Subjects," *Journal of Political Economy* 84 (Feb. 1981): 116–51.

94. William M. Landes, "An Economic Study of U.S. Aircraft Hijacking, 1961–1976," *Journal of Law and Economics* 21 (Apr. 1978): 1–29.

95. Alfred Blumstein and Daniel Nagin, "The Deterrent Effect of Legal Sanctions on Draft Evasion," *Stanford University Law Review* 28 (1977): 241–76.

96. For a particularly well-done piece that uses data from another country, see Kenneth Wolpin, "An Economic Analysis of Crime and Punishment in England and Wales, 1894–1967," *Journal of Political Economy* 86 (1978): 815–40. For a recent survey of papers in this area, see Isaac Ehrlich, "Crime, Punishment, and the Market for Offenses," *Journal of Economic Perspectives* 10 (Winter 1996): 43–67.

97. Alfred Blumstein, Jacqueline Cohen, and Daniel Nagin, eds., *Deterrence and Incapacitation: Estimating the Effects of Criminal Sanctions on Crime Rates* (Washington, DC: National Academy of Sciences, 1978), pp. 4, 7. Economists have responded to this report; see Isaac Ehrlich and Randall Mark, "Fear of Deterrence: A Critical Evaluation of the 'Report of the Panel on Research on Deterrent and Incapacitation Effects,'" *Journal of Legal Studies* 6 (June 1977): 293–316.

98. Wallace P. Mullin, "Will Gun Buyback Programs Increase the Quantity of Guns?" Michigan State University working paper (Mar. 1997), and Martha R. Plotkin, ed., *Under Fire: Gun Buy-Backs, Exchanges, and Amnesty Programs* (Washington, DC: Police Executive Research Forum, 1996).

CHAPTER TWO

1. The Supreme Court Justices would not uphold broad protections for gun ownership "if they thought blood would flow in the streets." This point was made by Professor Daniel Polsby in a talk given at the University of Chicago, February 20, 1997. As he points out, the Supreme Court would not have allowed the publication of the Pentagon Papers, despite the arguments about the freedom of the press, if it had posed a severe military risk to the United States. It is not the role of this book to debate the purpose of the Second Amendment. However, the argument that the Second Amendment implies broad protection of gun ownership seems quite strong. William Van Alstyne argues that the reference to a "well-regulated Militia" refers to the "ordinary citizen" and that it was emphatically not an allusion to "regular armed soldiers." It was ordinary citizens who were to bring their own arms to form an army when the Republic was in danger. The amendment was viewed as the ultimate limit on a government's turning against the will of the people. See William Van Alstyne, "The Second Amendment Right to Arms," *Duke Law Review* 43 (Apr. 1994): 1236–55.

2. The opposite of endogenous is exogenous. An exogenous change in something is an independent change, not a response to something else. In reality, almost everything is to some extent related to something else, so the distinction between exogenous and endogenous is a matter of degree. Since models and statistical methods must put a limit on how much to include, some variables will always be treated as "exogenously given" rather than dependent on other variables. For the social sciences, this is a constant headache. Virtually any study is open to the criticism that "if variable X depends upon variable

Y, your results are not necessarily valid." In general, larger studies that rely on more data have better chances of reliably incorporating more relationships. Part of the process of doing research is determining which relationships may raise important concerns for readers and then attempting to test for those concerns.

3. With purely cross-sectional data, if one recognizes that differences may exist in crime rates even after all the demographic and criminal-punishment variables are accounted for, there are simply not enough observations to take these regional differences into account. One cannot control for more variables than one has observations to explain.

The problem with time-series data is the same. Time-series studies typically assume that crime follows a particular type of time trend (for example, they may simply assume that crime rises at a constant rate over time, or they may assume more complicated growth rates involving squared or cubic relationships). Yet almost any crime pattern over time is possible, and, as with cross-sectional data, unexplained differences over time will persist even after all the demographic and criminal-punishment variables are accounted for. Ideally, one could allow each year to have a different effect, but with time-series data we would again find that we had more variables with which to explain changes than we had observations to explain.

4. Gary Kleck and E. Britt Patterson, "The Impact of Gun Control and Gun-Ownership Levels on Violence Rates," *Journal of Quantitative Criminology* 9 (1993): 249–87.

5. David McDowall, Colin Loftin, and Brian Wiersema, "Easing Concealed Firearm Laws: Effects on Homicide in Three States," *Journal of Criminal Law and Criminology* 86 (Fall 1995): 193–206.

6. Arthur L. Kellermann, et al., "Gun Ownership as a Risk Factor for Homicide in the Home," *New England Journal of Medicine* (Oct. 7, 1993): 1084–91.

7. Ibid., p. 1084.

8. The interesting letter that provoked this response from Kellermann et al. was written by students in a graduate statistics class at St. Louis University. See the *New England Journal of Medicine* (Feb. 3, 1994): 366, 368.

9. Recent attempts to relate the crime rate to the prison population concern me. Besides difficulties in relating the total prison population to any particular type of crime, I think it is problematic to compare a stock (the prison population) with a flow (the crime rate). See, for example, Steven Levitt, "The Effect of Prison Population Size on Crime Rates: Evidence from Prison Overcrowding Litigation," *Quarterly Journal of Economics* 111 (1996): 144–67.

10. Gary S. Becker, "Crime and Punishment: An Economic Approach," *Journal of Political Economy* 76 (Mar./Apr. 1968): 169–217. See also, for example, Isaac Ehrlich, "Participation in Illegitimate Activities: A Theoretical and Empirical Investigation," *Journal of Political Economy* 81 (1973): 521–65; Michael K. Block and John Heineke, "A Labor Theoretical Analysis of Criminal Choice," *American Economic Review* 65 (June 1975): 314–25; William M. Landes, "An Economic Study of U.S. Aircraft Hijacking, 1961–1976," *Journal of Law and Economics* 21 (Apr. 1978): 1–29.; John R. Lott, Jr., "Juvenile Delinquency and Education: A Comparison of Public and Private Provision," *International Review of Law and Economics* 7 (Dec. 1987): 163–75; James Andreoni, "Criminal Deterrence in the Reduce Form: A New Perspective on Ehrlich's Seminal Study," *Economic Inquiry* 33 (July 1995): 476–83; Morgan O. Reynolds, "Crime and Punishment in America," (Dallas: National Center for Policy Analysis, June 1995); and Levitt, "Effect of Prison Population Size on Crime Rates."

11. John R. Lott, Jr., "Do We Punish High-Income Criminals Too Heavily?" *Economic Inquiry* 30 (Oct. 1992): 583–608.

12. John R. Lott, Jr., "The Effect of Conviction on the Legitimate Income of Criminals," *Economics Letters* 34 (Dec. 1990): 381–85 ; John R. Lott, Jr., "An Attempt at Measuring the Total Monetary Penalty from Drug Convictions: The Importance of an Individual's Reputation," *Journal of Legal Studies* 21 (Jan. 1992): 159–87.

13. This approach is also known as controlling for "fixed effects," where a separate dummy variable is used to account for each county.

14. James Q. Wilson and George L. Kelling, "Making Neighborhoods Safe," *Atlantic Monthly*, Feb. 1989, and "Broken Windows," *Atlantic Monthly*, Mar. 1982.

15. Arson was excluded because of a large number of inconsistencies in the data and the small number of counties reporting this measure.

16. Robbery includes street robbery, commercial robbery, service station robbery, convenience store robbery, residence robbery, and bank robbery. (See also the discussion of burglary regarding why the inclusion of residence robbery creates difficulty with this broad measure.) After I wrote the original paper, two different commentators attempted to argue that "If 'shall-issue' [a synonym for "nondiscretionary"] concealed-carrying laws really deter criminals from undertaking street crimes, then it is only reasonable to expect the laws to have an impact on robberies. Robbery takes place between strangers on the street. A high percentage of homicide and rape, on the other hand, occurs inside a home—where concealed-weapons laws should have no impact. These findings strongly suggest that something else—not new concealed-carry laws—is responsible for the reduction in crime observed by the authors." See, for example, Doug Weil, "Response to John Lott's Study on the Impact of 'Carry-Concealed' Laws on Crime Rates," *U.S. Newswire*, Aug. 8, 1996. The curious aspect of the emphasis on robbery over other crimes like murder and rape is that if robbery is the most obvious crime to be affected by gun-control laws, why have virtually no gun-control studies examined robberies? In fact, Kleck's literature survey only notes one previous gun-control study that examined the issue of robberies ("Guns and Violence: An Interpretive Review of the Field," Social Pathology 1 [Jan. 1995]: 12–47). More important, given that the FBI includes many categories of robberies besides those that "take place between strangers on the street," it is not obvious why this category should exhibit the greatest sensitivity to concealed-handgun laws.

17. "NRA poll: Salespeople No. 1 for Permit Applications," *Dallas Morning News*, Apr. 19, 1996, p. 32A.

18. For example, see Arnold S. Linsky, Murray A. Strauss, and Ronet Bachman-Prehn, "Social Stress, Legitimate Violence, and Gun Availability," Paper presented at the annual meetings of the Society for the Study of Social Problems, 1988; and Clayton E. Cramer and David B. Kopel, "'Shall Issue': The New Wave of Concealed-Handgun Permit Laws," *Tennessee Law Review* 62 (Spring 1995): 680–91.

19. Among those who made this comment to David Mustard and me were Bob Barnhart, Manager of the Intelligence/Concealed Handgun United of Multnomah County, Oregon; Mike Woodward, of the Oregon Law Enforcement Data System; Joe Vincent of the Washington Department of Licensing Firearms Unit; Alan Krug, who provided us with the Pennsylvania Permit data; and Susan Harrell of the Florida Department of State Concealed Weapons Division. Evidence for this point with respect to Virginia was obtained from Eric Lipton, "Virginians Get Ready to Conceal Arms: State's New Weapon Law Brings a Flood of Inquiries," *Washington Post*, June 28, 1995, p. A1, who notes that "analysts say the new law, which drops the requirement that prospective gun carriers show a 'demonstrated need' to be armed, likely won't make much of a difference in rural areas, where judges have long issued permits to most people who applied for them. But in urban areas such as Northern Virginia—where judges granted few permits because few residents could justify a need for them—the number of concealed weapon permits issued is expected to soar. In Fairfax, for example, a county of more than 850,000 people, only 10 now have permits." See also Cramer and Kopel, "New Wave of Concealed-Handgun Permit Laws," pp. 679–758.

20. For example, see Kleck and Patterson, "Impact of Gun Control and Gun-Ownership Levels on Violence Rates."

21. The sex ratios in Alaska are quite large. For example, white males outnumber

white females in the 20–29 age range by 19 percent, while the difference for the United States as a whole is 3 percent. The same ratio for the 30–39 age range is 12 percent in Alaska and 1 percent nationally. Yet the greatest differences occur for blacks. In Alaska black males outnumber black females in the 20–29 age range by 40 percent, while in the rest of the United States the reverse is true, with black females outnumbering (nonincarcerated) black males by 7 percent.

22. While no reliable data are available on this question, a couple of polls indicate that the number of otherwise law-abiding citizens who carry concealed handguns may be substantial. The results of a recent Oklahoma poll showed that up to 6 percent of Oklahoma residents already carry concealed handguns either on their persons or in their cars; see Michael Smith, "Many Permits to Go to Lawbreakers," *Tulsa World,* May 5, 1996, p. A15. The margin of error in the poll was 3.5 percent, which is substantial, given the small value with which this error is compared.

23. Sam Peltzman, "The Effects of Automobile Safety Regulation," *Journal of Political Economy* 83 (Aug. 1975): 677–725.

24. Steven Peterson, George Hoffer, and Edward Millner, "Are Drivers of Air-Bag-Equipped Cars More Aggressive? A Test of the Offsetting-Behavior Hypothesis," *Journal of Law and Economics* 38 (Oct. 1995): 251–64.

25. Kieran Murray, "NRA Taps into Anger of Mid-American Gunlovers," *Reuters Newswire,* dateline Dallas, Apr. 21, 1996.

26. At least since the work of Isaac Ehrlich, economists have also realized that potential biases exist from using the offense rate as both the variable that one is seeking to explain and as the denominator in determining the arrest rate. To see this, suppose that mistakes are made in measuring the crime rate (and mistakes are certainly made) because of recording inaccuracies or simply because citizens may change the rates at which they report crime over time. Accidentally recording a crime rate that is too high will result in our recording an arrest rate that is too low, since the arrest rate is the total number of arrests divided by the total number of crimes. The converse is also true: When too low a crime rate is recorded, the arrest rate that we observe will be too high. Obviously, this problem will make it appear that a negative relationship exists between arrest rates and crime even if no relationship exists. There is also the concern that increasing crime rates may lower arrest rates if the same resources are being asked to do more work. See Isaac Ehrlich, "Participation in Illegitimate Activities: A Theoretical and Empirical Investigation," *Journal of Political Economy* 81 (1973): 548–53.

CHAPTER THREE

1. The 1988 poll's margin of error was 1.1 percent, while that of the 1996 poll was 2.2 percent.

2. In order to obtain the rate at which people in the general population owned guns, I weighted the respondents' answers to give less weight to groups that were overrepresented among voters compared to their share in the overall population, and to give greater weight to those groups that were underrepresented. Twenty-four categories of personal characteristics were used to compute these weightings: white males and females, and black males and females, aged 18–29; neither black nor white males and females 18–29; white males and females, and black males and females 30–44; neither black nor white males and females 30–44; white males and females, and black males and females 45–59; neither black nor white males and females 45–59; white males and females, and black males and females over 59; neither black nor white males and females over 59.

3. This argument has been made explicitly in the press many times. See, for example, Scott Baldauf, "As Crime Shrinks, Security Is Still Growth Industry," *Christian Science Monitor,* Oct. 2, 1996, p. 1.

4. Alix M. Freedman, "Tinier, Deadlier Pocket Pistols Are in Vogue," *Wall Street Journal*, Sept. 12, 1996, P. B1.

5. The primary concern here is that letting people check those parts of a list that apply will result in fewer positive responses than asking people to answer individual questions about each item. As one way of checking the importance of this concern, I examined whether other questions that changed in a similar way between the two polls experienced a change in the same direction as that shown for gun ownership. The two questions that I looked at—regarding marriage and whether children less than 18 lived with the respondent—moved in the opposite direction. Relatively more people indicated these responses in the 1988 poll when the questions were presented in a list than did so when they were presented with separate questions about these characteristics. I have also done extensive research using other questions involving marriage and children under 18 living with the respondent that were part of a "check as many as apply" question. That research provides extremely strong evidence that these questions were answered consistently between 1988 and 1996. See John R. Lott, Jr. and Larry W. Kenny, "How Dramatically Did Women's Suffrage Change the Size and Scope of Government?" University of Chicago School of Law working paper (1997). The relative differences in gun ownership across groups is also consistent with recent work using other polls by Edward Glaeser and Spencer Glendon, "Who Owns Guns?" *American Economic Review* 88 (May 1998).

The empirical work that will be done later will allow us to adjust for the changes in the reported level of gun ownership that might result from the change in this question.

6. I appreciate Tom Smith's taking the time to talk to me about these issues on May 30, 1997.

7. Gun owners within each of the twenty-four categories listed in note 2 above may have particular characteristics that cause them to vote at rates that differ from the rates at which other people vote. One would hope that some of that difference would be accounted for in the detailed demographic characteristics, but there is a good chance that this may not occur. Several attempts were made to see how large this effect might be by asking, for example, whether gun owners were more or less likely not to have voted in previous elections. This question has also been broken down to account for those who are old enough to have voted previously. For 1988, the difference in gun ownership between those who were voting for the first time and those who had voted previously was 3 percent (23.2 percent of those voting for the first time and 26.2 percent of those who were not owned guns). Limiting this question to people who were 30 years of age or older produced an even smaller difference: 28.9 percent of first-time voters owned guns versus 27.5 percent of those who had voted previously. Similarly, for the question of whether voters in 1988 had also voted in 1984, the difference was also 3 percent (23 percent of those who did not vote in 1984 and 26.4 percent of those who did owned guns).

Because most people voted, a 13 percent increase in the proportion of the general population owning guns would require an even greater drop in gun ownership among those who didn't vote in order for gun ownership to have remained constant. For some groups, such as women, for whom gun ownership among voters increased by over 70 percent, the increase is so large and the percent of women voting so high that an 80 percent drop in gun ownership among nonvoting women would have been required for gun ownership among women to have remained constant.

8. Indeed, making this adjustment produces a number that is much closer to that found in other polls of the general population, such as the National Opinion Research Center's 1996 National Gun-Policy Survey, which finds that 42 percent of the general adult population owns guns.

9. The previous peak in murder rates occurred at the end of Prohibition in the early 1930s, with the peak of 9.7 murders per 100,000 people being reached in 1933. The 1996 murder rate of 7.3 murders per 100,000 people seems tame by comparison. Indeed many people, such as Milton Friedman, have argued that much of the change in murder rates

over time has been driven by the country's war on drugs and its earlier war on alcohol. Even the gradual increase in murder rates leading up to the Nineteenth Amendment's adoption in 1991 corresponds with passage of individual state laws. Kansas, Maine, and North Dakota enacted prohibition laws between 1880 and 1890. Five states enacted prohibition in 1907–1909, followed by twelve more between 1912 and 1915 and another twelve between 1916 and 1918. Obviously, all this points to the importance of other factors in the murder rate, and that is part of the reason why I include a measure of drug prices in my estimates to explain why crime rates change over time. See Ernest H. Cherrington, *The Evolution of Prohibition in the United States of America* (Westerville, OH: Tem-Press, 1920); Edward B. Dunford, *The History of the Temperance Movement* (Washington, DC: Tem-Press, 1943); D. Leigh Colvin, *Prohibition in the United States,* (New York: George H. Doran, 1926); as well as state statutes (as a check).

10. While I will follow Cramer and Kopel's definition of what constitutes a "shall-issue" or a "do-issue" state (see "'Shall Issue': The New Wave of Concealed-Handgun Permit Laws," *Tennessee Law Review* 62 [Spring 1995]), one commentator has suggested that it is not appropriate to include Maine in these categories (Stephen P. Teret, "Critical Comments on a Paper by Lott and Mustard," School of Hygiene and Public Health, Johns Hopkins University, mimeo, Aug. 7, 1996). Neither defining Maine so that the "shall-issue" dummy equals zero nor removing Maine from the data set alters the findings shown in this book.

11. While the intent of the 1988 legislation in Virginia was clearly to institute a "shall-issue" law, the law was not equally implemented in all counties in the state. To deal with this problem, I reran the regressions reported in this paper with the "shall-issue" dummy equal to both 1 and 0 for Virginia.

12. I rely on Cramer and Kopel for this list of states. Some states, known as "do-issue" states, are also included in Cramer and Kopel's list of "shall-issue" states, though these authors argue that for all practical purposes these two groups of states are identical. See Cramer and Kopel, "New Wave of Concealed-Handgun Permit Laws," pp. 679–91.

13. The Oregon counties providing permit data were Benton, Clackamas, Columbia, Coos, Curry, Deschutes, Douglas, Gilliam, Hood River, Jackson, Jefferson, Josephine, Klamath, Lane, Lincoln, Linn, Malheur, Marion, Morrow, Multnomah, Polk, Tillamook, Umatilla, Washington and Yamhill.

14. In economics jargon I would say that I am interacting the sentence length with year-dummy variables.

15. These variables are referred to as county fixed-effects, where a separate dummy variable is set equal to 1 for each individual county.

16. See appendix 4 for the list and summary statistics.

17. For example, see James Q. Wilson and Richard J. Herrnstein, *Crime and Human Nature* (New York: Simon and Schuster, 1985), pp. 126–47.

18. However, the effect of an unusually large percentage of young males in the population may be mitigated because those most vulnerable to crime may be more likely to take actions to protect themselves. Depending upon how responsive victims are to these threats, the coefficient for a variable like the percent of young males in the population could be zero even when the group in question poses a large criminal threat.

19. Edward L. Glaeser and Bruce Sacerdote, "Why Is There More Crime in Cities?" Harvard University working paper, Nov. 14, 1995.

20. For a discussion of the relationship between income and crime, see John R. Lott, Jr., "A Transaction-Costs Explanation for Why the Poor Are More Likely to Commit Crime," *Journal of Legal Studies* 19 (Jan. 1990): 243–45.

21. A brief survey of the laws, excluding the changes in the rules regarding permits, reveals the following: Alabama made no significant changes in these laws during the period. Connecticut law gradually changed its wording from "criminal use" to "criminal possession" from 1986 to 1994. Florida has the most extensive description of penalties; the

same basic law (790.161) persists throughout the years. An additional law (790.07) appeared only in 1986. In Georgia, a law (16-11-106) that does not appear in the 1986 edition appears in the 1989 and 1994 editions. The law involves possession of a firearm during commission of a crime and specifies the associated penalties. Because this legal change might have occurred at the same time as the 1989 changes in the rules regarding permits, I used a Lexis search to check the legislative history of 16-11-106 and found that the laws were last changed in 1987, two years before the permit rules were changed (*Official Code of Georgia, Annotated,* at 16-11-106 [1996]). Idaho has made no significant changes over time. In Indiana and Maine no significant changes occurred in these laws during the period. In Mississippi, Law 97-37-1 talks explicitly about penalties. It appears in the 1986 version but not in the 1989 or the 1994 versions. Montana enacted some changes in punishments related to unauthorized carrying of concealed weapons, but no changes in the punishment for using a weapon in a crime. New Hampshire, North Dakota, Oregon, Pennsylvania, and Washington made no significant changes in these laws during period. In South Dakota, Law 22-14-13, which specifies penalties for commission of a felony while armed, appears in 1986 but not 1989. In Vermont, Section 4005, which outlines the penalties for carrying a gun when committing a felony, appears in 1986 but not in 1989 or 1994. Virginia and Washington made no significant changes in these laws during the period. West Virginia had Law 67-7-12 on the books in 1994, but not in the earlier versions. It involves punishment for endangerment with firearms. Removing Georgia from the sample, which was the only state that enacted changes in its gun laws near the year that the "shall-issue" law went into affect, eliminates the chance that the other changes in gun laws might affect my results and does not appreciably alter those results.

22. Thomas B. Marvell and Carlisle E. Moody, "The Impact of Enhanced Prison Terms for Felonies Committed with Guns," *Criminology* 33 (May 1995): 247, 258–61.

23. Marvell and Moody's findings (see note 22 above) show that the shortest time period between these sentencing enhancements and changes in concealed-weapon laws is seven years (Pennsylvania). Twenty-six states passed their enhancement laws prior to the beginning of my sample period, and only four states passed such laws after 1981. Maine, which implemented its concealed-handgun law in 1985, passed its sentencing-enhancement laws in 1971.

24. The states that had waiting periods prior to the beginning of the sample are Alabama, California, Connecticut, Illinois, Maryland, Minnesota, New Jersey, North Carolina, Pennsylvania, Rhode Island, South Dakota, Washington, and Wisconsin. The District of Columbia also had a waiting period prior to the beginning of my sample. The states that adopted this rule during the sample period are Hawaii, Indiana, Iowa, Missouri, Oregon, and Virginia.

CHAPTER FOUR

1. More precisely, it is the percentage of a one-standard-deviation change in the crime rate that can be explained by a one-standard-deviation change in the endogenous variable.

2. All the results are reported for the higher threshold required with a two-tailed t-test.

3. One possible concern with these initial results arises from my use of an aggregate public-policy variable (state right-to-carry laws) on county-level data. See Bruce C. Greenwald, "A General Analysis of the Bias in the Estimated Standard Errors of Least Squares Coefficients," *Journal of Econometrics* 22 (Aug. 1983): 323–38; and Brent R. Moulton, "An Illustration of a Pitfall in Estimating the Effects of Aggregate Variables on Micro Units," *Review of Economics and Statistics* 72 (1990): 334. Moulton writes, "If disturbances are correlated within the groupings that are used to merge aggregate with micro data, however, then even small levels of correlation can cause the standard errors from the ordinary

least squares (OLS) to be seriously biased downward." Yet this should not really be a concern here because of my use of dummy variables for all the counties, which is equivalent to using state dummies as well as county dummies for all but one of the counties within each state. Using these dummy variables thus allows us to control for any disturbances that are correlated within any individual state. The regressions discussed in table 4.2 reestimate the specifications shown in table 4.1 but also include state dummies that are interacted with a time trend. This should thus not only control for any disturbances that are correlated with the states, but also for any disturbances that are correlated within a state over time. Finally, while right-to-carry laws are almost always statewide laws, there is one exception. Pennsylvania partially exempted its largest county (Philadelphia) from the law when it was passed in 1989, and it remained exempt from the law during the rest of the sample period. However, permits granted in the counties surrounding Philadelphia were valid for use in the city.

4. However, the increase in the number of property crimes is larger than the decrease in the number of robberies.

5. While I adopt the classifications used by Cramer and Kopel in "'Shall Issue': The New Wave of Concealed-Handgun Permit Laws," Tennessee Law Review 62 (Spring 1995), some are more convinced by other classifications of states (for example, see Doug Weil, "Response to John Lott's Study on the Impact of 'Carry-Concealed' Laws on Crime Rates," U.S. Newswire, Aug. 8, 1996; and Stephen P. Teret, "Critical Comments on a Paper by Lott and Mustard," School of Hygiene and Public Health, Johns Hopkins University, mimeo, Aug. 7, 1996). Setting the "shall-issue" dummy for Maine to zero and rerunning the regressions shown in table 4.1 results in the "shall-issue" coefficient equaling –3% for violent crimes, –8% for murder, –6% for rape, –4.5 for aggravated assault, –1% for robbery, 3% for property crimes, 8.1% for automobile theft, 0.4% for burglary, and 3% for larceny. Similarly, setting the "shall-issue" dummy for Virginia to zero results in the "shall-issue" coefficient equaling –4% for violent crimes, –9% for murder, –5% for rape, –5% for aggravated assault, –0.11% for robbery, 3% for property crimes, 9% for automobile theft, 2% for burglary, and 3% for larceny. As a final test, dropping both Maine and Virginia from the data set results in the "shall-issue" coefficient equaling –2% for violent crimes, –10% for murder, –6% for rape, –3% for aggravated assault, 0.6% for robbery, 3.6% for property crimes, 10% for automobile theft, 2% for burglary, and 4% for larceny.

6. This information is obtained from Mortality Detail Records provided by the U.S. Department of Health and Human Services.

7. This assumption is implausible for many reasons. One reason is that accidental handgun deaths occur in states without concealed-handgun laws.

8. Given the possible relationship between drug prices and crime, I reran the regressions in table 4.1 and included an additional variable for cocaine prices. One argument linking drug prices and crime is that if the demand for drugs is inelastic and if people commit crimes in order to finance their habits, higher drug prices might lead to increased levels of crime. Using the Drug Enforcement Administration's STRIDE data set from 1977 to 1992 (with the exceptions of 1988 and 1989), Michael Grossman, Frank J. Chaloupka, and Charles C. Brown, ("The Demand for Cocaine by Young Adults: A Rational Addiction Approach," NBER working paper, July 1996), estimate the price of cocaine as a function of its purity, weight, year dummies, year dummies interacted with eight regional dummies, and individual city dummies. There are two problems with this measure of predicted prices: (1) it removes observations during a couple of important years during which changes were occurring in concealed-handgun laws, and (2) the predicted values that I obtained ignored the city-level observations. The reduced number of observations provides an important reason why I do not include this variable in the regressions shown in table 4. 1. However, the primary impact of including this new variable is to make the "shall-issue" coefficients in the violent-crime regressions even more negative and more

significant (for example, the coefficient for the violent-crime regression becomes –7.5%, –10% for the murder regression, –7.7% for rape, and –11% for aggravated assault, with all of them significant at more than the 0.01 level). Only for the burglary regression does the "shall-issue" coefficient change appreciably: it becomes negative and insignificant. The variable for drug prices itself is negatively related to murders and rapes and positively and significantly related, at least at the 0.01 level for a one-tailed t-test, to all the other categories of crime. I would like to thank Michael Grossman for providing me with the original regressions on drug prices from his paper.

9. In contrast, if we had instead inquired what difference it would make in crime rates if either all states or no states adopted right-to-carry concealed-handgun laws, the case of all states adopting concealed-handgun laws would have produced 2,000 fewer murders; 5,700 fewer rapes; 79,000 fewer aggravated assaults; and 14,900 fewer robberies. In contrast, property crimes would have risen by 336,410.

10. Ted R. Miller, Mark A. Cohen, and Brian Wiersema, *Victim Costs and Consequences: A New Look* (Washington, DC: National Institute of Justice, Feb. 1996).

11. See Sam Peltzman, "The Effects of Automobile Safety Regulation," *Journal of Political Economy* 83 (Aug. 1975): 677–725.

12. To be more precise, a one-standard-deviation change in the probability of arrest accounts for 3 to 11 percent of a one-standard-deviation change in the various crime rates.

13. Translating this into statistical terms, a one-standard-deviation change in the percentage of the population that is black, male, and between 10 and 19 years of age explains 22 percent of the ups and downs in the crime rate.

14. This is particularly observed when there are more black females between the ages of 20 and 39, more white females between the ages of 10 and 39 and over 65, and females of other races between 20 and 29.

15. In other words, the second number shows how a one-standard-deviation change in an explanatory variable explains a certain percent of a one-standard-deviation change in the various crime rates.

16. While I believe that such variables as the arrest rate should be included in any regressions on crime, one concern with the results reported in the various tables is over whether the relationship between the "shall-issue" variable and the crime rates occurs even when all the other variables are not controlled for. Using weighted least squares and reporting only the "shall-issue" coefficients, I estimated the following regression coefficients.

How do average crime rates differ among states with and without nondiscretionary laws?

Crime rates	Crime rates in states with nondiscretionary concealed-handgun laws compared to those without the law (regressing the crime rate only on the variable for the law)	Crime rates in states with nondiscretionary concealed-handgun laws compared to those without the law after adjusting for national trends (regressing the crime rate on the variable for the law and year-dummy variables)
Violent crimes	−40%	−57%
Murder	−48	−52
Rape	−16	−28
Aggravated assault	−38	−57

Crime rates	Crime rates in states with nondiscretionary concealed-handgun laws compared to those without the law (regressing the crime rate the law)	Crime rates in states with nondiscretionary concealed-handgun laws compared to those without the law after adjusting for national trends (regressing the crime rate on the variable for the law and year-dummy variables)
Robbery	−62	−75
Property crime	−17	−20
Auto theft	−31	−43
Burglary	−28	−24
Larceny	−11	−15

Note: The only factors included are the presence of the law and/or year-specific effects. All these differences are statistically significant at least at the 1 percent level for a two-tailed t-test. To calculate these percentages, I used the approximation 100 [exp(coefficient) − 1).

17. The time-trend variable ranges from 1 to 16: for the first year in the sample, it equals 1; for the last year, it is 16.

18. Other differences arise in the other control variables, such as those relating to the portion of the population of a certain race, sex, and age. For example, the percent of black males in the population between 10 and 19 is no longer statistically significant.

19. If the task instead had been to determine the difference in crime rates when either all states or no states adopt the right-to-carry handgun laws, the case of all states adopting concealed-handgun laws would have produced 2,048 fewer murders, 6,618 fewer rapes, 129,114 fewer aggravated assaults, and 86,459 fewer robberies. Non-arson property crimes also would have fallen by 511,940.

20. Generally, aggregation is frowned on in statistics anyway, as it reduces the amount of information yielded by the data set. Lumping data together into a group cannot yield any new information that did not exist before; it only reduces the richness of the data.

21. Eric Rasmusen, "Stigma and Self-Fulfilling Expectations of Criminality," *Journal of Law and Economics* 39 (Oct. 1996): 519–44.

22. In January 1996, women held 118,728 permits in Washington and 17,930 permits in Oregon. The time-series data available for Oregon during the sample period even indicate that 17.6 percent of all permit holders were women in 1991. The Washington state data were obtained from Joe Vincent of the Department of Licensing Firearms Unit in Olympia, Washington. The Oregon state data were obtained from Mike Woodward of the Law Enforcement Data System, Department of State Police, Salem, Oregon. Recent evidence from Texas indicates that about 28 percent of applicants were women ("NRA poll: Salespeople No. 1 for Permit Applications," *Dallas Morning News,* Apr. 19, 1996, p. 32A).

23. For an interesting discussion of the benefits to women of owning guns, see Paxton Quigley, *Armed and Female* (New York: E. P. Dutton, 1989).

24. Unpublished information obtained by Kleck and Gertz in their 1995 National Self-Defense Survey implies that women were as likely as men to use handguns in self-defense in or near their homes (defined as in the yard, carport, apartment hall, street adjacent to home, detached garage, etc.), but that women were less than half as likely to use a gun in self-defense away from home. See Gary Kleck and Marc Gertz, "Armed Resistance to Crime: The Prevalence and Nature of Self-Defense with a Gun," *Journal of Criminal Law and Criminology* 86 (Fall 1995): 249–87.

25. Counties with real personal income of about $15,000 in real 1983 dollars experienced 8 percent drops in murder, while mean-income counties experienced a 5.5 percent drop.

26. Lori Montgomery, "More Blacks Say Guns Are Answer to Urban Violence," *Houston Chronicle,* July 9, 1995, p. A1. This article argues that while the opposition to guns in the black community is strong, more people are coming to understand the benefits of self-protection.

27. For an excellent overview of the role of race in gun control, see Robert J. Cottrol and Raymond T. Diamond, "The Second Amendment: Toward an Afro-Americanist Reconsideration," *Georgetown Law Review* 80 (Dec. 1991): 309.

28. See William Van Alstyne, "The Second Amendment Right to Arms," *Duke Law Review* 43 (Apr. 1994): 1236–55. In slave states prior to the Civil War, the freedoms guaranteed under the Bill of Rights were regularly restricted by states because of the fear that free reign might lead to an insurrection. As Akhil Reed Amar writes, "In a society that saw itself under siege after Nat Turner's rebellion, access to firearms had to be strictly restricted, especially to free blacks." See Akhil Reed Amar, "The Bill of Rights and the Fourteenth Amendment," *Yale Law Journal* 101 (Apr. 1992): 1193.

29. *Associated Press Newswire,* May 9, 1997, 4:37 P.M. EDT. As the *Washington Times* recently noted, this story "comes at an awkward time for the administration, since President Clinton has spent the last week or two berating Republicans for failing to include in anti-crime legislation a provision requiring that child safety locks be sold with guns to keep children from hurting themselves" (Editorial, "The Story of a Gun and a Kid," *Washington Times,* May 22, 1997, p. A18).

30. The conversation took place on March 18, 1997, though regrettably I have misplaced the note containing the representative's name.

31. John Carpenter, "Six Other States Have Same Law," *Chicago Sun-Times,* Mar. 11, 1997, p. 8.

32. John J. DiIulio, Jr., "The Question of Black Crime," *The Public Interest* 117 (Fall 1994): 3–24. Similar concerns about the inability of minorities to rely on the police was also expressed to me by Assemblyman Rod Wright (D–Los Angeles) during testimony before the California Assembly's Public Safety Committee on November 18, 1997.

33. One additional minor change is made in two of the earlier specifications. In order to avoid any artificial collinearity either between violent crime and robbery or between property crimes and burglary, violent crimes net of robbery and property crimes net of burglary are used as the endogenous variables when robbery or burglary are controlled for.

34. The Pearson correlation coefficient between robbery and the other crime categories ranges between .49 and .80, and all are so statistically significant that a negative correlation would only appear randomly once out of every ten thousand times. For burglary, the correlations range from 0.45 to 0.68, and they are also equally statistically significant.

35. All the results in tables 4.1 and 4.4 as well as the regressions related to both parts of figure 4.1 were reestimated to deal with the concerns raised in chapter 3 over the "noise" in arrest rates arising from the timing of offenses and arrests and the possibility of multiple offenders. I reran all the regressions in this section by limiting the sample to those counties with populations over 10,000, over 100,000, and then over 200,000 people. The more the sample was restricted to larger-population counties, the stronger and more statistically significant was the relationship between concealed-handgun laws and the previously reported effects on crime. This is consistent with the evidence reported in figure 4.1. The arrest-rate results also tended to be stronger and more significant. I further reestimated all the regressions by redefining the arrest rate as the number of arrests over the last three years divided by the total number of offenses over the last three years. Despite the reduced sample size, the results remained similar to those already reported.

36. More formally, by using restricted least squares, we can test whether constraining

the coefficients for the period before the law produces results that yield the same pattern after the passage of the law. Using both the time-trend and the time-trend-squared relationships, the F-tests reject the hypothesis that the before and after relationships are the same, at least at the 10 percent level, for all the crime categories except aggravated assault and larceny, for which the F-tests are only significant at the 20 percent level. Using only the time-trend relationship, the F-tests reject the hypothesis in all the cases.

37. The main exception was West Virginia, which showed large drops in murder but not in other crime categories.

38. See Thomas B. Marvell and Carlisle E. Moody, "The Impact of Enhanced Prison Terms for Felonies Committed with Guns," *Criminology* 33 (May 1995): 259–60.

39. I should note, however, that the "nondiscretionary" coefficients for robbery in the county-level regressions and for property crimes using the state levels are no longer statistically significant.

40. Toni Heinzl, "Police Groups Oppose Concealed-Weapons Bill," *Omaha World-Herald,* Mar. 18, 1997, p. 9SF.

41. A simple dummy variable is used for whether the limit was 18 or 21 years of age.

42. Here is one example: "Mrs. Elmasri, a Wisconsin woman whose estranged husband had threatened her and her children, called a firearms instructor for advice on how to buy a gun for self-defense. She was advised that, under Wisconsin's progressive handgun law, she would have to wait 48 hours so that the police could perform the required background check.

"Twenty-four hours later, . . . Mrs. Elmasri's husband murdered the defenseless woman and her two children" (William P. Cheshire, "Gun Laws No Answer for Crime," *Arizona Republic,* Jan. 10, 1993, p. C1.) Other examples can be found in David B. Kopel, "Background Checks and Waiting Periods," in *Guns: Who Should Have Them,* ed. David B. Kopel (Amherst, NY: Prometheus Books, 1995.) Other examples tell of women who successfully evaded these restrictions to obtain guns.

> In September 1990, mail carrier Catherine Latta of Charlotte, N. C., went to the police to obtain permission to buy a handgun. Her ex-boyfriend had previously robbed her, assaulted her several times, and raped her. The clerk at the sheriff's office informed her that processing a gun permit would take two to four weeks. "I told her I'd be dead by then," Latta recalled.
>
> That afternoon, Latta bought an illegal $20 semiautomatic pistol on the street. Five hours later, her ex-boyfriend attacked her outside her house. She shot him dead. The county prosecutor decided not to prosecute Latta for either the self-defense homicide or the illegal gun. (Quoted from David B. Kopel, "Guns and Crime: Does Restricting Firearms Really Reduce Violence?" *San Diego Union-Tribune,* May 9, 1993, p. G4.)

For another example where a woman's ability to defend herself would have been impaired by a waiting period, see "Waiting Period Law Might Have Cost Mother's Life," *USA Today,* May 27, 1994, p. 10A.

43. Quoted in David Armstrong, "Cities' Crime Moves to Suburbs," *Boston Globe,* May 19, 1997, pp. 1 and B6.

CHAPTER FIVE

1. While county-level data were provided in the *Supplementary Homicide Reports,* matching these county observations with those used in the *Uniform Crime Reports* proved unusually difficult. A unique county identifier was used in the *Supplementary Homicide Reports* that was not consistent across years. In addition, some caution is necessary in using both the Mortality Detail Records and the *Supplementary Homicide Reports,* since the murder rates reported

in both sources have relatively low correlations of less than .7 with the murder rates reported in the *Uniform Crime Reports*. This is especially surprising for the supplementary reports, which are derived from the *Uniform Crime Reports*. See U.S. Department of Justice, FBI staff, *Uniform Crime Reports* (Washington, DC: U.S. Govt. Printing Office) for the years 1977 to 1992.

2. Indeed, the average age of permit holders is frequently in the mid- to late forties (see, for example, "NRA poll: Salespeople No. 1 for Permit Applications," *Dallas Morning News*, Apr. 19, 1996, p. 32A.) In Kentucky the average age of permit holders is about fifty (see Terry Flynn, "Gun-Toting Kentuckians Hold Their Fire," *Cincinnati Enquirer*, June 16, 1997, p. A1).

3. This is the significance for a two-tailed t-test.

4. Similar breakdowns for deaths and injuries are explored in much more depth in a paper that I have written with William Landes; see William Landes and John R. Lott, Jr., "Mass Public Shootings, Bombings, and Right-to-Carry Concealed-Handgun Laws," University of Chicago working paper, 1997.

5. A second change was also made. Because of the large number of observations noting no deaths or injuries from mass public shootings in a given year, I used a statistical technique known as Tobit that is particularly well suited to this situation.

6. The results shown below provide the estimates for the simple linear time trends before and after the adoption of the law. They demonstrate that for each year leading up to the passage of the law, total deaths or injuries from mass public shootings rose by 1.5 more per 10 million people and that after the passage of the law, total deaths or injuries fell by 4 more per 10 million people. The difference in these two trends is statistically significant at the 1 percent level for a two-tailed t-test. It is interesting to note that higher murder arrest rates, although they deter murderers, do not seem to deter perpetrators of mass public shootings.

Linear time trends for deaths and injuries from mass public shootings before and after adoption of concealed-handgun law

	Total deaths and injuries per 100,000 population
Average annual change for years after adoption of the law	−0.04*
Average annual change for years before adoption of the law	0.015*
Arrest rate for Murder	−0.0003

*Statistically significant at least at the 10 percent level for a two-tailed t-test
Note: numbers are negative; years furthest beyond adoption are the largest

7. See appendix 4 for the means and standard deviations of the variables used in these regressions.

8. Again, this is stating that a one-standard-deviation change in arrest rates explains more than 15 percent of a one-standard-deviation change in crime rates.

9. Running the regressions for all Pennsylvania counties (not just those with more than 200,000 people) produced similar signs for the coefficient for the change in concealed-handgun permits, though the coefficients were no longer statistically significant for violent crimes, rape, and aggravated assault. Alan Krug, who provided us with the Pennsylvania handgun-permit data, told us that one reason for the large increase in concealed-handgun permits in some rural counties was that people used the guns for

hunting. He told us that the number of permits issued in these low-population, rural counties tended to increase most sharply in the fall around hunting season. If people were in fact getting large numbers of permits in low-population counties (which already have extremely low crime rates) for some reason other than crime, it would be more difficult to pick up the deterrent effect of concealed handguns on crime that was occurring in the larger counties.

10. A one-standard-deviation change in conviction rates explains 4 to 20 percent of a one-standard-deviation change in the corresponding crime rates.

11. I reran these regressions using the natural logs of the arrest and conviction rates, and I consistently found statistically larger and even economically more important effects for the arrest rates than for the conviction rates.

12. For example, see Dan M. Kahan, "What Do Alternative Sanctions Mean?" *University of Chicago Law Review* 63 (1996): 591–653.

13. See John R. Lott, Jr., "The Effect of Conviction on the Legitimate Income of Criminals," *Economics Letters* 34 (Dec. 1990): 381–85; John R. Lott, Jr., "An Attempt at Measuring the Total Monetary Penalty from Drug Convictions: The Importance of an Individual's Reputation," *Journal of Legal Studies* 21 (Jan. 1992): 159–87; John R. Lott, Jr., "Do We Punish High-Income Criminals Too Heavily?" *Economic Inquiry* 30 (Oct. 1992): 583–608.

14. Put differently, six of the specifications imply that a one-standard-deviation change in the number of concealed-handgun permits explains at least 8 percent of a one-standard-deviation change in the corresponding crime rates.

15. Philip Heymann, a former deputy attorney general in the Clinton administration and currently a law professor at Harvard University, wrote, "None of this [the drop in crime rates] is the result of . . . the Brady Act (for most guns were never bought by youth from licensed gun dealers)." See "The Limits of Federal Crime-Fighting," *Washington Post*, Jan. 5, 1997, p. C7.

16. For a discussion of externalities (both benefits and costs) from crime, see Kermit Daniel and John R. Lott, Jr., "Should Criminal Penalties Include Third-Party Avoidance Costs?" *Journal of Legal Studies* 24 (June 1995): 523–34.

17. Alix M. Freedman, "Tinier, Deadlier Pocket Pistols Are in Vogue," *Wall Street Journal*, Sept. 12, 1996, pp. B1, B16.

18. One hundred and eighty-two million people lived in states without these laws in 1991, so the regressions would have also implied nine more accidental deaths from handguns in that year.

19. Given the very small number of accidental deaths from handguns in the United States, the rate of such deaths in the vast majority of counties is zero, and the last two columns of table 5.6 again use Tobit regressions to deal with this problem. Limitations in statistical packages, however, prevented me from being able to control for all the county dummies, and I opted to rerun these regressions with only state dummy variables.

20. For example, see Nicholas D. Kristof, "Guns: One Nation Bars, the Other Requires," *New York Times*, Mar. 10, 1996, sec. 4, p. 3. For some evidence on international gun ownership rates see Munday and Stevenson, *Guns and Violence* (1996): 30.

21. See Ian Ayres and Steven Levitt, "Measuring Positive Externalities from Unobservable Victim Precaution: An Empirical Analysis of Lojack," NBER working paper 5928 (1997); and John Donohue and Peter Siegelman, "Is the United States at the Optimal Rate of Crime?" *Journal of Legal Studies* 27 (Jan. 1998).

22. See notes 12 and 13 above.

CHAPTER SIX

1. Isaac Ehrlich, "Participation in Illegitimate Activities: A Theoretical and Empirical Investigation," *Journal of Political Economy* 81 (1973): 548–51. Except for the political variables, my specification accords fairly closely with at least the spirit of Ehrlich's specification,

though some of my variables, like the demographic breakdowns, are much more detailed, and I have a few other measures that were not available to him.

2. See also Robert E. McCormick and Robert Tollison, "Crime on the Court," *Journal of Political Economy* 92 (Apr. 1984): 223–35, for a novel article testing the endogeneity of the "arrest rate" in the context of basketball penalties.

3. These last two variables are measured at the state level.

4. Phil Cook suggested this addition to me. In a sense, this is similar to Ehrlich's specification, except that the current crime rate is broken down into its lagged value and the change between the current and previous periods. See Ehrlich, "Participation in Illegitimate Activities," p. 557.

5. The natural logs of the rates for violent crime and property crime were used.

6. These estimates are known as two-stage least squares.

7. Ehrlich raises the concern that the types of two-stage, least-squares estimates discussed above might still be affected by spurious correlation if the measurement errors for the crime rate were serially correlated over time. To account for this, I reestimated the first-stage regressions predicting the arrest rate without the lagged crime rate, which made the estimated results for the nondiscretionary law dummy even more negative and more statistically significant than those already shown. See Ehrlich, "Participation in Illegitimate Activities," p. 552 n. 46.

8. Still another approach would be to estimate what are known as Tobit regressions, but unfortunately no statistical package is available that allows me both to control for all the different county dummy variables and to use the Tobit procedure.

CHAPTER SEVEN

1. The Violence Policy Center grew out of the National Coalition to Ban Handguns.

2. Douglas Weil, the research director for Handgun Control, Inc., has publicly disagreed with the claim that most gun-control advocates initially refused to comment on my study. In a letter to the Washington Times, Weil wrote,

> The *Washington Times* editorial ("Armed and Safer," Aug. 14) is misinformed and misguided. The *Times* falsely claims that gun-control proponents "initially refused to read" John Lott's and David Mustard's study of the impact of laws regarding the right to carry concealed guns, and that I attacked the researchers' motivations rather than challenge the study "on the merits." This charge is untrue.
>
> One look at the study would prove the *Times* wrong. On the title page of the study, several pro–gun-control researchers are credited for their comments "on the merits" of the study. Included in this list are David McDowall, a criminologist at the University of Maryland; Philip Cook, an economist at Duke University; and myself, research director for the Center to Prevent Handgun Violence.
>
> Upon reviewing the study, I found Mr. Lott's methodology to be seriously flawed. I told Mr. Lott that his study did not adequately control for the whole range of ways that state and local governments attempt to lower the crime rate. In Oregon, for example, the same legislation that made it easier to carry a concealed handgun included one of the toughest new handgun-purchase laws in the country—a 15-day waiting period and fingerprint-background check on all purchases. . . .
>
> I gladly shared my critique of this study with Mr. Lott and will now reiterate it here; as someone fully credentialed to evaluate Mr. Lott's and Mr. Mustard's work, I would have recommended that the paper be rejected. (See Douglas Weil, "A Few Thoughts on the Study of Handgun Violence and Gun Control," *Washington Times,* Aug. 22, 1996, p. A16.)

While it is true that I thanked Mr. Weil in my paper for a comment that he made, his single comment was nothing like what his letter to the *Times* claimed. Before he explained his concerns to the press, he and I had no discussions about whether I had controlled for "ways that state and local governments attempt to lower the crime rate," possibly because my study not only controls for arrest and conviction rates, prison sentences, the number of police officers and police payroll, but also waiting periods and criminal penalties for using a gun in the commission of a crime.

Mr. Weil's sole comment to me came after two previous telephone calls over a month and a half in which Mr. Weil had said that he was too busy to give me any comments. His sole comment on August 1 was that he was upset that I had cited a study by a professor, Gary Kleck, with whom Weil disagreed. I attempted to meet this unusual but minor criticism by rewriting the relevant sentence on the first page in a further attempt to dispassionately state the alternative hypotheses.

Mr. Weil's claims are particularly difficult to understand in light of a conversation that I had with him on August 5. After hearing him discuss my paper on the news, I called him to say how surprised I was to hear about his telling the press that the paper was "fundamentally flawed" when the only comment that he had given me was on the reference to Kleck. Mr. Weil then immediately demanded to know whether it was true that I had thanked him for giving comments on the paper. He had heard from people in the news media who had seen a draft with his name listed among those thanked. (On August 1, I had added his name to the list of people who had given comments, and when the news of the paper suddenly broke on August 2 with the story in *USA Today*, it was this new version that had been faxed to the news media.) He wanted to know if I was trying to "embarrass" him with others in the gun-control community, and he insisted that had not given me any comments. I said that I had only done it to be nice, and I mentioned the concern that he raised about the reference to Kleck. Weil then demanded that I "immediately remove [his] name" from the paper.

3. This was not my only experience with Ms. Glick. On August 8, 1996, six days after the events of August 2 described above, I appeared with her on MSNBC. After I tried to make an introductory statement setting out my findings, Ms. Glick attacked me for having my study funded by "gun manufacturers." She claimed that I was a "shill" for the gun manufactures and that it was important that I be properly identified as not being an objective academic. She also claimed that there were many serious problems with the paper. Referring to the study, she asserted that it was a fraud.

I responded by saying that these were very serious charges and that if she had some evidence, she should say what it was. I told her that I didn't think she had any such evidence, and that if she didn't, we should talk about the issues involved in the study.

At this point the moderator broke in and said to Ms. Glick that he agreed that these were very serious charges, and he asked her what evidence she had for her statements. Glick responded by saying that she had lots of evidence and that it was quite obvious to her that this study had been done to benefit gun manufacturers.

The moderator then asked her to comment further on her claim that there were serious problems with the study, and she stated that one only had to go to page 2 before finding a problem. Her concern was that I had used data for Florida that was a year and a half old. The moderator then asked her why this was a problem, since I couldn't be expected to use data that was, say, as recent as last week. Ms. Glick responded by saying that a lot of things could have changed since the most recent data were available. I then mentioned that I had obtained more recent data since the study had been written and that the pattern of people not using permitted guns improperly had held true from October 1987 to December 31, 1995.

A more recent exchange that I had with the Violence Policy Center's President, Josh Sugarmann, on MSNBC on February 24, 1997, involved the same accusations.

4. Douglas Weil, from the Center to Prevent Handgun Violence, a division of Handgun Control, wrote the following to the *Washington Times:* "Given that Mr. Lott has published 70 papers in peer-reviewed journals, it is curious that he has chosen a law review for his research on concealed-gun-carrying laws" (*Washington Times,* Aug. 22, 1996, p. A16).

5. Scott Harris, "To Build a Better America, Pack Heat," *Los Angeles Times,* Jan. 9, 1997, p. B1. In many ways, my study was indeed fortunate for the coverage that it received. It appears that no other study documenting the ability of guns to deter crime has received the same level of coverage. MediaWatch, a conservative organization tracking the content of television news programs, reviewed every gun-control story on four evening shows (ABC's *World News Tonight,* CBS's *Evening News,* CNN's *The World Today,* and NBC's *Nightly News*) and three morning broadcasts (ABC's *Good Morning America,* CBS's *This Morning,* and NBC's *Today*) from July 1, 1995 through June 30, 1997. MediaWatch categorized news stories in the following way: "Analysts counted the number of pro- and anti-gun-control statements by reporters in each story. Pieces with a disparity of greater than 1.5 to 1 were categorized as either for or against gun control. Stories closer than the ratio were deemed neutral. Among statements recorded as pro-gun control: violent crime occurs because of guns, not criminals, and gun control prevents crime. Categorized as arguments against gun control: gun control would not reduce crime; that criminals, not guns are the problem; Americans have a constitutional right to keep and bear arms; right-to-carry concealed weapons laws caused a drop in crime." MediaWatch concluded that "in 244 gun policy stories, those favoring gun control outnumbered stories opposing gun control by 157 to 10, or a ratio of almost 16 to 1 (77 were neutral). Talking heads were slightly more balanced: gun-control advocates outnumbered gun-rights spokesmen 165 to 110 (40 were neutral)." The news coverage of my study apparently accounted for 4 of the 10 "anti-gun control" news reports. (*Networks Use First Amendment Rights to Promote Opponents of Second Amendment Rights: Gun Rights Forces Outgunned on TV,* MediaWatch, July 1997.)

6. One of the unfortunate consequences of such attacks is the anger that they generate among the audience. For example, after Congressman Schumer's letter to the *Wall Street Journal,* I received dozens of angry telephone calls denouncing me for publishing my *Wall Street Journal* op-ed piece on concealed-handgun laws without first publicly stating that the research had been paid for by gun manufacturers. Other letters from the Violence Policy Center making these funding claims produced similar results.

Understandably, given the seriousness of the charges, this matter has been brought up by legislators in every state in which I have testified before the state legislature. Other politicians have also taken up these charges. Minnesota State Rep. Wes Skoglund (DFL–Minneapolis) provided one of the milder statements of these charges in the *Minneapolis Star Tribune* (Mar. 29, 1997, p. A13): "Betterman [a Minnesota state representative] uses a much-publicized study by John Lott Jr., of the University of Chicago, to back up her claims about the benefits of her radical gun-carry law. . . . But what no one has told you about Lott's study is that it has been found to be inaccurate and flawed. And Betterman didn't tell you that the study was funded by the Olin Foundation, which was created by the founder of Winchester Arms."

7. I telephoned Ms. Rand to ask her what evidence she had for her claim that the study was "the product of gun-industry funding" and reminded her that the public relations office at the University of Chicago had already explained the funding issue to her boss, Josh Sugarmann, but Ms. Rand hung up on me within about a minute.

8. Alex Rodriquez, "Gun Debate Flares; Study: Concealed Weapons Deter Crime," *Chicago Sun-Times,* Aug. 9, 1996, p. 2. Kotowski made his remark at a press conference organized by the Violence Policy Center, whose president, Josh Sugarmann, had been clearly told by the press office at the University of Chicago on August 6 that these charges were not true (as the letter by William E. Simon shown later will explain). Catherine Behan in the press office spent an hour trying to explain to him how funding works at Universities.

9. *Chicago Tribune,* Aug. 15, 1996.

10. "Study: Concealed Guns Deterring Violent Crime," *Austin American Statesman,* Aug. 9, 1996, p. A12.

11. The brief correction ran in the *Austin American Statesman,* Aug. 10, 1996.

12. As Mr. Simon mentions, one journalist who looked into these charges was Stephen Chapman of the *Chicago Tribune.* One part of his article that is particularly relevant follows:

> Another problem is that the [Olin] foundation didn't (1) choose Lott as a fellow, (2) give him money, or (3) approve his topic. It made a grant to the law school's law and economics program (one of many grants it makes to top universities around the country). A committee at the law school then awarded the fellowship to Lott, one of many applicants in a highly competitive process.
>
> Even the committee had nothing to do with his choice of topics. The fellowship was to allow Lott—a prolific scholar who has published some 75 academic articles—to do research on whatever subject he chose. . . .
>
> To accept their conspiracy theory, you have to believe the following: A company that derives a small share of its earnings from sporting ammunition somehow prevailed on an independent family foundation to funnel money to a scholar who was willing to risk his academic reputation (and, since he does not yet have tenure, his future employment) by fudging data to serve the interests of the firearms lobby—and one of the premier research universities in the world cooperated in the fraud. (See Stephen Chapman, "A Gun Study and a Conspiracy Theory," *Chicago Tribune,* Aug. 15, 1996, p. 31.)

13. A Gannett Newswire story quoted a spokeswoman for the Coalition to Stop Gun Violence who made similar statements: "But Katcher said the study . . . was funded by the Olin Foundation, which has strong ties to the gun industry. The study has 'been proven by a series of well-known, well-respected researchers to be inaccurate, false, junk science,' she said." (Dennis Camire, "Legislation before Congress Would Allow Concealed Weapons Nationwide," Gannett News Service, June 6, 1997.)

14. John R. Lott, Jr., "Should the Wealthy Be Able to 'Buy Justice'?" *Journal of Political Economy* 95 (Dec. 1987): 1307.

15. "Notebook," *The New Republic,* Apr. 14, 1997, p. 10.

16. After much effort, Randy was eventually able to get Cynthia Henry Thielen, a Hawaiian State Representative, to participate in the radio program.

17. Richard Morin, "Unconventional Wisdom: New Facts and Hot Stats from the Social Sciences," *Washington Post,* Mar. 23, 1997, p. C5.

18. It is surely not uncommon for academics to write letters to their local newspapers or to national or international publications, and indeed such letters were also written (see, for example, *The Economist,* Dec. 7, 1996, p. 8). But to track down the letters of everyday citizens to local newspapers and send replies is unusual.

19. The *Springfield State Journal-Register,* Nov. 26, 1996. Steven Teret, director of the Center for Gun Policy and Research wrote dozens of letters to newspapers across the country. They usually began with statements like the following: "Recently in a letter to the editor dated October 19, Kurt Amebury cited the work of two University of Chicago professors" (*Orlando Sentinel,* Nov. 16, 1996, p. A18); "Recently the *Dispatch* published a letter to the editor citing the work of two researchers" (*Columbus Dispatch,* Nov. 16, 1996, p. A11); "The *State Journal-Register* Oct. 28 published two letters citing research by the University of Chicago's John Lott" (*Springfield State Journal-Register,* Nov. 13, 1996, p. 6); or "A recent letter to the editor . . ." (*Buffalo News,* Nov. 17, 1996, p. H3). In late November, I asked Stephen Teret how many newspapers he had sent letters to. He would not give me an exact count, but he said "dozens" and then listed the names of some major newspapers to which they had

written. It is curious that none of the effort put into responding to my paper by the Center has gone into writing a comment for submission to the *Journal of Legal Studies*, where my original paper was published. Nor has the Center prepared a response for any other scholarly journal.

20. My opinion piece appeared in the *Omaha World-Herald*, Mar. 9, 1997, p. B9.

21. *Virginia Code Annotated*, § 18.2-3088 (1988).

22. This discussion relies on conversations with Clayton Cramer.

23. This point is similar to the "broken-window" argument made by Wilson and Kelling; see James Q. Wilson and George L. Kelling, "Making Neighborhoods Safe," *Atlantic Monthly*, Feb. 1989.

24. Some robberies also involve rape. While I am not taking a stand on whether rape or robbery is the primary motivation for the attack, there might be cases where robbery was the primary motive.

25. Information obtained from Kathy O'Connell at the Illinois Criminal Justice Information Authority.

26. For example, see Douglas Weil, "A Few Thoughts on the Study of Handgun Violence and Gun Control," *Washington Times*, Aug. 22, 1996, p. A16.

27. The durability of these initial false claims about Florida's crime rates can be seen in more recent popular publications. For example, William Tucker, writing in the *Weekly Standard*, claims that "Florida crime rates remained level from 1988 to 1990, then took a big dive. As with all social phenomena, though, it is difficult to isolate cause and effect." See William Tucker, "Maybe You Should Carry a Handgun," *Weekly Standard*, Dec. 16, 1996, p. 30.

28. In an attempt to facilitate Black's and Nagin's research, I provided them not only with all the data that they used but also computer files containing the regressions, in order to facilitate the replication of each of my regressions. It was thus very easy for them to try all possible permutations of my regressions, doing such things as excluding one state at a time or excluding data based on other criteria.

29. Dan Black and Dan Nagin, "Do 'Right-to-Carry' Laws Deter Violent Crime?" Carnegie-Mellon University working paper, Dec. 18, 1996, p. 5.

30. In addition, because the regressions use individual county dummy variables, so that they are really measuring changes in crime rates relative to each county's mean, one need not be concerned with the possibility that the average crime rates for the years that are farthest beyond the adoption of the concealed-handgun laws are being pulled down by relatively low crime rates in some states.

31. Ian Ayres and Steven Levitt, "Measuring Positive Externalities from Unobservable Victim Precaution: An Empirical Analysis of Lojack," NBER working paper 5928 (1997). The main issue with their empirical estimates, however, is whether they might be overestimating the impact from Lojack because they do not control for any other responses to higher auto-theft rates. For example, while higher auto theft rates might trigger implementation of Lojack, they might also increase purchases of other antitheft devices like The Club. In addition, the political support for altering the distribution of police resources among different types of crimes might also change. Unfortunately, neither Ayres and Levitt nor Lojack has made the information on the number of Lojacks installed available to other researchers. My attempts to replicate their results with dummy variables have found insignificant effects.

32. Ultimately, however, the levels of significance that I have tested for are the final arbiters in deciding whether one has enough data, and the results presented here are quite statistically significant.

33. Daniel W. Webster, "The Claims That Right-to-Carry Laws Reduce Violent Crime Are Unsubstantiated," The Johns Hopkins Center for Gun Policy and Research, copy obtained March 6, 1997, p. 5.

34. Jens Ludwig, "Do Permissive Concealed-Carry Laws Reduce Violent Crime?" Georgetown University working paper (Oct. 8, 1996), p. 12.

35. "Battered Woman Found Not Guilty for Shooting Her Husband Five Times," *San Francisco Examiner,* Apr. 9, 1997.

36. In Chicago from 1990 to 1995, 383 murders (or 7.2 percent of all murders) were committed by a spouse.

37. For a detailed discussion of how Black's and Nagin's arguments have changed over time, see my paper entitled "If at First You Don't Succeed . . ." : The Perils of Data Mining When There Is a Paper (and Video) Trail: The Concealed-Handgun Debate," *Journal of Legal Studies* 27 (January 1998), forthcoming.

38. Black and Nagin, "Do 'Right-to-Carry' Laws Deter Violent Crime?" Carnegie-Mellon working paper, version of December 18, p. 5, n. 4.

39. The December 18, 1996, version of their paper included a footnote admitting this point:

> Lott and Mustard weight their regression by the county's population, and smaller counties are much more likely to have missing data than larger counties. When we weight the data by population, the frequencies of missing data are 11.7% for homicides, 5.6% for rapes, 2.8% for assaults, and 5% for robberies.

In discussing the sample comprising only counties with more than 100,000 people, they write in the same paper that "the (weighted) frequencies of missing arrest ratios are 1.9% for homicides, 0.9% for rapes, 1.5% for assaults, and 0.9% for robberies."

40. For rape, 82 percent of the counties are deleted to reduce the weighted frequencies of missing data from 5.6 to 0.9 percent. Finally, for robbery (the only other category that they examine), 82 percent of the observations are removed to reduce the weighted missing data from 5 to 0.9 percent.

41. The reluctance of gun-control advocates to share their data is quite widespread. In May 1997 I tried to obtain data from the Police Foundation about a study that they had recently released by Philip Cook and Jens Ludwig, but after many telephone calls I was told by Earl Hamilton on May 27, "Well, lots of other researchers like Arthur Kellermann do not release their data." I responded by saying that was true, but that it was not something other researchers approved of, nor did it give people much confidence in his results.

42. See William Alan Bartley, Mark Cohen, and Luke Froeb, "The Effect of Concealed-Weapon Laws: Estimating Misspecification Uncertainty," Vanderbilt University working paper (1997).

CHAPTER EIGHT

1. Allison Thompson, "Robber Gets Outgunned on Westside," *Jacksonville (Florida) Times-Union,* Sept. 24, 1997, p. B1.

2. Craig Jarvis, "Pizza Worker's Husband Shoots Masked Bandit," *Raleigh News and Observer,* Dec. 11, 1996, p. B3.

3. Other work that I have done indicates that while hiring certain types of police officers can be quite effective in reducing crime rates, the net benefit from hiring an additional police officer is about a quarter of the benefit from spending an equivalent amount on concealed handguns. See John R. Lott, Jr., "Does a Helping Hand Put Others At Risk? Affirmative Action, Police Departments, and Crime," University of Chicago working paper (July 1997).

4. The cost of public prisons runs about twice this rate; see Mike Flaherty, "Prisons for Profit; Can Texas System Work for Wisconsin's Overflowing System," *Wisconsin State Journal,* Feb. 16, 1997, p. A1.

5. Fox Butterfield, "Serious Crime Decreased for Fifth Year in a Row," *New York Times,* Jan. 5, 1997, p. 10.

6. Michael Fumento, "Are We Winning the Fight Against Crime?" *Investor's Business Daily,* Feb. 5, 1997, p. A34.

7. Yet there never was much controversy over this issue: when Congress debated the law, no one, not even the National Rifle Association, opposed background checks. The dispute was over a five-day waiting period versus an "instant check."

8. Fumento, "Fight Against Crime," p. A34.

9. After the Supreme Court decision, Arkansas completely stopped the background checks, while Ohio has essentially gutted the rules by making background checks voluntary. In addition, as "Ohio Deputy Attorney General Mark Weaver said, the responsibility for conducting background checks rests with counties and cities in most states—rather than with statewide agencies—and . . . 'hundreds of counties' stopped doing checks after the Supreme Court ruling." (Joe Stumpe, "Arkansas Won't Touch Gun Checks 'Unwarranted,' Chief Cop Says," *Arkansas Democrat-Gazette,* July 29, 1997, p. 1A.

10. Bureau of Alcohol, Tobacco, and Firearms, *A Progress Report: Gun-Dealer Licensing and Illegal Gun Trafficking,* Washington, D.C.: Department of the Treasury, Bureau of Alcohol, Tobacco, and Firearms (Jan. 1997).

11. Many other restrictions on gun use have prevailed during the last couple of years, even some that appear fairly trivial. For example, in 1996 alone thirteen states voted on initiatives to restrict hunting. The initiatives were successful in eleven of the states. Congressman Steve Largent from Tulsa, Oklahoma, claims that the new rules are "part of a national effort to erode our ability to hunt. . . . It wasn't a local effort. It was a national effort." Not only were the initiatives strongly supported by animal rights activists, but they also received strong support from gun-control advocates. It is probably not lost on gun-control advocates that support for gun control seems to be strongest among those who grew up in households without guns and that making hunting less attractive is one long-term way to alter support for these initiatives. See Janet Pearson, "A 'Fair Chase': Keep the Sport in Hunting," *Tulsa World,* Nov. 17, 1996, p. G1.

12. For most government agencies that try to obtain higher funding, exaggerating the problems helps justify such higher funding. Michael Fitzgerald, a spokesman for the BATF in Chicago, is quoted as saying that 1 percent of federal license holders are estimated to be illegally running guns. "If that figure is accurate, the reduction of . . . dealers should eliminate a substantial number of traffickers." See Jim Adams, "Number of Licenses Falls Dramatically: Crime Law Puts Squeeze on Gun Dealers; Zoning Can Be Used to Keep Gun Sales Out of Private Homes," *Louisville Courier-Journal,* Mar. 20, 1997, p. A1.

13. During the last few years, the BATF has been much more aggressive in harassing law-abiding gun owners and retailers. A recent study using 1995 data, by Jim Couch and William Shughart, claims not only that the BATF refers dramatically more criminal firearm violations to prosecutors in states that have more National Rifle Association members, but that Clinton's own U.S. attorneys have declined to prosecute a much greater percentage of the cases referred to them in these states. They estimate that 54 percent of the variation across states in the BATF's criminal referrals is explained simply by the number of NRA members in a state, and that about a quarter of these higher requests for prosecutions are declined by U.S. attorneys. See Jim F. Couch and William F. Shughart I, "Crime, Gun Control, and the BATF: The Political Economy of Law Enforcement," University of Mississippi working paper presented at the March, 1997, Public Choice Meetings in San Francisco.

14. Alix M. Freedman, "Tinier, Deadlier Pocket Pistols Are in Vogue," *Wall Street Journal,* Sept. 12, 1996, p. B1.

15. Three different types of devices are under development: X-rays, ultrasound, and radar. The first devices capable of functioning on the street are expected in 2001. See Fox Butterfield, "New Devices May Let Police Spot People on the Street Hiding Guns," *New York Times,* Apr. 7, 1997, p. A1.

16. James Q. Wilson sees these devices as an effective means of disarming criminals

while allowing law-abiding citizens to keep their guns. In his view, they will provide us with the best of both worlds, allowing us to retain the benefits of private protection and to disarm criminals. See James Q. Wilson, "Just Take Away Their Guns," *New York Times,* Mar. 20, 1994, sec. 6, p. 47.

17. In airports or courts, for example, such searches would probably be allowed. Whether these devices will be deemed constitutional if used on the street is less clear.

18. I cannot end, however, without at least mentioning several excellent law-review articles on the issue of what was intended in the Second Amendment: see Nelson Lund, "The Second Amendment, Political Liberty, and the Right to Self-Preservation," *Alabama Law Review* 33 (1988): 103–47; Robert J. Cottrol and Raymond T. Diamond, "The Fifth Auxiliary Right," *Yale Law Journal* 104 (1995): 309–42; Don B. Kates, "Handgun Prohibition and the Original Meaning of the Second Amendment," *University of Michigan Law Review* 82 (1983): 204–68; William Van Alstyne, "The Second Amendment Right to Arms," *Duke Law Review* 43 (Apr. 1994): 1236–55; and Sanford Levinson, "The Embarrassing Second Amendment," *Yale Law Journal* 99 (Dec. 1989): 637–89. Legal scholars seem to be in general agreement on the way the Second Amendment's use of the word *militia* is so completely misinterpreted in current discussions of what the amendment means. The only twentieth-century case in which the Supreme Court directly interpreted the Second Amendment was *United States v. Miller,* 307 US 174 (1939). The court was quite clear that historical sources "showed plainly enough that the Militia comprised all males physically capable of acting in concert for the common defense." The court accepted "the common view . . . that adequate defense of the country and laws could be secured through the Militia—citizens primarily, soldiers on occasion."

The framers of the Constitution were also very clear on this issue. James Madison wrote in the Federalist papers that if a standing army threatened citizens' liberties, it would be opposed by "a militia amounting to near a half-million citizens with arms in their hands" ; see Clinton Rossiter, ed., *The Federalist* no. 46 (1961): 299. An excellent discussion of this and related issues is presented by David L. Franklin and Heather L. O'Farrell in their University of Chicago Moot Court brief on *Printz and Mack v United States,* Apr. 18, 1997.

CHAPTER NINE

1. Editorial, "Why Sharon Laid Down Her Arms," *New York Post,* Aug. 19, 1999, p. 8.

2. Ruth Teichroeb, "Hearing Today for Boy Expelled over Squirt Gun," *Seattle Post-Intelligencer,* Sept. 22, 1998, p. B1. To show how extreme these cases have gotten, young students have been suspended even for taking toenail clippers to school (Carolyn Bower, "Huffman School Suspends Student for Possessing Toenail Clippers," *St. Louis Post-Dispatch,* Sept. 28, 1999).

3. This statement was in response to the following question: "Now there does not seem to be that much that this kind of program works to reduce crime, in fact, no evidence, as far as I can tell, at all. How do you respond to that?" (Thalia Assuras, "Andrew Cuomo, Secretary of HUC, Explains President Clinton's Gun Buyback Program," CBS's *This Morning,* Sept. 9, 1999.

4. "Special Report: America under the Gun: What Must Be Done," *Newsweek,* Aug. 23, 1999.

5. Brian Rooney and Ted Koppel, "Guns—an American Way of Life and/or Death," ABC's *Nightline,* Aug. 10, 1999.

6. These reactions are hardly limited to the United States. United Nations Secretary-General Kofi Annan proposes that nations "adopt gun control laws including a prohibition of unrestricted trade and private ownership of small arms" ("UN Targets Small Arms," *BBC News,* Sept. 25, 1999, 0723 GMT).

7. Dates were established by doing a Nexis search. During 1996, Kentucky, Louisiana,

and South Carolina enacted "shall-issue" laws. However, these did not go into effect until extremely late in the year. Louisiana did not even start issuing applications until the end of September (Lisa Roland, "Applications for Concealed Handgun Permits to Be Issued This Week," *Gannett News Service*, Sept. 20, 1999). In Kentucky, permits were also not issued until the very end of the year (Michael Quinlan, "Concealed Guns: Permits Will Take Time, Law Will Go into Effect Tomorrow," *Louisville Courier-Journal*, Sept. 30, 1996, p. A1). South Carolina's law went into effect August 22, 1996, but its permitting process also took a couple of months to start actually issuing permits (Kathy Steele, "Women with Guns on Rise," *Augusta (GA) Chronicle*, Apr. 11, 1997, p. B2).

8. While I believe the much more interesting question is how crime rates change before and after the adoption of right-to-carry laws, the states with right-to-carry laws in effect for at least one year in 1996 had an average violent crime rate of 446.6 per 100,000 people, while the states with more restrictive "may-issue" rules had a violent crime rate of 592.6, and states banning concealed handguns a rate of 789.7. The main reason for not focusing on these numbers is simply that it ignores whether these states tended to be the lowest-crime-rate states even before they adopted right-to-carry laws. One method that partially accounts for this concern is to examine the cross-sectional data using the demographic, poverty, income, and other variables that have been employed throughout the book. After controlling for these other factors, the presence of a right-to-carry law implies a violent crime rate 15 percent lower than the absence of a law implies, and the effect is quite statistically significant, with a t-statistic that is significant at better than the .01 percent level for a two-tailed t-test.

9. David Hemenway, "Book Review of *More Guns, Less Crime*," *New England Journal of Medicine*, Dec. 31, 1998, pp. 2029–30.

10. Jens Ludwig, "Concealed-Gun-Carrying Law and Violent Crime: Evidence from State Panel Data," *International Review of Law and Economics* 18 (Sept. 1998): 239–54.

11. The Northeast includes Connecticut, Delaware, the District of Columbia, Maine, Maryland, Massachusetts, New Hampshire, New Jersey, New York, Pennsylvania, Rhode Island, and Vermont; the South includes Alabama, Arkansas, Florida, Georgia, Louisiana, Mississippi, Missouri, North Carolina, Oklahoma, South Carolina, Tennessee, Texas, and Virginia; the Midwest includes Illinois, Indiana, Iowa, Kansas, Kentucky, Michigan, Minnesota, Nebraska, North Dakota, Ohio, South Dakota, West Virginia, and Wisconsin; the Rocky Mountains include Arizona, Colorado, Idaho, Montana, Nevada, New Mexico, Utah, and Wyoming; and the Pacific states include Alaska, California, Hawaii, Oregon, and Washington.

12. Because of the criticism that it is unrealistic to use a simple dummy variable, I have decided to focus from the beginning on the more realistic approach that examines the before- and after-law trends in crime rates.

13. The results using the old specifications also continue to be very similar.

14. As another test of the sensitivity of the results, I also reestimated the before-and-after trends by limiting them to ten years before and after the adoption of the right-to-carry laws. The results equivalent to table 9.1 are −3.1 percent for violent crime, −0.8 percent for murder, −2.0 percent for rape, −2.6 percent for robbery, −3.3 percent for aggravated assault, and −0.4 percent for property crime. All the violent-crime category results are significant at least at the .01 percent level except for murder, which is significant at the 4 percent level.

15. See also figures 7.7–7.9.

16. Glenn Puit, "Survey: Gun Sales Increasing since Grocery Store Shooting," *Las Vegas Review-Journal*, June 24, 1999, p. 4A; and "Gun Sales up 30 Percent This Year," *Associated Press Newswire*, dateline San Francisco, Aug. 28, 1999. The *Las Vegas Review-Journal* article mentions that "Firearms instructors also said they have seen a jump in the number of people wanting to know the requirements to carry a concealed weapon. And, Las Vegas police have

seen an increase in requests for concealed weapons permits in recent weeks." The Associated Press story mentions that "Others say recent crime stories in the news, from the shooting rampage at a Los Angeles Jewish day camp to the tourist killings in Yosemite National Park, have motivated gun buyers."

17. The average murder rate for states over this period is 7.57 per 100,000; for rapes, 33.8; for aggravated assaults, 282.4; and for robberies, 161.8. A 4 percent change in murders is 0.3 per 100,000, a 7 percent change in rape is 2.4 per 100,000, a 5 percent change in aggravated assaults is 14.1 per 100,000, and a 13 percent change in robberies is 21 per 100,000. By contrast, a one-percentage-point increase in the population with permits is 1,000 per 100,000.

18. While small, lightweight guns are available and new materials have also made it possible to make lighter guns, most handguns weigh about the same as a laptop computer. Carrying them around requires some significant inconvenience.

19. More precisely, I replaced the predicted percentage of the population with permits with the predicted percentage of the population with permits divided by the permit fee. This is the same as the interactions done earlier looking at the percentage with permits multiplied by county demographics.

20. Ideally, one would also want to use the expected variation in permit rates across counties (though those data were not available at the time that I put these results together), but since I am examining all counties in the state, the state permitting rates at least allow us to rank the relative impact of right-to-carry laws across states.

21. The different drafts of their paper also went through different specifications.

22. Edward E. Leamer, "Let's Take the Con Out of Econometrics," *American Economic Review* 173 (Mar. 1983): 31–43; and Walter S. McManus, "Estimates of the Deterrent Effect of Capital Punishment: The Importance of the Researcher's Prior Beliefs," *Journal of Political Economy* 93 (Feb. 1985): 417–25.

23. I also included a tenth variable that examined the percentage of the adult population that was in prison, but there were sufficient theoretical objections to including this that I have decided not to report these results in the text. The major theoretical problem is that this variable is a "stock" while the crime rate is a "flow." In other words, the prison population is created by the number of people who are convicted and sentenced over many years and not just how harsh the current sentences are. In fact, if tough sentencing in the past makes it more likely that current criminals will not be sentenced to prison terms as long as those of past criminals (e.g., because of a takeover of the prison system by the courts), it is possible that there might even be a negative relationship between the prison population and the current toughness of the system. The bottom line is that past punishment is only roughly related to current punishment, particularly when average state differences are already being taken into account through fixed effects and when regional yearly fixed effects have also been added.

24. In a powerful piece, Isaac Ehrlich and Zhiqiang Liu show that classic economics papers concerning the law of demand, production theory, and investment theory would fail this test (Isaac Ehrlich and Zhiqiang Liu, "Sensitivity Analyses of the Deterrence Hypothesis: Let's Keep the Econ in Econometrics," *Journal of Law and Economics* 42 [Apr. 1999]: 455–88). Because of this strong bias toward not finding "true" relationships, Leamer and McManus have dropped off the 10 percent most extreme values on both ends of their estimates when they have reported their results. Yet even this does not protect most studies from having their results determined to be "fragile" by this test.

25. One problem from excluding the arrest rate was never clearly made in the first edition of this book. The reason using the arrest rate forces some county observations to be dropped is that when the number of crimes is zero, the arrest rate is "undefined." Including counties with zero crime rates biases the results toward not finding an effect because crime rates cannot fall below zero. Since these counties already have a zero crime

rate, the passage of the right-to-carry law can produce no benefit. The more counties with zero crime rates that are included, the more the estimated benefit from the law will move toward zero.

My work with Steve Bronars also examined whether replacing the crime-specific arrest rates with the overall violent-crime or property-crime arrest rates altered the results, and we found that it had no impact on the results. There are few counties which have no violent crimes of any type, so there are few missing observations for the violent-crime arrest rate (Stephen G. Bronars and John R. Lott, Jr., " Criminal Deterrence, Geographic Spillovers, and Right-to-Carry Laws," *American Economic Review* 88 (May 1998): 475–79).

26. While I find it difficult to believe that anyone would argue that demographic factors are not important in explaining crime rates, I did try a couple of specification tests. Paring the demographic variables down to the percentage of the population that is black, the percentage of the population that is white, the percentage of the population that is male, and the percentage of the population in the six different age classifications leaves the results essentially unchanged. Eliminating the demographic variables entirely reduces the estimated drop in violent-crime rates from right-to-carry laws by at most one percentage point.

27. The way that the county-level data were compiled was changed in 1994. Prior to that time those jurisdictions within a county which provided data for fewer than six months were estimated to have the same offense rates as the rest of the county. From 1994 onward, the imputation method was applied only to counties with less than three months of data. For jurisdictions with at least six months of data prior to 1994 and at least three months of data after that time, the jurisdiction was calculated to have $12/N$ offenses, where N is the number of months reported.

Because of concerns that this might affect estimates using data after 1993, I reran the regressions reported in table 9.1 by including a variable for the change in a county's crime rate between 1993 and 1994. This change variable was included for the 1994–1996 observations to account for the relative differences that this change in measurement might have had across different counties. The results are similar to those already reported. The annual difference in the trends in violent-crime rates before and after the passage of a right-to-carry law are −1.4 percent for murder, −2.94 percent for rape, −2.8 percent for robbery, and −3.12 percent for aggravated assault. All the results are significant at better than the .01 percent level with F-tests of 17.36, 83.33, 87.38, and 87.31, respectively.

28. These data draw on research that I am currently conducting with Kevin Cremin. Kevin collected all the data used here on policing policies.

29. "[The] problem-solving effort began essentially as directed patrol operations designed to identify patterns of offending or known offenders and to deploy police to catch the offenders. All gradually evolved into quite different efforts that involved activities other than arrest and agencies other than the police. The attack on burglaries in the housing projects involved surveying tenants, cleaning the projects, creating a multiagency task force to deal with particular problems in the housing projects, and organizing the tenants not only to undertake block watches but also to make demands on city agencies. The attack on thefts from cars eventually involved the inclusion of police officers in the design of new parking lots to make them less vulnerable to theft. The attack on prostitution and robbery involved enhanced code enforcement against hotels and bars that provided the meeting places for prostitutes and their customers as well as decoy operations" (Christopher Slobogin, "Why Liberals Should Chuck the Exclusionary Rule," *University of Illinois Law Review* 99 (1999): 363.

30. The data on community-oriented policing, problem-oriented policing, and the broken-windows strategy were primarily obtained by using the Westlaw "News" database. For community policing, the search took the form [name of city] & "community policing" & DA(BEF 1/1/1997) & DA(AFT 1/1/1975). For problem-oriented policing, the search

took the form ("Problem Solving Policing" or "Problem-Solving Policing" or "Problem Oriented Policing" or "Problem-Oriented Policing") & DA(AFT 1/1/1975) & DA(BEF 1/1/ 1997). Finally, for the broken-windows strategy, the search consisted of "Broken Window" & Crime & DA(AFT 1/1/1975) & DA(BEF 1/1/1997) AND NOT "Broken Windows." Other sources were also investigated. For community policing, the sources included Robert C. Trojanowicz and Hazel A. Harden, "The Status of Contemporary Community Policing Programs," National Center for Community Policing, 1985; Washington State University, Division of Governmental Studies and Services (DGSS), surveys of police administrators conducted at three-year intervals between 1978 and 1994; Anna Sampson, "National Survey of Community Policing Strategies, 1992–93"; and Robert C. Trojanowicz et al., "Community Policing: A Survey of Police Departments in the United States," 1994. However, the only one of these studies which identifies the cities is the 1985 Trojanowicz and Harden study. The authors of the other studies were unwilling to identify the cities in their samples. For the broken-windows strategy, George Kelling's book was also used to identify additional cities (George L. Kelling, *Fixing Broken Windows: Restoring Order and Reducing Crime in Our Communities* [New York: Free Press, 1998]).

31. John R. Lott, Jr., "Does a Helping Hand Put Others at Risk? Affirmative Action, Police Departments, and Crime," *Economic Inquiry* (forthcoming).

32. For example, policing policies may have changed because of concerns about future crime rates. Not adopting the change might have resulted in even more crime.

33. Bartholomew Sullivan, "Students Recall 'Unreal' Rampage," *Commercial Appeal*, June 11, 1998, p. A1.

34. Lance Gay, "New Gun Measure Wouldn't Have Halted School Tragedies," *Cleveland Plain Dealer*, May 30, 1999, p. 19A.

35. Pam Belluck and Jodi Wilgoren, "Shattered Lives—a Special Report: Caring Parents, No Answers, in Columbine Killers' Pasts," *New York Times*, June 29, 1999, p. A1; and Virginia Culver, "Pastor Comforts Gunman's Family," *Arizona Republic*, May 1, 1999, p. D7.

36. Evelyn Larrubia, Ted Rohrlich, and Andrew Blankstein, "Suspect Scouted 3 Prominent L.A. Jewish Sites as Targets," *Los Angeles Times*, Aug. 13, 1999, p. 1.

37. An earlier attempt by Congress to pass this law was never really enforced and was struck down by the Supreme Court in 1995. The 1995 law put in simple "boiler plate" language requiring that prosecutors make a finding that the gun or parts of the gun had been involved in interstate commerce.

38. To illustrate, let the probability that a single individual is carrying a concealed handgun equal .10. Assume further that there are 10 individuals in a public place. Then the probability that at least one of them is armed is $1 - .9^{10}$, or about .65.

39. *Baltimore Sun*, Apr. 30, 1999.

40. Greg Pierce, "Professional Viewpoint," *Washington Times*, Sept. 3, 1999, p. A5.

41. Even so-called smart locks, which are activated by one's fingerprint or by a special ring with a computer, pose several types of risks. With locks activated by fingerprints, a spouse would be unable to use the gun to come to the other person's rescue if the gun were coded for the other person. The person must also correctly position the finger on the fingerprint reader. Small differences in the angle of the finger may leave the gun inoperable even for the designated user.

42. This discussion is based upon research that I am currently doing with John Whitley.

43. Peter Cummings, David C. Grossman, Frederick P. Rivara, and Thomas D. Koepsell, "State Gun Safe Storage Laws and Child Mortality Due to Firearms," *Journal of the American Medical Association* 278 (Oct. 1, 1997): 1084–86.

44. U.S. General Accounting Office, "Accidental Shootings: Many Deaths and Injuries Caused by Firearms Could Be Prevented" (Washington, DC: U.S. General Accounting Office, Mar. 1991).

45. An article in the *Journal of the American Medical Association* does not control for any other factors but claims that 23 percent of the accidental gun deaths for children under fifteen would have been prevented by these storage rules. In 1996, this would have amounted to thirty-two lives if the laws had been in effect for the entire country. One obvious mistake that this article made was that it made no attempt to account for the normal downward trend in accidental gun deaths that would have continued to at least some extent even without these safe-storage laws. Since no other variables were being controlled for, all of the drop was being attributed to the new law (Cummings et al., "State Gun Safe Storage Laws").

46. As of this writing, the Violence Policy Center still has a section of its Web site entitled "Funder of the Lott CCW Study Has Links to the Gun Industry" at http://www.vpc.org/fact_sht/lottlink.htm.

47. M. W. Guzy, "Soft Logic on Hard Facts on Guns," *St. Louis Post-Dispatch*, July 22, 1998, p. B7.

48. Shelley Kiel [state senator in Nebraska], "Some Gun Restrictions Needed," *Omaha World-Herald*, July 11, 1998, p. 11.

49. Kevin Beck, "Conceal Carry," *St. Louis Post-Dispatch*, Aug. 12, 1998.

50. Minnesota Representative Wesley Skoglund on PBS's *Almanac*, Sept. 26, 1998.

51. Take for example a June 21, 1999, discussion between two people on talk.politics.guns:

> *"Dutch Courage"*: hey, did you know Lott's study was funded by a gun manufacturer? I did. That's a little suspicious, don't you think?
>
> *"Shawn Wilson"*: You're right, it was a foundation founded by the owner of a gun company, which is now an ammunition company, and further the foundation has large holdings in this company, and several of the directors of this foundation are men with standing within the company which shares the name. So much for his reputation as an honest scholar and academic reputation, eh?

52. Linnet Myers, " Go Ahead . . . Make Her Day," *Chicago Tribune*, May 2, 1999, p. C12. See also Diane Carman, "Gun-Bill Premise Is Bogus," *Denver Post*, Mar. 23, 1999, p. B1: "While gun-control activists have criticized Lott's work because it is funded in part through a grant from the Olin Foundation, which was founded by the largest manufacturer of ammunition in the U.S., [Jens] Ludwig argues that the debate about the grant money 'only distracts people. The study fails on its merits.'"

53. This quote is from the Web site of Handgun Control, Inc. (http://www.handgun-control.org/lott.htm). The Violence Policy Center's claim that I believe that "increases in the percent of minority police officers increase crime rates" can be found at http://www.vpc.org/fact_sht/wholott.htm. Of course, the Violence Policy Center fails to mention the rest of the abstract in question, which points out that the paper (Lott, "Does a Helping Hand Put Others at Risk?") will investigate "whether these increases in crime are due to changes in the quality of all new police officers or just minority officers."

54. The previous footnote provides references for this claim on gun-control Web sites. Similar statements were made by Luis Tolley, the western regional director for Handgun Control, Inc., at a debate that I participated in at Claremont College, and Tom Diaz, an analyst for the Violence Policy Center, has made this claim a couple of times when we appeared on radio shows together.

55. Lott, "Does a Helping Hand Put Others at Risk?"

56. The selective quoting was obviously a well-orchestrated campaign, with newspaper editorials also getting involved in repeating the statements by Handgun Control. Consider the following editorial attack on me: "In May 1998, for instance, he published the following in a police research journal: 'Increasing black officers' share of the police force by one percentage point increases murders by four percent, the violent crimes by

seven percent, and property crimes by eight percent. . . . More black and female officers are also associated with declines in both the arrest and conviction rates'" (Editorial, "A Lott More Guns," *St. Louis Post-Dispatch*, Mar. 23, 1999, p. B6). They failed to quote some other sentences in this same piece, such as "Not all black officers nor all white officers nor all officers of any other race are of the same quality. Some black officers are undoubtedly better at reducing crime than most potential white officers, and some white officers are probably better than most potential black officers. The question is how to select those officers who will do the best job. There is the possibility that choosing applicants by race or sex could work against hiring the best officers available. . . . One must be very clear about what is happening, however. The large impact of more black officers indicates that more than just the quality of new minority recruits or new minority promotions are affected. Indeed, changing tests to employ a greater percentage of blacks appears to make it more difficult to screen out lower-quality candidates generally, including whites and other racial groups" (John R. Lott, Jr., "Who Is Really Hurt by Affirmative Action?" *Subject to Debate*, May 1998, pp. 1, 3).

57. William F. Shughart II, "More Guns, Less Crime: Understanding Crime and Gun Control Laws: Review," *Southern Economic Journal* 65, no. 4 (Apr. 1, 1999): 978.

58. Bruce L. Benson, "Review of *More Guns, Less Crime*," *Public Choice* 100 (Sept. 1999), nos. 3–4: 309.

59. Stan Liebowitz, "Handgun Argument Is Loaded," *Dallas Morning News*, June 21, 1998.

60. Nelson Lund, "Gunning Down Crime: The Statistics of Concealed Weapons," *Weekly Standard*, June 1, 1998.

61. Joanne Eisen and Paul Gallant, "Scientific Proof That Gun Control Increases the Cost of Crime," *Shield*, Summer 1998, p. 42.

62. I really don't take most threats very seriously, and I believe that it is just people blowing off steam. The worst threats usually come over the telephone, though I did have some regular writers from Canada who would express the hope that someone would get a gun and kill either me or my family members. The one E-mail threat that was forwarded to me by one of the editors at the University of Chicago Press gives some idea of the types of comments I received:

> Pass along the word, to that soulless weasel and absolutely irresponsible chickenshit John M. Lott that he better change his name and get some plastic surgery because his days of [obscenities deleted] of the NRA's [obscenities deleted] will be quickly coming to a crashing close if he keeps trying to pass off unethical, and second rate statistics with his pseudoscience rhetorical sylogisms.
>
> My point—someone is going to become very angered by the view of this imbecile, and is going to get a concealed hand-gun permit and find where he lives and make a point. I won't lose sleep knowing that one more moron is dead, but I feel that he should be warned none-the-less. Also, if John Lott had any integrity he'd make it possible to reach him. Since the little scatmuncher is playing hide and seek by having no-available e-mail adress, whoever reads this please forward this too him. This is not a threat, just a warning.
>
> Sometimes when views of cretins like this are expressed I think "love it or leave it," and man, if our scholars get any stupider and any more immoral than Mr. Lott I'm out of this shit house. I nearly packed my bags.

63. Matt Bai, "Is He the Smoking Gun?" *Newsweek*, Jan. 25, 1999, Business section.

64. "According to the Federal Bureau of Investigation's Uniform Crime Report, from 1992 to 1997, states which made it easier for citizens to carry concealed handguns had a significantly smaller drop in their crime rates than states which chose not to loosen their conealed weapons laws" (Brian Morton [associate director of communications for Hand-

gun Control and the Center to Prevent Handgun Violence], "John Lott's Gun Research Doesn't Hold Up to Review," *Fort Wayne Journal Gazette*, Aug. 15, 1999, p. 3C).

Even when others would state that the FBI indeed did not produce these claims, Handgun Control's press release was put on the same footing as my research. Consider the following: "The Center to Prevent Handgun Violence did a 1999 analysis of crime statistics that came to a conclusion opposite of Mr. Lott's, and their study (like his) is open to review by experts in many fields" (Molly Ivins, "More Guns, Less Crime? Are You Sure?" *Fort Worth Star-Telegram*, Aug. 15, 1999). For clarification, the Center to Prevent Handgun Violence is part of Handgun Control, and Sarah Brady serves as the head of both organizations. Many similar statements were made by the media in Missouri during the debate over the concealed-handgun law.

65. For example, a December 1998 press release on children and gun violence had South Carolina and Colorado ranking similarly in terms of how liberal their right-to-carry laws were, but by January 1999, in a press release examining the change between 1992 and 1997, Colorado was listed as having a more restrictive law than South Carolina. The only motivation that I can conjecture for the change was that it helped get them the different results that they wanted.

66. "In stark contrast, a review of the national Uniform Crime Reporting data, which is compiled by the FBI each year from state and local law enforcement agencies, indicates that the violent crime rate has fallen in all states by an average of 19 percent from 1992–97" (Richard Cook, "Don't Buy the Pro-Gun Arguments," *Kansas City Star*, Mar. 11, 1999, p. B7).

67. Peter Squires, "Review of More Guns, Less Crime," *British Journal of Criminology* 39, no. 2 (Spring 1999): 318–20.

68. My book does not even cite this quotation, though I mentioned it in an earlier research paper because it was "quite relevant" to the debate over concealed handguns: it illustrates both the possibility of deterrence and the fears about the possible disasters that such laws could lead to.

Still other recent discussions in medical journals continue claiming that the nondiscretionary concealed-handgun laws for "several counties . . . were misclassified" and that the National Academy of Sciences deemed it inappropriate to account for arrest rates when researchers tried to explain changes in crime (see Arthur Kellermann and Sheryl Heron, "Firearms and Family Violence," *Emergency Medicine Clinics of North America*, Aug. 1999, pp. 699–708). Of course, responses 4 and 9 on pages 132–33 and 142 in this book addressed the first concern and page 18 discussed the second one.

69. http://www.handguncontrol.org/gunowner/statflaw.htm.

70. Doug Weil, Handgun Control's research director, provided the only response that I know of to my research on the Brady law by claiming that "Since John's data does not cover the years following implementation of the Brady Act, it's hard to know how he can claim to have studied the impact of the Brady law on crime rates or criminal access to guns" ("More Guns, Less Crime?: A Debate between John Lott, Author of *More Guns, Less Crime*, and Douglas Weil, Research Director of Handgun Control, Inc.," an online debate sponsored by *Time* magazine, transcript from July 1, 1998.) In fact, my book examined data up through 1994, the first year that the Brady law was in effect.

71. Romesh Ratnesar, "Should You Carry A Gun? A New Study Argues for Concealed Waspons," *Time*, July 6, 1998, p. 48.

72. I responded by saying that he was doing more than simply reporting these statements as claims when he used phrases like "Lott dropped" or "the book does not account." More importantly, readers were likely to believe that he had looked at the material and that he would not print something, even if the critics claimed it was true, unless it was true. Again, he emphasized that his role was that of a reporter and not to take sides in the debate.

I had called Romesh in part to tell him that I planned to send in a letter clarifying these points, and *Time* magazine did print a letter. Undoubtedly he played some role in guaranteeing that the letter was published, but it seems doubtful that the letter carried the same weight as a statement by the reporter about whether he could verify if the claims made against me were true. The letter in *Time* magazine was printed in the Aug. 3, 1998, issue under the heading "More about Concealed Weapons." It read:

> While your piece "Should You Carry a Gun?" [July 6] was generally favorable toward my new book, *More Guns, Less Crime,* it contained seriously misleading statements. Despite accusations by some critics, my study on the effect that carrying concealed weapons has on crime absolutely did not ignore "counties that had no reported murders or assaults for a given year." In contrast to the tiny samples in previous work by others, I used data on all the counties in the U.S. that were available when I did the study on the years from 1977 to 1994. It is likewise false that I did "not account for fluctuating factors like poverty levels and police techniques." Among the factors I included in the analysis were poverty, income, unemployment, arrest and conviction rates, the number of police officers and police expenditures per capita, as well as the impact that the prevention of less serious crimes has on more serious ones.

73. Ivins, "More Guns, Less Crime? Are You Sure?"

74. Tom Teepen, "A Modest Proposal: Let's Arm the Teachers," *Atlanta Journal and Constitution,* Sunday, May 17, 1998, p. 2G.

75. The following letter of mine appeared in the *Atlanta Journal and Constitution,* May 24, 1998, p. 6B:

> Tom Teepen's column "A modest proposal: Let's arm the teachers," Perspective, May 17), an attack on my new book "More Guns, Less Crime" (University of Chicago Press), contained misleading information. He claimed that "Lott can't fairly compare 1988 and 1996 exit polls on gun ownership, as he does, because the questions were asked differently." Yet on pages 36–37 in my book, I point out this fact and discuss in detail what impact this has on estimates of changing gun ownership.
>
> Citing a paper in the *Journal of Legal Studies,* Teepen claimed that I make a "fundamental gaffe" by failing to consider other anti-crime variables. My book provides the first systematic national evidence and examines the crime, accidental gun death, and suicide rates for all 3,054 counties in the United States by year from 1977 to 1994. No other study on crime has attempted to account for anywhere near as many different factors that could have affected crime rates over time. Unlike the Centers for Disease Control and Prevention's claim that homes with guns were "more likely to experience suicide," or have "a member of the family killed by another member or by an acquaintance," I did not focus on data from only one or a few cities for only one year. There is no evidence that these claims are correct.
>
> Obviously, bad things can happen with guns, but guns also prevent bad things from happening to people. The evidence in my book indicates that many more lives are saved than lost from gun ownership.

76. An editor at the *Fort Worth Star-Telegraph,* Bob Davis, was very helpful, and he took the time to read my book to evaluate whether a mistake had been made. He printed a response by me in his newspaper, and he asked Creators Syndicate, which distributes Ms. Ivins's commentary, to make the response available to other newspapers around the country that carried Ms. Ivins's column. Unfortunately, despite repeated promises by Creators to do so, they never followed through on this.

77. Let me just give a couple of other examples.

Even John Lott admits that 58 percent of homicides are committed either by family members or friends and acquaintances, not criminals. (Richard Scribner, [director of the Injury Control Research Center], "More Guns Don't Mean a Safer Society," *New Orleans Times-Picayune,* Apr. 28, 1999, p. B6)

Dr. Lott's own analysis accounts for only about 10 percent of why some crime rates have fallen. We need to explain the other 90 percent before concluding that the "best" social policy is to carry more handguns. (Shela Van Ness, "More Guns, Less Crime? This Isn't Just a 'Good Guy' vs. 'Bad Guy' Issue," *Chattanooga Times / Chattanooga Free Press,* May 9, 1999, p. H1)

For the first point, not only do I not "admit" this, but my book points out that this claim is extremely misleading because the term "acquaintances" primarily includes rival gang members killing each other or drug buyers and drug sellers killing each other. As to the second point, the estimates shown in this book explain about 80–95 percent of the variation in crime rates.

78. The *Chronicle of Higher Education* noted that the opposition to my book also showed up in the University of Chicago Press, this book's publisher. The *Chronicle* reported that "The book also caused a mini-revolt at Chicago, where salespeople initially blanched at the prospect of pitching it to bookstores. Some cited personal views about guns; others thought that the book would alienate booksellers" (Christopher Shea, "'More Guns, Less Crime': A Scholar's Thesis Inflames Debate over Weapons Control," *Chronicle of Higher Education,* June 5, 1998, p. A14).

79. In this case, the dummy must be interpreted as whether the law raised or lowered the crime rate as quickly as the quadratic time trend would predict.

80. This example is taken from David D. Friedman's Web site, www.best.com/~ddfr/Lott_v_Teret/Lott_Mustard_Controversy.html.

81. Virtually identical complaints have been posted on the Handgun Control, Inc., Web site, where Handgun Control writes: "To this day, John Lott has failed to provide any statistical evidence of his own that counters Black and Nagin's finding that Lott's conclusions are inappropriately attributed to changes in concealed-carry laws. Until Lott can do this, it is inappropriate for him to continue to claim that allowing more people to carry concealed handguns causes a drop in crime."

82. Dan A. Black and Daniel S. Nagin, "Do Right-to-Carry Laws Deter Violent Crime?" *Journal of Legal Studies* 27 (Jan. 1998): p. 213.

83. What is mystifying to me is how others have also continued to make this claim. Hashem Dezbakhsh and Paul H. Rubin claim that "We believe that Lott and Mustard's findings are suspect, mainly because of the way they parameterize and measure the effect of permissive handgun laws on crime. They model the effect as a shift in the intercept of the linear crime equation they estimate at the county level. This approach is predicated on two assumptions: (i) all behavioral (response) parameters of this equation (slope coefficients) are fixed (unaffected by the law), and (ii) the effect of the law on crime is identical across counties" (Hashem Dezbakhsh and Paul H. Rubin, "Lives Saved or Lives Lost? The Effects of Concealed-Handgun Laws on Crime," *American Economic Review Papers and Proceedings,* May 1998, p. 468).

84. http://www.best.com/~ddfr/Lott_v_Teret/Friedman_on_B_and_N.html. A great deal of debate about my research and other gun-related research takes place on the Internet in discussion groups such as talk.politics.guns or on Web sites such as David Friedman's, which allows for a very detailed discussion of the issues. The give and take also allows people to ferret out the weaknesses and strengths of different arguments.

85. Benson, "Review of *More Guns, Less Crime,*" p. 312.

86. Ayres and Donohue mention in a footnote that "Lott was not unaware of the possibility that crack influenced the level of crime and some regressions in the book control for the price data for cocaine (p. 201, fn. 8), but the quantity of crack sold in

discrete geographic markets instead of its national price would be much more probative." Even though I had given them the price data, they apparently had not had time to examine it and realize that it was county-level data.

While simply using the price does not allow one to perfectly disentangle local differences in demand and supply, arbitrage basically assures that, except for short periods of time, the differences in prices between these local markets will equal differences in selling costs. If the total cost of selling cocaine were the same in two different cities, any price differentials resulting from sudden shifts in demand would cause distributors to send cocaine to the city with the higher price until the price had fallen enough that the prices between the two cities were equal. Distributors could even remove cocaine from the low-price city and move it to where it could obtain a higher price. Sellers in a city could also hold inventories and not sell their cocaine during periods with unusually low demand. To the extent that it is costly to move drugs instantly between different cities or to store drugs, any price differentials in the short run can be due to demand shifts, but since we are dealing with a period of a year, it seems difficult to believe that any non-cost-based price differentials will not be arbitraged away.

The bottom line is that if price differentials exist for long periods of time (and we would pick up precisely these differences by using average yearly prices), any price differentials will be cost based. Now cost differences can arise for many reasons (e.g., differences in law enforcement, wage differentials for workers, differences in rental prices for "business" spaces, etc.). The concern is not why these cost differentials exist, but simply that they do and that this will be related to the accessibility of drugs.

Suppose, for example, that it costs $8 to sell an ounce of cocaine in Atlanta and $3 in Washington, DC. If the price of a one-ounce bag of cocaine were $10 in Washington and $13 in Atlanta, then minus these selling costs an importer of illegal drugs would make $7 in Washington and $5 in Atlanta. Where is he going to ship more of his drugs? Clearly Washington, and he will continue doing so until the relative price net of these costs in Washington falls until the difference between the two markets is $5.

87. An example of one of the other criticisms is by Ayres and Donohue where they write that "the ultimate criticism of Lott will be that the model is too flawed to provide any information on the effect of the law. . . . One of the strongest results to emerge from Lott's book is that shall issue laws, as he models them, lead to higher property crime. If you don't believe this, then you cannot endorse any of Lott's findings. But, to believe that property crime rose you must believe that the rate of robbery fell, because the only reason that more concealed handguns would cause property crime to go up is that some other money-generating activity became less available or less attractive. One would hardly expect that someone desiring to beat up an individul would instead decide to steal a car if the assaultive option were foreclosed. But since the robbery results are arguably weak, it is hard to tell a convincing story that would explain the alleged shift from violent crime to property crime that the Lott model attributes to shall issue laws" (Ian Ayres and John J. Donohue III, "Nondiscretionary Concealed Weapons Laws: A Case Study of Statistics, Standards of Proof, and Public Policy," *American Law and Economics Review* 1, nos. 1–2 (Fall 1999): 436–70.

88. The "recidivism" referred to by Ayres and Donohue is actually not a good measure for what they are discussing, since recidivism refers to whether criminals keep on committing a crime after they have been punished by the legal system.

89. Ayres and Donohue raise another issue that should be discussed at least briefly, and that is the use of the percentage of a state's population that is in prison as an enforcement variable. They find that including this variable strengthens the results, but while the variable provides some information, there are some important theoretical problems with it. One problem is that the prison population and the crime rate are simply in different units. The prison population measures a "stock," while the crime rate represents a "flow." The simplest comparison is between the amount of water in a bathtub (a stock)

and the rate at which water is flowing into the bathtub (a flow). The amount of water in the bathtub is only loosely related to the current flow into it because it depends upon not only flows in previous periods but also the rate at which water is flowing out of it. A second problem is that I have focused on county-level data because of the heterogeneity in law enforcement across counties within a state, and this variable is available only at the state level.

90. For example, Sarah Brady, "Q: Would New Requirements for Gun Buyers Save lives? Yes: Stop Deadly, Unregulated Sales to Minors, at Gun Shows and on the Internet," *Insight,* June 21, 1999, p. 24; or "More Guns, Less Crime? A Debate between John Lott and Douglas Weil."

91. Gary Kleck, *Targeting Guns: Firearms and Their Control* (Hawthorne, NY: Aldine de Gruyter Publishers, 1997), p. 371.

92. This is true whether one uses the 430,000 instances in 1997 in which crimes with guns were reported to police in the Uniform Crime Report or the number that is about twice as large from the National Crime Victimization Survey.

93. Stephanie Elizondo Griest, "Group: Arrest Data Show Flaw in Concealed-Gun Law: Permit Holders Have Been Arrested 2,080 times: NRA Says Low Conviction Rate Proves Licensees Abide by Law," *Austin American-Statesman,* Mar. 23, 1999, p. B2.

94. John Lott, Jr., "License to Kill? Careful Look at Critical Study Actually Backs Gun Permit Holders," *Dallas Morning News,* Feb. 8, 1998, p. J6.

95. Jonathan Rauch, "And Don't Forget Your Gun," *National Journal,* Mar. 20, 1999.

96. Based upon a telephone conversation with the Alaska bureau responsible for issuing permits.

97. Source: Lt. Bill Whalen, Arizona Department of Public Safety, 602–223-2704. Peak issuance of permits was November 1998, when 63,040 permits were issued. The renewal rate is about 42 percent. Based on that number and the fact that about 26,000 permits were issued by July 1995, over 76,000 permits must have been issued during the period.

98. http://licgweb.dos.state.fl.us/stats/cw_monthly.html.

99. Based upon a telephone conversation with the Indiana State Firearms Bureau.

100. Revocation rate obtained from "North Carolina Handgun Permit Statistics by County from Dec. 1, 1995 and Aug. 4, 1999" (available on the North Carolina state government Web site). The other information is based upon a telephone conversation with Julia Nipper and Susan Grissom.

101. James N. Thurman, "As More Carry Hidden Guns, Who's Safer?" *Christian Science Monitor,* Sept. 1, 1999, p. 1.

102. Information from Steve Anderson with the Utah State Firearms Bureau.

103. Based on an E-mail message sent to me by Mr. Wilson of the Criminal Department of Investigation, Wyoming). His telephone number is 307-777-7181.

104. Frank Main, "Taxpayers Pay Big Part of Gunshot Victims' Bills," *Chicago Sun-Times,* Aug. 4, 1999, p. 30.

105. Another survey by gun-control advocates claims that "four million legal handgun owners sometimes carried guns for protection 'in connection with work.' Two-thirds of those who carried handguns said they kept them in their vehicles, while the others said they sometimes carried them. . . . The researchers said about 56 percent of those who carried handguns outside of work did so fewer than 30 days per year, while 22 percent said they rarely left home without a gun" (Will Hacker, "Majority of Owners Cite Security Concerns," *South Bend Tribune,* June 29, 1997, p. A6).

106. Unlike the critical papers by Black and Nagin as well as Ludwig, the paper by Dezhbakhsh and Rubin also critically examined my data, but I did not think it would be of general enough interest to discuss in the text (Dezhbakhsh and Rubin, "Lives Saved or Lives Lost?" pp. 468–74). What they do is run a regression over only those observations in which the right-to-carry law is in effect; they then take this regression and plug in

those observations during 1992 for which the right-to-carry laws are not in effect. This last step generates what they claim are predicted values for what the crime rates would be in those counties without the laws if they had the laws. They then compare what the actual crime rates were in the counties without the laws with their predicted crime rates and take the difference. If the actual crime rate is greater than the predicted, they claim that this shows that the law would have lowered the crime rate. If the actual crime rate is less than the predicted value, they claim that this shows the law would have raised the crime rate.

This approach makes no sense to me. It is throwing out all the information on the before-and-after change in crime rates that occurs when states change their laws. The method also eliminates the role of fixed effects. All the predicted crime rates in the counties without right-to-carry laws in 1992 are assumed to have the same intercept value from the regression, since there is no county dummy to use in making the predicted value. If the left-out county that is represented by the intercept happens to have a low crime rate, it will make the right-to-carry laws look good. If the reverse is true, the right-to-carry laws will look as if the law is increasing the crime rate. On average, randomly picking one will produce no systematic effect and the predicted values will lie on both sides of the actual crime rates.

107. William Bartley and Mark Cohen, "The Effect of Concealed Weapons Laws: An Extreme Bound Analysis," *Economic Inquiry* 36 (Apr. 1998): 259. See also William Alan Bartley, "Will Rationing Guns Reduce Crime?" *Economics Letters* 62 (1999): 241–43; and Carlisle E. Moody, "Testing for the Effects of Concealed Weapons Laws: Specification Errors and Robustness," William and Mary College, Department of Economics, working paper, December 1999, p. 13.

108. David Olson and Michael Maltz, "Magic Bullets, Deterrence, and Gun Laws," Loyola University Chicago working paper, December 1999.

109. Florenz Plassman and T. Nicolaus Tideman, "Does the Right to Carry Concealed Handguns Deter Countable Crimes? Only a Count Analysis Can Say," State University of New York at Binghampton working paper, May 19, 1999, p. 22. See also Glenn W. Harrison, David Kennison, and Katherine M. Macedon, "Legal Guarantee of the Right to Bear Arms: Can It Be Justified Empirically?" University of South Carolina working paper, December 1999.

110. Florenz Plassman and T. Nicholaus Tideman, "Geographical and Temporal Variation in the Effects of Right-to-Carry Laws on Crime," Virginia Polytechnic Institute and State University working paper, November 17, 1999. Both of Plassman and Tideman's papers use a Poisson process to handle the low number of expected crimes per county observation and this allows them to solve the problem of missing observations that has plagued other papers using this data.

111. William F. Shughart II, "More Guns, Less Crime: Understanding Crime and Gun Control Laws: Review," pp. 978–80; and Benson, "Review of *More Guns, Less Crime*," pp. 309–13.

112. Benson, "Review of *More Guns, Less Crime*," p. 309.

113. These reviews during 1998 have appeared in the *Dallas Morning News* (Stan Liebowitz at the University of Texas at Dallas), *American Enterprise* (Robert Cottrol at George Washington University), the *Weekly Standard* (Nelson Lund at George Mason University Law School), *National Review* (John O. McGinnis at Cardozo School of Law), and *Reason Magazine* (Dan Polsby at Northwestern University).

114. Janelle Hartman, "Assailant Gets Shot by Victim," *Eugene (OR) Register Guard*, Mar. 11, 1998, p. 1.

115. Nicole Marshall, "Concealed Gun Carrier Subdues Suspect: Man Reportedly Had Snatched Toddler," *Tulsa World*, Jan. 31, 1998.

116. Frank J. Murray, "Arizona Gun Owner's Courage Led to Scary Arrests," *Washington Times*, May 2, 1999, p. C8.

117. Laurie Mason, "Customer Stops Would-Be Robber," *Bucks County Courier Times,* Dec. 13, 1998, p. 7C.

118. Edward W. Lempinen, "Robber Shot Dead," *Newsday,* Aug. 3, 1999, p. A3; "Concealed Carry Permit Pays Off," *Local Cincinnati-Northern Kentucky TV 9 Evening News,* Aug. 19, 1999; Tom Jackman and Maria Glod, "A Glimmer of Hope, Then Violent Death," *Washington Post,* June 21, 1999, p. B1; "Carjacking Suspect Critically Wounded," *Arizona Republic,* June 5, 1999, p. B2; and Joe Brogan, "Rent Collector Shoots, Kills Riviera Robber," *Palm Beach Post,* Jan. 14, 1999, p. B1.

A case from the end of 1998 that deserves some mention involved an eighty-one-year-old Chicago native who defended himself by illegally carrying a concealed handgun—a gun that he wasn't even allowed to own legally in Chicago, let alone carry with him.

In the pre-dawn hours Tuesday, 81-year-old Bruno Kosinski looked like an easy mark for a robbery. Kosinski, a frail man with thinning white hair who shuffles his feet as he walks slightly hunched over, was getting into his car in Ukrainian Village when he felt something wet on his head. In a few brief moments, two teenagers allegedly squirted pepper spray in his face, pushed him to the ground, took his wallet and, still unsatisfied, threatened to kill him, police said. Kosinski did something authorities said was rare: The 5-foot-5 elderly man used a concealed handgun he carries in his pants. Without saying a word, he got to his feet and fired once.... Kosinski, admitting he illegally carried a concealed handgun, was unapologetic. "I don't feel at all sorry that it happened," said Kosinski.... "The least that I could do was defend myself." (Bechetta Jackson and Todd Lightly, "Aged Hold-Up Victim Shoots Teen Suspect," *Chicago Tribune,* Dec. 8, 1998, sec. 2, p. 8)

119. Mene Tekel Upharsin, "Homeowner Grabs Gun for Self-Defense, Assists Police in Capture of Escaped Murderer," *Associated Press Newswire,* Aug. 21, 1999, 8:37 EDT. What would have become a multiple-victim public shooting at a business in July 1999 was stopped by a person with a concealed handgun ("Gunman Turns Weapon on Gun Store Employees, Is Wounded in Shootout," *St. Louis Post-Dispatch* (from Reuters), July 7, 1999, p. A11; and see also Thomas Sowell, "Why Does Media Hide Benefits of Arming Citizens?" *Bergen County (NJ) Record,* July 19, 1999, p. L3). Typical is the story of a Greenville, North Carolina, restaurant owner who prevented a robbery with a gun that he carried with him all the time "in the small of his back" (Travis Fain, "Man Shot, Killed in Attempted Robbery," *Daily Reflector,* June 2, 1999, p. B1). Other articles on prevented robberies from June 1999 can be found in the *Providence Journal,* June 18, 1999; the *Prescott (AZ) Daily Courier,* June 13, 1999; the *Augusta (GA) Chronicle,* June 16, 1999; and the *Aiken (SC) Standard,* June 2, 1999.

120. "Man Charged in Robbery Hurt in Intimidation Bid," *Buffalo News,* Jan. 16, 1999; "Cops: Woman Shot by Man She Tried to Rob," *Orlando Sentinel* (from Associated Press), Jan. 10, 1999, p. B4; Seth Muller, "Homeowner Fires .357 at Night Burglar," *Martinsburg (WV) Journal,* Mar. 2, 1999; Valerie Bauertein, "Woman Kills an Intruder in Her Home," *Winston-Salem Journal,* Mar. 2, 1999, p. A1; "Woman Shoots Golf Stalker to Death during Attack," *Palm Beach Post* (from Associated Press), May 12, 1999, p. A11; Kirk Swauger, "Shooter's Brother: Break-in Not First," *Johnstown (PA) Tribune-Democrat,* Apr. 10, 1999, p. A1; Bill Blair, "West End Man Slays Intruder," *Johnstown (PA) Tribune-Democrat,* Apr. 9, 1999, p. A1; Bill Hanna, "Robbery Victim Shoots Suspect," *Fort Worth Star-Telegram,* June 15, 1999; Mark Duncan, "Hall of Fame Cowboy Stems Tragedy at Ranch: Family Survives Knife Attack," *Yavapai County (AZ) Daily Courier,* June 13, 1999, p. A1; Dan Richardson, "Armed Homeowner Drives Off Intruder," *Valley News (VT),* July 2, 1999; Heather Romero, "Intruder Is Wounded As Shots Fly 'All Over,'" *Arizona Daily Star,* July 3, 1999, p 1B; Beena A. Hyatt, "Intruder Is Killed in Home," *Chattanooga Times,* July 22, 1999, p. B1; Kate Folmar and Luise Roug, "Late-Night Intruder Gets More Than He Bargained For," *Los Angeles Times,* Aug. 2, 1999, Orange

County edition, p. B1; and "Homeowner Shoots Man Climbing into Window," *Knoxville (TN) Knox-News Sentinel,* Aug. 1, 1999.

121. While I find the claims greatly exaggerated, another recent study has come out claiming that sixty-four children under the age of two die every year from sleeping with their parents (Shari Roan, "Baby's First Year: Dangerous to Doze with Baby Alongside?" *Los Angeles Times,* Oct. 4, 1999, p. S1).

122. Brenda Rodriguez, "Notes Begin to Tell Story of Rampage in Atlanta: Killer Wanted to Exact Revenge," *Dallas Morning News,* July 31, 1999, p. 1A.

123. Rhonda Cook, "To the Rescue: Salesman Grabs Gun, Prevents Tragedy," *Atlanta Journal and Constitution,* Aug. 3, 1999, 1B; Lyda Longa and David Pendered, "Armed Patient Shot in Grady," *Atlanta Journal and Constitution,* Aug. 4, 1999, p. 1B; Hannity and Colmes, Fox News Network, Aug. 11, 1999 (21:30 EST); and "Armed Georgia Defenders Thwart Two Gunmen," *Washington Times* (from Reuters), Aug. 4, 1999, p. A9.

124. Carol Robinson, "Gunman Opens Fire at Alabama Business," *New Orleans Times-Picayune,* Aug. 6, 1999 p. A17.

125. Editorial, "Lethal Weapon," *Daily News of Los Angeles,* May 6, 1999, p. N20.

126. Elaine Gale, "Grieving Mother Haunted by Crash Scene," *Los Angeles Times,* May 6, 1999, p. A1.

127. A Nexis search of news stories for the one week after both incidents indicates that Buford Furrow was mentioned in the news about five times as often as Steve Abrams, and that while news accounts of Furrow tended to be full-feature news stories, virtually all of the mentions of Mr. Abrams were fairly minor recounts of the Associated Press story that ran on him. Later in the day it was discovered that Furrow had killed a U.S. Post Office worker, but the initial news coverage was based upon the attack at the community center.

Other writers have done an excellent job of pointing out these biases (Sowell, "Why Does Media Hide Benefits of Arming Citizens?" p. L3; Jeff Jacoby, "Media Bias Revealed by Crimes That Go Unnoticed," *San Jose Mercury News,* Aug. 24, 1999).

128. This total includes 427 incendiary bombings. Eleven deaths and 29 injuries were classified as "noncriminal" (Bureau of Alcohol, Tobacco, and Firearms, "Arson and Explosives: Incidents Report, 1997" [Department of the Treasury, 1999]). For an example of a recent knife attack that injured several people on an Amtrak train see Editorial, "Speak Up," *Dayton Daily News,* Sept. 2, 1999.

129. For example, CNN's *Late Edition with Wolf Blitzer,* May 2, 1999, 12:00 A.M. EST.

130. Fox Butterfield, "Study Exposes Illegal Traffic in New Guns," *New York Times,* Feb. 21, 1999, sec. 1, p. 22.

131. Tom Diaz, *Making a Killing: The Business of Guns in America* (New York: New Press, 1999).

132. Teichroeb, "Hearing Today for Boy Expelled over Squirt Gun," p. B1; Mike Martindale, "OU Acts after Police Take Youth into Custody after Call," *Detroit News,* Aug. 13, 1999; Pete Falcone, "Student Expelled for Toting BB Gun," *Bloomington (IL) Pantagraph,* May 27, 1999, p. A2; Cathy Cummins, "Expulsion Law's Author Says Schools Have Gone Too Far," *Rocky Mountain News,* Feb. 23, 1998, p. A4; and "Howitzer Picture Cut From Yearbook," *Associated Press Newswire,* Oct. 28, 1999, 3:16 EDT. These different incidents were said to violate schools' "zero tolerance" policy.

133. This information on the number of words in different gun-control laws was compiled by Alan Korwin (Alan Korwin, *The California Gun Owner's Guide* [Phoenix: Bloomfield Press, 1999], *The Texas Gun Owner's Guide* [Phoenix: Bloomfield Press, 1998]; and *Gun Laws of America* [Phoenix: Bloomfield Press, 1997]).

134. From the Web site of the Australia Bureau of Statistics at www.abs.gov.au.

135. Nicholas Rufford, "Official: More Muggings in England Than US," *Sunday Times (London),* Oct. 11, 1998.

136. Ken Hamblin, "Gun Makers in the Crosshairs," *Denver Post,* Oct. 5, 1999, p. B11.

137. Paul M. Barrett, "Lawsuits Trigger Gun Firms' Bankruptcy Filings," *Wall Street Journal*, Sept. 13, 1999, p. B10. The story lists three major gun makers filing for bankruptcy: Sundance Industries, Davis Industries, and Lorcin Engineering Company.

138. Vanessa O'Connell and Douglas A. Blackman, "New UPS Rules Are Latest Jolt to Gun Makers," *Wall Street Journal*, Oct. 7, 1999, p. B1. There is at least some skepticism of UPS's motives. As one large handgun dealer said, "We get as many handguns from UPS here as anybody. We haven't missed a handgun in years. This is not a problem. It is just window dressing to make a political statement" (Timothy Burn, "UPS Won't Ship Guns on Ground: Air Delivery OK," *Washington Times*, Oct. 8, 1999, p. A1).

139. Terry L. Anderson, Charles W. Baird, Randy E. Barnett, et al. [letter signed by 290 academics], "Disarming Good People," *Washington Times*, June 16, 1999, p. A17. The correct number of 294 signatories was noted in John R. Lott, Jr., "More Gun Controls? They Haven't Worked in the Past," *Wall Street Journal*, June 17, 1999, p. A26.

140. Dale Anema, "A Father at Columbine High," *American Enterprise*, Sept./Oct. 1999, pp. 48–50.

APPENDIX ONE

1. Although this jargon may appear overwhelming, it is actually fairly simple. Consider the following example. Suppose we wish to present findings that height and SAT scores are correlated among college-bound students. Instead of reporting that an additional inch is related to an increase in test scores of so many points, we can compare standard-deviation changes, which would be equivalent to reporting the results as comparisons of changes in percentile height with percentile changes in the SAT-scores.

2. To phrase this in terms of the earlier discussion of standard deviations, with a symmetric distribution, there is a 32 percent probability that a variable will take on a value that is more than one standard deviation different from its mean, and only a five percent probability that it will be more than two standard deviations away from the mean.

APPENDIX THREE

1. U.S. Department of Justice, *Crime in the United States, 1994* (Washington, DC: U.S. Department of Justice, 1994.) I also wish to thank Tom Bailey of the FBI and Jeff Maurer of the Department of Health and Human Services for answering questions concerning the data used in this paper.

2. The Inter-University Consortium for Political and Social Research number for this data set was 6387, and the principle investigator was James Alan Fox of Northeastern University College of Criminal Justice.

3. Dropping the zero crime values from the sample made the "shall-issue" coefficients larger and more significant, but doing the same thing for the accident-rate regressions did not alter "shall-issue" coefficients. (See also the discussion at the end of the section headed "Using County and State Data for the United States" in chapter 4.

4. For further descriptions of the procedures for calculating intercensus estimates of population, see ICPSR (8384): U.S. Department of Commerce, Bureau of the Census, *Intercensal Estimates of the Population of Counties by Age, Sex, and Race (United States), 1970–1980* (Ann Arbor, MI: ICPSR, Winter 1985). See also Bureau of the Census, *Methodology for Experimental Estimates of the Population of Counties by Age and Sex: July 1, 1975*, Current Population Reports, series P-23, no. 103, and *Census of Population, 1980: County Population by Age, Sex, Race, and Spanish Origin (Preliminary OMB-Consistent Modified Race)*.

5. U.S. Department of Commerce, Bureau of the Census, *Methodology for Experimental Estimates of the Population of Counties by Age and Sex: July 1, 1975*, Current Population Reports,

series P-23, no. 103; see also Bureau of the Census, *Census of Population, 1980: County Population by Age, Sex, Race, and Spanish Origin (Preliminary OMB-Consistent Modified Race)*, pp. 19–23.

6. U.S. Department of Commerce, *Statistical Abstract of the United States,* 114th ed., table 746, p. 487.

7. Thomas B. Marvell and Carlisle E. Moody, "The Impact of Enhanced Prison Terms for Felonies Committed with Guns," *Criminology* 33 (May 1995): 259–60.

Bibliography

Akhil Reed Amar. "The Bill of Rights and the Fourteenth Amendment." *Yale Law Journal* 101 (Apr. 1992).

Andreoni, James. "Criminal Deterrence in the Reduce Form: A New Perspective on Ehrlich's Seminal Study." *Economic Inquiry* 33 (July 1995).

Annest, J. L.; J. A. Mercy; D. R. Gibson; and G. W. Ryan. "National Estimates of Nonfatal, Firearm-Related Injuries: Beyond the Tip of the Iceberg." *Journal of the American Medical Association* (June 14, 1995).

Ayres, Ian, and Steven Levitt. "Measuring Positive Externalities from Unobservable Victim Precaution: An Empirical Analysis of Lojack." NBER working paper 5928 (1997).

Bartley, William Alan; Mark A. Cohen; and Luke Froeb. "The Effect of Concealed-Weapon Laws: Estimating Misspecification Uncertainty." Vanderbilt University working paper (1997).

Battalio, Raymond C.; John H. Kagel; and Owen R. Phillips. "Optimal Prices and Animal Consumers in Congested Markets." *Economic Inquiry* 24 (Apr. 1986).

————. "Optimal Prices and Animal Consumers in Congested Markets: A Reply." *Economic Inquiry* 25 (Oct. 1987).

Battalio, Raymond C.; John H. Kagel; Howard Rachlin; and Leonard Green. "Commodity Choice Behavior with Pigeons as Subjects." *Journal of Political Economy* 84 (Feb. 1981).

Becker, Gary S. "Crime and Punishment: An Economic Approach." *Journal of Political Economy* 76 (Mar./Apr. 1968).

Block, Michael K., and Vernon E. Gerety. "Some Experimental Evidence on the Differences between Student and Prisoner Reactions to Monetary Penalties." *Journal of Legal Studies* 24 (Jan. 1995).

Block, Michael K., and John Heineke. "A Labor Theoretical Analysis of Criminal Choice." *American Economic Review* 65 (June 1975).

Blumstein, Alfred, and Daniel Nagin. "The Deterrent Effect of Legal Sanctions on Draft Evasion." *Stanford University Law Review* 28 (1977).

Blumstein, Alfred; Jacqueline Cohen; and Daniel Nagin, eds. *Deterrence and Incapacitation: Estimating the Effects of Criminal Sanctions on Crime Rates.* Washington, DC: National Academy of Sciences, 1978.

Bureau of Alcohol, Tobacco, and Firearms. *A Progress Report: Gun-Dealer Licensing and Illegal Gun Trafficking.* Washington, DC: Department of the Treasury, Bureau of Alcohol, Tobacco, and Firearms, Jan. 1997.

Bureau of Justice Statistics Special Reports." Murder in Large Urban Counties, 1988." Washington, DC: U.S. Department of Justice, 1993.

————. "Murder in Families. Washington, DC: U.S. Department of Justice, 1994.

Cherrington, Ernest H. *The Evolution of Prohibition in the United States of America.* Westerville, OH: Tem-Press, 1920.

Colvin, D. Leigh. *Prohibition in the United States.* New York: George H. Doran Co., 1926.

Cook, P. J. "The Role of Firearms in Violent Crime," in M. E. Wolfgang and N. A. Werner, eds., *Criminal Violence.* Newbury, NJ: Sage Publishers, 1982.

————. "The Technology of Personal Violence." *Crime and Justice: Annual Review of Research* 14 (1991).

Cottrol, Robert J., and Raymond T. Diamond. "The Second Amendment: Toward an Afro-Americanist Reconsideration." *Georgetown Law Review* 80 (Dec. 1991).

Cramer, Clayton E., and David B. Kopel. "'Shall Issue': The New Wave of Concealed-Handgun Permit Laws." *Tennessee Law Review* 62 (Spring 1995). A longer version of this study is available from the Independence Institute, 14142 Denver West Parkway, Suite 185, Golden, Colorado, 80401–3134.

Daly, Martin, and Margo Wilson. *Homicide.* Hawthorne, NY: Aldine de Gruyter Publishers, 1988.

Davis, James A., and Tom W. Smith. *General Social Surveys, 1972–1993: Cumulative Codebook.* Chicago: National Opinion Research Center, 1993.

Donohue, John, and Peter Siegelman. "Is the United States at the Optimal Rate of Crime?" *Journal of Legal Studies* 27 (Jan. 1998).

DiIulio, John J., Jr. "The Question of Black Crime." *The Public Interest* 117 (Fall 1994).

————. "White Lies About Black Crime." *The Public Interest* 118 (Winter 1995).

Dunford, Edward B. *The History of the Temperance Movement.* Washington, DC: Tem-Press, 1943.

Ehrlich, Isaac. "Participation in Illegitimate Activities: A Theoretical and Empirical Investigation." *Journal of Political Economy* 81 (1973).

————. "Crime, Punishment, and the Market for Offenses." *Journal of Economic Perspectives* 10 (Winter 1996).

Ehrlich, Isaac, and Randall Mark. "Fear of Deterrence: A Critical Evaluation of the Report of the Panel on Research on Deterrent and Incapacitation Effects." *Journal of Legal Studies* 6 (June 1977).

Geller, William A., and Michael S. Scott. *Deadly Force: What We Know.* Washington, DC: Police Executive Research Forum, 1992.

Glaeser, Edward L., and Bruce Sacerdote. "Why Is There More Crime in Cities? (Harvard University working paper, Nov. 14, 1995).

Glaeser, Edward, and Spencer Glendon. "Who Owns Guns?" *American Economic Review* 88 (May 1998).

Greenwald, Bruce C. "A General Analysis of the Bias in the Estimated Standard Errors of Least Squares Coefficients." *Journal of Econometrics* 22 (Aug. 1983).

Grossman, Michael; Frank J. Chaloupka; and Charles C. Brown. "The Demand for Cocaine by Young Adults: A Rational Addiction Approach." NBER working paper, July 1996.

Kagel, John H.; Raymond C. Battalio; Howard Rachlin; and Leonard Green. "Experimental Studies of Consumer Demand Behavior Using Laboratory Animals." *Economic Inquiry* 13 (Jan. 1975).

————. "Demand Curves for Animal Consumers." *Quarterly Journal of Economics* 96 (Feb. 1981).

Kahan, Dan M. "What Do Alternative Sanctions Mean?" *University of Chicago Law Review* 63 (1996).

Kahan, Dan, and Martha Nussbaum. "Two Conceptions of Emotion in Criminal Law." *Columbia Law Review* 96 (Mar. 1996).

Kates, Don B., and Dan Polsby. "The Background of Murders." Northwestern University Law School working paper (1997).

Kates, Don, and Dan Polsby. "Of Genocide and Disarmament." *Journal of Criminal Law and Criminology* 86 (Fall 1995).

Kellermann, Arthur L., et al. "Gun Ownership as a Risk Factor for Homicide in the Home." *New England Journal of Medicine* (Oct. 7, 1993).

Kennedy, David M.; Anne M. Piehl; and Anthony A. Braga. "Youth Violence in Boston: Gun Markets, Serious Youth Offenders, and A Use-Reduction Strategy." *Law and Contemporary Problems* 59 (Winter 1996).

Kermit, Daniel, and John R. Lott, Jr. "Should Criminal Penalties Include Third-Party Avoidance Costs?" *Journal of Legal Studies* 24 (June 1995).

Kleck, Gary. *Point Blank: Guns and Violence in America.* Hawthorne, NY: Aldine de Gruyter Publishers, 1991.

———. *Targeting Guns.* Hawthorne, NY: Aldine de Gruyter Publishers, 1997.

———. "Guns and Violence: An Interpretive Review of the Field." *Social Pathology* 1 (Jan. 1995).

Kleck, Gary, and Marc Gertz. "Armed Resistance to Crime: The Prevalence and Nature of Self-Defense with a Gun." *Journal of Criminal Law and Criminology* 86 (Fall 1995).

Kleck, Gary, and E. Britt Patterson. "The Impact of Gun Control and Gun-Ownership Levels on Violence Rates." *Journal of Quantitative Criminology* 9 (1993).

Kopel, David B. *The Samurai, the Mountie, and the Cowboy.* Amherst, NY: Prometheus Books, 1992.

———. *Guns: Who Should Have Them?* Amherst, NY: Prometheus Books, 1995.

Landes, William M. "An Economic Study of U.S. Aircraft Hijacking, 1961–1976." *Journal of Law and Economics* 21 (Apr. 1978).

Law Enforcement Technology magazine. "Gun-Control Survey." *Law Enforcement Technology* (July–Aug. 1991).

Levinson, Sanford. "The Embarrassing Second Amendment." *Yale Law Journal* 99 (Dec. 1989).

Levitt, Steven. "The Effect of Prison Population Size on Crime Rates: Evidence from Prison Overcrowding Litigation." *Quarterly Journal of Economics* 111 (1996).

Lott, John R., Jr. "Juvenile Delinquency and Education: A Comparison of Public and Private Provision." *International Review of Law and Economics* 7 (Dec. 1987).

———. "Should the Wealthy Be Able to 'Buy Justice'?" *Journal of Political Economy* 95 (Dec. 1987).

———. "The Effect of Conviction on the Legitimate Income of Criminals." *Economics Letters* 34 (Dec. 1990).

———. "A Transaction-Costs Explanation for Why the Poor Are More Likely to Commit Crime." *Journal of Legal Studies* 19 (Jan. 1990).

———. "An Attempt at Measuring the Total Monetary Penalty from Drug Convictions: The Importance of an Individual's Reputation." *Journal of Legal Studies* 21 (Jan. 1992).

———. "Do We Punish High-Income Criminals Too Heavily?" *Economic Inquiry* 30 (Oct. 1992).

———. "The Concealed-Handgun Debate." *Journal of Legal Studies* 27 (Jan. 1998): forthcoming.

Lott, John R., Jr., and Larry W. Kenny. "How Dramatically Did Women's Suffrage Change the Size and Scope of Government?" University of Chicago Law School working paper (1997).

Lott, John R., Jr., and William M. Landes. "Multiple Victim Public Shootings, Bombings, and Right-to-Carry Concealed Handgun Laws." University of Chicago Law School Working Paper (1997).

Lott, John R., Jr., and Stephen G. Bronars. "Criminal Deterrence, Geographic Spillovers, and Right-to-Carry concealed Handgun Laws." *American Economic Review* 88 (May 1998).

Lund, Nelson. "The Second Amendment, Political Liberty, and the Right to Self-Preservation." *Alabama Law Review* 33 (1988).

Marvell, Thomas B., and Carlisle E. Moody. "The Impact of Enhanced Prison Terms for Felonies Committed with Guns." *Criminology* 33 (May 1995).

McCormick, Robert E., and Robert Tollison. "Crime on the Court." *Journal of Political Economy* 92 (Apr. 1984).

McDowall, David; Colin Loftin; and Brian Wiersema. "Easing Concealed-Firearm Laws: Effects on Homicide in Three States." *Journal of Criminal Law and Criminology* 86 (Fall 1995).

Miller, Ted R.; Mark A. Cohen; and Brian Wiersema. *Victim Costs and Consequences: A New Look.* Washington, DC: National Institute of Justice, Feb. 1996.

Moulton, Brent R. "An Illustration of a Pitfall in Estimating the Effects of Aggregate Variables on Micro Units." *Review Economics and Statistics* 72 (1990).

Mullin, Wallace P. "Will Gun Buyback Programs Increase the Quantity of Guns?" Michigan State University working paper (Mar. 1997).

Munday, R. A. I., and J. A. Stevenson. *Guns and Violence: The Debate Before Lord Cullen.* Essex, England: Piedmont Publishers, 1996.

Peltzman, Sam. "The Effects of Automobile Safety Regulation." *Journal of Political Economy* 83 (Aug. 1975).

Peterson, Steven; George Hoffer; and Edward Millner. "Are Drivers of Air-Bag-Equipped Cars More Aggressive? A Test of the Offsetting-Behavior Hypothesis." *Journal of Law and Economics* 38 (Oct. 1995).

Plotkin, Martha R., ed. *Under Fire: Gun Buy-Backs, Exchanges, and Amnesty Programs.* Washington, DC: Police Executive Research Forum, 1996.

Polsby, Daniel D. "From the Hip: The Intellectual Argument in Favor of Restrictive Gun Control Is Collapsing. So How Come the Political Strength of Its Advocates Is Increasing?" *National Review,* Mar. 24, 1997.

Quigley, Paxton. *Armed and Female.* New York: St. Martin's, 1989.

Rasmusen, Eric. "Stigma and Self-Fulfilling Expectations of Criminality." *Journal of Law and Economics* 39 (Oct. 1996).

Reynolds, Morgan O. "Crime and Punishment in America." Dallas: National Center for Policy Analysis, June 1995.

Sandler, Todd. "Optimal Prices and Animal Consumers in Congested Markets: A Comment." *Economic Inquiry* 25 (Oct. 1987).

Shields, Pete. *Guns Don't Die, People Do.* New York: Arbor, 1981.

Singular, Stephen. *Talked to Death.* New York: Beech Tree Books, 1987.

Smith, Tom W. "1996 National Gun-Policy Survey of the National Opinion Research Center: Research Findings." Chicago: National Opinion Research Center, Mar. 1997.

Smith, Tom W., and Robert J. Smith. "Changes in Firearm Ownership Among Women, 1980–1994." *Journal of Criminal Law and Criminology* 86 (Fall 1995).

Southwick, Lawrence, Jr. "Self-defense with Guns: The Consequences." *Journal of Criminal Justice* (forthcoming).

Teret, Stephen P. "Critical Comments on a Paper by Lott and Mustard." School of Hygiene and Public Health, Johns Hopkins University, mimeo, Aug. 7, 1996.

U.S. Department of Commerce, Bureau of the Census. *Statistical Abstract of the United States.* Washington, DC: U.S. Government Printing Office, 1995.

Uviller, H. Richard. *Virtual Justice: The Flawed Prosecution of Crime in America.* New Haven, CT: Yale University Press, 1996.

Van Alstyne, William. "The Second Amendment Right to Arms." *Duke Law Review* 43 (Apr. 1994).

Viscusi, W. Kip. "The Lulling Effect: The Impact of Child-Resistant Packaging on Aspirin and Analgesic Ingestions." *American Economic Review* (May, 1984).

Wilson, James Q., and Richard J. Herrnstein. *Crime and Human Nature.* Simon and Schuster, New York, N.Y. 1985.

Wilson, James Q., and George L. Kelling. "Making Neighborhoods Safe." *Atlantic Monthly,* Feb. 1989.

Wolpin, Kenneth. "An Economic Analysis of Crime and Punishment in England and Wales, 1894–1967." *Journal of Political Economy* 86 (1978).

Wright, James D., and Peter Rossi. *Armed and Considered Dangerous: A Survey of Felons and Their Firearms.* New York: Aldine de Gruyter Publishers, 1986.

Zimring, Franklin. "The Medium Is the Message: Firearm Caliber as a Determinant of Death from Assault." *Journal of Legal Studies* 1 (1972).

SUPPLEMENTARY ENTRIES FOR SECOND EDITION

Ayres, Ian, and John J. Donohue III. "Nondiscretionary Concealed Weapons Laws: A Case Study of Statistics, Standards of Proof, and Public Policy." *American Law and Economics Review* 1, nos. 1–2 (Fall 1999): 436–70.

Bartley, William Alan. "Will Rationing Guns Reduce Crime?" *Economics Letters* 62 (1999): 241–43.

Bartley, William, and Mark Cohen. "The Effect of Concealed Weapons Laws: An Extreme Bound Analysis." *Economic Inquiry* 36 (Apr. 1998): 258–65.

Benson, Bruce L. "Review of More Guns, Less Crime." *Public Choice* 100, nos. 3–4 (Sept. 1999): 309–13.

Black, Dan A., and Daniel S. Nagin. "Do Right-to-Carry Laws Deter Violent Crime?" *Journal of Legal Studies* 27 (Jan. 1998): 209–19.

Bronars, Stephen G., and John R. Lott, Jr. " Criminal Deterrence, Geographic Spillovers, and Right-to-Carry Laws." *American Economic Review* 88 (May 1998): 475–79.

Cummings, Peter, David C. Grossman, Frederick P. Rivara, and Thomas D. Koepsell. "State Gun Safe Storage Laws and Child Mortality Due to Firearms." *Journal of the American Medical Association* 278 (Oct. 1, 1997): pp. 1084–86.

Dezbakhsh, Hashem, and Paul H. Rubin. "Lives Saved or Lives Lost? The Effects of Concealed-Handgun Laws on Crime." *American Economic Review Papers and Proceedings* 88 (May 1998): 468–74.

Diaz, Tom. *Making a Killing: The Business of Guns in America.* New York: New Press, 1999.

Ehrlich, Isaac, and Zhiqiang Liu. "Sensitivity Analyses of the Deterrence Hypothesis: Let's Keep the Econ in Econometrics." *Journal of Law and Economics* 42 (Apr. 1999): 455–88.

Eisen, Joanne, and Paul Gallant. "Scientific Proof That Gun Control Increases the Cost of Crime." *Shield,* Summer 1998, p. 42.

Harrison, Glenn W., David Kennison, and Katherine M. Macedon. "Legal Guarantee of the Right to Bear Arms: Can It Be Justified Empirically?" University of South Carolina working paper, December 1999.

Hemenway, David. "Book Review of More Guns, Less Crime." *New England Journal of Medicine,* Dec. 31, 1998, pp. 2029–30.

Kellermann, Arthur, and Sheryl Heron. "Firearms and Family Violence." *Emergency Medicine Clinics of North America* 17 (Aug. 1999): 699–708.

Kelling, George L. *Fixing Broken Windows: Restoring Order and Reducing Crime in Our Communities.* New York: Free Press, 1998.

Korwin, Alan. *The California Gun Owner's Guide.* Phoenix: Bloomfield Press, 1999.

———. *Gun Laws of America.* Phoenix: Bloomfield Press, 1997.

———. *The Texas Gun Owner's Guide.* Phoenix: Bloomfield Press, 1998.

Leamer, Edward E. "Let's Take the Con Out of Econometrics." *American Economic Review* 73 (Mar. 1983): 31–43.

Lott, John R., Jr. "Does a Helping Hand Put Others at Risk? Affirmative Action, Police Departments, and Crime." *Economic Inquiry,* vol. 38 (April 2000), forthcoming.

———. "Who Is Really Hurt by Affirmative Action?" *Subject to Debate,* May 1998, pp. 1, 3.

Lott, John R., Jr., and John E. Whitley. "Safe Storage Gun Laws: Accidental Deaths, Suicides, and Crime." Yale Law School working paper, October 1, 1999.

Ludwig, Jens. "Concealed-Gun-Carrying Law and Violent Crime: Evidence from State Panel Data." *International Review of Law and Economics* 18 (Sept. 1998): 239–54.

McManus, Walter S. "Estimates of the Deterrent Effect of Capital Punishment: The Importance of the Researcher's Prior Beliefs." *Journal of Political Economy* 93 (Feb. 1985): 417–25.

Miron, Jeffrey A. "Violence, Guns, and Drugs: A Cross-Country Analysis." Boston University working paper, December 9, 1999.

Moody, Carlisle E. "Testing for the Effects of Concealed Weapons Laws: Specification Errors and Robustness." College of William and Mary, Department of Economics, working paper, December 19, 1999.

Mustard, David B. "The Impact of Gun Laws on Police Deaths." University of Georgia working paper, November 1999.

Olson, David, and Michael Maltz. "Magic Bullets, Deterrence, and Gun Laws." Loyola University Chicago working paper, December 1999.

Plassman, Florenz, and T. Nicolaus Tideman. "Does the Right to Carry Concealed Handguns Deter Countable Crimes? Only a Count Analysis Can Say." State University of New York at Binghamton working paper, May 19, 1999.

————. "Geographical and Temporal Variation in the Effects of Right-to-Carry Laws on Crime." Virginia Polytechnic Institute and State University working paper, November 19, 1999.

Shughart, William F., II. "More Guns, Less Crime: Understanding Crime and Gun Control Laws: Review." *Southern Economic Journal* 65, no. 4 (Apr. 1, 1999): 978–81.

Slobogin, Christopher. "Why Liberals Should Chuck the Exclusionary Rule." *University of Illinois Law Review* 99 (1999): 363–446.

Squires, Peter. "Review of More Guns, Less Crime." *British Journal of Criminology* 39, no. 2 (Spring 1999): 318–20.

U.S. General Accounting Office. "Accidental Shootings: Many Deaths and Injuries Caused by Firearms Could Be Prevented." Washington, DC: U.S. General Accounting Office, Mar. 1991.

Index

A "t" indicates material is located in a table or other figure; an "n" indicates material in an endnote.